THE SPANISH-SPEAKING WORLD

An Anthology of Cross-Cultural Perspectives

Louise Fiber Luce

National Textbook Company
a division of NTC *Publishing Group* • Lincolnwood, Illinois USA

Published by National Textbook Company, a division of NTC Publishing Group.
© 1992 by NTC Publishing Group, 4255 West Touhy Avenue,
Lincolnwood (Chicago), Illinois 60646-1975 U.S.A.
Manufactured in the United States of America.

1 2 3 4 5 6 7 8 9 0 VP 9 8 7 6 5 4 3 2 1

Contents

The culture capsule involves members of at least two cultures in a situation of conflict. Of the two scenarios the authors present, both are set in the U.S. The first involves a Puerto Rican mother and the local schoolteachers; the second, a Colombian mother and her Anglo landlord.

An ongoing debate in the U.S. and Mexico deals with bilingualism and whether to support minority languages. What are the needs and responsibilities of those who speak minority languages on the one hand and the interests of national, state, and local governments on the other?

Medical and legal ethics are at risk in a case that began at the Los Angeles Medical Center and continued in a subsequent jury trial. The reader learns about the stresses affecting minority groups and the majority in a pluralistic society.

Two of Spain's ethnic minorities, the Catalans and the Basques, are testing Spain's new parliamentary democracy and redefining the complex economic and ideological relationship between periphery and center.

By studying male social interactions in rural Andalusian bars, the author identifies why the bar is central to male socialization in this rural setting. We also discover how masculine display rituals are linked to contradictions between ideal and actual sex roles.

Introduction

Among the concerns that led to the present volume, *The Spanish-Speaking World: An Anthology of Cross-Cultural Perspectives*, certainly the most important relates to contemporary events—political, cultural, social, and economic. They have occurred around the world during the past two decades, and they have had a profound effect on how we think about culture, about other societies, and about ourselves. Within a Spanish-speaking context, the events include the impact of demographic shifts in the U.S. on our political and cultural institutions, post-Franco Spain and its place in the European community's coming-of-age in 1992, and Latin America's economic and political malaise throughout the decades of the 1970s and '80s. Inevitably these events have drawn us, as individuals and citizens, into the complexities of global economies, cultural pluralism, and human rights.

Taking only the United States (and I refer here, albeit inaccurately, to the forty-eight states north of the United States of Mexico), it is estimated that over 500,000 immigrants are arriving here annually, the majority from Latin and Asian countries. In fact, among the Spanish-speaking countries in the world, the U.S. now ranks fifth—after Spain, Argentina, Mexico, and Colombia. Thus, when one speaks about the "browning of America," it is in part because of the influx of immigrants, documented or otherwise, who now reside in the U.S. and who, along with U.S.-born Hispanics, make up the growing population of Spanish-speaking people. Houston, Texas, offers a good example. It is a U.S. community where Spanish is used as a mother tongue by a large segment of its citizens. There are seven Spanish-language radio stations broadcasting regularly; there are Spanish-language billboards and magazine and newspaper advertisements; and city agencies hire Spanish speakers as teachers, paramedics, nurses, fire fighters, and police officers (Holcomb, 14).

1

Elsewhere, events that have occurred in Spain and Latin America are no less critical to our understanding of these societies and what they are today. In some instances, there is a record of immense creativity and growth; in others, an overwhelming record of repression, censorship, and for ethnic groups like the Basques of Spain or the Quechua Indians of Peru, ongoing marginalization. Certainly one outcome from reading the articles in *The Spanish-Speaking World* will be an overwhelming sense of the long-term effects of political upheaval and tyranny in many regions and countries.

A second major concern of *The Spanish-Speaking World* is to engage the intellect and creativity of the readers and to provide them with opportunities to reflect, discuss, question, and participate. It is a strategy reaffirmed only last August at a conference held by educators to discuss the current and future status of the secondary and elementary school curriculum. Although the participants represented such diverse fields as English, foreign languages, geography, history, mathematics, science, and social studies, they identified common themes underlying course content. Among them were more active learning, more small-group learning, the use of original materials and "real-life" contexts, more time spent working cooperatively rather than competitively, and more critical and creative thinking and problem solving (Franklin, 4). The mature learner, no less than the high school student, is motivated to learn in similar ways. The material I have selected aims at drawing the interest of a diverse group of readers, including traditional and nontraditional learners.

Finally, another important feature of *The Spanish-Speaking World* is its comparative focus. I have chosen to frame our discussion of the Spanish-speaking world within a cross-cultural perspective. I use the term *cross-cultural* in the broadest sense, including not only comparative views between the Spanish-speaking world and "mainstream" U.S. cultural practices, but generational, ethnic, and gender comparisons within Spain, Mexico, the Caribbean, or Latin America. I take this approach for two reasons. First, when we use such a rich and diverse cultural base, we have greater opportunity to see how meaning is generated in various contexts. It allows us, as Catharine Stimpson has said, to "explore the laws and processes through which a culture generates meaning and significance" (Stimpson, 2). Second, for U.S. readers to bring a cross-cultural perspective to the articles, they will first have to explore their own culture-bound view of reality, what implicit assumptions and values they bring with them when they experience another culture. All too frequently we tend to impose our parochial meanings on another society's cultural artifacts and practices. This in turn leads to cross-cultural misunderstanding and a breakdown in the communication process. Furthermore, when we examine our cultural origins dispassionately and critically, we gain greater insight into who we are. Leslie Fishbein said recently that "comparing the U.S. with other nations will compel us to find a new prism of interpretation through which to view American culture." And we are the richer for this.

KEY FEATURES OF *THE SPANISH-SPEAKING WORLD*

The Spanish-Speaking World, growing from the aforementioned concerns, offers an exploration of some major events of the past two decades. The regions highlighted in the twenty articles are Mexico, Spanish-speaking communities of the U.S., the Caribbean, Spain, Venezuela, Chile, Colombia, and Argentina. The texts seek committed readers who are willing to engage in dialogue and explore often complex and difficult issues from a cross-cultural frame of reference, including how cultural biases and stereotypes hinder our understanding of other cultures. Although they were selected with the nonspecialist reader in mind, the articles are intellectually solid and written by leading scholars from both the U.S. and abroad. Several of the articles come from what will perhaps be new sources, like the Intercultural Press, the American Forum for Global Education, The Urban Institute, *International Journal of Comparative Sociology*, or *Anthropological Quarterly*.

Descriptive Overview

Section I of the collection, "Reading Strangers: The Cultural Context," introduces readers to the concept of cultural difference by examining several basic U.S. cultural practices along with those of other nations. In this critical section, the readers discover (1) how one's perception of reality is culturally determined and (2) why we need to move outside a single cultural frame of reference when we meet cultural difference.

The opening essay, a penetrating study by Daniel J. Boorstin, a former head of the U.S. Library of Congress, reflects on how the traveler of past centuries who sought new experiences has evolved into today's tourist, unwilling to take risks in unfamiliar territory. Robert Hanvey's article builds on Boorstin's by discussing ways one can prepare to encounter a new cultural environment, whether through travel to another country or by meeting cultural difference here at home. William Gudykunst and Young Yun Kim, in a concluding essay, introduce the concept of "contexting" and give a cross-cultural appraisal of how communication styles change from high-context groups, like those of Latin countries, to low-context groups like the United States.

Thus, the purpose of this first section is to encourage American readers to reflect on their own culture, to prepare them to meet several alternative cultural patterns of Spanish-speaking peoples, and finally, to help them become more comfortable with the reality of cultural pluralism.

Like each of the subsequent sections, Section I concludes with discussion questions and activities. These allow the readers to react to the material they have just read and to apply it to situations in their own communities or schools. The preferred work mode is in small groups.

The next three sections of the text focus on Spanish-speaking peoples in North and South America. Section II, "Mexico and the Caribbean," opens with a well-known essay by Octavio Paz, the recent recipient of the Nobel Prize in literature. He suggests that the profound cultural differences between the U.S. and Mexico grow from their respective origins in Spain and England. In Peter Berger's tale of two moralities faced by a young Mexican woman, the values of a technologically advanced society are contrasted with those of a rural traditional society. Louis Zurcher and Arnold Meadow offer a cross-cultural "reading" of U.S. baseball games and Mexican bullfights, demonstrating how each activity corresponds with the individual's need to contest authority in a culturally appropriate way in the two settings.

Turning to the Caribbean, Catherine Sunshine gives a comparative view of what separates and unites Caribbean societies. Her discussion is framed by the event of colonialism. Jan Carew choses a pre- and postcolonial perspective from which to look at the crisis of self-identity in the Caribbean today.

Section III, "Latin America," opens with a comparative view of U.S. nationals and Colombians. John Fieg and John Blair base their comments on extensive interviews with Colombians visiting the U.S. Carmen García shares her research on how American and Venezuelan women differ in communication and interpersonal styles.

Only by stretching our notion of what "cross-cultural" implies can we include Fernando Reati's important article in the collection. It is in fact a look at the impact of political events in Argentina on contemporary film productions. We see recorded in the films new images of the collective imagination which grew from the terrors of the previous military regime. Authoritarian governments are again called into question with the Manuel Alcides Jofré piece on cultural productions in Chile. The author examines his society's worldview reflected in its art, literature, and the mass media after an extended period of political trauma.

A comparative Anglo-Hispanic viewpoint gives focus to Section IV, "Spanish-Speaking Communities in the U.S." Walker Connor opens the section by identifying the diversity of the Spanish-speaking immigrant groups and discussing their legitimacy in the U.S. A striking example of linguistic and cultural imperialism is found in the scenarios of the culture capsules edited by M. Eileen Hansen and Robbie Peguese. The role-plays show how cultural assumptions from a single perspective can lead to communication failure. Shirley Brice Heath in turn studies the complex and highly charged issue of national language policies in Mexico and the U.S., where "minorities are fighting not only linguistic but cultural absorption as well, and language becomes a major symbol of separate identity" (Lambert). The closing article of the section, by Carlos G. Velez-I., deals with the moral and ethical dilemma surrounding an incident of nonconsenting sterilization of Mexican women in Los Angeles.

In the last section of *The Spanish-Speaking World*, "Iberia: The Emerging Contexts of New Spain," all of the contributing authors offer comparative readings of several aspects of contemporary, post-Franco Spain. Salvador Giner brings a comparative political viewpoint to questions involving Spain's emerging ethnic groups on the one hand and mainstream political forces on the other. Henk Driessen and Stanley Brandes focus on male and female roles in southern Spain and the social and economic forces that shape these roles. Finally, Nissa Torrents compares the Franco and post-Franco eras with respect to censorship and civil liberties in the cinema and media. She, too, suggests that national minorities such as the Basques and Catalans are not yet free of the legacy of censorship from Franco's reign.

The reader will note that the emphasis throughout *The Spanish-Speaking World* is on contexts. Meaning, of course, grows from the context in which the cultural discourse is produced. Further, whether in Colombia, Puerto Rico, New York, post-Franco Spain, or the Dominican Republic, the discourse is relational, involving the participation of both a sender and a receiver; it is dynamic, not static, continually generating

new messages; it is, in short, a process. The reader is invited to participate in the process and the discovery of meaning within the several
worlds explored in *The Spanish-Speaking World.*

Louise Fiber Luce
Oxford, Ohio

Works Cited

Fishbein, Leslie. "The Field of American Studies Is Too Parochial: It Needs
    More Cross-Cultural Perspectives." *Chronicle Higher Education* 36, 48
    (August 15, 1990): A36.
Franklin, Phyllis. "Editor's Column." *MLA Newsletter* 22, 4 (Winter 1990): 4–5.
Holcomb, Betty. "The Browning of America." *The Tarrytown Newsletter* 51
    (September 1985): 14–15.
Lambert, Richard. *Language Policy: An International Perspective.* NFLC
    Occasional Papers #8. Washington, D.C.: National Foreign Language
    Center at Johns Hopkins University, 1990.
Stimpson, Catharine R. "President's Column." *MLA Newsletter* 22, 4 (Winter
    1990): 2–3.

SECTION I

Reading Strangers:
The Cultural Context

DANIEL J. BOORSTIN

From Traveler to Tourist:
The Lost Art of Travel

(Travel as cultural praxis reflects how our social structures and values have changed over the past century.)

"You're just 15 gourmet meals from Europe on the world's fastest ship."
                    —ADVERTISEMENT FOR THE UNITED STATES LINES

During recent decades we have come to think that our new technology can save us from the inexorable laws of familiarity. By magical modern machinery we hope to clear the world of its commonplaceness—of its omnipresent tree sparrows, starlings, and blue jays—and fill it with rare Sutton's warblers, ivory-billed woodpeckers, whooping cranes, and rufous hummingbirds. Every bird-watcher knows how hard it is to reconcile oneself to the fact that the common birds are the ones most usually seen and that rare birds are really quite uncommon. Now all of us frustrate ourselves by the expectation that we can make the exotic an everyday experience (without its ceasing to be exotic); and can somehow make commonplaceness itself disappear.

The word "adventure" has become one of the blandest and emptiest in the language. The cheap cafeteria at the corner offers us an "adventure in good eating"; a course in self-development ($13.95) in a few weeks will transform our daily conversation into a "great adventure"; to ride in the new Dodge is an "adventure." By continual overuse, we wear

Reprinted with permission of Atheneum Publishers, an imprint of Macmillan Publishing Company, from *The Image* by Daniel J. Boorstin. Copyright © 1961 by Daniel J. Boorstin.

out the once-common meaning of "an unusual, stirring, experience, often of romantic nature," and return "adventure" to its original meaning of a mere "happening" (from the Latin, *adventura*, and *advenire*). But while an "adventure" was originally "that which happens without design; chance, hap, luck," now in common usage it is primarily a contrived experience that somebody is trying to sell us. Its changed meaning is both a symptom of the new pervasiveness of pseudo-events and a symbol of how we defeat ourselves by our exaggerated expectations of the amount of unexpectedness—"adventure"—as of everything else in the world.

There is no better illustration of our newly exaggerated expectations than our changed attitude toward travel. One of the most ancient motives for travel, when men had any choice about it, was to see the unfamiliar. Man's incurable desire to go someplace else is a testimony of his incurable optimism and insatiable curiosity. We always expect things to be different over there. "Traveling," Descartes wrote in the early seventeenth century, "is almost like conversing with men of other centuries." Men who move because they are starved or frightened or oppressed expect to be safer, better fed, and more free in the new place. Men who live in a secure, rich, and decent society travel to escape boredom, to elude the familiar, and to discover the exotic.

They have often succeeded. Great stirrings of the mind have frequently followed great ages of travel. Throughout history by going to far places and seeing strange sights men have prodded their imagination. They have found amazement and delight and have reflected that life back home need not always remain what it has been. They have learned that there is more than one way to skin a cat, that there are more things in heaven and earth than was dreamt of in their philosophy, that the possibilities of life are not exhausted on Main Street.

In the fifteenth century the discovery of the Americas, the voyages around Africa and to the Indies opened eyes, enlarged thought, and helped create the Renaissance. The travels of the seventeenth century around Europe, to America, and to the Orient helped awaken men to ways of life different from their own and led to the Enlightenment. The discovery of new worlds has always renewed men's minds. Travel has been the universal catalyst. It has made men think faster, imagine larger, want more passionately. The returning traveler brings home disturbing ideas. Pascal (three centuries before television) said that man's ills came from the fact that he had not yet learned to sit quietly in a room.

In recent decades more Americans than ever before have traveled outside our country. In 1854 about thirty-odd thousand Americans went abroad; a century later in 1954 almost a million American citizens left the United States for foreign parts other than Canada and Mexico. After allowing for the increase in population, there is about five times as much foreign travel by Americans nowadays as there was a hundred years ago. As a nation we are probably the most traveled people of our time, or of any time. What is remarkable, on reflection, is not that our foreign travel has increased so much. But rather that all this travel has made so little difference in our thinking and feeling.

Our travels have not, it seems, made us noticeably more cosmopolitan or more understanding of other peoples. The explanation is not that Americans are any more obtuse or uneducable than they used to be. Rather, the travel experience itself has been transformed. Many Americans now "travel," yet few are travelers in the old sense of the word. The multiplication, improvement, and cheapening of travel facilities have carried many more people to distant places. But the experience of going there, the experience of being there, and what is brought back from there are all very different. The experience has become diluted, contrived, prefabricated.

The modern American tourist now fills his experience with pseudo-events. He has come to expect both more strangeness and more familiarity than the world naturally offers. He has come to believe that he can have a lifetime of adventure in two weeks and all the thrills of risking his life without any real risk at all. He expects that the exotic and the familiar can be made to order: that a nearby vacation spot can give him Old World charm, and also that if he chooses the right accommodations he can have the comforts of home in the heart of Africa. Expecting all this, he demands that it be supplied to him. Having paid for it, he likes to think he has got his money's worth. He has demanded that the whole world be made a stage for pseudo-events. And there has been no lack of honest and enterprising suppliers who try to give him what he wants, to help him inflate his expectations, and to gratify his insatiable appetite for the impossible.

Until almost the present century, travel abroad was uncomfortable, difficult, and expensive. The middle-class American did not go for "fun." Foreign capitals offered sophisticated pleasures: conversation with the great and the witty, views of painting, sculpture, and architecture, romantic musings in the ruins of vanished civilizations, pilgrimages to the birthplaces of poets, to the scenes of glory of statesmen and orators. Men seeing the "Wonders of the World" felt a wonderment for which they usually were well prepared. This had long been the pattern of European travel by Euopeans. "As soon as we have got hold of a bit of Latin," the French wit Saint-Évremond caricatured in one of his comedies in the seventeenth century, "we prepare to start on our travels. . . . When our travellers are of a literary turn of mind, they invariably take with them a book consisting solely of blank pages nicely bound, which they call an *Album Amicorum*. Armed with this, they make a point of calling on the various learned men of the locality they happen to be visiting, and beg them to inscribe their names in it."

The serious attitude in the late eighteenth century was expressed by an aristocratic scholar, the Comte de Volney, who explained that, having received a small inheritance:

> On reflection, I thought the sum too inconsiderable to make any sensible addition to my income and too great to be dissipated in frivolous expenses. Some fortunate circumstances had habituated me to study; I had acquired a taste, and even a passion for knowledge, and the accession to my fortune appeared to me a fresh means of gratifying my inclination, and opening a new way to improvement. I had read and frequently heard repeated, that of all methods of adorning the mind, and forming the judgment, travelling is the most efficacious; I determined, therefore, on a plan of travelling, but to what part of the world to direct my course remained still to be chosen: I wished the scene of my observations to be new, or at least brilliant.

Volney decided to go to the Middle East, and his journey through Syria and Egypt (1783–85) produced a travel classic. Arthur Young, the English agriculturalist, took three trips to nearby France in 1787, 1788, and 1789, as a self-appointed surveyor of farming ways; his journal (published 1792) helped revolutionize the agronomy of England and reached its influence far out to the young United States. Jefferson, in France and Italy about the same time, earnestly sought out new plants for Virginia and found the architectural models which shaped the University of Virginia.

The young aristocrat went abroad also to grow up and to sow his wild oats. He could enjoy his rakish pleasures at a comfortable distance from home and reputation. Adam Smith, in *The Wealth of Nations* (1776), recorded that in his day it was the custom among those who could afford it "to send young people to travel in foreign countries immediately upon their leaving school, and without sending them to any university. Our young people, it is said, generally return home much improved by their travels. A young man who goes abroad at seventeen or eighteen, and returns home at one-and-twenty, returns three or four years older than he was when he went abroad; and at that age it is very difficult not to improve a good deal in three or four years." Smith objected, however, that this was a risky practice which often corrupted the young; the custom, he said, could not have arisen except for the low state of English universities. The wealth of England had enabled her young people on the continent (as a German observer somewhat enviously remarked in 1760) to "give a loose to their propensities to pleasure, even in Italy ... having a great deal of money to lavish away, it not only gives them more spirit to engage in adventures, but likewise furnishes them with means for removing impediments, or buying off any ill-consequences." Casanova's amorous *Memoirs* (1826–38), we sometimes forget, were a record of travels which had taken him through the capitals of Europe—to Venice, Paris, Berlin, Warsaw, Madrid, and as far east as Constantinople.

In the seventeenth and eighteenth centuries many European men of culture liked to boast of having made more than one country their own. To travel was to become a man of the world. Unless one was a man of the world, he might not seem cultivated in his own country. The young Italian, Antonio Conti, for example (as Paul Hazard recalls), was born in Padua, lived for a while in Paris, then in London in 1715 joined a discussion of the recently invented infinitesimal calculus, afterwards stopped to pay his respects to Leeuwenhoek, the naturalist and microscope maker, in Holland—all on his way to meet the philosopher Leibniz in Hanover. In the old Grand Tour (recounted, for example, in Laurence Sterne's *Sentimental Journey*) the young gentleman rounded off his education. Locke, Gibbon, and Hume knew France from extended visits. Gibbon did much of his writing in Switzerland. Monarchs often went abroad, and not only when they abdicated or were banished. Prince Hamlet went abroad to study. Christina of Sweden lived for a while in Paris, and died in Rome in 1689. Peter the Great at the end of the seventeenth century traveled in Germany, Holland, England, and Austria. For Europeans foreign travel was an institution of exiled monarchs, adventuring aristocrats, merchant princes, and wandering scholars.

For Americans, too, until nearly the end of the nineteenth century foreign travel (still mostly European travel) was the experience of a privileged few. Franklin's great overseas success was in the committee rooms of the House of Commons and in the salons (and bedrooms) of Paris. Jefferson and other cultivated Americans, who still believed in a worldwide "Republic of Letters," were eager to meet their European fellow citizens. Henry Adams in Berlin, Rome, London, Paris was an idealized American version of the European on Grand Tour. All the success that Adams or his father or grandfather achieved, so Henry said, "was chiefly due to the field that Europe gave them," and it was more than likely that without the help of Europe they would have all remained local politicians or lawyers, like their neighbors, to the end. When a Franklin, a Jefferson, a Charles Sumner, or a Henry Adams arrived in Europe, he was armed with introductions to the great and famous. Henry Adams called the European journey his third or fourth attempt at education. Like other means of education, such travel had its delights, but it was hard work.

The scarcity of postal facilities and the lack of newspapers gave an added incentive to travel. At the same time, the hardships of a virtually roadless landscape restricted the foreign journey to those with a serious or at least earnestly frivolous purpose, who were willing to risk robbers, cutthroats, and disease, and to find their own way through trackless heath, vast swamps, and mud that came up to the carriage axles. "Under the best of conditions," one historian of the eighteenth century records, "six horses were required to drag across country the lumbering coaches of the gentry, and not infrequently the assistance of oxen was required." It was not until nearly 1800—and the work of two Scottish engineers, Thomas Telford and John Macadam—that the modern science of roadbuilding was developed and cheap and effective hard-surfacing became possible.

The travel experience was an adventure, too, simply because so few could afford or would dare its hardships. The modern hotel—the place which George Bernard Shaw later praised as "a refuge from home life"—had not been invented. In the picturesque inn of the travel books every comfort had to be specially negotiated. The luxury of a private bed was hard to come by, not only because of the constant companionship of cockroaches, bedbugs, and fleas, but because innkeepers felt free to assign more than one guest to a bed. Englishmen traveling in France noted how rare it was to encounter fellow travelers, much less fellow countrymen. Arthur Young in the late eighteenth century found "a paucity of travellers that is amazing"; he traveled a whole day on a main road thirty miles outside of Paris and "met but a single gentleman's carriage, nor anything else on the road that looked like a gentleman." Even later, when sleeping accommodations had improved, the traveler on the continent might expect to find "comfortable hotels, but no uncomfortable crowds." As late as the 1860's an English traveler to Holland noted that "tourists were comparatively rare and there were no cheap trippers."

(After describing the democratization of travel in the nineteenth century, the author turns to today's tourists and the obstacles that prevent them from seeing the world they were supposed to discover.)

... The traveler, then, was working at something; the tourist was a pleasure-seeker. The traveler was active; he went strenuously in search of people, of adventure, or experience. The tourist is passive; he expects interesting things to happen to him. He goes "sight-seeing". . . . He expects everything to be done to him and for him.

The self-conscious effort to provide local atmosphere is itself thoroughly A merican. And an effective insulation from the place where you have gone. Out-of-doors the real Turkey surrounds the Istanbul Hilton. But inside it is only an imitation of the Turkish style. The hotel achieves the subtle effect, right in the heart of Turkey, of making the experience of Turkey quite secondhand.

A similar insulation comes from all the efforts of different countries which are or hope to become "Tourist Meccas" to provide attractions for tourists. These "attractions" offer an elaborately contrived indirect experience, an artificial product to be consumed in the very places where the real thing is [as] free as air. They are ways for the traveler to remain out of contact with foreign peoples in the very act of "sight-seeing" them. They keep the natives in quarantine while the tourist in air-conditioned comfort views them through a picture window. They are the cultural mirages now found at tourist oases everywhere.

Oddly enough, many of these attractions came into being, rather accidentally, as by-products of democratic revolutions. But soon they were being carefully designed, planned in large numbers and on a grand scale by national tourist agencies eager to attract visitors from far away.

The modern museum, like the modern tourist himself, is a symp-tom of the rise of democracy. Both signal the diffusion of scientific knowledge, the popularization of the arts, the decline of private patronage of artists, and the spread of literacy among the middle classes. Collections of valuable, curious, and beautiful objects had always been gathered by men of wealth and power. There had long been private museums, but these were seldom open to the public. In ancient days, and especially before the printed book, museums and libraries had been closely allied, as in Alexandria, for example. Of course, there had always been some works of art especially designed for public display, as in the Pinacotheca (a marble hall of the propylaeum on the Athenian

Acropolis) or in the forum of Augustus in Rome. At least since Roman times, the best collections of the works of art and of learning were privately owned. And the first modern public museum was the British Museum, established by Act of Parliament in 1753. It had been inspired by the will of Sir Hans Sloane, who on his death that year left the nation his remarkable collection of books, manuscripts, and curiosities. On the European continent most of the great art museums are part of the booty which the rising middle classes have captured for themselves in the revolutions since the late eighteenth century. The Louvre, which had been a royal palace, became a public art museum after the French Revolution of 1789.

Nowadays a visit to the best art museums in Europe is often a tour of the vacated residences of magnates, noblemen, and monarchs of the pre-democratic age: in Florence, the Uffizi and Pitti Palaces; in Venice, the Doge's Palace; in Paris, the Louvre; in Vienna, Schönbrunn. Beautiful objects, taken from scores of princely residences, are crowded together for public display in the grandest of defunct palaces. Painting, sculpture, tapestries, tableware, and other *objects d'art* (once part of the interior decoration or household equipment of a working aristocracy) were thus "liberated" by and for the people. Now they were to be shown to the nation and to all comers. Common people could now see treasures from the inner sanctums of palaces, treasures originally designed to adorn the intimate dining tables, bedrooms, and bathrooms of a well-guarded aristocracy. At last everyone could take a Cook's Tour* of the art of the ages for a nominal admission fee or free of charge. Statesmen saw these new museums as symbols of wide-spreading education and culture, as monuments and catalysts of national pride. So they were. Today they remain the destination of tourist-pilgrims from afar.

To bring the paintings of Botticelli, Rubens, and Titian into a room where one could see them in a few minutes, to gather together the sculpture of Donatello and Cellini from widely dispersed churches, monasteries, and drawing rooms for chronological display in a single hall, to remove the tapestries designed for wall-covering in remote mansions and hunting lodges, and spread them in the halls of centrally located museums—this was a great convenience. But there was one unavoidable consequence. All these things were being removed from their context. In a sense, therefore, they were all being misrepresented. Perhaps more was gained in the quantity of people who could see them

---

* Thomas Cook is a famous British tourist agency dating from the nineteenth century. (Editor's note)

at all than was lost in the quality of the experience. This is not the question. The effect on experience is plain and undeniable.

Inevitably these museums—and others made later on the defunct-palace model—become major tourist attractions. They still are. It remains true, however, that, almost without exception, whatever one sees in a museum is seen out of its proper surroundings. The impression of individual works of art or of a country's past culture as a whole, whenever it is formed from museum visits, is inevitably factitious. It has been put together for your and my convenience, instruction, amusement, and delight. But to put it together the art commissioners have had to take apart the very environment, the culture which was once real, and which actually created and enjoyed these very works. The museum visitor tours a warehouse of cultural artifacts; he does not see vital organs of living culture. Even where (as in the Prado in Madrid or the Hermitage in Leningrad) one visits what was once a private museum, the original collection has been so diluted or expanded and the atmosphere so changed that the experience is itself a new artifact. Only the museum itself is quite real—a functioning part of a going concern. The ribbon across the chair, the ancestral portrait no longer viewed by its descendant, is a symbol of the change. Each living art object, taken out of its native habitat so we can conveniently gaze at it, is like an animal in a zoo. Something about it has died in the removal.

Of course, there remain sites all over the world—Windsor Castle, the Medici Palace in Florence, the Hindu rock carvings at Elefanta, Japanese Imperial Palaces, and countless churches, shrines and temples—where works of art remain in their original sites. But in nearly all Tourist Meccas much of the tourist's sight-seeing is museum-seeing. And most museums have this unreal, misrepresentative character.

The museum is only one example of the tourist attraction. All tourist attractions share this factitious, pseudo-eventful quality. Formerly when the old-time traveler visited a country whatever he saw was apt to be what really went on there. A Titian, a Rubens or a Gobelin tapestry would be seen on a palace wall as background to a princely party or a public function. Folk song and folk dance were for the natives themselves. Now, however, the tourist sees less of the country than of its tourist attractions. Today what he sees is seldom the living culture, but usually specimens collected and embalmed especially for him, or attractions specially staged for him: proved specimens of the artificial.

Since the mid-nineteenth century, international expositions have increased in number and grown in prominence. They usually have some solid purposes—to promote trade, to strengthen world peace, to exchange technological information. But when expositions become tourist attractions they acquire an artificial character. From the London Crystal Palace Exposition of 1851 and the Exposition on the Champs Elysées in 1855 down to Chicago's Century of Progress Exposition in 1933–34, the New York World's Fair of 1939–40, the Brussels World's Fair of 1958, and the annual Cinema Festivals in Venice, modern expositions have been designed for propaganda, to attract foreign tourists and their currency. An exposition planned for tourists is a self-conscious and contrived national image. It is a pseudo-event for foreign consumption.

The rise of tourist traffic has brought the relatively recent phenomenon of the tourist attraction pure and simple. It often has no purpose but to attract in the interest of the owner or of the nation. As we might expect, this use of the word "attraction" as "a thing or feature which 'draws' people; especially, any interesting or amusing exhibition" dates only from about 1862. It is a new species: the most attenuated form of a nation's culture. All over the world now we find these "attractions"—of little significance for the inward life of a people, but wonderfully salable as [a] tourist commodity. Examples are Madame Tussaud's exhibition of wax figures in London (she first became known for her modeled heads of the leaders and victims of the French Revolution) and the Tiger Balm Gardens in Hong Kong. Disneyland in California—the American "attraction" which tourist Khrushchev most wanted to see—is the example to end all examples. Here indeed Nature imitates Art. The visitor to Disneyland encounters not the two-dimensional comic strip or movie originals, but only their three-dimensional facsimiles.

Tourist attractions serve their purpose best when they are pseudo-events. To be repeatable at will they must be factitious. Emphasis on the artificial comes from the ruthless truthfulness of tourist agents. What they can really guarantee you are not spontaneous cultural products but only those made especially for tourist consumption, for foreign cash customers. Not only in Mexico City and Montreal, but also in the remote Guatemalan Tourist Mecca of Chichicastenango and in far-off villages of Japan, earnest honest natives embellish their ancient rites, change, enlarge, and spectacularize their festivals, so that tourists will not be disappointed. In order to satisfy the exaggerated expectations of tour agents and tourists, people everywhere obligingly become dishonest mimics of themselves. To provide a full schedule of events at the best seasons and at convenient hours, they travesty their most solemn rituals, holidays, and folk celebrations—all for the benefit of tourists.

In Berlin, in the days before the First World War, legend tells us that precisely at the stroke of noon, just as the imperial military band would begin its daily concert in front of the Imperial Palace, Kaiser Wilhelm used to interrupt whatever he was doing inside the palace. If he was in a council of state he would say, "With your kind forbearance, gentlemen, I must excuse myself now to appear in the window. You see, it says in Baedeker that at this hour I always do."

Modern tourist guidebooks have helped raise tourist expectations. And they have provided the natives—from Kaiser Wilhelm down to the villagers of Chichicastenango—with a detailed and itemized list of what is expected of them and when. These are the up-to-date scripts for actors on the tourists' stage. The pioneer, of course, was Karl Baedeker (1801–1859) of Leipzig, whose name long since has entered our language as a synonym for his product. He began offering his packaged tours in print at the same time that Thomas Cook in England was perfecting the personally conducted packaged tour. Baedeker issued a guidebook to Coblenz in 1829, first in German; then in 1846 came his first foreign-language edition (in French); in 1861 appeared his first English-language edition. By the beginning of World War II the Baedeker firm had sold more than two million copies of about a hundred different guides in English, French, and German, the languages that reached those nations with rising middle classes who were now strenuously adapting the Grand Tour to their more meager budgets and more limited education. Despite the setback of the war and the destruction of the Baedeker plant in Leipzig by the Royal Air Force, fifty new editions were published in the decade after 1950. In the single year 1958 about 80,000 Baedeker guides were sold at a price of nearly five dollars apiece. At this rate, within twenty-five years as many Baedekers would be sold as in the whole previous century.

Karl Baedeker himself was a relentless sight-seer. In the beginning he refused to describe anything he had not personally seen. His guide-books have held a reputation for scrupulous accuracy, leading many tourists to share A.P. Herbert's faith:

> For kings and governments may err
> But never Mr. Baedeker.

A testimony to Baedeker's incorruptibility was his statement in an early edition that "Hotels which cannot be accurately characterized without exposing the editor to the risk of legal proceedings are left unmentioned." Baedeker saved his readers from unnecessary encounters with the natives, warned against mosquitoes, bedbugs, and fleas, advised wariness of unwashed fruit and uncooked salads, told the price of a postage stamp, and indicated how much to tip (overtipping was a cardinal sin in Baedeker's book).

Eventually Baedeker actually instructed the tourist how to dress and how to act the role of a decent, respectable, tolerant member of his own country, so as not to disappoint or shock the native spectators in the country he was visiting. By the early years of the twentieth century Baedeker was prompting the English reader to play this role "by his tact and reserve, and by refraining from noisy behaviour and contemptuous remarks (in public buildings, hotels, etc.), and especially from airing his political views." "The Englishman's customary holiday attire of rough tweeds, 'plus fours,' etc., is unsuitable for town wear in Italy." "The traveller should refrain from taking photographs of beggars, etc."

Baedeker's most powerful invention was the "star system," which soon had as much charm over sight-seers as its namesake later came to have over movie-goers. His system of rating gave two stars (**) to sights that were extraordinary (the Louvre, Yellowstone Park, Windsor Castle, St. Peter's, the Uffizi, the Pyramids, the Colosseum), one star (*) to sights of lesser rank (merely noteworthy), and no stars at all to the mine-run tourist attractions. This scheme, later copied or adapted by Baedeker's successors (Russell Muirhead of the successful *Blue Guides* and *Penguin Guides*, and numerous American authors of guides), has dominated the uneasy, half-cultivated modern tourist. Hermann Göring, instructing his *Luftwaffe* in 1942, is said to have directed them to destroy "every historical building and landmark in Britain that is marked with an asterisk in Baedeker." These were sometimes called the "Baedeker raids."

Anyone who has toured with Baedeker knows the complacent feeling of having checked off all the starred attractions in any given place, or the frustration of having gone to great trouble and expense to see a sight only to discover afterward that it had not even rated a single asterisk. Tourists versed in one-upmanship who visit some frequented place like Paris or Florence have been known to concentrate their sight-seeing on unstarred items, so that in conversation back home they can face-down their plodding acquaintances who go by the book. But the star system, like the public museums and the whole phenomenon of middle-class touring, has been a by-product of the democratic revolutions. It, too, has helped blaze "an easy path to cultural sophistication for millions." As Ivor Brown shrewdly observes, this star system has tended to produce star-gazers rather than explorers.

The tourist looks for caricature; travel agents at home and national tourist bureaus abroad are quick to oblige. The tourist seldom likes the authentic (to him often unintelligible) product of the foreign culture; he prefers his own provincial expectations. The French chanteuse singing English with a French accent seems more charmingly French than one who simply sings in French. The American tourist in Japan looks less for what is Japanese than for what is Japanesey. He wants to believe that geishas are only quaint oriental prostitutes; it is nearly impossible for him to imagine they can be anything else. After all, he hasn't spent all that money and gone all the way over there to be made a fool of. The Noh or Kabuki or Bunraku (which have long entertained the Japanese in their distinctive theatrical idiom) bore him, but he can grasp the Takarazuka girlie show, a Japanesey musical extravaganza on the Ziegfeld-Billy Rose model, distinguished from its American counterparts mainly by the fact that all the performers are women. The out-of-dateness of its manner he mistakes for an oriental flavor. Even the official Japanese Tourist Bureau guidebook, anxiously reminding the American that in Japan he will not fail to find what he wants, notes that "strip tease . . . performances are advancing somewhat artistically." The Takarazuka extravaganza is described at length as "an opera peculiar to Japan, known as the girls' opera." Like its Frenchy counterpart, the Folies Bergères which is sometimes featured in Las Vegas, a Takarazuka-type show from any country will be a box-office success in the United States.

As the obliging foreign producers work harder to give Americans just what they expect, American tourists, in turn, oblige by becoming more and more naive, to the point of gullibility. Tourists, however, are willing gulls, if only because they are always secretly fearful their extravagant (and expensive) expectations may not be fulfilled. They are determined to have their money's worth. Wherever in the world the American tourist goes, then, he is prepared to be ruled by the law of pseudo-events, by which the image, the well-contrived imitation, out-shines the original.

Everywhere, picturesque natives fashion papier-maché images of themselves. Yet all this earnest picturesqueness too often produces only a pallid imitation of the technicolor motion picture which the tourist goes to verify. The Eternal City becomes the site of the box-office hit *Roman Holiday*; tourist-pilgrims are eager to visit the "actual" scenes where famous movies like *Ben Hur* and *Spartacus* were really photographed. Mount Sinai becomes well-known as the site about which *The Ten Commandments* was filmed. In 1960 a highly successful packaged tour was organized which traced the route of events in Leon Uris' novel *Exodus*; the next year El Al Israel Airlines announced a new sixteen-day tour which promised to cover the very places where Otto Preminger and his film crew had shot scenes for the movie version.

The problems of satisfying the tourist expectations of a great middle-class market were summarized in a government study (1936) under the auspices of the Union of South Africa and the South African Railways and Harbours:

Supply of Tourist Attractions

In the wake of advertising and demand, creation must ordinarily follow an organized and systematic supply. If publicity has been given in foreign countries to the national tourist attractions of a country and if a demand has been created therefore, then it is imperative not only that that which has been advertised should come up to reasonable expectations but that it should also be ordinarily available and normally accessible. So, for example, if animal or native life is made to feature in foreign publicity then as such it must be ordinarily available to tourists. Under no circumstances should any aspect of animal or native life which is not ordinarily present be made to feature in a country's tourist publicity. Thus it is wrong to make a feature of native initiation ceremonies or native dances which are only seen on rare occasions since in their true character they have ritual significance.

The sight-seeing items which can be confidently guaranteed and conveniently and quickly delivered to tourists on arrival have these merchandisable qualities precisely because they are *not* naive expressions of the country. They cannot be the real ritual or the real festival; that was never originally planned for tourists. Like the hula dances now staged for photographer-tourists in Hawaii (courtesy of the Eastman Kodak Company), the widely appealing tourist attractions are apt to be those specially made for tourist consumption.

And the tourist demands more and more pseudo-events. The most popular of these must be easily photographed (plenty of daylight) and inoffensive—suitable for family viewing. By the mirror-effect law of pseudo-events, they tend to become bland and unsurprising reproductions of what the image-flooded tourist knew was there all the time. The tourist's appetite for strangeness thus seems best satisfied when the pictures in his own mind are verified in some far country.

ROBERT G. HANVEY

Cross-Cultural Awareness

(The author describes the obstacles that keep us from understanding other cultures and identifies some options for those who wish to improve their cross-cultural awareness.)

Cross-cultural awareness may be one of the more difficult dimensions [of internationalism] to attain. It is one thing to have some knowledge of world conditions. The air is saturated with that kind of information. It is another thing to comprehend and accept the consequences of the basic human capacity for creating unique cultures—with the resultant profound differences in outlook and practice manifested among societies. These differences are widely known at the level of myth, prejudice, and tourist impression. But they are not deeply and truly known—in spite of the well-worn exhortation to "understand others." Such a fundamental acceptance seems to be resisted by powerful forces in the human psychosocial system. Attainment of cross-cultural awareness and empathy at a significant level will require methods that circumvent or otherwise counter those resisting forces. Let us think afresh about what such methods might be, with a full recognition of how difficult the task will be and a corresponding willingness to discard ideas that don't work.

From Robert G. Hanvey, *An Attainable Global Perspective* (New York: American Forum for Global Education, 1976), 8–12, by permission of the publisher.

DOES UNDERSTANDING FOLLOW CONTACT

One of the cherished ideas of our own times and of earlier times is that contact between societies leads to understanding. The durability of this notion is awesome considering the thousands of years of documented evidence to the contrary. Consider the following example. When the French began to explore North America they came into contact with a number of aboriginal groups. At various times they attempted to muster the males of these groups into fighting units. The Indians clearly had no aversion to fighting; they were warriors, skilled in the use of arms, proud of triumphs over an enemy. But they would not take orders. French commanders had no control and the so-called chiefs of these groups depended on persuasion, which might or might not be successful. Every individual Indian warrior made his own decisions about whether to join a raid or war party, worked out his own battle strategy, and left the fray when he chose.

This kind of contact between the French and the Indians provided the French with detailed information on the ways of their Indian allies—information they noted scornfully in their journals, sometimes sputtering in rage and frustration. But the behavior they described was incomprehensible to them. By virtue of the concrete experiences that the French had with the Indians, the French had rich data—but no understanding. The French were able to see Indian behavior only in the light of their own hierarchical social system, where it is natural for the few to command and the many to obey. Social systems that worked on other principles were literally unimaginable.

Of course, now we are more sophisticated. What happens when the nature of the contact between groups is not one of exploitation or domination but rather one of sympathetic assistance, and where there is at least some preparation for the cultural differences that will be encountered? Here is an account of Peace Corps experience in the Philippines:

> Most human relationships in the world are governed by a pervasive fatalism, in the Philippines best described by the Tagalog phrase, *bahala na*, which means, "never mind" or, "it will be all right" or, "it makes no difference." Americans, more than any other people in history, believe man can control his environment, can shape the forces of nature to change his destiny. That peculiarity, which is essentially Western, is quintessentially American.
>
> Most of the peoples of the world also value dependency and harmony relationships within the in-group. Rather than stress independence in relationships—freedom from restraint and free-

dom to make choices—they emphasize reciprocity of obligation and good will within the basic group and protection of that group against outsiders. It is the group—family, tribe or clan—which matters and not the individual. In the Philippines, this phenomenon is perhaps best described by the term *utang na loob* which means a reciprocal sense of gratitude and obligation.

The value of independence in relationships and getting a job done makes us seem self-reliant, frank, empirical, hardworking, and efficient to ourselves. To Filipinos, the same behavior sometimes makes us seem to be unaware of our obligations, insensitive to feelings, unwilling to accept established practices, and downright aggressive. . . .

Nearly all volunteers had to struggle to understand and deal with Filipino behavior that, when seen from our peculiar stress on independence in relationships as opposed to Filipino *utang na loob*, was deeply distressing. . . . Filipinos wanted to be dependent on others and have others dependent on them; they were often ashamed in the presence of strangers and authority figures; they were afraid of being alone or leaving their families and communities; they showed extreme deference to superiors and expected the same from subordinates; they veiled true feelings and opinions in order not to hurt others or be hurt by them. . . .

It is one thing to study and understand *utang na loob*. It is another to have a principal treat you as a status figure and to insist that you tell him how to run his school, or to have children in your class cower in what seems to be shame, or to have neighbors who care much more that you should like them and that you should have a pleasurable experience than that you should get your job done.

Filipinos, with their incessant hospitality and curiosity, repeatedly made it plain that for them the main job of Peace Corps volunteers was to enjoy themselves and to enhance pleasure for those around them, an approach to life best described by the Filipino phrase, *pakikisama*. . . . Nothing was more difficult for volunteers to understand or accept than that Filipinos wanted them for pleasure in relationships and not to achieve the tasks to which they had been assigned. . . .

It was not just the Filipino's stress on *utang na loob* and *pakikisama* which interfered with getting the job done. It was also *bahala na*, the widespread fatalism of the barrio which showed itself in the lack of emotion at the death of little children, the persistent and nearly universal beliefs that ghosts and spirits control life and death, and the failure of Filipinos to keep promises and appointments. Why should the job matter when fate governs human existence? . . .

During the first two years, four volunteers resigned and twenty-six others were sent home, usually by mutual agreement, because they were not able or willing to cope with the extraordinary psychological burdens of being Peace Corps volunteers. Some volunteers developed a "what's the use" attitude and failed to appear at school, or made short unauthorized trips away from their barrios. Withdrawal was sometimes followed in the same volunteer by extremely hostile behavior against the Philippine Bureau of Public Schools, Washington, and the Peace Corps staff. Some volunteers, particularly those in the first group, wished there was some honorable way for them to cut short their tour of duty without an overwhelming sense of personal failure. [1]

The American Peace Corps volunteers, like the French officers of the 17th Century, could not escape the powerful influence of their own culture, especially since that culture was so deeply embedded in the very definition of the mission. The task was to render assistance. And success was measured by some kind of closure, "getting the job done." Filipino behavior stood in the way of getting the job done. There were distractions, delays, and detours. And the positive reinforcements that a busy, efficient American would have received in his home setting were nowhere to be found. The result: puzzlement and frustration equivalent to that of the French in their relations with Indian groups.

ACHIEVING UNDERSTANDING

But some volunteers did solve the cultural puzzle.

A male volunteer from South Carolina, D was as much admired by Filipinos and volunteers as any volunteer in the project. Almost from the first, he accepted people for what they were, learned the dialect, made friends, and seemed to enjoy that more than anything else. After two years, he wrote, "I consistently believed and followed a life based on getting away from all identity or entanglement with the Peace Corps. My reasons were . . . to figure out a little bit about what was going on in the Philippines, to see what was really significant in my own place, to try to understand life here, and to learn to function in a way that could be meaningful to me and the community. I burrowed into life here unmindful of anything but my community and involvement and survival. . . ."

Although everyone had thought that he epitomized the ability of a volunteer to live deeply in the culture after just six months, he wrote toward the end of his third year, "I have continued to change here and have now sort of reached a point of being able to feel with others. This is different from understanding how they feel. I am able to be a part of them as they do things with each other and me . . . " (Fuchs, p. 253).

D was a success in both Filipino and Peace Corps terms. So was another volunteer.

> A male volunteer from Massachusetts ran what appears to have been highly successful in-service training classes on English and science for teachers. He also had effective adult education classes and a successful piggery-poultry project. He seemed to blend into his community almost from the beginning, becoming one of the first volunteers to learn the dialect from his region and use it extensively. He enjoyed serenading at night with the gang from the *sari-sari* store and drank tuba with the older men who, as he put it "had the pleasure of learning they could drink the American under the proverbial table"(Fuchs, p. 250).

These two cases teach us some useful things. Both volunteers genuinely joined their communities. They learned the language, sought to "burrow in." Most importantly, they accepted the Filipinos on their own terms and made friends with them, presumably long before their own understanding of the local culture had developed. D wrote, "The people are different, but willing to take me in. . . ." Somehow or other, the Filipino traits that so frustrated other volunteers were not an obstacle to these two. Instead, these two accepted not only the worth of the Filipinos but the worth of their ways, enough to practice them joyfully. And out of that long practice came D's remarkable statement that he was now able to feel *with* others.

Did the two volunteers "go native"? In a sense. Perhaps the most important respect in which this is true lies in the acceptance of the worth and authority of the local community's standards of conduct. These volunteers *participated* in Filipino life. That participation was reinforced in two ways. First, it must have been intrinsically enjoyable to these particular young men. It was satisfying to drink tuba with the local males. Second, that participation must have won social approval from the Filipinos *and that approval must have mattered* to these volunteers. Conceivably the approval of Peace Corps staff became less important (remember that D chose to shake off "entanglement" with the Peace Corps) as the approval of the local community became more important.

The sequence of events seem[s] to go like this:

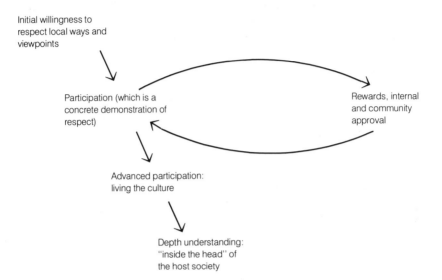

Initial willingness to
respect local ways and
viewpoints

Participation (which is a
concrete demonstration of
respect)

Rewards, internal
and community
approval

Advanced participation:
living the culture

Depth understanding:
"inside the head" of
the host society

It is worth noting that it was only after three years of intense, 24-hour-a-day experience that D felt that he was inside the Filipino head, seeing and feeling in Filipino ways. This, of course, should be no surprise, especially to Americans with their centuries of experience in the difficulties of immigrant assimilation. Stories of immigrants are replete with the difficulties of adjustment, the persistence of old-country ways and attitudes, the stress between parents and the children born in the new country. Many immigrants never made the cultural shift emotionally, even after decades of living in the new setting. But many did.

RESPECT AND PARTICIPATION—MISSING ELEMENTS

What the Peace Corps examples—and the American immigrant experience—show us is that it is not easy to attain cross-cultural awareness or understanding of the kind that puts you into the head of a person from an utterly different culture. Contact alone will not do it. Even sustained contact will not do it. There must be a readiness to respect and accept, and a capacity to participate. The participation must be reinforced by rewards that matter to the participant. And the participation must be sustained over long periods of time. Finally, one may assume that some plasticity in the individual, the ability to learn and change, is crucial. In general, the young will be more flexible and able to achieve this.

This kind of cross-cultural awareness is not reached by tourists nor, in the days of empire, was it reached by colonial administrators or missionaries, however long their service on foreign soil. In American schools, despite integration and black and Chicano study programs, whites do not achieve such an awareness of minority world-views. The missing elements are respect and participation. The society offers limited gratifications for reinforcement of respect for minorities—and very limited penalties for disrespect. And it offers absolutely no rewards to those of the white majority who might seek to participate in minority behavior patterns. The situation for the minority groups is somewhat different; there are social rewards for participating in the majority culture and many individuals shuttle more or less successfully between the two worlds or work out some kind of synthesis.

OPTIONS

If cross-cultural awareness of a profound sort is extremely difficult to attain, what are the options? Are there lesser varieties of awareness that might nonetheless be said to contribute to a global perspective? Are there better methods than have typically been employed to reach awareness? Is the goal itself worthwhile; i.e., does cross-cultural awareness matter?

Let me talk to that last question first. Yes, cross-cultural awareness does matter, for the following major reason if for no other. Several million years of evolution seem to have produced in us a creature that does not easily recognize the members of its own species. That is stated in rather exaggerated form, but it refers to the fact that human groups commonly have difficulty in accepting the humanness of other human groups.

> [We] call a group of primitives in northern North America Eskimos; this name, originated by certain Indians to the south of the Eskimos, means "Eaters of Raw Flesh." However, the Eskimos' own name for themselves is not Eskimos but Inupik, meaning "Real People." By their name they provide a contrast between themselves and other groups; the latter might be "people" but are never "real." [2]

This practice of naming one's own group "the people" and by implication relegating all others to not-quite-human status has been documented in nonliterate groups all over the world. But it is simply one manifestation of a species trait that shows itself in modern populations as well. It is there in the hostile faces of the white parents demonstrating against school busing. You will find it lurking in the background as Russians and Chinese meet at the negotiating table to work out what is ostensibly a boundary dispute. And it flares into the open during tribal disputes in Kenya.

It must, once, have been an adaptive trait. Perhaps, in ways that we now tend to deprecate, it still is. We call it chauvinism rather than self-esteem. Clearly, there are positive effects associated with a strong sense of group identity. Loyalty is a virtue everywhere, disloyalty abhorred everywhere. The inner harmony of groups is strengthened if aggression can be displaced, diverted to external targets. And if aggression is to be justified, then it helps if the enemy is not quite human. It helps even more if the enemy can be shown to be engaging in practices that are so outrageously different from one's own that they can be credibly labeled inhuman.

There was a time when the solidarity of small groups of humans was the basis for the survival of the species. But in the context of mass populations and weapons of mass destructiveness, group solidarity and the associated tendency to deny the full humaneness of other peoples pose serious threats to the species. When we speak of "humans" it is important that we include not only ourselves and our immediate group but all four billion of those other bipeds, however strange their ways.

This is the primary reason for cross-cultural awareness. If we are to admit the humanness of those others, then the strangeness of their ways must become less strange. Must, in fact, become believable. Ideally, that means getting inside the head of those strangers and looking out at the world through their eyes. Then the strange becomes familiar and totally believable. As we have seen, that is a difficult trick to pull off. But there may be methods that will increase the probability of success. Further, there are lesser degrees of cross-cultural awareness than getting inside the head; these more modest degrees of awareness are not to be scorned.

LEVELS OF CROSS-CULTURAL AWARENESS

We might discriminate between four levels of cross-cultural awareness as follows:

Level	Information	Mode	Interpretation
I	Awareness of super-ficial or very visible cultural traits: stereotypes	Tourism, textbooks, National Geographic	Unbelievable, i.e., exotic, bizarre
II	Awareness of signifi-cant and subtle cultural traits that contrast markedly with one's own	Culture conflict situations	Unbelievable, i.e., frustrating, irrational
III	Awareness of signifi-cant and subtle cultural traits that contrast markedly with one's own	Intellectual analysis	Believable, cognitively
IV	Awareness of how another culture feels from the standpoint of the insider	Cultural immersion: living the culture	Believable beacuse of subjective familiarity

At level I, a person might know that Japanese were exaggerated in their politeness and gestures of deference. At level II are those who know, through either direct or secondhand experience, of cultural traits that significantly (and irritatingly) contrast with one's own practices. The French in their relations with some Indian tribes and the Peace Corps volunteers who failed to adjust might be at this level. So, too, might those who despair over the seeming inability of many developing countries to control population growth. At level III are those who might know, for example, that the really distinctive aspect of the Japanese social hierarchy has nothing to do with the forms of politeness but rather exists in the keen sense of mutual obligation between superior and inferior. The level III person accepts this cultural trait intellectually; it makes sense to him. Peace Corps volunteers might have had this kind of intellectual understanding before actual contact with host cultures. After that contact, some of them slipped to level II and some moved to level IV.

According to this scheme, "believability" is achieved only at levels III and IV. And I have argued that believability is necessary if one group of humans is to accept other members of the biological species as human. I have also noted the rigors of the climb to level IV. This seems to leave level III as the practical goal. But is level III enough?

My position is that level III is indeed more attainable than level IV, and it is a reasonably worthy goal. But not quite enough. We should try to attain at least some aspects of level IV awareness. We can. There are new methods to be explored. And there is a more general reason for encouragement. The evolutionary experience that seemed to freeze us into a small-group psychology, anxious and suspicious of those who were not "us," also made us the most adaptive creature alive. That flexibility, the power to make vast psychic shifts, is very much with us. One of its manifestations is the modern capacity for empathy.

BEYOND EMPATHY

Daniel Lerner in *The Passing of Traditional Society* writes:

> Empathy . . . is the capacity to see oneself in the other fellow's situation. This is an indispensable skill for people moving out of traditional settings. Ability to empathize may make all the difference, for example, when the newly mobile persons are villagers who grew up knowing all the extant individuals, roles and relationships in their environment. Outside his village or tribe, each must meet new individuals, recognize new roles, and learn new relationships involving himself. . . .
>
> High empathic capacity is the predominant personal style only in modern society, which is distinctively industrial, urban, literate and participant. Traditional society is nonparticipant—it deploys people by kinship into communities isolated from each other and from a center. . . .
>
> Whereas the isolate communities of traditional society func- tioned well on the basis of a highly constrictive personality, the interdependent sectors of modern society require widespread participation. This in turn requires an expansive and adaptive self- system, ready to incorporate new roles and to identify personal values with public issues. This is why modernization of any society has involved the great characterological transformation we call psychic mobility. . . . In modern society *more* individuals exhibit *higher* empathic capacity than in any previous society.[3]

If Lerner is correct, modern populations have a dramatically different outlook, a dramatically different readiness for change, than traditional populations. That difference must have been learned—and by millions of people. If the latent capacity for empathy can be learned or activated, then it may not be too much to work toward a psychic condition that reaches a step beyond empathy. Magoroh Maruyama, an anthropologist-philosopher, describes that next step as *transspection.*

> "Transspection is an effort to put oneself in the head . . . of another person. One tries to believe what the other person believes, and assume what the other person assumes. . . ." Transspection differs from analytical "understanding." Empathy is a projection of feelings between two persons with one epistemology. Transspection is a trans-epistemological process which tries to learn a foreign belief, a foreign assumption, a foreign perspective, feelings in a foreign context, and consequences of such feelings in a foreign context. In transspection a person temporarily believes whatever the other person believes. It is an understanding by practice. [4]

Empathy, then, means the capacity to imagine oneself in another role within the context of one's own culture. Transspection means the capacity to imagine pupils in a role within the context of a foreign culture. Putting Lerner and Maruyama together, we might chart the psychic development of humanity as follows:

Traditional peoples   Unable to imagine a viewpoint other than that associated with fixed roles in the context of a local culture.

Modern peoples   Able to imagine and learn a variety of roles in the context of a national culture.

Postmodern peoples   Able to imagine the viewpoint of roles in foreign cultures.

Or, we might show the sequence of development in a more graphic way, as involving a movement from the constrictions of local perspectives through the expanded psychological flexibility necessary for role learning in large, heterogeneous national societies, to the advanced versatility of "global psyches" that travel comfortably beyond the confines of the home culture. (The gray zone is home culture.)

The modern personality type did not develop because it was planned. It emerged in the context of changing social conditions. The postmodern personality type, similarly, is not likely to be produced by educational strategies. But if there is a broad social movement, an essentially unplanned intensification of human interaction on the world stage, then educators and other interested parties can play their minor but nonetheless useful roles in the unfolding drama. For educators, that will mean providing students with maximum experience in transspection. And maximum experience means more than time. It means a climate in which transspection is facilitated and expected—and in which the expectations are reinforced. Under such circumstances the schools might produce a slightly higher proportion of persons with the kind of psychic mobility displayed by D, the Peace Corps worker who could feel *with* others. That would be a gain.

If more and more individuals reach the vantage point of level IV awareness, there will be another kind of gain. Dispelling the strangeness of the foreign and admitting the humanness of all human creatures is vitally important. But looking at ourselves from outside our own culture is a possibility for those who can also see through the eyes of the foreigner—and that has significance for the *perspective consciousness* discussed earlier. Native social anyalysts can probe the deep layers of their own culture, but the outside eye has a special sharpness: if the native for even a moment can achieve the vision of the foreigner, he will be rewarded with a degree of self-knowledge not otherwise obtainable.

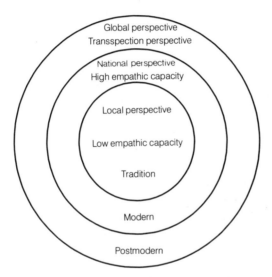

Notes

1. Lawrence H. Fuchs, "The Role and Communication Task of the Change Agent—Experiences of the Peace Corps in the Philippines," in Daniel Lerner and Wilbur Schramm (eds.), *Communication and Change in the Developing Countries*, pp. 242–245, East-West Center Press, Honolulu, 1967.

2. Wendell H. Oswalt, *Understanding Our Culture*, p. 19, Holt, Rinehart and Winston, Inc., 1970.

3. Daniel Lerner, *The Passing of Traditional Society*, pp. 50, 51, Free Press, 1958.

4. Magoroh Maruyama, "Toward a Cultural Futurology," Cultural Futurology Symposium, American Anthropology Association national meeting, Training Center for Community Programs, University of Minnesota, 1970.

WILLIAM B. GUDYKUNST and
YOUNG YUN KIM

Cultural Variations
in Message Decoding

(The authors of the previous articles in this section suggest that we tend to seek our own reflection in intercultural encounters. Gudykunst and Young Kim help the reader understand how perception and interpretation of what we see keep us culture-bound.)

What has been thought of as mind is actually internalized culture. The mind-culture process which has evolved over the past four or more million years is primarily concerned with "organization" and, furthermore, the organization of "information" as it is channeled (and altered by the senses) to the brain.

—Edward T. Hall

Humans are active organisms. In making sense of our environment, we create as much as we define. A large class of social objects, such as our concepts of love, friendship, beauty, and freedom, "exist" only as created and collectively understood meanings. The perception of our environment as offering opportunities, as threatening, or as irrelevant and the imputation to it of qualities more generally are somewhat arbitrary from the standpoint of their "objective" reality. In many cases such meanings cannot be derived simply from knowledge of such objective qualities. Through the process of decoding, we appraise the things and people around us and strive to assess what meanings they may have for the fulfillment of our needs. Since other people and objects are perceived and interpreted in terms of their meanings for us, it follows that our definitions and classifications reflect only in part the "real" nature of things.

Cross-cultural research has revealed much concerning the ways people in various cultures decode messages from their physical and

From Gudykunst and Young, *Communicating with Strangers* (New York: McGraw-Hill Publishing Company, 1984), 119–133, by permission of the publisher.

psychological environments. The term *subjective culture* has been used often as a theoretical construct in comparing various cultures. This concept focuses on those aspects of culture manifested in the commonalities of perceptual-cognitive patterns in individuals within a given cultural group. It was introduced by Osgood (1964; 1965), who explored the notion of a universal framework for some affective and connotative aspects of language. Triandis (1972) further extended the concept to include values, beliefs, and attitudes in an attempt to construct a model to guide cross-cultural research on how people in different cultures perceive and interpret their social reality.

In [what follows] we describe some of the variations in subjective cultures. We are interested particularly in cognitive differences across cultures in decoding communication messages. We first discuss the patterns of receiving and organizing information from the environment, which we refer to as perception. Next, we explore cultural variations in mental processing (interpreting, evaluating, abstracting, etc.) of the perceived information (i.e., thinking). Finally, we examine some of the characteristics of interpersonal orientation directly influencing the way people in various cultures perceive and think, as well as express themselves verbally and nonverbally.

PERCEPTION

In understanding perceptual variations across cultures, the concept of *contexting*, introduced by Hall (1976), provides a useful point of view. . . . Hall states that culture provides a selective screen between individuals and the outside world and different cultures "program" their members to pay attention to different aspects of the environment with a greater or lesser attachment of significance. Based on this observation, Hall uses the term *contexting* to describe the perceptual process of recognizing, giving significance to, and incorporating contextual cues in interpreting the total meaning of any stimulus in a particular communication transaction. Here contextual cues refer to all the messages implicit in a communication transaction, including the nature of the interpersonal relationship between the communicators, the nonverbal expressions of the communicators, the physical setting, and the social circumstances. Verbal messages are viewed as explicitly coded messages that *stand out against* the background of various contextual cues. For example, the act of uttering the verbal message "how wonderful!" can convey different meanings depending on the contextual cues accompanying it. The circumstances, facial expression, and vocal tone that are simultaneously emanating implicit messages help us to interpret the overall meaning of a particular communication.

Hall applies this concept of contexting to the cross-cultural comparision of communication patterns. Based on the contexting patterns of individuals, Hall distinguishes cultures as either high-context cultures or low-context cultures. Of course, such dichotomous terms as *high-context* and *low-context* should not be interpreted literally. Rather, they should be seen as extreme ends of the same continuum, on which cultures can be placed according to the relative degree of implicitness or explicitness in perceptual and message patterns. Thus cultures that tend to place greater emphasis on sensitivity to and the significance of subtle contextual cues can be characterized as high-context cultures. On the other hand, low-context cultures tend to emphasize spoken or written verbal messages that are explicitly coded. Generally speaking, many of the Western cultures that are technologically advanced tend to be low-context cultures. Among low-context cultures, according to Hall, are the cultures of the United States, Canada, England, Switzerland, Germany, and the Scandinavian nations. Other European cultures (such as French, Italian, and Spanish) and many non-European cultures (such as Asian, African, native American, and South American) are characterized as high-context cultures. One can further observe that as a high-context culture such as Japan undergoes a rapid technological advancement, its social dynamics also go through changes toward less implicit, lower-context communication patterns.

A number of other cross-cultural studies have provided supportive evidence to Hall's observation of high-context and low-context cultures. Ouchi (1981), for example, compares Japanese and North American business organizational cultures and characterizes the basic mechanisms of management control in a Japanese company as much more "subtle, implicit, and internal," so they often appear to be nonexistent to strangers from a low-context culture. Such a conclusion would be a mistake since the Japanese management mechanisms are clearly recognizable among the Japanese employees; these mechanisms are highly disciplined, thorough, demanding, and yet very flexible. Also, Adelman and Lustig (1981), in their study of the perceptions of the communication problems between Saudi Arabian and North American business personnel, observe Saudi Arabians tend to fault North Americans for their inattention to implicit social rituals. For the North Americans, the Saudi Arabians lack the explicitness and objectivity felt to be necessary in business transactions. The North American business personnel working in these two high-context cultures, Japanese and Saudi Arabian, react to the local modes of communication based on the conditioning of their low-context culture. They tend to place less significance on subtle contextual cues in business transactions, while to their Japanese and Saudi Arabian counterparts the contextual messages are an integral part of the total business transaction process.

THINKING

Cross-cultural variations in message decoding also are found in patterns of "thinking," in the sense of sustained mental processes. Once we perceive information from the environment, we "process" it; that is, we engage in such mental activities as abstracting, analyzing, evaluating, and synthesizing, among others. In other words, we make "sense" out of the perceived information through reasoning.

Just as individuals in divergent cultures perceive the environment differently, so are they observed to differ in their thinking patterns. One of the variations most widely recognized in cognitive psychology is that between *field-dependence* and *field-independence*. This concept originally was formulated to refer to how people rely on visual or other information in space in making judgments about the orientations of themselves and of objects in space (Witkin et al., 1962). This bipolarity, of course, defines only the extremes of a continuum along which people in different cultures may be ordered and compared. The concept has since been generalized to other cognitive patterns, such as global versus analytical style. Recently it has been expanded further to include personality characteristics, such as the degree to which a person differentiates between self and nonself. Jahoda (1980) summarizes relevant research findings to describe the salient features of field-independent individuals:

> Field-independent people have a higher ability to extract a constituent part than field-dependent people who find it difficult to break up such an organized whole analytically. Similarly, in the intellectual sphere, relative field-independent people display greater skill in solving the particular type of problem which requires isolating certain elements from their context and making use of [them] in a different context. It was also originally suggested that field-dependent individuals were more sensitive to the prevailing social field and therefore more likely to respond to social cues or conform to social pressures. (p. 100)

Note the close linkage between the above characterization of the field-dependent and field-independent cognitive styles and the earlier description of perceptual styles in high-context and low-context cultures. The field-dependent cognitive style corresponds closely to the perceptual mode of the high-context cultures, while the field-independent cognitive style is related closely to the perceptual pattern of the low-context cultures. Both perspectives provide useful conceptual tools for understanding cross-cultural variations in information decoding patterns.

Keeping the general conceptual frameworks in mind, let us now examine some specific cross-cultural patterns of thinking. Observers of Western cultures . . . characterize their predominant mode of thinking as "logical," "analytic," "action mode," and "linear"—all of which fit the description of the field-independent cognitive style. Their most characteristic form is known as scientific induction, which emphasizes concentrated attention on the "raw materials" provided by the senses and applying rational principles to those raw materials to bring them into a more or less orderly and self-consistent whole. Gulick (1962), in his comparative analysis of Eastern and Western cultures, describes Western thinking in the main as "the effort to make a coherent and verifiable 'world construct,' and to impose man's will on nature and society" (p. 127). Such mental characteristics of the Western peoples have given great impetus to the development of natural science and technology.

An associated characteristic of Western cultures, particularly that of the United States, is the tendency to see the world in terms of dichotomies (Stewart, 1972). This characteristic is illustrated by the Western tendency to think in terms of good-evil, right-wrong, true-false, and beautiful-ugly. Stewart describes this tendency to polarize as "simplifying the view of the world, predisposing to action and providing individuals with a typical method of evaluating and judging by means of a comparison" (p. 29).

While sharing a great deal of commonality with thinking in Western cultures in general, thinking by the people in the United States is distinguishable from that of Europeans by its heavier emphasis on empirical facts, induction, and operationalism. Stewart (1972) comments:

> For Americans, the world is composed of facts—not ideas. Their process of thinking is generally inductive, beginning with facts and then proceeding to ideas. But the movement from the concrete to the more abstract is seldom a complete success, for Americans have a recurrent need to reaffirm their theories and . . . their ideas require validation by application and by becoming institutionalized. (pp. 22–23)

The operational style of thinking tends to produce a stress on consequences and to result in a disregard for the empirical world as such. What is important is the ability of the individual to affect the empirical world. Such operationally oriented thinking in the United States has led to the prevailing cultural values of pragmatism and functionalism.

In contrast, Europeans are characterized as attaching primacy to ideas and theories. Their deductive and abstract style of thinking gives priority to the conceptual world. Although the empirical world is not necessarily ignored, it often is treated with a symbolic and demonstrational attitude. Deductive thinkers are likely to have much more confidence in their ideas and theories, so it suffices for them to show one or two connections between their concepts and the empirical world. They do not feel compelled to amass facts and statistics, as is the way in the United States, and they tend to generalize from one concept to another concept, or to facts, by means of logic. Europeans have a greater faith and trust in the powers of thought, while people in the United States place a greater significance on their methods of empirical observation and measurement (Stewart, 1972). Although the cultures of the United States and Western Europe are in some respects dissimilar, they share certain basic characteristics of field-independent, low-context cultures. Even though the relative significance placed on empirical observation and verification and on the deductive and the inductive processes of deriving knowledge differs between the two cultural groups, they both emphasize a fundamental cognitive pattern that is logical, categorical, linear, and analytic.

Compared to those of Western cultures, the thinking patterns of non-Western cultures are often characterized as "relational," "integrative," "holistic," and "intuitive." Asians, in general, are observed to have a central mode of thinking that is not concerned as much with logic and analysis as it is with intuitive "knowing" and meditative introspection and contemplation. Asians tend to emphasize the unity between the subjective and the objective realms of the inner and the outer conditions, and thus engage less in analyzing a topic divisively by breaking it down into smaller units as Westerners often do. What seems to be of central importance in Asian thinking is a certain repose of the personality in which it "feels" it is "grasping" the inner significance of the object of contemplation. The direct sense of rapport with the outer object—whether a person, idea, or thing—is the primary end result of Asian thinking (Gulick, 1962, p. 127).

The intuitive thinking of non-Westerners tends to deemphasize the power of analysis, classification, precision, and abstraction, and the result is perhaps not as effective in attaining accurate "facts" about the object.

On the other hand, intuitive thinking allows holistic and intimate identification with all of the contextual cues in a communication transaction, thus making the perceptual patterns of non-Westerners highly contextual. Their intuitive style of thinking provides a powerful cognitive mechanism for developing a harmonious rapport with the other person and the environment. This mechanism enables the non-Westerner to be sensitive to the most subtle undercurrents of emotion and mood in a particular communication event and interpersonal relationship without having to engage in a deliberate attempt to logically analyze the situation. Such an Asian sensibility, more intuitive than analytic, may appear to many people from Western cultures to be ambiguous and illogical. For strangers from Asia, it may be almost impossible to explain some of these inner experiences to their North American friends. Such cross-cultural differences in the process of experiencing external phenomena can create much frustration and frequent misunderstanding when we communicate with strangers.

Ornstein (1972), in summarizing evidence from split brain research by Sperry and his colleagues, suggests a possible physiological explanation for the observed perceptual and cognitive variations across cultures. He believes the two cerebral hemispheres of the human brain process different kinds of information and the operating characteristics of the two likewise differ. The left hemisphere is involved predominantly with analytic, logical thinking, speech, and mathematical functions. Its mode of operation is primarily linear; it seems to process information sequentially. The right hemisphere is more holistic, direct, and relational in its mode of operation. It is responsible for orientation in space, intuition, and imagination and is able to integrate information in a nonlinear, diffused fashion. In normal people, of course, the two hemispheres operate interdependently, integrating both sides of the brain. The differential emphasis in the specialized hemispheric functions, however, appears to correspond very closely to the variations in the patterns of information processing in Western and Eastern cultures.

In recognizing the above cultural variations in thinking, one must keep in mind that these identified cultural patterns do not mean Westerners think using only logic and reason or non-Westerners think using only intuition. What we have presented so far is the *relative* emphasis that different cultures place on particular methods of thinking, rather than absolute differences in kind. While non-Westerners do think and reason, as well as use their intuitive mode of "seeing" things without logical analysis, the significance of knowledge through intuition is accepted and valued more extensively in the East than in the West.

Similarly, Western thinking involves intuitive processes, but Westerners tend to deemphasize the importance of such awareness through intuition and to value instead the outcome of logical, analytic thinking processes.

INTERPERSONAL ORIENTATION

As well as showing observed differences in patterns of perception and thinking, individuals in different cultures vary in their conception of self, of others, and of human relationships in various social contexts. All interpersonal communication is based on a relationship of some sort, ranging from strangers, to casual acquaintances, to intimate friends, to family relationships. A culture conditions its members to orient themselves toward specific interpersonal relationships in certain patterned ways. In this section we examine some of the culturally determined variations in individuals' orientations in their social relationships.

Relationship of the Individual to the Group

In all societies individuals belong to a number of significant groups, such as family, co-workers, and friends. These groups provide individuals with emotional support and a sense of security. At the same time they espouse in their members a respect for authority, acceptance of standards, a tendency to behave in accord with established norms, and a desire to cooperate to achieve group goals. It also has been observed that some degree of tension between the competing values of conformity and autonomy must therefore exist in every society (Segall, 1979, p. 140).

Although many group functions are universal, the extent to which an individual is dependent on the group and the equilibrium point of optimal balance between dependency and autonomy of individual members in a primary group vary across cultures and subcultures. . . . To . . . illustrate, Berry (1967) reports that the Eskimos, whose food-getting practices should result in training for independence, were much less conformist than the agricultural African group the Temne, whose subsistence activities demand cooperation and whose socialization practices, therefore, should stress conformity. On a continuum of the dependency (or conformity) of the individual on the group, the position of the culture of the United States is represented by the attitude that the individual is more important than the group. Francis Hsu (1981), a noted anthropologist, describes individualism as a central theme of the North American personality. In comparing the cultures of the United States and China, Hsu believes individualism is a master key to the North

American character and the rest of the Western world and distinguishes the Western world from the non-Western.

Generally speaking, people in the United States stress the individual as a primary point of reference. This tendency begins at a very early age, when children are encouraged to be autonomous. The self-directedness of the child is seldom questioned. It is accepted implicitly that "each child or person should be encouraged to decide for himself, developing his own opinions, solve his own problems, have his own things, and learn to view and deal with the world from the point of view of the self" (Stewart, 1972, p. 70). Accordingly, one's social conduct is viewed as a reflection of one's own character, i.e., the internal system of moral and ethical systems. Any serious misconduct by an individual brings social disgrace to that individual and only that individual, and little to the family or other primary groups. Mir-Djalali (1980) provides a supportive finding from his comparative study of United States and Iranian samples: Iranians tend to perceive the word *me* with a heavy emphasis on "human beings" and future-oriented concerns, such as ambition and aim, while the North American responses emphasize the concept of self as "individual." Similarly, Yousef (1974) finds a difference in the basic attitudes toward life in the United States and Arab societies. North Americans value individual centeredness and self-reliance, and the Arabic attitude is one of mutual dependence.

Many non-Western cultures commonly are characterized by their relatively greater degree of submission of individual identity, individualism, and self-expression to the groups to which one belongs. The concept of *amae* is pointed out by Doi (1976) as being illustrative of the intimate nature of individual-group interdependence in Japan. It refers to the individual's emotional dependency on other members of primary groups, in much the same way as a child is dependent on the parents. In many non-Western cultures, members of a family or a company are expected to submerse their personal interests and desires in favor of those of the total group. The members are expected to behave in a manner that will not disgrace the honor of the family or the company. Thus, as Glidden (1972) and Yousef (1974) observe, the interplay between honor and shame dictates much of Middle Eastern interpersonal behavior. Also, Ouchi (1981), in comparing the corporate systems in Japan and the United States, emphasizes the collective sense of responsibility among Japanese employees. Benedict's (1934) description of the Japanese culture as a "shame culture," in contrast to the "sin culture" of the United States, appears to be still relevant, in spite of many apparent changes in the two societies. This means that, in Japan, parents often admonish their children by saying, "If you do that, people will laugh at you," implying, "If you are laughed at, you are bringing shame to your family." When North American parents say the same thing to their children, they mean, "It is wrong for you to do that and you will be punished for it." Japanese children who go through such a socialization process develop a strong "group-ego," which often supercedes their individualistic orientation. North American children, on the other hand, learn to develop a strong sense of self-reliance and independence.

The intense interdependency observed in many of the non-Western cultures, however, cannot be generalized to outside the primary group settings. In fact, there exists a tendency in these cultures to discriminate in-group members from out-group members. . . . People in non-Western cultures often behave in an aloof and indifferent manner to strangers, which may be perceived by Westerners as impoliteness (Morsbach, 1976, p. 255). Or, sometimes, we see them behave with exaggerated politeness to strangers or casual acquaintances, which may be perceived as being either "inappropriate" or "insincere" by Westerners. The well-known notion of "face-saving" among Japanese, for example, illustrates the psychological "distancing" of out-group members through being formal and polite. Whether one acts in an impolite manner or with exaggerated politeness, the underlying psychological tendency seems to be a concentrated involvement with in-group members and a relative distancing from out-group members. The interpersonal behavior in many Western cultures, particularly that of the United States, displays a less discriminating orientation with respect to in-group and out-group associations. People in Western cultures are generally more willing to develop relationships with strangers, without imposing too rigid a screening process. Such an orientation toward others characterizes the Westerners as friendly, open, informal, and outgoing and is typified in common social rituals such as cocktail parties, where individuals are introduced to one another for the first time. In such social gatherings, people are expected to find ways to reach out to others and to begin to develop relationships with them, if mutually agreeable. For a stranger from a non-Western culture, this Western style of social interaction can be perceived as "awkward," "unnatural," "superficial," and difficult to participate in actively. On the other hand, a stranger from the United States in an Eastern country may find the reserve and social rigidity of non-Westerners uncomfortable and difficult to penetrate.

It appears then there is a close relationship between culturally patterned in-group and out-group relationships. For Westerners, the relatively less intense interpersonal involvement and interdependency among members of primary groups appear to allow them to be more open toward out-group members. For non-Westerners, the relatively discriminatory and concentrated involvement within primary groups tends to make them distant toward out-group members.

Interpersonal Relationships

In any interpersonal relationship there are certain expectations individuals develop regarding each other's attitudes and behaviors and toward the relationship itself. Such interpersonal expectations are shaped substantially by cultural rules, norms, and values. . . .

In the United States relationships are developed and maintained primarily according to activities (Stewart, 1972, p. 54). Time spent with a friend (meaning anyone, from a passing acquaintance to a lifelong intimate) centers around activity, a thing, an event, or a shared history. Thus North Americans have friendships that originate around work, children's schools, political activities, charities, leisure activities, and various occasions for sharing food and drink. This activity-oriented nature of friendship reflects one of the central Western values—the importance of each individual and the maximization of the fulfillment of individual needs. For North Americans a relationship is considered healthy to the extent it serves the expected function for each of the involved parties. The activity-oriented and functional approach, coupled with a greater degree of social mobility, tends to contribute to the relatively unstable and impermanent nature of interpersonal relationships in the United States and other technologically advanced Western societies. As people move from one residence or job to another, few old friends are retained in a lasting relationship. Instead, people tend to look forward to establishing a new circle of friends with whom they share mutually helpful and satisfying social functions and activities.

Compare such a functional, impermanent orientation toward interpersonal relationships to the more stable and lasting one found in many non-Western cultures. For people in a relatively homogeneous and less technological environment, relationships are often "given" to them according to their birth, schooling, work, and/or residence. Intimate relationships tend to develop as a consequence of prolonged affiliation rather than of actively seeking them out. The primary basis for many interpersonal relationships in non-Western cultures lies not so much in specific functions that individuals do for and with each other as in mutual liking and affection for each other's disposition and temperament and a more generalized acceptance of the whole person. Once a relationship has developed into an intimate one, it often is expected to last throughout life.

A related characteristic of the relatively stable and permanent interpersonal relationship is the strong psychological involvement and loyalty toward each other. In non-Western cultures close friends and family members are closely intertwined in their sharing of their private lives. Such intense commitment between intimates is the source of an emotional stability and security and often transcends individual needs and desires. In financial matters the distinction of material things as "yours" and "mine" is often unclear or suppressed among intimates. The common Western practice of "Dutch treat" by close friends is not as prevalent in many non-Western cultures and is encountered by non-Westerners with much discomfort and feeling of "unnaturalness." Splitting the bill according to the respective meals when two friends eat in a restaurant is considered rather impersonal and businesslike. Even on making decisions about personal affairs, such as choosing a career or a marriage partner, the opinions of family members, especially parents, exert a stronger influence in the group-oriented cultures. It is not too unusual, for instance, for a son to forsake his choice of a spouse because of the opposition of his parents, and even the opinions of his intimate friends exert a substantial influence on his choice of a mate. Further, the non-Westerners' loyalty in intimate relationships sometimes leads them to "bend the system," willingly or unwillingly, making them more likely to engage in such practices as nepotism or favoritism. It should be noted, however, that these practices may not be negatively evaluated as they are in the West.

In line with the observed intimacy, commitment, and latitude for each other's interests among non-Western intimates, the breakup of such a relationship commonly is accompanied by a great sense of tragedy. Once the emotionally based relationship reaches a point of "no return," it is difficult for the involved parties to talk things over rationally and to attempt to mend the "broken" relationship. In the United States, on the other hand, it is not uncommon to find intimate friends or married couples who remain friends even after they decide to terminate their current arrangement. Such a redefining of the nature of an existing relationship can be seen as an expression of the functional orientation many North Americans have toward interpersonal relationships. The specialized nature of a relationship makes it possible for the involved parties to terminate a relationship with relative ease and, if necessary and mutually agreeable, to redefine the function of the relationship to something more feasible. In this cultural context, the functions themselves, rather than *who* performs the functions, often take priority. If two people in a relationship cannot agree on their mutual functions, then the most logical thing for them to do is to redefine the functions or to find someone else who can more readily perform them. Comparatively, such redefining of an intimate relationship is rarely practiced in cultures where intimates expect and demand full and lasting commitment. These same patterns exist with respect to the resolution of conflict. . . .

Hall (1976) interprets these contrasting approaches to interpersonal relationships as characteristic of high-context and low-context cultures. The emotionally based, person-oriented approach is viewed as characteristic of high-context cultures, while the functionally based, specialized approach is seen as characteristic of low-context cultures. Hall sees interpersonal bonds in a low-context culture as fragile and notes that people in such a culture move away or withdraw with relative ease if a relationship is not developing satisfactorily. On the other hand, according to Hall, the bonds between people in a high-context culture are stronger, and thus there is a tendency to allow for considerable "bending" of individual interests for the sake of the relationship.

The specialized approach to interpersonal relationships can be extended to the prevailing reliance of people in the United States and other Western cultures on specialists and experts, who are available for almost all functions that need to be performed. This pattern seems to reflect the logical, rational thinking of Westerners, who desire the "best" solution to a given problem from an expert who is qualified in that particular area. Thus, if someone is experiencing a serious emotional distress, the person is encouraged to see a professional psychologist or counselor in order to deal with the problem more rationally. In contrast, help for many of the social and emotional problems in high-context cultures is sought from members of one's family and from close friends.

Some variations in interpersonal relationship patterns must be noted among Western cultures. Whereas North Americans tend to limit friendship to an area of common interest, Russians and other Eastern and Southern Europeans tend to be more person-oriented, embracing the whole person. . . . In contrast to the North American, the Russian expects to form a deep bond of friendship with another person, assumes the obligation of almost constant companionship, and avoids any reticence or secretiveness toward friends (Stewart, 1972, pp. 54–55). The French, on the other hand, according to Stewart, exhibit contradictions stemming from simultaneous demands for privacy, independence, and long, close friendships. Combining features of both the North American and Russian styles, the French styles of friendship are specialized but are also organized in patterns of long duration, often with an expectation that family friendships will extend over more than one generation.

A similar observation is made by Hall (1976), who examined the French business practice of being generally much more involved with their employees, customers, and clients than are their American counterparts. . . .

Interpersonal Status

Another aspect of interpersonal orientation influencing communication processes is the culturally defined nature and the interpersonal functions of social status. . . . In the United States status generally is achieved. It depends very much on what we do and how other people respond to what we accomplish, and very little on what we are as persons. It is not too difficult in the United States to find successful self-made individuals who have gained higher status fairly rapidly. In many traditional non-Western cultures, status is often ascribed; it depends on the family into which one is born and is not likely to change drastically during one's lifetime. Consequently, there is less need for behavior designed to change one's status. Foa (1967) reports empirical evidence of the ascriptive, relatively permanent nature of social status among Middle Easterners. Similar results are reported by D. Levine (1965) and Korten (1972) in their studies of Ethiopian culture. Both Levine and Korten stress the extreme degree to which one's rank in Ethiopian society is determined by the rank of one's parents rather than by one's personal achievements. Korten also documents the Ethiopians' "obsessive fear" of incurring the disfavor of another person and the potentially disastrous effects of doing so. Other observations of the qualities of social status are reported in studies of Japanese and other Asian cultures. Bennett and McKnight (1966), for example, note that in Japan a superior, such as one's professor, retains strong "symbolic hierarchical precedence throughout the life of both parties, even when the student has become a professional equal in productivity, rank, and pay" (p. 600).

Comparatively, Western cultures, particularly the United States, tend to foster an initial egalitarian response toward others; two persons are presumed to be equal unless proven otherwise. Interpersonal relations are typically horizontal, conducted between presumed equals. This egalitarian principle of North American interpersonal behavior leads to what Asians and other non-Westerners consider to be fluidity and unpredictability in interactions and a highly variable, or at least less apparent, concern for status (Bennett and McKnight, 1966, p. 602).

The relative lack of a rigid status distinction in the United States and other Western cultures also is observed in the informality and directness with which people in those cultures tend to treat others. The

North American refers to everyone in essentially the same way; the preferred mode is equality. International students in the United States (strangers) find it more difficult than their North American classmates do to call their professors by their first names. On the other hand, North Americans working overseas (strangers) frequently find it difficult to adapt to the flowery language, complex methods of address, and ritualistic manners reflecting the hierarchical social structure and interpersonal orientation of the local people. Whereas the average North American considers formality, style, and protocol as unnatural and unnecessary in many interpersonal encounters, in some cultures these cues provide a dependable basis for predicting others' behavior.

Some of the variations in interpersonal orientation discussed so far are not limited to cross-cultural comparisons but can be discerned among subcultural groups within a culture. A most noticeable difference in interpersonal orientation exists between urban and rural communities. Generally speaking, a less technological and less complex rural community provides a subcultural environment in which interpersonal relationships are more stable, more involved, and less specialized. In cohesive rural areas, individuals tend to rely more on interpersonal sources for information and advice than on mass media or specialists. Research findings provide strong evidence that interpersonal relationships in rural areas tend to be more "global" and less function-specific. The "opinion leaders" in urban centers, for example, are noted more for the specialized nature of their influence on others than are their rural counterparts (Rogers and Shoemaker, 1971). Of course, there is a gradual diminishing of urban-rural distinctions in cultural and communication patterns as both areas increasingly are exposed to a similar information environment as a result of the pervasive networking of the mass media and transportation systems. Haselden (1968) goes so far as to say, "In the cultural sense there is no longer a rural America, no longer pockets where you find strange customs and people unacquainted with what occurs in the rest of the world" (p. 66). This obviously is not totally true, since groups like the Hutterites still exist in the United States today. This observation, however, points to a likely direction of change in the United States, as well as in many other countries of the world.

SUMMARY

In this [discussion], we presented some of the basic cross-cultural differences in patterns of message decoding in interpersonal communication. Emphasizing the importance of recognizing individual differences within a cultural group, we described variations in subjective culture, the fundamental way people in different cultures perceive and cognitively experience their physical and social environments. We also discussed variations in orientation toward primary groups, normative characteristics of interpersonal relationships in general, and the ways in which social status plays a role in interpersonal communication processes.

The main conceptual framework instrumental in comparing perceptual and thinking patterns of various cultures is Hall's construct of contexting and the identification of cultures on the bipolar continuum of high-context to low-context. We compared cultures according to the degree of field-dependence or field-independence in their cognitive patterns of information processing. A close correspondence exists between Hall's anthropological perspective and that of cognitive psychology. Both perspectives, when applied to the characterization of different cultures, describe essentially the same variation in message-decoding patterns. Individuals in high-context cultures tend to rely more heavily on subtle, implicit contextual cues, such as the social and relational context, knowledge about the other person, situational characteristics, and nonverbal cues. Some characteristics are identified with field-dependent individuals whose perception and cognitive processes are heavily embedded in the social and physical field.

Other associated cognitive characteristics in high-context and low-context cultures also were examined. Compared to low-context cultures, high-context cultures were described as more readily accepting and valuing intuitive, holistic, direct modes of thinking. We also discussed how the observed perceptual and cognitive differences between high-context and low-context cultures closely correspond to variations in the patterns of individual-group interdependence, the basic nature of interpersonal relationships, and the significance of social status in interpersonal communication. Individuals in high-context cultures tend to have a stronger group orientation, more explicit in-group and out-group distinctions, and more intense involvement with intimates than do people in low-context cultures, who have a stronger individualistic orientation.

It often requires a long and difficult process of trial and error before someone from a low-context culture develops an accurate understanding of the perceptual and cognitive patterns of a stranger from a high-context culture. Because our decoding process occurs mostly beyond our conscious control, we cannot easily recognize the specific discrepancies between our decoding patterns and those of the stranger. Recognizing the variations discussed . . . can help us to better understand the different message-decoding patterns used by strangers and thereby increase our ability to interpret and predict their behavior correctly.

Works Cited

Adelman, M. B., and Lustig, W. Intercultural communication problems as perceived by Saudi Arabian and American managers. *International Journal of Intercultural Relations*, 1981, 5, 365–381.

Benedict, R. *Patterns of culture*. Boston: Houghton Mifflin, 1934.

Bennett, J., and McKnight, R. Social norms, national imagery and interpersonal relations. In A. Smith (ed.), *Communication and culture*. New York: Holt, Rinehart, and Winston, 1966.

Berry, J. Independence and conformity in subsistence-level societies. *Journal of Personality and Social Psychology*, 1967, 7, 415–418.

Doi, T. The Japanese patterns of communication and the concept of *amae*. In L. Samovar and R. Porter (eds.), *Intercultural communication: A reader*, 2nd ed. Belmont, CA: Wadsworth, 1976.

Foa, U. Differentiation in cross-cultural communication. In L. Thayer (ed.), *Communication: Concepts and perspectives*. Washington, D.C.: Spartan Books, 1967.

Glidden, H. The Arab world. *American Journal of Psychiatry*, 1972, 128, 984–988.

Gulick, S. *The East and the West: A study of their psychic and cultural characteristics*. Rutland, VT: Charles E. Tuttle, 1962.

Hall, E. T. *Beyond culture*. New York: Doubleday, 1976.

Haselden, K. *Morality and the mass media*. Nashville, TN: Broadman Press, 1968.

Hsu, F. *Americans and Chinese*, 3rd ed. Honolulu: U. of Hawaii Press, 1981. (First published in 1953.)

Jahoda, G. Theoretical and systematic approaches. In H. Triandis and W. Lambert (eds.), *Handbook of cross-cultural psychology*, vol. 1. Boston: Allyn and Bacon, 1980.

Korten, D. *Planned change in a traditional society*. New York: Praeger, 1972.

Levine, D. *Wax and gold*. Chicago: U. of Chicago Press, 1965.

Mir-Djalali, E. The failure of language to communicate. *International Journal of Intercultural Relations*. 1980, 4, 307–328.

Morsbach, H. Aspects of nonverbal communication in Japan. In L. Samovar and R. Porter (eds.), *Intercultural communication: A reader*, 2nd ed. Belmont, CA: Wadsworth, 1976.

Ornstein, R. *The psychology of consciousness*. New York: Holt, Rinehart, and Winston, 1978.

Osgood, C. Semantic differential technique in the comparative study of cultures. *American Anthropologist*, 1964, 66, 171–200.

Osgood, C. Cross-cultural comparability in attitude measurement via multilingual semantic differentials. In I. Steiner and M. Fishbein (eds.), *Current studies in social psychology*. New York: Holt, Rinehart, and Winston, 1965.

Ouchi, W. *Theory Z*. Reading, MA: Addison-Wesley, 1981.

Rogers, E. M., and Shoemaker, F. *Communication of innovations*, 2nd ed. New York: Free Press, 1971.

Segall, M. H. *Cross-cultural psychology: Human behavior in global perspective.* Monterey, CA: Brooks/Cole, 1979.

Stewart, E. C. *American cultural patterns: A cross-cultural perspective.* Chicago: Intercultural Network, 1972.

Triandis, H. C., et al. *The analysis of subjective culture.* New York: Wiley, 1972.

Witkin, H. A., Dyk, R. B., Faterson, H. F., Goodenough, D. R., and Karp, S. A. *Psychological differentiation.* New York: Wiley, 1962.

Yousef, F. S. Cross-cultural communication. *Human Organization,* 1974, 33, 383–387.

*

DISCUSSION QUESTIONS AND ACTIVITIES

Boorstin

1. In his discussion of the transition from traveler to tourist, Daniel Boorstin evokes certain "pseudo-events." What are other pseudo-events that you can name? Look through magazines and newspapers with travel sections and find evidence of travel described as "adventures."

2. What are some reasons for travel in your family? Why did family members choose a particular destination? Their mode of transportation? Their accommodations during the trip? Consider great-grandparents, grandparents, your parents and their generation, your sibling.

3. Boorstin wrote this classic and articulate reflection on the cultural shift from travel to tourism in 1960, well before the ERA and the women's rights movements. Working with a partner, find gender-specific references ("man's incurable desire," "men who move"). How would you restate them using ungendered terms?

4. Define traveler and tourist. What distinguishes a traveler from a tourist? Plan itineraries for both a traveler and a tourist.

5. Go to a travel bureau for brochures advertising several trips. What do the brochures highlight? What trip is most tempting for you? Why?

6. Find a list of the Seven Wonders of the World in an encyclopedia or other reference book. Generate a new list in light of today's international realities. Explain your choices and compare them to those made by others in your group.

7. Take the position of a devil's advocate and refute Boorstin's concern that museums show works out of context and thus deprive the viewer of a considerable portion of their meaning.

8. What are some "tourist meccas" in your region? Are they located in their natural context or have they been elsewhere? What does the traveler gain by visiting them?

52

Hanvey

9. Apply Hanvey's "levels of cross-cultural awareness" to your own experiences with Spanish-speaking cultures in the U.S., Latin America, and Spain. Describe one or more experiences and identify the level of awareness you have achieved for each experience.

10. How does Hanvey distinguish between "empathy" and "transspection"?

11. Reread the section of the article that describes the Peace Corps experience. What are some of the characteristics of those who adjusted best to the new cultural environment? Of those who had difficulty? Interview a former Peace Corps volunteer about his or her experience and report on your findings. Write the Peace Corps for material describing the volunteers' work and inquire about the several areas in which they receive training before they begin their assignment.

Gudykunst and Kim

12. Professors Gudykunst and Kim stress the importance of "contexting" when discussing communication. How do you define the term in light of their article?

13. Gudykunst and Kim state that "Western cultures, particularly that of the United States, [have] the tendency to see the world in terms of dichotomies" (good-evil, right-wrong, true-false, etc.). Find some examples of this in today's society. Consider areas as diverse as politics, movies, sports, and child-rearing.

14. What other characteristics would you add to the authors' profile of the American?

15. Interview a person from one of the countries mentioned in the Gudykunst-Kim article. Frame some of your interview questions around the distinctions drawn by the authors on perception, thinking, and interpersonal relations. Share the results of your interview.

Mexico and the Caribbean

*

OCTAVIO PAZ
Translated by Rachel Phillips Belash

Mexico and the United States

(A respected Nobel prize winner argues that Mexico and the U.S. are two distinct versions of Western civilization. They differ not because of an imbalance of political or economic power, but because of profound cultural differences.)

When I was in India, witnessing the never-ending quarrels between Hindus and Muslims, I asked myself more than once this question: What accident or misfortune of history caused two religions so obviously irreconcilable as Hinduism and Muhammadanism to coexist in the same society? The presence of the purest and most intransigent form of monotheism in the bosom of a civilization that has elaborated the most complex polytheism seemed to me a verification of the indifference with which history perpetrates its paradoxes. And yet I could hardly be surprised at the contradictory presence in India of Hinduism and Muhammadanism. How could I forget that I myself, as a Mexican, was (and am) part of a no less singular paradox—that of Mexico and the United States.

Our countries are neighbors, condemned to live alongside each other; they are separated, however, more by profound social, economic, and psychic differences than by physical and political frontiers. These differences are self-evident, and a superficial glance might reduce them to the well-known opposition between development and underdevelop-

Reprinted by permission; © Octavio Paz. Originally in *The New Yorker* magazine (September 17, 1979).

ment, wealth and poverty, power and weakness, domination and dependence. But the really fundamental difference is an invisible one, and in addition it is perhaps insuperable. To prove that it has nothing to do with economics or political power, we have only to imagine a Mexico suddenly turned into a prosperous, mighty country, a superpower like the United States. Far from disappearing, the difference would become more acute and more clear-cut. The reason is obvious: We are two distinct versions of Western civilization.

Ever since we Mexicans began to be aware of national identity—in about the middle of the eighteenth century—we have been interested in our northern neighbors. First with a mixture of curiosity and disdain; later on with an admiration and enthusiasm that were soon tinged with fear and envy. The idea the Mexican people have of the United States is contradictory, emotional, and impervious to criticism; it is a mythic image. The same can be said of the vision of our intellectuals and writers.

Something similar happens with Americans, be they writers or politicians, businessmen or only travellers. I am not forgetting the existence of a small number of remarkable studies by various American specialists, especially in the fields of archeology and ancient and modern Mexican history. The perceptions of the American novelists and poets who have written on Mexican themes have often been brilliant, but they have also been fragmentary. Moreover, as a critic who has devoted a book to this theme (Drewey Wayne Gunn: *American and British Writers in Mexico*) has said, they reveal less of the Mexican reality than of the authors' personalities. In general Americans have not looked for Mexico in Mexico; they have looked for their obsessions, enthusiasms, phobias, hopes, interests—and these are what they have found. In short, the history of our relationship is the history of a mutual and stubborn deceit, usually involuntary though not always so.

Of course, the differences between Mexico and the United States are not imaginary projections but objective realities. Some are quantitative, and can be explained by the social, economic, and historical development of the two countries. The more permanent ones, though also the result of history, are not easily definable or measurable. I have pointed out that they belong to the realm of civilization, that fluid zone of imprecise contours in which are fused and confused ideas and beliefs, institutions and technologies, styles and morals, fashions and churches, the material culture and that evasive reality which we rather inaccurately call *le génie des peuples*. The reality to which we give the name of civilization does not allow of easy definition. It is each society's vision of the world and also its feeling about time; there are nations that are hurrying toward the future, and others whose eyes are fixed on the past. Civilization is a society's style, its way of living and dying. It embraces the erotic and the culinary arts; dancing and burial; courtesy and curses; work and leisure; rituals and festivals; punishments and rewards; dealings with the dead and with the ghosts who people our dreams; attitudes toward women and children, old people and strangers, enemies and allies; eternity and the present; the here and now and the beyond. A civilization is not only a system of values but a world of forms and codes of behavior, rules and exceptions. It is society's visible side—institutions, monuments, works, things—but it is especially its submerged, invisible side: beliefs, desires, fears, repressions, dreams.

The points of the compass have served to locate us in history as well as in space. The East-West duality soon acquired a more symbolic than geographical significance, and became an emblem of the opposition between civilizations. The East-West opposition has always been considered basic and primordial; it alludes to the movement of the sun, and is therefore an image of the direction and meaning of our living and dying. The East-West relationship symbolizes two directions, two attitudes, two civilizations. The North-South duality refers more to the opposition between different ways of life and different sensibilities. The contrasts between North and South can be oppositions within the same civilization.

Clearly, the opposition between Mexico and the United States belongs to the North-South duality as much from the geographical as the symbolic point of view. It is an ancient opposition which was already unfolding in pre-Columbian America, so that it antedates the very existence of the United States and Mexico. The northern part of the continent was settled by nomadic, warrior nations; Mesoamerica, on the other hand, was the home of an agricultural civilization, with complex social and political institutions, dominated by warlike theocracies that invented refined and cruel rituals, great art, and vast cosmogonies inspired by a very original vision of time. The great opposition of pre-Columbian America—all that now includes the United States and Mexico—was between different ways of life: nomads and settled peoples, hunters and farmers. This division greatly influenced the later development of the United States and Mexico. The policies of the English and the Spanish toward the Indians were in large part determined by this division; it was not insignificant that the former established themselves in the territory of the nomads and the latter in that of the settled peoples.

The differences between the English and the Spaniards who founded New England and New Spain were no less decisive than those that separated the nomadic from the settled Indians. Again, it was an opposition within the same civilization. Just as the American Indians' world view and beliefs sprang from a common source, irrespective of their ways of life, so Spanish and English shared the same intellectual and technical culture. And the opposition between them, though of a different sort, was as deep as that dividing an Aztec from an Iroquois. And so the new opposition between English and Spaniards was grafted onto the old opposition between nomadic and settled peoples. The distinct and divergent attitudes of Spaniards and English have often been described before. All of them can be summed up in one fundamental difference, in which perhaps the dissimilar evolution of Mexico and the United States originated: in England the Reformation triumphed, whereas Spain was the champion of the Counter-Reformation.

As we all know, the reformist movement in England had political consequences that were decisive in the development of Anglo-Saxon democracy. In Spain, evolution went in the opposite direction. Once the resistance of the last Muslim was crushed, Spain achieved a precarious political—but not national—unity by means of dynastic alliances. At the same time, the monarchy suppressed regional autonomies and municipal freedoms, closing off the possibility of eventual evolution into a modern democracy. Lastly, Spain was deeply marked by Arab domination, and kept alive the notion of crusade and holy war, which it had inherited from Christian and Muslim alike. In Spain, the traits of the modern era, which was just beginning, and of the old society coexisted but never blended completely. The contrast with England could not be sharper. The history of Spain and of her former colonies, from the sixteenth century onward, is the history of an ambiguous approach—attraction and repulsion—to the modern era.

The discovery and conquest of America are events that inaugurated modern world history, but Spain and Portugal carried them out with the sensibility and tenor of the Reconquest. Nothing more original occurred to Cortes's soldiers, amazed by the pyramids and temples of the Mayans and Aztecs, than to compare them with the mosques of Islam. Conquest and evangelization: these two words, deeply Spanish and Catholic, are also deeply Muslim. Conquest means not only the occupation of foreign territories and the subjugation of their inhabitants but also the conversion of the conquered. The conversion legitimized the conquest. This politico-religious philosophy was diametrically opposed to that of English colonizing; the idea of evangelization occupied a secondary place in England's colonial expansion.

The Christianity brought to Mexico by the Spaniards was the syncretic Catholicism of Rome, which had assimilated the pagan gods, turning them into saints and devils. The phenomenon was repeated in Mexico: the idols were baptized, and in popular Mexican Catholicism the old beliefs and divinities are still present, barely hidden under a veneer, of Christianity. Not only the popular religion of Mexico but the Mexicans' entire life is steeped in Indian culture—the family, love, friendship, attitudes toward one's father and mother, popular legends, the forms of civility and life in common, the image of authority and political power, the vision of death and sex, work and festivity. Mexico is the most Spanish country in Latin America; at the same time it is the most Indian. Mesoamerican civilization died a violent death, but Mexico is Mexico thanks to the Indian presence. Though the language and religion, the political institutions and the culture of the country are Western, there is one aspect of Mexico that faces in another direction—the Indian direction. Mexico is a nation between two civilizations and two pasts.

In the United States, the Indian element does not appear. This, in my opinion, is the major difference between our two countries. The Indians who were not exterminated were corralled in "reservations." The Christian horror of "fallen nature" extended to the natives of America: the United States was founded on a land without a past. The historical memory of Americans is European, not American. For this reason, one of the most powerful and persistent themes in American literature, from Whitman to William Carlos Williams and from Melville to Faulkner, has been the search for (or invention of) American roots. We owe some of the major works of the modern era to this desire for incarnation, this obsessive need to be rooted in American soil.

Exactly the opposite is true of Mexico, land of superimposed pasts. Mexico City was built on the ruins of Tenochtitlán, the Aztec city that was built in the likeness of Tula, the Toltec city that was built in the likeness of Teotihuacán, the first great city on the American continent. Every Mexican bears within him this continuity, which goes back two thousand years. It doesn't matter that this presence is almost always unconscious and assumes the naïve forms of legend and even superstition. It is not something known but something lived. The Indian presence means that one of the facets of Mexican culture is not Western. Is there anything like this in the United States? Each of the ethnic groups making up the multiracial democracy that is the United States has its own culture and tradition, and some of them—the Chinese and Japanese, for example—are not Western. These traditions exist alongside the dominant American tradition without becoming one with it.

They are foreign bodies within American culture. In some cases, the most notable being that of the Chicanos, the minorities defend their traditions against or in the face of the American tradition. The Chicanos' resistance is cultural as well as political and social.

If the different attitudes of Hispanic Catholicism and English Protestantism could be summed up in two words, I would say that the Spanish attitude is inclusive and the English exclusive. In the former, the notions of conquest and domination are bound up with ideas of conversion and assimilation; in the latter, conquest and domination imply not the conversion of the conquered but their segregation. An inclusive society, founded on the double principle of domination and conversion, is bound to be hierarchical, centralist, and respectful of the individual characteristics of each group. It believes in the strict division of classes and groups, each one governed by special laws and statutes, but all embracing the same faith and obeying the same lord. An exclusive society is bound to cut itself off from the natives, either by physical exclusion or by extermination; at the same time, since each community of pure-minded men is isolated from other communities, it tends to treat its members as equals and to assure the autonomy and freedom of each group of believers. The origins of American democracy are religious, and in the early communities of New England that dual, contradictory tension between freedom and equality which has been the leitmotiv of the history of the United States was already present.

The opposition that I have just outlined is expressed with great clarity in two religious terms: "communion" and "purity." This opposition profoundly affects attitudes toward work, festivity, the body, and death. For the society of New Spain, work did not redeem, and had no value in itself. Manual work was servile. The superior man neither worked nor traded. He made war, he commanded, he legislated. He also thought, contemplated, wooed, loved, and enjoyed himself. Leisure was noble. Work was good because it produced wealth, but wealth was good because it was intended to be spent—to be consumed in those holocausts called war, in the construction of temples and palaces, in pomp and festivity. The dissipation of wealth took different forms: gold shone on the altars or was poured out in celebrations. Even today in Mexico, at least in the small cities and towns, work is the precursor of the fiesta. The year revolves on the double axis of work and festival, saving and spending. The fiesta is sumptuous and intense, lively and funereal; it is a vital, multicolored frenzy that evaporates in smoke, ashes, nothingness. In the aesthetics of perdition, the fiesta is the lodging place of death.

The United States has not really known the art of the festival, except in the last few years, with the triumph of hedonism over the old Protestant ethic. This is natural. A society that so energetically affirmed the redemptive value of work could not help chastising as depraved the cult of the festival and the passion for spending. The Protestant rejection was inspired by religion rather than economics. The Puritan conscience could not see that the value of the festival was actually a religious value: communion. In the festival, the orgiastic element is central; it marks a return to the beginning, to the primordial state in which each one is united with the great all. Every true festival is religious because every true festival is communion. Here the opposition between communion and purity is clear. For the Puritans and their heirs, work is redemptive because it frees man, and this liberation is a sign of God's choice. Work is purification, which is also a separation: the chosen one ascends, breaks the bonds binding him to earth, which are the laws of his fallen nature. For the Mexicans, communion represents exactly the opposite: not separation but participation, not breaking away but joining together; the great universal commixture, the great bathing in the waters of the beginning, a state beyond purity and impurity.

In Christianity, the body's status is inferior. But the body is an always active force, and its explosions can destroy a civilization. Doubtless for this reason, the Church from the start made a pact with the body. If the Church did not restore the body to the place it occupied in Greco-Roman society, it did try to give the body back its dignity; the body is fallen nature, but in itself it is innocent. After all, Christianity, unlike Buddhism, say, is the worship of an incarnate god. The dogma of the resurrection of the dead dates from the time of primitive Christianity; the cult of the Virgin appeared later, in the Middle Ages. Both beliefs are the highest expressions of this urge for incarnation, which typifies Christian spirituality. Both came to Mesoamerica with Spanish culture, and were immediately fused, the former with the funeral worship of the Indians, the latter with the worship of the goddesses of fertility and war.

The Mexicans' vision of death, which is also the hope of resurrection, is as profoundly steeped in Catholic eschatology as in Indian naturalism. The Mexican death is of the body, exactly the opposite of the American death, which is abstract and disembodied. For Mexicans, death sees and touches itself; it is the body emptied of the soul, the pile of bones that somehow, as in the Aztec poem, must bloom again. For Americans, death is what is not seen: absence, the disappearance of the person. In the Puritan consciousness, death was always present, but as a moral entity, an idea. Later on, scientism pushed death out of the

American consciousness. Death melted away and became unmentionable. Finally, in vast segments of the American population of today, progressive rationalism and idealism have been replaced by neo-hedonism. But the cult of the body and of pleasure implies the recognition and acceptance of death. The body is mortal, and the kingdom of pleasure is that of the moment, as Epicurus saw better than anyone else. American hedonism closes its eyes to death and has been incapable of exorcising the destructive power of the moment with a wisdom like that of the Epicureans of antiquity. Present-day hedonism is the last recourse of the anguished and the desperate, an expression of the nihilism that is eroding the West.

Capitalism exalts the activities and behavior patterns traditionally called virile: aggressiveness, the spirit of competition and emulation, combativeness. American society made these values its own. This perhaps explains why nothing like the Mexicans' devotion to the Virgin of Guadalupe appears in the different versions of Christianity professed by Americans, including the Catholic minority. The Virgin unites the religious sensibilities of the Mediterranean and Mesoamerica, both of them regions that fostered ancient cults of feminine divinities, Guadalupe-Tonantzin is the mother of all Mexicans—Indians, mestizos, whites—but she is also a warrior virgin whose image has often appeared on the banners of peasant uprisings. In the Virgin of Guadalupe we encounter a very ancient vision of femininity which, as was true of the pagan goddesses, is not without a heroic tint.

When I talk about the masculinity of the American capitalist society, I am not unaware that American women have gained rights and posts still denied elsewhere. But they have obtained them as "subjects under the law"; that is to say, as neuter or abstract entities, as citizens, not as women. Now, I believe that, much as our civilization needs equal rights for men and women, it also needs a feminization, like the one that courtly love brought about in the outlook of medieval Europe. Or like the feminine irradiation that the Virgin of Guadalupe casts on the imagination and sensibility of us Mexicans. Because of the Mexican woman's Hispano-Arabic and Indian heritage, her social situation is deplorable, but what I want to emphasize here is not so much the nature of the relation between men and women as the intimate relationship of woman with those elusive symbols which we call femininity and masculinity. For the reasons I noted earlier, Mexican women have a very lively awareness of the body. For them, the body, the woman's and man's, is a concrete, palpable reality. Not an abstraction or a function but an ambiguous magnetic force, in which pleasure and pain, fertility and death are inextricably intertwined.

Pre-Columbian Mexico was a mosaic of nations, tribes, and languages. For its part, Spain was also a conglomeration of nations and races, even though it had realized political unity. The heterogeneity of Mexican society was the other face of Spanish centralism. The political centralism of the Spanish monarchy had religious orthodoxy as its complement, and even as its foundation. The true, effective unity of Mexican society has been brought about slowly over several centuries, but its political and religious unity was decreed from above as the joint expression of the Spanish monarchy and the Catholic Church. Mexico had a state and a church before it was a nation. In this respect also, Mexico's evolution has been very different from that of the United States, where the small colonial communities had from their inception a clear-cut and belligerent concept of their identity as regards the state. For North Americans, the nation antedated the state.

Another difference: In those small colonial communities, a fusion had taken place among religious convictions, the embryonic national consciousness, the political institutions. So harmony, not contradiction, existed between the North Americans' religious convictions and their democratic institutions; whereas in Mexico Catholicism was identified with the viceregal regime, and was its orthodoxy. Therefore, when, after independence, the Mexican liberals tried to implant democratic institutions, they had to confront the Catholic Church. The establishment of a republican democracy in Mexico meant a radical break with the past, and led to the civil wars of the nineteenth century. These wars produced the militarism that, in turn, produced the dictatorship of Porfirio Díaz. The liberals defeated the Church, but they could not implant true democracy—only an authoritarian regime wearing democracy's mask.

A no less profound difference was the opposition between Catholic orthodoxy and Protestant reformism. In Mexico, Catholic orthodoxy had the philosophical form of Neo-Thomism, a mode of thought more apologetic than critical, and defensive in the face of the emerging modernity. Orthodoxy prevented examination and criticism. In New England, the communities were often made up of religious dissidents or, at least, of people who believed that the Scriptures should be read freely. On one side, orthodoxy, dogmatic philosophy, and the cult of authority. On the other, reading and free interpretation of the doctrine. Both societies were religious, but their religious attitudes were irreconcilable. I am not thinking only of dogmas and principles but of the very ways in which the two societies practiced and understood religion. One society fostered the complex and majestic conceptual structure of orthodoxy, an equally complex ecclesiastical hierarchy, wealthy and militant religious orders, and a ritualistic view of religion, in which the sacraments occupied a central place. The other fostered free discussion of the Scriptures, a small and often poor clergy, a tendency to eliminate the hierarchical boundaries between the simple believer and the priest, and a religious practice based not on ritual but on ethics, and not on the sacrament but on the internalizing of faith.

If one considers the historical evolution of the two societies, the main difference seems to be the following: the modern world began with the Reformation, which was the religious criticism of religion and the necessary antecedent of the Enlightenment; with the Counter-Reformation and Neo-Thomism, Spain and her possessions closed themselves to the modern world. They had no Enlightenment, because they had neither a Reformation nor an intellectual religious movement like Jansenism. And so, though Spanish-American civilization is to be admired on many counts, it reminds one of a structure of great solidity—at once convent, fortress, and palace—built to last, not to change. In the long run, that construction became a confine, a prison. The United States was born of the Reformation and the Enlightenment. It came into being under the sign of criticism and self-criticism. Now, when one talks of criticism one is talking of change. The transformation of critical philosophy into progressive ideology came about and reached its peak in the nineteenth century. The broom of rationalist criticism swept the ideological sky clean of myths and beliefs; the ideology of progress, in its turn, displaced the timeless values of Christianity and transplanted them to the earthly and linear time of history. Christian eternity became the future of liberal evolutionism.

Here is the final contradiction, and all the divergencies and differences I have mentioned culminate in it. A society is essentially defined by its position as regards time. The United States, because of its origin and its intellectual and political history, is a society oriented toward the future. The extraordinary spatial mobility of America, a nation constantly on the move, has often been pointed out. In the realm of beliefs and mental attitudes, mobility in time corresponds to physical and geographical displacement. The American lives on the very edge of the now, always ready to leap toward the future. The country's foundations are in the future, not in the past. Or, rather, its past, the act of its founding, was a promise of the future, and each time the United States returns to its source, to its past, it rediscovers the future.

Mexico's orientation, as has been seen, was just the opposite. First came the rejection of criticism, and with it rejection of the notion of change: its ideal is to conserve the image of divine immutability. Second, it has a plurality of pasts, all present and at war within every Mexican's soul. Cortes and Montezuma are still alive in Mexico. At the time of that great crisis the Mexican Revolution, the most radical faction, that of Zapata and his peasants, proposed not new forms of social organization but a return to communal ownership of land. The rebelling peasants were asking for the devolution of the land; that is, they wanted to go back to a pre-Columbian form of ownership which had been respected by the Spaniards. The image the revolutionaries instinctively made for themselves of a Golden Age lay in the remotest past. Utopia for them was not the construction of a future but a return to the source, to the beginning. The traditional Mexican attitude toward time has been expressed in this way by a Mexican poet, Ramón López Velarde: "Motherland, be still the same, faithful to each day's mirror."

In the seventeenth century, Mexican society was richer and more prosperous than American society. This situation lasted until the first half of the eighteenth century. To prove that it was so, one need only glance at the cities of those days, with their monuments and buildings—Mexico City and Boston, Puebla and Philadelphia. Then everything changed. In 1847, the United States invaded Mexico, occupied it, and imposed on it terrible and heavy conditions of peace. A century later, the United States became the dominant world power. An unusual conjunction of circumstances of a material, technological, political, ideological, and human order explains the prodigious development of the United States. But in the small religious communities of seventeenth-century New England, the future was already in bud: political democracy, capitalism, and social and economic development. In Mexico, something very different has occurred. At the end of the eighteenth century, the Mexican ruling classes—especially the intellectuals—discovered that the principles that had founded their society condemned it to immobility and backwardness. They undertook a twofold revolution: separation from Spain and modernization of the country through the adoption of new republican and democratic principles. Their examples were the American Revolution and the French Revolution. They gained independence from Spain, but the adoption of new principles was not enough: Mexico changed its laws, not its social, economic, and cultural realities.

During much of the nineteenth century, Mexico suffered an endemic civil war and three invasions by foreign powers—the United States, Spain, and France. In the latter part of the century, order was re-established, but at the expense of democracy. In the name of liberal ideology and the positivism of Comte and Spencer, a military dictatorship was imposed which lasted more than thirty years. It was a period of peace and appreciable material development—also of increasing penetration by foreign capital, especially from England and the United States. The Mexican Revolution of 1910 set itself to change direction. It succeeded only in part: Mexican democracy is not yet a reality, and the great advances achieved in certain quarters have been nullified or are in danger because of excessive political centralization, excessive population growth, social inequality, the collapse of higher education, and the actions of the economic monopolies, among them those from the United States. Like all the other states of this century, the Mexican state has had an enormous, monstrous development. A curious contradiction: The state has been the agent of modernization, but it has been unable to modernize itself entirely. It is a hybrid of the Spanish patrimonialist state of the seventeenth century and the modern bureaucracies of the West. As for its relationship with the United States, that is still the old relationship of strong and weak, oscillating between indifference and abuse, deceit and cynicism. Most Mexicans hold the justifiable conviction that the treatment received by their country is unfair.

Above and beyond success and failure, Mexico is still asking itself the question that has occurred to most clear-thinking Mexicans since the end of the eighteenth century: the question about modernization. In the nineteenth century, it was believed that to adopt the new democratic and liberal principles was enough. Today, after almost two centuries of setbacks, we have realized that countries change very slowly, and that if such changes are to be fruitful they must be in harmony with the past and the traditions of each nation. And so Mexico has to find its own road to modernity. Our past must not be an obstacle but a starting point. This is extremely difficult, given the nature of our traditions—difficult but not impossible. To avoid new disasters, we Mexicans must reconcile ourselves with our past: only in this way shall we succeed in finding a route to modernity. The search for our own model of modernization is a theme directly linked with another: today we know that modernity, both the capitalist and the pseudo-socialist versions of the totalitarian bureaucracies, is mortally wounded in its very core—the idea of continuous, unlimited progress. The nations that inspired our nineteenth-century liberals—England, France, and especially the United States—are doubting, vacillating, and cannot find their way. They have ceased to be universal examples. The Mexicans of the nineteenth century turned their eyes toward the great Western democracies; we have nowhere to turn ours.

Between 1930 and 1960, most Mexicans were sure of the path they had chosen. This certainty has vanished, and some people ask themselves if it is not necessary to begin all over again. But the question is not relevant only for Mexico; it is universal. However unsatisfactory our country's situation may seem to us, it is not desperate—especially compared with what prevails elsewhere. Latin America, with only a few exceptions, lives under military dictatorships that are pampered and often supported by the United States. Cuba escaped American domination only to become a pawn of the Soviet Union's policy in Africa. A large number of the Asian and African nations that gained their independence after the Second World War are victims of native tyrannies often more cruel and despotic than those of the old colonial powers. In the so-called Third World, with different names and attributes, a ubiquitous Caligula reigns.

In 1917, the October Revolution in Russia kindled the hopes of millions; in 1979, the world "Gulag" has become synonymous with Soviet socialism. The founders of the socialist movement firmly believed that socialism would put an end not only to the exploitation of men but to war; in the second half of the twentieth century, totalitarian "socialisms" have enslaved the working class by stripping it of its basic rights and have also covered the whole planet with the threatening uproar of their disputes and quarrels. In the name of different versions of "socialism," Vietnamese and Cambodians butcher each other. The ideological wars of the twentieth century are no less ferocious than the wars of religion of the seventeenth century. When I was young, the idea that we were witnessing the final crisis of capitalism was fashionable among intellectuals. Now we understand that the crisis is not of a socioeconomic system but of our whole civilization. It is a general, worldwide crisis, and its most extreme, acute, and dangerous expression is found in the situation of the Soviet Union and its satellites. The contradictions of totalitarian "socialism" are more profound and irreconcilable than those of the capitalist democracies.*

The sickness of the West is moral rather than social and economic. It is true that the economic problems are serious and that they have not been solved. Inflation and unemployment are on the rise. Poverty has not disappeared, despite affluence. Several groups—women and racial, religious, and linguistic minorities—still are or feel excluded. But the real, most profound discord lies in the soul. The future has become the

---

* This essay was written before the stunning events of 1989–1990 in the U.S.S.R. and Warsaw Pact countries. (Editior's note)

realm of horror, and the present has turned into a desert. The liberal societies spin tirelessly, not forward but round and round. If they change, they are not transfigured. The hedonism of the West is the other face of desperation; its skepticism is not wisdom but renunciation; its nihilism ends in suicide and in inferior forms of credulity, such as political fanaticisms and magical chimeras. The empty place left by Christianity in the modern soul is filled not by philosophy but by the crudest superstitions. Our eroticism is a technique, not an art or a passion.

I will not continue. The evils of the West have been described often enough, most recently by Solzhenitsyn, a man of admirable character. However, although his description seems to me accurate, his judgment of the causes of the sickness does not, nor does the remedy he proposes. We cannot renounce the critical tradition of the West; nor can we return to the medieval theocratic state. Dungeons of the Inquisition are not an answer to the Gulag camps. It is not worthwhile substituting the church-state for the party-state, one orthodoxy for another. The only effective arm against orthodoxies is criticism, and in order to defend ourselves against the vices of intolerance and fanaticism our only recourse is the exercise of the opposing virtues: tolerance and freedom of spirit. I do not disown Montesquieu, Hume, Kant.

The crisis of the United States affects the very foundation of the nation, by which I mean the principles that founded it. I have already said that there is a leitmotiv running throughout American history, from the Puritan colonies of New England to the present day; namely, the tension between freedom and equality. The struggles of the blacks, the Chicanos, and other minorities are an expression of this dualism. An external contradiction corresponds to this internal contradiction: the United States is a republic and an empire. In Rome, the first of these contradictions (the internal one between freedom and equality) was resolved by the suppression of freedom; Caesar's regime began as an egalitarian solution, but, like all solutions by force, it ended in the suppression of equality also. The second, external contradiction brought about the ruin of Athens, the first imperial republic in history.

It would be presumptuous of me to propose solutions to this double contradiction. I think that every time a society finds itself in crisis it instinctively turns its eyes toward its origins and looks there for a sign. Colonial American society was a free, egalitarian, but exclusive society. Faithful to its origins, in its domestic and foreign policies alike, the United States has always ignored the "others." Today, the United States faces very powerful enemies, but the mortal danger comes from within: not from Moscow but from that mixture of arrogance and opportunism, blindness and short-term Machiavellianism, volubility and stubbornness which has characterized its foreign policies during recent years and which reminds us in an odd way of the Athenian state in its quarrel with Sparta. To conquer its enemies, the United States must first conquer itself—return to its origins. Not to repeat them but to rectify them: the "others"—the minorities inside as well as the marginal countries and nations outside—do exist. Not only do we "others" make up the majority of the human race, but also each marginal society, poor though it may be, represents a unique and precious version of mankind. If the United States is to recover fortitude and lucidity, it must recover itself, and to recover itself it must recover the "others"—the outcasts of the Western World.

PETER L. BERGER

A Tale of Two Moralities

(After working in California for a year and saving money, Manuela plans to return to Mexico. She now faces the difficult choice of moving back to her village and its collective solidarity or leaving it behind to seek economic and social advancement in Mexico City.)

Manuela keeps dreaming about the village.[1] She does not think about it very much in the daytime. Even when she thinks about Mexico, it is not usually about the village. In any case, during the day it is the brash, gleaming reality of California that dominates, its loud demand for full attention pushing into the background the old images and feelings. It is at night that the village comes back, reclaiming its power over Manuela. It is then as if she had never left it—or, worse, as if she must inevitably return to it.

It is often very hot in the village, though at night one may freeze. The earth is dry. Time moves very slowly, as the white clouds move through the brightly blue sky over the brown and arid hills. Time moves slowly in the faces of the people, too, and the faces too are brown and arid. Even the faces of the very young seem to hold old memories. The children do not smile easily. The day is measured by the halting motion

From *Pyramids of Science: Political Ethics and Social Change*, by Peter L. Berger. Copyright © 1974 by Peter L. Berger. Reprinted by permission of Basic Books, Inc., Publishers, New York.

1. Manuela's story is fiction, made up as a composite from several true stories. Manuela does not exist. But many Manuelas do exist, not only in Mexico but all over the Third World. Their moral dilemma must be understood if one is to understand "development."

of shadows over houses and trees. The years are mostly measured by calamities. The past is powerfully present, although there are few words for it. No one in the village speaks an Indian language, though everyone has Indian blood. Can the blood speak, without words? Do the dead speak from the earth? Somewhere in this blue sky and in these brown hills there are very old presences, more threatening than consoling. Some years ago the schoolteacher dug up some Indian artifacts and wanted to take them to the city, to sell them to a museum. Calamity struck at once, all over the village. The dead do not want to be disturbed, and they are dangerous.

The village is distant. Distant from what? Distant from everything, but most importantly distant from the places where time moves quickly and purposefully. There is no paved road, no telephone, no electricity. Even the schoolteacher only comes on two days of the week. He has two other villages to take care of, and he lives somewhere else. To get to the nearest bus station, one rides on a donkey for three hours over footpaths of trampled dirt. Time and distance determine the world of the village, in fact and in Manuela's dreams. If she were to put it in one sentence, this world, she would have to say: It is very far away, and life there moves very slowly. On the maps the village is in the state of Guerrero, in a very specific location between Mexico City and the Pacific Ocean. In Manuela's dreams the village is located in the center of her self, deep down inside rather than out there somewhere.

Manuela was born in the village twenty-two years ago. Her mother died shortly afterward. Her father, already married to another woman with seven legitimate children, never acknowledged Manuela. Indeed, he has never spoken with her. She was raised by one of her mother's brothers, a man without land and much of the time without work, with a large family of his own that he barely managed to support. There was never any question about the family obligation to take care of Manuela; the only question at the time, lengthily discussed by her grandfather and the three uncles still living in the area, was which of the three would take the baby in. But this obligation did not greatly exceed supplying the bare necessities of life. There was never the slightest doubt about Manuela's status in her uncle's household as the unwanted bastard who took the food out of the mouths of her more deserving cousins—and she was told so in no uncertain terms on many occasions. If there was little food, she would be the hungriest. If there was hard work, she would be the one to do it. This does not mean that she received no affection. She was a very pretty, winsome child, and often people were kind to her. But she always knew that affection and kindness were not her right, were given to her gratuitously—and, by the same token, could be gratuitously taken away again. As a child Manuela wished for someone who would love her all the time, reliably, "officially." However, she was only dimly unhappy in her uncle's household, since she knew nothing else. She was often hungry, sometimes beaten. She did not have shoes until her tenth birthday, when her grandfather made her a present of a pair. This was also the first occasion when she went outside the village, accompanying her grandfather on a visit to the doctor in the nearest town.

Her grandfather and one of her uncles in the village were *ejidatarios*, belonging to the minority that owned parcels of land under the village *ejido* (agricultural cooperative). Most of the time the uncle with whom she stayed worked on this land, too, though he would hire himself out for work elsewhere when there was an opportunity. When she was not working in the house or taking care of her little cousins, Manuela also worked in the fields or with the animals belonging to her family. After her tenth birthday she sometimes worked for outsiders, but she was expected to turn over the money she received for this. Sometimes she succeeded in keeping a few coins for herself, though she knew that she would be beaten if found out. She was allowed to go to school and, being very bright, she learned to read and write well. It was her brightness that attracted her grandfather, who was amused by her and took a liking to her (much to the annoyance of her cousins).

"Bad blood will show." "You will come to no good end, like your mother." Manuela must have heard this hundreds of times during her childhood. The prophecy was fulfilled when she was fifteen and made pregnant by the secretary of the *ejido*, one of the most affluent farmers in the village. When her condition could no longer be concealed, there was a terrible scene and her uncle threw her out of the house. Her grandfather, after slapping her a couple of times rather mildly, gave her the address of an aunt in Acapulco and enough money to pay her bus fare there. It was thus that she left the village.

Manuela marveled at Acapulco and its astonishing sights, but, needless to say, she lived there in a world far removed from that experienced by the tourists. Her aunt, a gentle widow with two children and a maid's job in one of the big hotels, took Manuela in very warmly (at least in part because she could use some help in the house). Manuela's baby was born there, a healthy boy whom she named Roberto. Not much later Manuela also started to work outside the house.

A Mexican *campesino*, when he migrates, normally follows an itinerary taken before him by relatives and *compadres*. When he arrives, the latter provide an often intricate network of contacts that are indispensable for his adjustment to the new situation. They will often provide initial housing, they can give information and advice, and, perhaps most important, they serve as an informal labor exchange. Such a network awaited Manuela in Acapulco. In addition to the aunt she was staying with, there were two more aunts and an uncle with their respective families, including some twelve cousins of all ages. This family system, of course, was transposed to the city from the village, but it took on a quite different character in the new context. Freed from the oppressive constraints of village life, the system, on the whole, was more benign. Manuela experienced it as such. Several of her cousins took turns taking care of little Roberto when Manuela started to work. Her aunt's "fiancé" (a somewhat euphemistic term), who was head clerk in the linen supply department of the hotel, found Manuela a job in his department. The uncle, through a *compadre* who was head waiter in another hotel, helped her get a job there as a waitress. It was this uncle, incidentally, who had gone further than any other member of the Acapulco clan, at least for a brief time. An intelligent and aggressive man, he worked himself up in the municipal sanitation department to the rank of inspector. Through a coup, the details of which were shrouded in mystery but which were safely assumed by everyone to involve illegality of heroic proportions, Uncle Pepe amassed the equivalent of about one thousand U.S. dollars in a few months' time, a staggering sum in this ambience. With this money he set out for Mexico City, ostensibly to look into a business proposition. In fact he checked into one of the capital's finest hotels, made the rounds of nightclubs and luxury brothels, and returned penniless but not overly unhappy a month later. The clan has viewed him with considerable awe ever since.

Manuela now had a fairly steady cash income, modest to be sure, but enough to keep going. This does not mean, however, that she could keep all of it for herself and her child. The family system operated as a social insurance agency as well as a labor exchange, and there was never a shortage of claimants. An aunt required an operation. An older cousin set up business as a mechanic and needed some capital to start off. Another cousin was arrested and a substantial *mordida* was required to bribe his way out of jail. And then there were always new calamities back in the village, requiring emergency transfers of money back there. Not least among them was the chronic calamity of grandfather's kidney ailment, which consumed large quantities of family funds in expensive and generally futile medical treatments.

Sometimes, at the hotel, Manuela did babysitting for tourists with children. It was thus that she met the couple from California. They stayed in Acapulco for a whole month, and soon Manuela took care of their little girl almost daily. When they left, the woman asked Manuela whether she wanted a job as a maid in the States. "Yes," replied Manuela at once, without thinking. The arrangements were made quickly. Roberto was put up with a cousin. Uncle Pepe, through two trusted intermediaries, arranged for Manuela to cross the border illegally. Within a month she arrived at the couple's address in California.

And now she has been here for over a year. California was even more astonishing than Acapulco had been when she first left the village, but now she had more time to explore this new world. She learned English in a short time and, in the company of a Cuban girl who worked for a neighbor, she started forays into the American universe, in ever-wider circles from her employers' house. She even took bus trips to Hollywood and San Francisco. For the first time in her life she slept in a room all by herself. And, despite her regular payments for Roberto's keep, she started to save money and put it in a bank account. Most important, she started to think about her life in a new way, systematically. "What will become of you when you go back?" asked the American woman one day. Manuela did not know then, but she started to think. Carmelita, the Cuban girl, discussed the matter with her many times—in exchange for equal attention paid to her own planning exercises. Eventually, one project won out over all the alternatives: Manuela would return to go to commercial school, to become a bilingual secretary. She even started a typing course in California. But she would not return to Acapulco. She knew that, to succeed, she would have to remove herself from the family there. She would go to Mexico City, first alone, and then she would send for Roberto.

This last decision was made gradually. It was the letters that did it. Manuela, some months before, had mentioned the amount of money she had saved (a very large amount, by her standards, and enough to keep her and Roberto afloat for the duration of the commercial course). Then the letters started coming from just about everyone in the Acapulco clan. Most of the contents were family gossip, inquiries about Manuela's life in the States, and long expressions of affectionate feelings. There were frequent reminders not to forget her relatives, who took such good care of Roberto. Only gradually did the economic infrastructure emerge from all this: There was to be a *fiesta* at the wedding of a cousin, and could Manuela make a small contribution. The cousin who had been in jail was still to be tried, and there were lawyer's expenses. Uncle Pepe was onto the most promising business opportunity of his "long and distinguished career in financial activities" (his own words), and just three hundred American dollars would make it possible for him to avail himself of this never-to-recur opportunity—needless to say, Manuela would be a full partner upon her return. Finally, there was even a very formal letter from grandfather, all the way from the village, containing an appeal for funds to pay for a trip to the capital so as to take advantage of a new treatment that a famous doctor had developed there. It took a while for Manuela to grasp that every dollar of her savings had already been mentally spent by her relatives.

The choice before Manuela now is sharp and crystal-clear: She must return to Mexico—because she wants to, because of Roberto, and because the American authorities would send her back there sooner or later anyway. She can then return to the welcoming bosom of the family system, surrender her savings, and return to her previous way of life. Or she can carry through her plan in the face of family opposition. The choice is not only between two courses of action, but between two moralities. The first course is dictated by the morality of collective solidarity, the second by the morality of personal autonomy and advancement. Each morality condemns the other—as uncaring self-ishness in the former case, as irresponsible disregard of her own potential and the welfare of her son in the latter. Poor Manuela's conscience is divided; by now she is capable of feeling its pangs either way.

She is in America, not in Mexico, and the new morality gets more support from her immediate surroundings. Carmelita is all for the plan, and so are most of the Spanish-speaking girls with whom Manuela has been going out. Only one, another Mexican, expressed doubt: "I don't know. Your grandfather is ill, and your uncle helped you a lot in the past. Can you just forget them? I think that one must always help one's relatives." Manuela once talked about the matter with the American woman. "Nonsense," said the latter, "you should go ahead with your plan. You owe it to yourself and to your son." So this is what Manuela intends to do, very soon now. But she is not at ease with the decision. Every time another letter arrives from Mexico, she hesitates before opening it, and she fortifies herself against the appeals she knows to be there.

Each decision, as dictated by the respective morality, has predict-able consequences: If Manuela follows the old morality, she will, in all likelihood, never raise herself or her son above the level she achieved in Acapulco—not quite at the bottom of the social scale, but not very far above it. If, on the other hand, she decides in accordance with the new morality (new for her, that is), she has at least a chance of making it up one important step on that scale. Her son will benefit from this, but probably no other of her relatives will. To take that step she must, literally, hack off all those hands that would hold her back. It is a grim choice indeed.

What will Manuela do? She will probably at least start out on her plan. Perhaps she will succeed. But once she is back in Mexico, the tentacles of the old solidarity will be more powerful. They will pull more strongly. It will be harder to escape that other village, the village of the mind within herself. The outcome of the struggle will decide whether the village will be Manuela's past or also her future. Outside observers should think very carefully indeed before they take sides in this contest.

LOUIS A. ZURCHER, JR. and ARNOLD MEADOW

On Bullfights and Baseball:
An Example of
Interaction of Social Institutions

(Like family structure, national sports reflect the social character of a society and provide an acceptable means to contest authority. Baseball in the United States of America and the *corrida de toros* in the United States of Mexico provide a cross-cultural example here.)

A "social institution," typically considered, is "a comparatively stable, permanent and intricately organized system of behavior formally enforced within a given society and serving social objectives regarded as essential for the survival of the group." Four major social institutions are found very widely in human society: (1) economic, (2) familial, (3) political, and (4) religious. Through these the society strives to achieve material well-being, an adequate population, organization, and some feeling of control over the unknown or unexpected. As a society becomes more urbanized, more "highly developed," it may evolve additional institutions, such as the recreational, the educational and the aesthetic, which take over functions no longer adequately performed by the basic four.

Since individuals have overlapping roles in a number of the society's institutions, and since each institution is a functional segment of the total, ongoing society, the interaction of institutions presents itself as a fruitful area for study. This interaction is a key variable in the process of social change and highlights cultural themes running through the structures of a society.

From *International Journal of Comparative Sociology.* 8, 1967: 99–117, by permission of the publisher.

The central institution of a society and its primary agent of socialization is the family—which interacts in various degrees with other
institutions. Whiting and Child, for example, have described the impact
of values learned in the family upon behavior in other social institutions
(1953). Kardiner has written of the ways in which the religious institution
is shaped by family patterns (1939). Tumin has described the interaction
between the family and the economic institution (1956).

In this paper the authors will focus their attention on some aspects
of the interaction between two social institutions: (1) the family and (2)
the institutionalized recreation form known as the "national sport." It is
hypothesized that the national sport symbolizes in its structure and
function the processes in the modal family that both engender and
restrict hostility toward authority, and that it also exemplifies a socially
legitimized means for the expression of that hostility.

As Dollard has described it, the socialization process itself engenders hostility toward authority. The demands of socialization, which of
course have their focal point in the family, conflict in many instances
with the child's own behavioral choices. The child is thus frustrated and
desires to move against the restrictive figure but does not do so because
he fears punishment. This fear acts as a catalyst, inciting further aggressive feelings toward the frustrating agent. Repression of this aggression
is not complete and the individual seeks sources for its legitimized
expression (1938).

Hostility toward authority is especially generated in the authoritarian family milieu, or when some characteristics of the parents create
for the child an uncertainty of or rejection of his or the parent's familial
role. Situations such as this not only arouse keen hostility but are also
usually unyieldingly restrictive and harshly punitive of any demonstration of that hostility.

From another view, it is quite possible that hostility toward authority
is a lesson of, as well as a reaction to, socialization. That is, the characteristics of the society may be such that a general distrust for or hatred of
authority has become part of the cultural value system. This is particularly the case in those societies which have undergone long periods of
manipulation and oppression under a tyrannical or exploitative power
structure.

Since every society depends, from the family up, on authority to
maintain relative consistency of behavior, and since not all the members
of the society will take well to that restrictive authority, it follows that the
society must provide as a further means of control some outlet for the
resultant hostility toward authority—not only that incited in the family

situation or learned in socialization, but also the generalized forms of hostility that are reawakened and intensified by the demands of interpersonal relations. The provisions for such expression, as well as the degree to which it is controlled, vary from society to society. As Dollard points out, "Each society standardizes its own permissive patterns, and differs from the next in the degree to which hostility may be expressed" (1938).

In the terminology of modern dynamic psychiatry, it can be said that the defense processes which societies employ to channel hostility differ from culture to culture. These defense processes will be differentially manifested not only in the families of different societies, but also, as we hypothesize, in their "national sports," since both are institutions of these societies.

PLAY, THE GAME, THE SPORT

Play has been considered by a number of social scientists to be of major importance in the socialization and personality formation of the individual. Other writers have seen the various forms of play as reflecting the particular traits, values, expectations, and the degree of social control in a given culture. In addition to the foregoing functions, play is a "permissive pattern," a "channel" serving as a legitimized means for the symbolic demonstration of hostility toward authority figures.

There is a hierarchy of play extending from seemingly purposeless, repetitive movements in the crib, through games (with competition, an "ethic" of some sort, elaborate rules and regulations, mutual player expectations, and an ostensible purpose), up to the highest level of complexity, the "organized sport" (with schedules, painstaking record keeping, large audiences, governing bodies supplying officials and dispensing rules, "seasons," recruiting, training, and if professional, the paying of participants). The "national sport" is an organized sport that has been adopted by a nation as its own special "home-owned" variety. When, for example, the "American Way" is alluded to, it implies, among other things, apple pie, hot dogs, mothers, Disneyland and *baseball*.

It is hypothesized, then, that the national sport, as the epitome of institutionalized recreation, maximally reflects that aspect of the "social character" of a society which establishes the degree of tolerance for the expression of hostility toward authority. Furthermore, it is hypothesized that the national sport replicates, on the playing field or in the arena, the family processes which engender, exacerbate or restrict that hostility, and will manifest the "societal ideal" for its expression.

Baseball is the national sport of the United States of America. Its counterpart in the United States of Mexico is the *corrida de toros*, the bullfight. It should be mentioned here that the *aficionado* (dedicated fan) would object to the association of the bullfight with the term "sport", and there are good arguments in support of his opinion. For the sake of parsimony, however, and since the bullfight approaches the criteria established in this paper, it will be considered, for analysis, the equivalent of a national sport. An analysis of baseball and the bullfight, and of the modal family patterns in their respective societies, should reveal, especially with regard to the dynamic of hostility toward authority, a facet of the interaction between the social institutions of family and recreation. In addition to the formation and legitimized expression of hostility, the analysis should reveal, as they appear in both the family and the sport, some of the characteristic defense mechanisms, values and social relationships shared by members in each of the two societies.

ANALYSIS OF FAMILY PATTERNS

The Mexican family typically is described as a proving ground for the dominance needs of the father. Though the family structure is essentially mother centered, the father compulsively strives to maintain his *macho* (manly) role and to prove that he has *huevos largos [grandes]* (large "eggs"), *muy [muchos] cojones* (abundant testicles) or "hair on his chest" by playing the role of the emotionally detached but severely authoritarian head of the household. He overtly disparages the achievements of, violently disapproves of any show of independence in, and physically punishes any demonstration of hostility by his wife or children. Often the children are punished by their father for sins (especially sexual) projected upon them from his own guilt-ridden repertoire. Drunkenness, promiscuity and abandonment, as components of *machismo*, further compound the overpowering image of father. This pattern of behavior has been detailed in the literature by Lewis (1961), Gillin (1961), Meadow et al., and Díaz-Guerrero (1961).

The question then arises, how do the children, especially the males, handle the hostility that they cannot direct against the mitigated feudalism of such an unyielding socialization figure as the Mexican father? It appears that the son attempts to recoup his identity by emulating the father's example, but he does so in other quarters (dominating his younger sisters and brothers, fighting, being sexually promiscuous). The wife and daughters seem to develop a solidly female "mutual protection society," adopt a passively controlling "martyr" role and wait patiently to seize control whenever the father's dominance falters. Thus exists a climate which fosters overcompensating sons, with ambivalence (passive-aggressive) toward the father, and daughters who, because of hostility toward a punishing father, distrust all men.

A safe but indirect manner for the Mexican male to express hostility against his father, then, seems to be one of "showing the old boy that I am as much, or more, [of a] man than he is." This, however, cannot be done in direct confrontation. Rather it is done in spheres away from the father's bailiwick—away from his watchful eye. As Jesús Sánchez puts it, "to grow up away from your parents helps you to become mature" (Lewis, 1961). The son can't compete with the father directly, so he acts out his hostility guided by his father's examples, but on his own terms in his own battlefield.

The family is, of course, a reflection of and the basis for culture. Mexican culture is, as is the family, authoritarian and hierarchical in structure. Though Mexican citizens have a general distrust of and disregard for the "officials" in government, church and other large-scale organizations, they are most hesitant to directly or overtly criticize them. This passiveness in the face of authority has, as the passiveness to the father, an aggressive counterpart. As a matter of fact, Meadow's, et al., in-depth studies of Mexican psychopathology, cite different degrees of passive-aggressiveness as a central feature of the modal personality of the Mexican. Does this aggressive component demonstrate itself in a socially acceptable manner in a Mexican institution? The premise here is that the bullfight will relive aspects of the frustration engendering conflict and provide an outlet for the resultant aggression. It would be expected, from observations of the Mexican family and from examination of the symptom-formation in Mexican psychopathology, that the legitimized expression would be of a type allowing "acting out" of hostility. But first, before considering the bullfight itself, let us examine by contrast the situation in the Anglo-American family.

If the Anglo-American father were to attempt to follow the dominance pattern of his Mexican counterpart, he would posthaste be imprisoned, divorced with the condemnation of the court, or at best, socially ostracized.

In the Anglo nuclear family, as in the Anglo culture, the ideological byword is equality. Mother, father, son and daughter are "members of the group" and have a *right* to be heard, to voice their opinion and to register their vote around the family conference table. Everyone "shares the responsibility" and "pulls his weight" in the "togetherness" of the family.

The Anglo ethic, loaded as it is with the popular meaning of "democracy," encourages an unrealistic muting of authority as it exists in the society. Fathers and mothers are not supposed to be authority figures but "pals," "buddies," "good heads" and "regular guys." They are still, however, expected to be the prime socialization agents of Anglo society, and as such, must impress upon the child an awareness of behavior which is accepted and expected by that society. This cannot be done without the exertion of authority. Socialization makes demands that often are contrary to the child's own preferences. Thus, the frustration-aggression cycle is manifested. But how can the child demonstrate overt hostility to a "pal," a "buddy" or an equal? Furthermore, the vagueness of the parental role in the Anglo family presents the child with a mercurial identification model. Should he be dependent upon or independent of his parents—and when? Mother preaches togetherness, but usually agrees with the television and movie stereotype of the well-meaning, bungling father who needs her subtle domination.

Authoritarianism from people who are not supposed to be authoritarian, vagueness of or conflict in role expectations, obscure role models, plus the restrictions of socialization, set the stage for hostility toward authority in the Anglo family. Typically, however, this hostility, and in fact most familial conflict, is intellectualized and abstracted into elaborate displacements and double-bind communications.

The Mexican child seems to have clear reason for hostility, but can't reveal it to the father because he may be beaten. He can't be hostile to the mother because she is a "saint." The Anglo child has difficulty showing overt hostility in his family because, first, he has a hard time tracing the basis for his frustration, and second, he can't be aggressive to two "buddies." But the hostility from socialization and role conflict is still there and needs expression.

The Mexican is forced to be passive to the frustrating agent, but along with this passiveness rides an aggressive component. If the Mexican has been shaped into a passive-aggressive, then it seems feasible to posit as a central feature of the Anglo modal personality the defense mechanism of intellectualization. The Anglo child learns from his parents to intellectualize conflict, to abstract hostility, to disengage it from painful affect, and to deal with it in a symbolic, ritualistic fashion. Whereas the Mexican acts out his hostility, the Anglo rationalizes it and elaborately disguises it with verbal repartee. Manuel Sánchez observed "life in the United States is too abstract, too mechanical. The people are like precision machines" (Lewis, 1961).

As does the Mexican family in the Mexican culture, the Anglo family reflects and maintains the Anglo culture. Anglo society has been characterized by a plethora of writers as being abstract, universalistic, materialistic, impersonal, unemotional and bureaucratic. One would expect, then, the ideal legitimized outlets for hostility to be similarly complex, elaborately diffuse, and intellectualized, impersonalized and de-affected after a bureaucratic fashion. The national sport of the United States, baseball, we have hypothesized, should fully reflect this pattern.

THE BULLFIGHT

Aficionados who are of a mind to describe the essence of the bullfight do so in terms that parallel the *corrida* with a Greek drama. Robinson writes that the theme of the bullfight lies "somewhere between the themes of fate and death" (1964). Allen proclaims the bullfight to be "the last drama of our times that has death as an immediate object" (1953). In *The Brave Bulls*, two of Lea's Mexican characters discuss the *fiesta brava* as follows:

> It is a form of drama as certainly as the works of Sophocles. But what a difference between the happenings on a stage or in a poem, and the happening in a plaza! . . .
> The festival of bulls is the only art form in which violence, bloodshed, and death are palpable and unfeigned. It is the only art in which the artist deals actual death and risks actual death that gives the art its particular power. . . . (Lea, 1949)

Who, then, do the principals in this drama represent? Who is killing, and who is being killed? We have hypothesized that the events in the bullfight will provide a socially legitimized symbolic vehicle for the aggression toward authority which has been developed mainly in and by the Mexican family situation.

Since the reader may be unfamiliar with the structure of the bullfight, we shall undertake here a brief description before proceeding to the analysis.

Prior to the appearance of any of the principals in the *corrida*, the *alguacil*, a mounted bailiff, rides across the bullring and, with a bow and a flourish, renders his respect to the *Presidente* (a national, state or local official), who is in charge of the conduct of the bullfight. The *alguacil* will thereafter be the courier for the *Presidente* and will transmit orders from him to the principals in the *corrida*. Thus is the hierarchical nature of Mexican society represented in the bullfight. No major shift in action, no new sequence is attempted without first gaining the nod of the *Presidente*. It is he who will pass final judgment upon the performance of the *matador*. He, and only he, can decide that the bull shall live (on rare occasions), or die. In essence he has the power of life and death. It is interesting to note that, though disapproval in the highly emotional framework of the *corrida* may incite the crowd eloquently and thoroughly to curse and insult the *matador*, his assistants, his mother, father, *compadres*, lovers, children and future children, there is seldom a harsh word directed toward the sacrosanct *Presidente*. This respect remains, ironically, while symbolically authority is about to be murdered in the ring!

Upon receiving the nod from the *Presidente*, the *alguacil* rides out of the ring to lead back the *paseo*, or parade, which consists of, in splendid order, the *matadors*, their *banderilleros* (assistants), the *picadors*, the ring attendants and the harnessed team whose task it will be to remove the dead bull from the ring. The *matadors* halt directly beneath the *Presidente* and bow their respect. Following this, all the principals, usually with the exception of a *banderillero*, leave the ring. The *Presidente* gives permission for the bull to be released, and the assistant receives the bull.

The bullfight itself consists of three major parts (*Los Tres Tercios de la Lidia*). In the first, the *banderilleros* work the bull with the cape, thus allowing the *matador* to observe the *toro*'s idiosyncracies (direction of hook, favored eye and straightness of charge). Then the *picadors* pic* the bull, this to demonstrate the bull's courage (by his charge to the horse) and to lower his head. Following this, the ring is cleared—the bull remains, having "conquered," for a moment, all his antagonists. The *banderilleros* (sometimes the *matador*), in the second major part, place the *banderillas* (barbed sticks), these to correct for the bull's tendency to hook in one or the other direction. The third part consists of *brindis*, or formal dedication of the bull to the *Presidente* (then to anyone else in the crowd the *matador* chooses), the work with the *muleta* (small red cloth), and, finally, the sword.

Since there are two bulls for each *matador*, and two or three *matadors* in each bullfight, these three segments are repeated from four to six times in an afternoon.

Such is the bare structure of the bullfight. This tells nothing of the key to, the vitality of, the drama in the ring, the feeling in the crowd or the symbolic expression of hostility.

---

* A pic is the *picador's* lance. (Editor's note)

Perhaps a discussion of this can best be introduced by quoting the *matador* protagonist in Ramsey's *Fiesta* as he describes, when facing the bull, "a fear that never quite left him, and that encompassed others too indefinite for him to understand or even name, a fear of authority, of the powerful, the *patrón.* . . ." (Ramsey, 1955), of the *father!* Freedom from this authority is granted, he contends, in those rare moments when fear is combated and overcome.

Characteristically, the Mexican son profoundly fears his father. Manuel Sánchez testifies that in order to become a man, the individual must escape his father. Yet it was not until he, himself, was twenty-nine years old that he smoked in his father's presence. At that time, Manuel, though fearful, felt himself to be acting most bravely by showing his father that he was a man—*at twenty-nine years of age!*

This need for "manhood" (courage, domination, sexual prowess) which we have mentioned many times above is crucial enough in the Mexican culture to claim a syndrome entity all its own—the *machismo. Macho* connotes maleness—demonstrable and blatant maleness. The individual who is *macho* is *muy hombre* (much man), abundantly endowed with sexual organs, and fears nothing. The most grave and threatening insult to the Mexican male is one that challenges his masculinity.

What more natural preoccupation could one expect from a son who has been subject to an emasculating father—to a father whose own fear of male competition has led him to use his physical size to dominate his son? We have mentioned that one way the son can compensate for his subordinate role is to emulate his father in another sphere, and later in his own home with his own wife and children. But through the bullfight another compensation is offered. As a spectator (or better, a principal) he can compensate symbolically, uninhibitedly, with all the hate, insult, and invective that he can muster. What clearer representative of the father than the bull with his flagrant masculinity, awesome power and potential to maim and kill? What clearer representative of the son than the delicate, almost fragile, *matador* whose protection obviously cannot be strength but must be courage? See how the bull charges the *banderilleros!* See how he hurls himself against the pic and the horse! How can the *matador* stand up to the bull? How can the son stand up to the father? Aha! *Toro!* Aha!

The *matador* provides the spectator with an amazingly flexible psychological figure. He can identify with the *matador*'s courage, with his expertise, with his kill, and yet he can project upon the *matadors,* especially in a bad performance, accusations of cowardice and powerlessness he has experienced himself in the constantly losing battle with his father. It is interesting that many bullfighters take nicknames with diminutive denotations—Joselito, Armillita *Chico*, Amoros *Chico*, Gallito, Machaquito, etc. Similarly, well over three hundred *matadors* whose names have been entered in the records have somewhere in their nickname the word *niño* (child)—El Niño de la Palma, etc. Thus is emphasized their smallness, their fragility *vis-à-vis* the bull. Thus is emphasized symbolically the helplessness of the child *vis-à-vis* the father. Strength is not nearly so valued an attribute of the *matador* as is demonstrable courage. The great *matadors* are not remembered for their muscle but for their *macho*. Belmonte was sickly, Maera had wrists so fragile that he often dislocated them in a *faena* (series of passes), Manolete was painfully thin. In fact, size and strength may be a disadvantage. Joselito, a tall, athletic and graceful man, often complained that he had to take more chances with the bull than the physically struggling Belmonte in order to make his *faenas* appear as difficult. When asked how he developed strength for the *corrida*, Gallo is said to have replied, "I smoke Havana cigars," adding that one cannot possibly match the bull for strength, but he can for courage. The *matador* must, then, appear finite when facing the awesome power of the bull. A sign of fear is acceptable, even desirable, if the *faena* is good. Thus is highlighted the fact that the *matador* has, in spite of his fears, faced, dominated and killed the bull. A too calm, too nonchalant, too perfect *matador*, without the emotion of fear (and pride in controlling that fear), who cannot convey to the crowd that his is in fact a struggle in which he has faced, averred and administered death to an overpowering force, may be viewed as a *matador* without *salsa*—without "sauce." The fact of the matter is that the Mexican father is threatening, does physically hurt and *does* strike fear in the heart of his sons. To dominate and destroy him *would* be a remarkable feat. If the bullfight is to provide symbolically a resolution of this one-sided affair then it must be representative of its acts, events and especially of its emotions.

We have mentioned earlier that the passive role forced upon the Mexican child brings with it an aggressive component—a dynamic seen again and again in the Mexican personality structure. This interaction is beautifully manifested in the three commandments for the *matador*'s conduct in the bullfight—*Parar! Templar! Mandar!* (Keep the feet quiet! Move the cape and *muleta* slowly! Dominate and control the bull!). The central feature is, in the modern bullfight, the domination of the bull. But domination is expressed in the *bonita corrida* with a studied parsimony of movement, with a deliberately slow tempo. Boyd writes that "the *matador* gains mastery by his cunning awareness of the power of the absence of movement" (1956). The most valued placing of the *banderillas* and the most honored kill both consist of the *matador* performing these tasks while passively standing his ground and receiving the charge of the bull. The *matador*'s knees may knock together with fright, and the crowd will understand—as long as he continues to *parar*.

Kluckhohn sees this passive element in another Mexican institution, religion. She describes the Mexican's dependence upon the saints and submissive and accepting attitude toward the supernatural (1961). Since the basic cultural values run through all of a society's institutions, it is not surprising to find this same passivity modifying the legitimized expression of hostility toward authority in the bullfight.

The *matador* demands submissive behavior from his own assistants. Traditionally, the latter have not been allowed to eat at the same table with the *matador*, must obey his orders immediately and without question and, regardless of the amount of the *matador*'s income, are paid very poorly. Hemingway writes ". . . a *matador* feels that the less he pays his subordinates the more man he is and in the same way the nearer he can bring his subordinates to slaves the more man he feels he is." Thus, out of the ring as well as in, the *matador* perpetuates the *machismo*. This is also observed in the sexual exploits of *matadors*, and highlighted especially by their blatant disregard for and high incidence of syphilis. "You cannot expect," Hemingway says, "a *matador* who has triumphed in the afternoon by taking chances not to take them in the night" (1945).

Often the *matador* will single out a woman in the crowd and dedicate the kill to her, expecting, of course, some token of appreciation in return. One of the authors witnessed a *matador* leaving the *Plaza de Toros* after a successful *corrida* survey a bevy of adoring females, make his selection with a toss of the head and beckoning gesture with his blood-stained arm, and walk off hand-in-hand with the amazed and grateful girl to her car.

It would seem from the *matador*'s point of view that the crowd is symbolically female. The matador (son) looks for approval to the crowd (mother) when he demonstrates his domination, his superiority over, the bull (father). The crowd continually calls on the *matador* to work closer to the bull. It *demands* that he take chances and promises in return to give him manifestations of approval. In his study of Mexican psychopathology, Meadow has observed that the Mexican mother subtly encourages the son to compete with the father, thus providing her an added element of control. It is not surprising, then, to see this dynamic represented in the *corrida*. The crowd (mother) calls for the *matador* (son) to challenge, to dominate, the bull (father), and offers love as a reward. *Matadors* who have been gored when responding to the crowd's urges have been reported to turn to the crowd, blaming it, shouting, for example, "See what you have done to me! See what your demands have done!" It may well be that the females in the crowd would enjoy seeing both the *matador* and the bull destroyed, thus expressing the generalized hostility that Mexican women have toward men. For the Mexican female, the *corrida* may be a legitimized way of acting out aggression toward dominating husbands, fathers and lovers.

A famous breeder of *toros* writes that "... certain of their (the fighting bulls) number will stay home to take care of the cows and carry on the breed with those formidable sacs that swing between their legs. But not our fighters to the death. They are virgins. It is a curious thing, our festival" (Lea, 1949). The bull has not experienced mating, and never will, because the *matador* will kill him. Perhaps the son will have dominated and killed that symbolic father before he can mate with the mother (the *matador* prays before each fight to the Virgin Mother).

In *capeas*, or informal street bullfights, the bull may be slaughtered by many people (if the town can afford the loss) and often the testicles will be cut off, roasted, and devoured. At one time it was customary in the *corrida* to remove the testicles (*criadillas*) of the first killed bull of the afternoon and serve them as a prepared meal to the *Presidente* during the killing of the fifth bull. Thus with one symbolic move were expressed and satisfied two needs—to dominate and render forever impotent the father and to incorporate the "source" of his strength. In the same vein, small children are often seen flooding the ring after the last kill, dipping their fingers in the fallen bull's blood and licking their fingers of this fluid of courage. If the *matador* has performed well and is acclaimed by the crowd the *Presidente* may award him the bull's ear, two ears, or two ears and a tail, in that ascending order of honor.

Thus through the *corrida* does the Mexican spectator, identifying with the *matador* and reenacting the family situation, not only symbolically dominate and destroy the unyielding and hated authority figure, but he captures some of that figure's awesome power.

The bullfight itself has undergone considerable change. What exists now, as "modern bullfighting," began with Belmonte in the early 1930's, and according to the *aficionado*, is considerably different from its earlier stages. Hemingway writes:

> As the *corrida* has developed and decayed, there has been less emphasis on the form of the killing, which was once the whole thing, and more on the cape work, the placing of the *banderillas*, and the

work with the *muleta*. The cape, the *banderillas*, and the *muleta* have all become ends in themselves rather than means to an end. . . .

A bullfighter is now judged, and paid much more on the basis of his ability to pass the bull quietly and closely with the cape than on his ability as a swordsman. The increasing importance and demand for the style of cape work and work with the *muleta*, that was invented or perfected by Juan Belmonte; the expectation and demand that each *matador* pass the pull, giving a complete performance with cape, in the *quites*; and the pardoning of deficiency in killing of a *matador* who is an artist with the cape and *muleta*, are the main changes in modern bullfighting. (Hemingway, 1945)

Pre-Belmonte, then, the "kill" was the focal point of the bullfight. The *matador* who could kill with lust and enjoyment was admired and loved. The earlier phases of the *corrida* were to demonstrate the bull's courage and power and to prepare him for the kill. The essence of the bullfight was the final sword thrust, the actual encounter between man and bull where for an interminable moment they became one figure and was called the "Moment of Truth." Now, to accommodate the emphasis on the cape and *muleta* work, the bulls are smaller and killing is barely a "third of the fight" and anticlimactic to the cloth work (Hemingway, 1945). As Boyd points out, the "Moment of Truth" is now at the highlight of domination with the cape and *muleta*, not at the kill (1956). Hemingway agrees, writing that the emphasis in the modern *corrida* is upon dominance rather than killing and that this has gone hand-in-glove with the padding of the horses, the smaller bulls and the changing of the *picador*'s function for lowering the bull's head and showing his courage to weakening him (Hemingway, 1945). There are, say the older *aficionados*, no longer *matadors*, but now only *toreadors* (Hemingway, 1945).

Mexico has been gradually evolving from the feudal social structure and caste system imposed by the *Conquistadors* toward urbanization and industrialization. The reference group emulated in this transition is, of course, the "advanced" Western world, especially the United States. The trend toward urbanization brings with it more emotionally restrictive patterns of socialization and more abstract channels for the expression of hostility. The position of father in the Mexican family has, with urbanization, also begun to shift toward the "advanced" Western model. It might be said that as the father figure becomes less fearsome, less overpowering, there is less need to "kill" him symbolically—domination alone is an adequate expression of hostility. Western Europeans and Anglo-Americans are usually "shocked," for example, by the "brutality" of the bullfight and tend to dub cultures of which it is a part as "primitive." The more urbanized cultures do not, however, deny the need for legitimized expression of hostility. Kemp, a leading opponent of the bullfight, writes: "One of the functions of civilization is to direct the expression of one's desires by early training and social pressures so that, ideally, we will receive the minimum harm and maximum value from that expression" (1954). He admits to the need for satisfaction of the appetite for violence in all members of society but thinks that they must be satisfied less grossly than in the bullfight.

The general disapproval of Western Europe and the United States concerning the "barbarism" of the bullfight certainly must have had considerable influence on its conduct. (The padding of the horses was instigated by the English-born wife of a King of Spain, following promptings from her own country.) Since the institutions of a society reflect its culture, since the culture is influenced by the demands of other more powerful societies, and since urbanization itself accounts in part for change in cultural patterns, we would expect to see corresponding changes in all of the subject society's institutions, including the bullfight. Thus is seen the shift in emphasis from the "primitive" killing of the bull to the more abstract, more aesthetic, and certainly more "acceptable" domination with the cape and *muleta*. Thus is seen the complete elimination of the kill in Portugal and Switzerland, and in Spain and Mexico, its secondary, almost apologetic status.

Urbanization not only demands more intellectualized dealing with hostility but also brings with it a need for task specialization. This too is reflected in the modern *corrida*. The well-rounded "generalist" *matador* is rare. Most are specialists—cape men, *muleta* men and a few who are known for their work with the *banderillas*.*

The shift in emphasis in the bullfight (some say, the emasculation of the bullfight) has not affected the average American spectator's reaction of being revolted, disgusted, even sickened by the *corrida*. In sounding the reactions of some American college students to their first (and usually last) attendance at a bullfight, the authors have noted the recurring theme: "It's too much," "too blatant," "overpowering." Robinson writes, "the bullfight allows the American, protected from reality all his life by the palliation of modern American society, to face up to the real thing" (1964). And the "real thing" is "too much."

No doubt the highly "civilized" Anglo-American is threatened by such a direct acting out of hostility and violence as is manifest in the

---

* Today one can find women bullfighters, although they are the exception. (Editor's note)

bullfight. But in addition to this he is very likely frightened by such a direct confrontation with death. Americans tend to deny death, even avoiding it in their speech (he "passed away," was "laid to rest," etc.). In Mexico, according to Robinson, "the bullfight spectacle is only one of the forms through which Mexicans make their obeisance to death" (1964). Brenner noted that concern for death is "an organic part of Mexican thought" (1929). The possibility of early or violent death is much greater for the average Mexican than for the average Anglo. To see death averted by the *matador* is pleasing to the Mexican, giving him some feeling of control over an event that he witnesses, not atypically, taking place in the streets. To the American the drama is a grim reminder of the inevitability of an event he seldom sees and chooses to deny. Hemingway writes, "We, in games, are not fascinated by death, its nearness and avoidance. We are fascinated by victory and we replace the avoidance of death by the avoidance of defeat" (1945). The symbolic "victory" over another team is certainly at a higher level of emotional abstraction than the symbolism of the domination and bloody killing of a bull.

Anglo-Americans, the authors have observed, tend to "root" for the bull during a *corrida*. The *picadors* are soundly hooted (Mexicans only demonstrate disapproval if the bull is "ruined") and a tremendous barrage of invective pummels the *matador* if it takes him more than one sword to make a kill (even if all his swords are perfectly "over the horns"). This may be the result of the proclivity of the American to identify with the underdog, or the revulsion at seeing an animal (who, in the American ethic, is also a "buddy") killed. This seemingly irrational preference to see the man rather than the bull killed may also be influenced by a degree of prejudice in the ethnocentric Anglo toward the Mexican *matador*. It may also be that the *corrida* does not present to the Anglo a perception of two "evenly matched" antagonists. The opponents are not "equal"—few *matadors* are killed, but the bull rarely lives. This may run counter to the "fair play" ethic of the Anglo.

If the bullfight's overt display of hostility with its overriding components of inevitable death, animal suffering and inequality, is not acceptable as a suitable means for the expression of aggression to the Anglo, what does he prefer? As mentioned earlier, the Anglo, too, is subject to socialization, and he, too, experiences conflict situations which engender hostility toward parents and parent surrogates. How, then, as reflected in the Anglo national sport of baseball, is the expression of hostility toward authority legitimized?

BASEBALL

It was presented above that the Anglo child is prevented from directly manifesting hostility toward parents by their representation as "good guys" and "pals." Verbal aggression, elaborately intellectualized, is usually the most overt form of hostility allowed to the child. Whereas the Mexican seems painfully aware of conflict, hates his father and acts out his hostility (displaces, projects), the Anglo appears hopelessly ambivalent toward the vague "buddy" father and represses the fact that conflict exists. A good part of his psychic life is spent sustaining this repression compulsively and obsessively. In general, the legitimized means of expressing hostility are just as subtle as is the subtlety of the hostility generating [a] conflict situation—this mutedness is manifest as we shall see in the national sport.

The *matador*'s servile bow to the *Presidente* is an obvious and undisguised move of deference. In the prelude to a baseball game, however, the players line up, facing the flag, and stand quietly during the playing of the national anthem. Tribute to authority here certainly is less direct than in the bullring. A flag is a considerably more abstract and less threatening symbol than the pompous gentlemen in the privileged box. The government official who, as *Presidente*, attends the *corrida*, controls its conduct and can directly interfere in the performance. Government officials who attend baseball games are in no way able to interfere with play—at most, they throw in the first ball.

While the observer need only take a quick glance at the "barbaric" *corrida* to see a dramatically overt display of violence and aggression, he is hard pressed, after considerable observation, to see any marked degree of hostility in the structure of the "good clean sport" of baseball. He looks out over the field and sees two teams (composed of an equal number of similarly uniformed men), patiently and systematically taking an equal number of turns (innings) in the attempt to score. The field is elaborately chalked, [delimiting] those areas of "fair" from "foul" play, and an elaborate system of rules dictates when a player can get a "hit," take or advance a base, score a run, be "safe" or "out." The observer becomes aware of the game's dramatic emphasis on numbers (the most abstract of symbols)—the scoreboard, the batting averages, the earned-run averages, the team win percentages, and even the players, who are granted relative impersonality by the numbers on their backs.

Unlike the *matador*, who constantly communicates with the crowd, the baseball players are seen to remain distinctly aloof from them. The player's allegiance is to the team, and he who performs ostentatiously for the crowd is ostracized as a "grandstander." Contrast, for example, the baseball player's downcast eye and turf-kicking toe after an outstanding move with the *matador's* haughty glance and proud posture following a good series of passes. Contrast the convertible or television set given ritualistically by the crowd to the ball player on "his day" with the immediate, spontaneous and extremely emotional reaction of the crowd following an appreciated *corrida*—they clamor for the *Presidente* to give him awards, throw him wine flasks, *sombreros* and often rush into the ring to carry him about on their shoulders. It might be said that in baseball, the crowd is expected to observe, in a relatively detached way, the spectacle being performed for them on the field. At the bullfight, however, the crowd is expected to be one with the *matador*, to participate, fully, in the emotions of the fight.

There is, by contrast to the *corrida*, a noticeable lack of heterosexuality in the game of baseball. While the *matador* often dedicates his bull or tosses an ear to a *señorita*, the baseball player, on the field anyway, limits his interaction to male teammates, chattering to them, shaking their hands in success, slapping their buttocks in encouragement, and mobbing and hugging them for superlative feats of play.

There is, of course, competition taking place in the game—but nothing that can parallel the direct, individual confrontation of the *matador* with the bull. In baseball, two "teams" meet and the more evenly matched they are, the better the "contest" is. There are fans for both sides, each rooting for his team, hoping that it will win the "contest." After the game is over there will be a winner and a "good loser." It is interesting that the participants in baseball are called "players." The *matador* is not "playing" at the *corrida*—it is a *fight*. The aggressive component that one would expect in competition is muted by the rules governing the conduct of play and by the expectations of the crowd. There are occasional emotional outbreaks between rival players, between players and umpires and between managers and umpires, but these "rhubarbs" are ephemeral and seem somehow distant and artificial. The shouts and jeers of the crowd, with an occasional "murder the bum," lack the emotional punch and especially the personal reference of the venomous insults hurled by the displeased Mexican *aficionado*.

Some psychoanalytically oriented behavioral scientists have written vividly of the symbolic castration represented in the baseball games. Stokes, for example, calls baseball "a manifest exercise in phallic deftness" (1956). Petty sees the contest as a safe re-creation of the battle between father and son for the sexual favors of the mother (1963).

However, if hostility generated in a father-son competition is manifested here, how safe, how muted, is its expression? Its release is legitimized only under the restrictions of elaborate rules, omnipresent umpires, and with the insistence that each team systematically take turns playing one role or the other. It is diffused throughout a "team," no one man taking full responsibility and is submerged in a morass of batting and pitching rituals and superstitions that are unsurpassed by the most extreme of religions and the military. Batters will use only certain bats, stand a certain way, pound home plate a certain number of times, spit, rub dust, rub resin (or all three) on their hands, pull their clothing into a certain position before batting, wear lucky numbers, lucky charms, lucky hats, lucky sox [sic] or use a lucky bat. Many pitchers have elaborate series of movements before delivering the ball—touch cap, rub ball, grab resin bag, scuff dirt, adjust glove, retouch hat, rerub ball. . . . Professional pitcher Lew Burdette has taken as long as a full minute to complete a series of irrelevant gestures, ticks, clutches, and tugs before throwing the ball. Similarly, an observer would be hard pressed to find a baseball player who doesn't ritualistically chew gum or tobacco.

Furthermore, the conduct of the game, and therefore any expression of hostility, is closely scrutinized by at least three umpires. Interestingly enough, the word *umpire* is derived from the Latin, meaning "not equal." Thus, on a playing field where equality is a central ethic, the umpires are unique. They are the only personnel on the field who, even during inning intermissions, cannot sit down or relax. Like the "superego" theirs is an unrelenting vigilance. Their word is law, and disrespect for them can bring an ousting from the game. But how different is the player-umpire relationship from that of the *matador-Presidente*? The *Presidente* is treated with deference, and the interaction between authority and *matador* is seen to be personal and direct. As in the Mexican society at large, the authority figure, though he may be hated, is shown the utmost respect. Mexican patients have described their fathers as drunkards, brutes, etc., but always add that they "respect" them. Tucson, Arizona, school teachers often report that the behavior of the Mexican-American students *vis-à-vis* the teacher is exemplary, though their dropout and absentee records indicate a low value for education.

The umpire, on the other hand, is an impersonal figure. How many "fans" know the names of big league umpires? So abstract is the black-suited authority that "kill the umpire" can be vociferously and safely shouted. How nonthreatening is the typical reaction of the umpire to the complaints, admonishments, and verbal aggressions of the players and managers—he turns his back and slowly walks away. Authority is challenged—and with impunity! There is, however, a carefully defined limit to the amount of abuse the umpire is expected to endure. Physical violence and certain profanities bring not only a removal from the game but severe fines to the offender. Since there are fixed fines for specific obscenities, angry players will often turn to the umpire and, escaping the fine by ascending a rung on the abstraction ladder, declare, "You're that five-hundred-dollar word!"

Another phenomenon, certainly cultural in nature, is the ritual hypochondriasis of baseball players. *Matadors* traditionally disregard wounds (the *macho* does not fear, avoid or show disability because of pain) and have even fought with assistants who tried to carry them out of the ring after a serious goring. Baseball players leave the field for a simple pulled muscle. Yards of tape, gallons of ointment, heat treatments, vitamin pills, "isometrics," "training rules," arm warmers, whirlpool baths and rubdowns pamper the ball player. Pitchers are carefully protected from the wind, rain, and cold "dugout" seats, and can ask to be relieved if they are feeling tired.

As the conduct of the bullfight has changed with the increasing urbanization in Mexico, so also has the conduct of baseball changed with the increasing bureaucratization in the United States. In the early twentieth century, fines for insulting (or even striking) the umpire were nonexistent. The crowd very often displayed displeasures by throwing bottles and cushions at specific individuals in the field. In general, the level of expression of hostility was more direct and involved somewhat more acting out. The farm club system, its scouting ties with organized collegiate athletics and the bureaucratic "front office" were far less expansive. Rules and regulations were less restricting, and the tobacco-chewing, swearing, sweating player was typical as contrasted with the "gentleman players" who grace our fields and television commercials today. Nine innings then took about two-thirds the time they do now, the ball was "dead" and the number of players on the team's roster was smaller. There were fewer substitutes, and pitchers as a rule stayed in for the entire game.

In the present situation even the abstract "team" concept has been made obsolete by increased bureaucratization. The authors witnessed members of the winning (1963) Los Angeles Dodgers speaking proudly of the "Dodger organization," and the good job the "front office" had done.

In a television interview, Bill Veeck, an ex-professional manager, expressed dismay with the unnecessary "dragging out" of the game by prolonged warm-up pitches, drawn-out sessions of verbal haranguing, "long" walks to the dugout and summit meetings of the pitcher, catcher and manager. He complained about the time-wasting rituals of motion indulged in by both pitcher and batter. Veeck thus testifies to the increasing obsessive quality in the game, as its emphasis shifts to more and more diffuse, indirect and disguised means for expressing hostility.

One wonders, in fact, if the restrictions in baseball are too many, if the fans aren't growing dissatisfied. The increasing public attendance at professional football games, reaching a point where some sports analysts predict that it will replace baseball as the national sport, may be an indication of the demand for a less abstract expression of hostility in spectator sports. Nevertheless, from the point of view of social control, baseball masterfully mutes aggression behind its reciprocity, rules, records and rituals. It duplicates the vagueness and intellectualization of the conflict situation in the American family and provides a markedly abstract and controlled expression of hostility toward authority. Macoby, et al., write that baseball represents the *ideal* of American society (1964). It remains to be seen whether or not this ideal can, in the face of a need for a clearer expression of hostility, remain intact.

SUMMARY

The passive-aggressive component of the Mexican modal personality can be traced to the dominant and harshly punitive role of the father and to the general authoritarian nature of the Mexican culture. The passive-aggressiveness is perpetuated in the *macho* pattern of the Mexican male and in the "martyr" pattern of the Mexican female. Any acting out of the resultant hostility to authority must be carried out in spheres safely distant from that authority's immediate control.

The bullfight is seen to depict, symbolically , the power of the father, the subtle demands of the mother and the fear of the child. Unlike the family situation, the awesome authority does not prevail, but rather is dominated and destroyed through the courage and daring of the *matador*. He, however, acting for the spectator, must accomplish this hostile act in a framework of "respect" for authority, and with a studied passiveness in and control of movement.

By contrast, the "intellectualization" component of the Anglo modal personality can be traced to the superficial ethic of "equality" among family members and to the general intellectualized nature of highly urbanized societies. The attempt to mute authority by a pseudo-philosophy of togetherness, when authority is in fact assumed by the father, the mother and by the society, engenders a vagueness in role definitions, confusion in behavioral expectations and an intellectualization of the resultant conflict. Hostility toward this intangible yet frustrating authority figure is expressed by the individual in a manner as abstract and as ritualized as its causative factors.

The national sport of baseball is set in a framework of equality. Hostility toward authority takes the symbolic form of competition and desire to win, and is smothered under a covering of rules, regulations and player rituals. Guided by the authority of umpires (who are sufficiently impersonal to be challenged with relative impunity), and protected in the safety of numbers as a member of a team, the players systematically alternate roles, allowing each to have an equal opportunity to "be aggressive."

Spectators of the baseball game view two similarly uniformed teams consisting of the same number of players vying for an abstract "victory." The spectators' emotional participation in the game is distant and safe — "murder the bum" or "kill the umpire" does not have enough of a personal referent to arouse guilt or anxiety. They can take sides in occasional and severely regulated conflicts on the field, because such conflicts have "meaning" only in the game, and are forgotten when the game is over.

Since 1920, the bullfight has gradually been modified to accentuate domination rather than the kill. Paralleling this, the position of the father in the Mexican family has, with gradual urbanization, come more closely in line with that of the "advanced" Western model. He is less threatening, less fearsome, and can be dominated to a degree sufficient to reduce the importance of his symbolic destruction.

Baseball, since 1920, has similarly undergone significant changes. With the increasing bureaucratization of Anglo society, and with the increasing emphasis upon "equality" and impersonality in the family, have come the more complex bureaucratization and the more elaborate ritualization of baseball.

The family and the institutionalized recreation form known as the national sport mutually reflect, as they appear in Mexico, the cultural centrality of death, dominance, "personal" relationships, respect for and fear and hatred of authority and the defense systems of the passive-aggressive character structure.

In the Anglo culture, these two institutions [of family and institutionalized recreation] mutually reflect the cultural importance of equality, impersonality, and the defense mechanism of intellectualization.

Both national sports provide a socially acceptable channel for the expression of hostility toward authority. This channel is modified by other cultural values and expectations, and is framed in an activity which duplicates, symbolically, aspects of the hostility-generating familial situation.

Related Literature

Allen, J. H. *Southwest*. New York, 1953.

Boyd, G. "On bullfight." Wright, M., ed. *The Field of Vision*. New York, 1956: 100–111.

Brenner, A. *Idols Behind Altars*. New York, 1929.

Díaz-Guerrero, R. *Estudios de Psicología del Mexicano*. Mexico, 1961.

––––––– . "Socio-cultural premises, attitudes, and cross-cultural research." *Cross-Cultural Studies of Attitude Structure and Search*. Proceedings of 17th International Congress of Psychology. Washington, D.C., 1963.

Dollard, J. "Hostility and fear in social life." *Social Forces*. 42, 1938: 15–25.

Gillin, J. P. "Ethos and cultural aspects of personality." Y. A. Cohen, ed. *Social Structure and Personality*. New York, 1961: 288–300.

Hemingway, E. *Death in the Afternoon*. New York, 1945.

Kardiner, A. *The Individual and His Society*. New York, 1939.

Kemp, L. *The Only Beast*. New York, 1954.

Kluckhohn, F., and Strodbeck, F. L. *Variations in Value Orientation*. New York, 1961.

Lea, T. *The Brave Bulls*. Boston, 1949.

Lewis, O. *Children of Sanchez*. New York, 1961.

Lundberg, G. A., Schrag, L. C., and Larsen, O. N. *Sociology*. New York, 1958.

Macoby, M., Modiano, N., and Lander, P. "Games and social character in a Mexican village." *Psychiatry*. 1964: 50–61.

Meadow, A., Zurcher, L., and Stoker, D. "Sex role and schizophrenia in Mexican culture." *International Journal of Social Psychiatry* (forthcoming).

Meadow, A., and Stoker, D. "Symptomatic behaviour of Mexican-American and Anglo-American child guidance patients." Unpub. paper, University of Arizona.

Ramsey, R. *Fiesta*. New York, 1955.

Robinson, C. *With the ears of strangers: The Mexican in American Literature*. Tucson, Ariz., 1964.

Stokes, A. "Psychoanalytic reflections on the development of ball games." *International Journal of Psycho-Analysis*. 37, 1956: 185–192.

Tumin, M. M. "Some disfunctions of institutional imbalance." *Bahavioral Science*. 1, 1956: 218–223.

Whiting, J. W., and Child, I. L. *Child Training and Personality: A Cross-Cultural Study*. New Haven, Conn., 1953.

CATHERINE SUNSHINE

Unifying Themes in Caribbean Cultures

(If the hallmark of the Caribbean is diversity of race, religion, language, and culture, the Caribbean nations are unified by their common past under colonial governments and their present struggle for economic and cultural survival.)

The overwhelming cultural characteristic of the Caribbean, taken as the sum of its parts, is diversity. In race, in culture, in language and religion, it is one of the most heterogeneous areas in the world. This stems from the complex population movements which created Caribbean societies: forced and voluntary migrations from Africa, Europe and Asia into the Caribbean, and the continuing migration within the region itself.

A cultural map of the Caribbean reveals rigid barriers and omnipresent interconnections. The main barriers are the ones imposed by colonialism, which carved the region into Spanish, British, French and Dutch empires. These divisions have persisted into the era of political independence. Thus the English-speaking Caribbean forms a community, the "Commonwealth Caribbean," with political and economic ties among its members. The Spanish-speaking peoples of Cuba, the Dominican Republic and Puerto Rico consider themselves part of Latin America, although U.S. control has blurred this identity for Puerto Rico. The French Antilles and French Guiana, still under colonial rule, look only toward France. The Netherlands Antilles [and Aruba] are part of

From Catherine Sunshine, *The Caribbean: Survival, Struggle, and Sovereignty* (Boston: EPICA/South End Press, 1988), 19–22, by permission of the author and publisher.

the Kingdom of the Netherlands, while Suriname, formally independent, retains strong ties to Holland.

The linkages are more subtle. Despite the colonial divisions, Caribbean histories are parallel and intertwined. What unity there is rests on this shared experience: of African or Asian origins (for the majority), of slavery and indentured servitude, of colonization by the European powers. This history sometimes links people in a way which transcends the colonial barriers. During the 1700s, runaway slaves moved between French-held Martinique and St. Lucia, forming rebel communities. When St. Lucia passed to British ownership in 1814, formal ties with the French colonies ended, but links of language, culture and migration continued. Today the official language of St. Lucia is English, but the mass vernacular remains French Creole, virtually identical to that spoken in neighboring Martinique and Guadeloupe.[1]

In the former French and British colonies, which knew plantation slavery for 150 years, the majority of the population traces its roots to Africa. This is a force for unity, although colonial ideology and education long conspired to deny its importance. While the Jamaican nationalist slogan—"Out of many, one people"—suggests an equal contribution from numerous groups, in reality Jamaica is Afro-Caribbean, with 95 percent of its people black or brown.

In Guyana and Trinidad and Tobago, Indian indentureship on a large scale led to biracial populations almost evenly divided between people of African and East Indian descent. Suriname follows a similar pattern, with the addition of a significant third group, the Indonesians.

The Spanish-speaking Greater Antilles stand somewhat apart from this variant of the Caribbean experience. They had plantation slavery, but it developed on a large scale only after two centuries of Spanish settler colonialism. During this time the Spanish, some African slaves and the surviving Arawak Indians mingled, forming racially blended populations sharing a common Spanish language. In Puerto Rico, where slavery was not extensive, a mainly light-skinned peasantry emerged. In Cuba, by contrast, the development of a huge sugar industry meant a large slave population, with less racial mingling. Many Cubans are Spanish in appearance, but many others are clearly of African descent. Blending was greatest in the Dominican Republic, due in part to continuous contact with the black population of neighboring Haiti. The Dominican Republic today is predominantly a mulatto nation.[2]

The Spanish-speaking countries have a cultural unity arising from their own historic links. The ties between Cuba and Puerto Rico were particularly strong. Their independence struggles were jointly planned in the 1860s, and many Puerto Ricans fought and died in Cuba's war against Spanish control. The U.S. takeover of Spain's colonies in 1898 created a barrier to this unity, but the nearly identical flags of the two countries testify to the closeness which once existed.

The struggle against colonial Spain did not mean a rejection of Spanish culture. Rather, nationalist movements stressed Latin identity as a counter to North American cultural and political pressures. In addition, the middle and upper classes emphasized their Spanish antecedents in order to downplay the reality of an African heritage. The most extreme example occurred in the Dominican Republic, where the dictator Trujillo promoted Latin culture and anti-black racism as a way of rejecting the country's experience under Haitian rule.

The African roots of the Afro-Latin cultures, and indeed of all Caribbean cultures, are most evident in music and religion. Santería, the popular religion of Cuba, Puerto Rico and the Dominican Republic, is based on West African Yoruba beliefs. It is closely linked to Shango in Trinidad and Candomble in Brazil, two other countries which received many Yoruba slaves. Black Puerto Ricans in rural areas still perform the traditional African [influenced] dances of *la bomba* and *la plena*. La bomba has Ashanti origins, and resembles dances in Jamaica and Haiti. Dominican peasants do drum dances called *los palos*; a festival involving the dance was outlawed by Trujillo in his campaign to de-Africanize the country. African influences permeate contemporary music as well. Cuban *son* and *rumba*, Dominican *merengue* and Puerto Rican *salsa* all feature the strong drum rhythms of Africa.

The one thing all Caribbean societies have in common is a colonial past. Through its components of migration, racism and class oppression, colonialism gave rise to three themes woven throughout the cultural tapestry. They are the **class basis** of Caribbean cultures, their use of creative **synthesis**, and **culture as resistance**.

THE CLASS-COLOR-CULTURE TRIANGLE

The correlation between skin shade and class has become a truism of Caribbean life. White (with admixtures of Middle Eastern and Chinese) equals upper-class; mulatto or "brown" is middle-class; while the African and East Indian majority occupies the base of the social pyramid. These broad divisions, however, underlie a more complex stratification resulting from social mobility through education, politics, property ownership and marriage.

The class-color correlates of the West Indian social structure are real. But they are not the absolutes of a rigid caste system. Skin color determines social class; but it is not an exclusive determinant. There are many fair-skinned persons who are not upper-class, and many dark-skinned persons who are. The real divisions of the society are the horizontal ones of social class rather than the vertical ones of color identification. [3]

Racial perceptions in the Caribbean differ somewhat from those in Europe, and, especially, the United States. In U.S. society persons are generally defined as either "white" or "black," unless they are Hispanic or Asian. The slightest trace of African ancestry usually qualifies even a light-skinned person as "black." In the Caribbean, by contrast, skin color is seen as part of a continuum in which small variations become socially important. Brown-skinned persons are distinguished from those who are black; indeed there has traditionally been a world of social distance between them.

These color/class divisions carry with them cultural implications. At the top of the pyramid, the white elite waves the banner of its European origins—the English mores of Jamaica's upper class, or the Frenchness of Martinique's native white *békés*. This sets the standard for the society, becoming the goal toward which the brown and black middle class aspires. Historically, Caribbean societies have idealized the culture of the colonizer and looked down upon the culture of the mass. Yet ironically, it is from the original and vibrant mass cultures—not the imitative culture of the elite—that a Caribbean identity has emerged.

For if there is a common West Indian culture, it has been created, first and foremost, by the social classes at the bottom. . . . They, more than any others, have been the culture carriers, for the higher rung groups have been inhibited by the hybrid form of European culture they have imbibed from playing that role. [4]

Use of language is a case in point. The Caribbean is a region of tremendous linguistic diversity, in which the division into "English-speaking," "French-speaking," "Spanish-speaking" and "Dutch-speaking" obscures a far more complex reality. [5] Only in the Spanish-speaking Antilles is the official language also the language of all the people.

Elsewhere, French, English and Dutch compete with the far more widely spoken Creole languages. These originated when Africans speaking related languages of the Niger-Congo family in Africa came to the Caribbean. To make slave revolts more difficult, slave owners mixed Africans of different ethnic groups on their plantations. . . . To communicate, the slaves preserved the grammatical core of their related mother tongues and infused into this structure vocabulary from the colonizers' European languages. [6]

In the French colonies, *Kreyol* based on French words and African syntax emerged as the national language. Some 85 percent of Haitians speak only Kreyol. Yet the official language of Haiti has always been French; French is used in the schools, the government, and courts of law. In Haiti more than elsewhere, language has become part of a vicious class system which discriminates against the black, Creole-speaking majority.

The situation differs somewhat in the anglophone Caribbean. Here a similar historical process produced *Patwa*, an English Creole. But in contrast to the clear separation between French and Kreyol, standard English and Patwa are two ends of a continuum, with many intermediate forms in between. The less education a person has, the more his or her speech will likely tend toward the Patwa end of the scale and vice versa.

Yet even this is too simple: in a country like Jamaica, where the Patwa tradition is strong, everyone, including the middle and upper classes, can and does speak it. They simply adapt their speech to the social context of the moment. Thus a West Indian politician will use standard English for policy discussions, then go out on the soapbox and regale the crowd with jokes in Patwa.

Colonial ideology defined the Creole languages as inferior "corruptions" of European languages, and for a long time most Caribbean people accepted this view. That image has changed somewhat in recent years, with language coming to be seen as important to national identity. This is particularly so in Haiti and the French Antilles, where political movements have made Kreyol a symbol of popular empowerment. Throughout the region there are efforts to systematize the writing of Creoles, enabling the growth of a Creole literature and strengthening their image as legitimate languages.

This process has gone farthest in the Netherlands Antilles, where the mass vernacular is a Portuguese-based Creole called *Papiamentu*. While Dutch remains the official language and is used throughout the school system, Papiamentu has virtually replaced it as the spoken language of daily use. This is true not only for the popular majority, but for all classes. No longer stigmatized, Papiamentu is increasingly the language of national literature and the press.

Religion is another area closely linked to class. Jamaican author Leonard Barrett tells of the division in his own family between his mother's relatives, who belong to the brown middle class, and his father's family, black Jamaicans from the peasantry. The former are Christian church-goers, while the latter follow the Afro-Christian Pocomania cult. [7] As people move up the social ladder, they tend to leave the African syncretic religions in favor of mainline denominations such as the

English Baptists, Methodists and Presbyterians. Each country also has its high-status denominations historically associated with the colonial ruling class: Anglicanism in territories colonized by Britain, Catholicism in those colonized by the French and in the Dominican Republic, U.S. Protestantism in Puerto Rico, and Dutch Protestantism in the Netherlands Antilles.

The "official" view of popular culture has changed somewhat in recent years. With political independence, the new black and brown leadership has turned to the people's culture as a reservoir of authenticity in the struggle to create a national identity. A major factor has been the international commercial success of Caribbean art forms. Reggae and steelband music, born in the poverty of Kingston and Port-of-Spain slums, are now highly commercialized. Carnival, likewise, was a working-class "bachanal," scorned as vulgar and rowdy by the middle class. But when its colorful pageantry started drawing thousands of tourists to Trinidad, the government gave Carnival official sponsorship and a new respect, which also served to bring the festival under closer control.

SYNTHESIS AND RESISTANCE

A second theme which marks Caribbean cultures is **synthesis**: the blending of diverse cultural elements into new, original forms. The merger of Africa and Europe is at the root of Caribbean cultures. Other strong influences include India, Latin America and the United States.

Carnival provides a rich example of this process. In colonial Trinidad, the French Catholic elite celebrated the pre-Lenten season with masked balls and parades. Black Trinidadians had their own "Canboulay" celebrations commemorating emancipation from slavery. Eventually these traditions merged into the Carnival of today.

> From its opening moment of *jour overt* and the "ole mas" costume bands to its finale, forty-eight hours later, in the dusk of Mardi Carnival, the Trinidadian populace gives itself up to the "jump up," the tempestuous abandon of Carnival . . . Port-of-Spain becomes a panic of mob art: the Sailor Bands, sometimes of five thousand or more . . . the Seabees groups, mocking their original United States Navy inspiration with their exaggerated high-ranking officer titles and overblown campaign ribbons . . . impertinent personifications of, variously, Texas Rangers, French Foreign Legionnaires, British Palace Guards and Nazi High Command officers. . . . [8]

And underneath it all runs "a powerful undercurrent of Shango, bamboo-tamboo, canboulay"—the African traditions in Caribbean culture. [9]

The West Indian music known as calypso provides another example of creative synthesis. Originating in Trinidad in the 1800s, calypso has roots in the African oral tradition. Early lyrics were in French Creole, then shifted to English toward the end of the century. Musical influences on calypso included French and Spanish music, . . . East Indian drumming, and black Revivalist spirituals. During World War Two, with hundreds of U.S. troops in Trinidad, calypso absorbed influences from rhythm and blues, swing and bebop, along with an increasing degree of commercialism.

The same blending process underlies the Afro-Latin cultures. The *merengue* of the Dominican Republic was originated by the peasantry using drums and other African instruments. Middle and upper class Dominicans scorned the merengue, preferring to dance the waltz. But gradually, a change occurred: Spanish instruments such as the *tres* and *cuatro*, the accordion and the *bandoneón* were incorporated into merengue alongside the drums. This Europeanized merengue was called *merengue de salón*—parlor merengue—and was popular with town-dwellers. Merengue is now a national passion spanning all classes in the Dominican Republic.

Closely connected to the theme of synthesis is the theme of **culture as resistance** which runs through Caribbean history. By borrowing elements of culture and transforming them, Caribbean people fought back against cultural domination. This often is expressed in satire, as in the ribald parodies of Carnival. The Jonkonnu parade which once flourished in Jamaica, Belize and the Bahamas combines African elements such as the horsehead, cowhead and devil costumes with grotesque masked caricatures of British royalty. Such irreverent humor has its roots in the slavery era, when one form of slave resistance was subtle mockery of the ruling class.

In West Indian cultural resistance, the drum has always held pride of place. Drums were used in Africa for long-distance communication, and slaves on the plantations continued this practice. Fearful of slave revolts, the planters outlawed the drum. After emancipation, the . . . [colonial authorities banned] drumming as subversive and an obstacle to the assimilation of the blacks. But they could never totally suppress it. In 1884 riots broke out in Port-of-Spain when the colonial authorities banned the use of drums for Carnival.

The ban on drumming gave rise to a substitute known as *bamboo-tamboo*, the practice of beating out rhythms on the ground with cured sticks. In the late 1930s, young men in the urban slums of Trinidad turned to using metal biscuit tins and old oil drums, and the modern steelband—"pan"—was born.

Notes

1. Morgan Dalphinis, *Caribbean & African Languages: Social History, Language, Literature and Education* (London: Karia Press, 1985), chapter 2.

2. H. Hoetink, " 'Race' and Color in the Caribbean," in Sidney W. Mintz and Sally Price, eds., *Caribbean Contours* (Baltimore: Johns Hopkins University Press, 1985), pp. 56–58.

3. Gordon K. Lewis, *The Growth of the Modern West Indies* (New York: Monthly Review Press, 1968), p. 20.

4. *Ibid*, p. 28.

5. Mervyn C. Alleyne, "A Linguistic Perspective on the Caribbean," in Mintz and Price, p. 155.

6. Dalphinis, pp. 1–2.

7. Leonard Barrett, *The Sun and the Drum: African Roots in Jamaican Folk Tradition* (Jamaica: Sangster's Book Stores Ltd., 1976), pp. 11–12.

8. Gordon K. Lewis, pp. 30–31.

9. *Ibid*, pp. 31–32.

JAN CAREW

The Caribbean Writer and Exile

(People of the Caribbean are a complex of several cultural fragments—
Amerindian, African, European, Asian. The problematic character of exile and
its several meanings are discussed in light of these multi-cultural origins.)

There was a traditional format in the classical Akan* theatre around
which all drama—comedy, tragedy, farce—evolved. The important
features of this drama were these: there was an archetypal middle man
and on either side of him were powerful spirits opposing one another.
The figure in the middle often stood between malevolent and benign
spirits of the ancestral dead, and a host of other spirits that were urbane
or demonic, creative or destructive, compassionate or cruel, surrogates
of the living or the dead, ethereal or earthy, part saint, part trickster.
These spirits were involved in eternal conflicts which could only be
resolved if the human being periodically renewed contact with communal wellsprings of rhythm, creation and life.

The Caribbean writer today is a creature balanced between limbo
and nothingness, exile abroad and homeless at home; between the
people on the one hand and the creole and the colonizer on the other.

* A language spoken over a wide area in Ghana and extending into the Ivory Coast.
(Editor's note)

Jan Carew, "The Caribbean Writer and Exile" (*Caribbean Studies* 19, 1 and 2 [1979–1980]),
111–132, by permission of the publisher.

Exile can be voluntary or it can be imposed by stress of circumstances; it can be a punishment or a pleasure. The exile can leave home for a short time or he can be expelled forever. The colonizing zeal of the European made indigenous peoples exiles in their own countries—Prospero made Caliban an exile in his. The Caribbean writer by going abroad is in fact searching for an end to exile.

This, at first, appears to be a contradiction until one lays bare some of the truths of Caribbean life. The Caribbean person is subjected to successive waves of cultural alienation from birth, a process that has its origins embedded in a mosaic of cultural fragments—Amerindian, African, European, Asian. The European fragment is brought into sharper focus than the others, but it remains a fragment. Hiding behind the screen of this European cultural fragment the Caribbean writer oscillates in and out of sunlight and shadows, exile abroad and home-lessness at home. At home, he is what C.L.R. James described very aptly as a "twentieth century man living in a seventeenth century economy," [1] while abroad he is a performer in a circus of civilization.

There are times when he claims that he is a nomad, but this is one of his clever evasions. The irony of it all is that he can only become a nomad when his place in the sun, the speck on the globe that is his home is freed from the economic, psychological and political clutches of usurpers, who had seized it since the beginning of the Columbian era. The spaces that the nomad's imagination encompass exist within a circumference of seasons, and national borders have no meaning for him.

For the Caribbean writer, therefore, to become a true nomad his feet must traverse a territory that his imagination encompasses without let or hindrance. In his country, however, the land, the air-space, the water, the minerals under the earth are owned from abroad and administered by local surrogates; the rights of passage are overtly or covertly restricted. Every new trespass, therefore, is a kind of reckless lurch into a wider indifference.

The term *Caribbean* in this essay describes the island archipelago, the countries on the Caribbean littoral and Guyana, Surinam and Cayenne. Cuba is the exception that proves the rule. Cuba belongs to the Cubans. In Cuba, the northeastern sheet anchor of the Caribbean archipelago, the pre-revolutionary economic relationship between expatriate owners, local surrogates and the majority of people, no longer exists. Cuba is, therefore, a point of reference for us, a living example of how in less than two decades, age-old problems of economic and cultural alienation, race and color, caste, class and identity, can be looked at afresh and in many instances successfully dealt with.

In order to deal with one's heritage of exile today, one must return to the beginnings of the Columbian era. Marx said that history always repeats itself; the first time is tragedy and the next time farce, and in the Caribbean we often appear to be like sleep-walkers reliving the history and repeating the farce.

The early accounts written by European colonizers about their apocalyptic intrusion into the Amerindian domains are characterized, with few exceptions, by romantic evasions of truth and voluminous omissions. Have we ever really examined the images that these historical fictions have created of us? If we do so empirically, then we can begin to understand this question of exile abroad and homelessness at home of the writer.

After Columbus and his sailors were discovered by the Arawakian Lucayos on their beaches in 1492, the Americas of the colonizer came into being as part of both a literary exercise and one of the most apalling acts of ethnocide in recorded history: First, there were Columbus' diaries (the first literary offering of the interlopers), which told us more about the man himself than about the islands he had stumbled upon; and the man revealed to us was a schizoid being, a Janus astride two worlds, one medieval, the other of the Renaissance. These diaries are a blend of fantasies fed by writings from the Middle Ages; obsessive ramblings about a new crusade to recapture Jerusalem from the infidel Turks; special pleadings to the sovereigns of Castile; a precise sailor's log and useful scientific observations about the flora, fauna and topography of the lands visited. His writings about the people he met are contradictory, inaccurate, biased and in the midst of pious declarations about converting "natives" to Christianity, sprinkled with asides of racial arrogance and a lust for gold.

Columbus led an early life that was very similar to the one that future Caribbean artists, vagabonds, sailors, writers and immigrants would lead centuries later. In his journey from a nameless street in Genoa to the Portuguese and Spanish courts, he had to cross two centuries. Son of a wool carder, he began his trespass into the fifteenth and sixteenth centuries with little more than great expectations, and his whole life, in fact, was to become a journey to new illusions. He had had to cross not only distances in time and space, but the almost immeasurable gulf between the lower middle class and the nobility. Having made this impossible leap, he carried with him a multitude of insecurities and a persistent fear of looking back and acknowledging his lowly beginnings.

On his first journey across the Atlantic, Columbus became prey to the medieval fantasies nurtured like fungus on his narrow Genoese street with its gloomy doorways yawning like entrances to minotaur caves, its shuttered windows and its persistent odours of decay which the sea breezes even now do not seem to dispel completely. As he became more and more convinced that he would survive the Atlantic crossing, his mind was filled with dreams of golden-roofed palaces on the one hand, and on the other, a bestiary inhabited by gryphons and by other fabulous creatures, some of which ate human flesh, had human bodies and the snouts of dogs. When he did not find the monsters that medieval writers had dreamed up, Columbus invented a monstrous racial slander: he declared that the Caribs were cannibals.

What we can prove about the Caribs is that they fought with surpassing courage and skill against the European intruders, and that this became the basis for a new kind of ideological arrangement. Those who welcomed the colonizers were praised, enslaved and exterminated, and those who resisted were damned. The contumely heaped upon the heads of the Caribs by Columbus led to interesting lexical and literary aberrations—from Carib derived the word *cannibal* and from cannibal Shakespeare gave us Caliban. The institutionalisation of racism and colonialism begins with the Carib, cannibal, Caliban slander, one that has persisted for five centuries. In the Caribbean, school children are still being taught from texts, some of which have ostensibly been written by eminent Caribbean historians, that the Caribs ate human flesh. Richard Moore, the Barbadian historian, refuted this calumny in a brilliant booklet and in an article, both very well researched. [2] Both the Carib cannibal and the African and other Third World species are fruit from the same tree of racism. Every time a Caribbean child reads about the ancestral cannibal it becomes an unconscious act of psychological self-mutilation. "Do we not know," José Martí had written, "that the same blow that paralyzes the Indian, cripples us." [3] But our children neither read the works of Martí nor know who he is. They are still taught to idolize the colonizer and in so doing hate themselves.

On his second voyage, Columbus found human bones, relics of ancestor worship, in Carib huts in Dominica. He used this as evidence to prove his racial slander. Had a group of Caribs "discovered" Rome and visited the catacombs, they too would have found certain Catholic Orders preserving human bones, and by the same curious logic that Columbus used, could have assumed that the Pope and his followers were cannibals.

If the Admiral of the Ocean Sea had stayed in Genoa, he would most likely have remained a part-time sailor and a worker in wool. His family had for generations been clothmakers. They took sheep's wool, spun it into thread and wove the thread into cloth which they finally sold.

Since ancient times, the Genoese youth, particularly those from the lower middle class, had gone to sea in search of fame and fortune. For if they were ambitious, it would be clear as bells of the angelus that for them their society was one of many dogs and few bones. So the urge to seasons of adventure was not entirely a romantic one. During the Renaissance the challenge of conquering the seemingly infinite spaces of the Atlantic beyond the Pillars of Hercules, began to excite the imaginations of those young Genoese as it had never done before. Many of them migrated to Portugal, the foremost centre of the nautical sciences in fifteenth-century Europe. There were so many Genoese in Portugal that the Cortes in 1481 petitioned the King to exclude them from his dominions.

Columbus arrived in Portugal when he was about thirty years old. He is a man with whom we should be well acquainted, for he had heaped so much suffering upon our ancestors that we would be betraying their dreams of freedom for all mankind if we did not mark him well. We should know not only the mythical Columbus, but also the real one. And, since knowing is not just an abstract concept for us, we should be able to divine clearly what he looked like. His son Ferdinand said of him:

> The Admiral was a well built man of more than medium stature, long visaged with cheeks somewhat high, but neither fat nor thin. He had an aquiline nose and his eyes were light in color; his complexion too was light, but kindling to a vivid red. In youth his hair was blond, but when he came to his thirtieth year it all turned white. [4]

Bartolomé de las Casas, the Dominican monk, amplifies this description telling us that

> He was more than middling tall; face long and giving an air of authority; aquiline nose, blue eyes, complexion light and tending to bright red; beard and hair bright red when young but very soon turned gray from his labours. . . . [5]

While Ferdinand, the Admiral's son, was writing his father's biography, he was receiving the revenue from four hundred African slaves in Hispaniola. It would be interesting to discover how many generations of the Columbus family subsequently rode on the backs of sweating and anonymous Africans.

But let us return to the impoverished Columbus setting himself up in Portugal. He did not remain in penury for long, because he soon married a noble, wealthy and well-connected lady, Beatriz Enríquez de Harana, and he was eventually able to plead for royal sponsorship of what he himself described as *La Empresa de las Indias*, the Enterprise of the Indies.

The King of Portugal turned him down, but nine years later Ferdinand and Isabella, the Rulers of Castile, became his patrons. Certain that he could sail to India and China via the Western Seas, he surprised the Indians on their island beaches in the Bahamas, believing for a while that these islands were in the Bay of Bengal.

Alberigo Vespucci—and I deliberately use his authentic Christian name—a Florentine dilettante and rascal, corrected Columbus' error, if error it really was, because Columbus and Vespucci remained on very close and friendly terms until the former's death in 1506. Vespucci, having sailed to the American mainland, declared that what Columbus had indeed stumbled upon was a New World—a surprising declaration about twin continents which had already been inhabited for over two hundred milleniums. Having returned from his travels, Vespucci wrote a number of letters to the Duc de Medici in Paris, using a lively and entertaining prose style, and causing a great stir when these letters were published.

Columbus' writings are intense, humourless, turgid, occasionally poetic. The intensity of his passions seems to burn through the dense prose and illuminate it for moments, until once again it becomes uneven, repetitive and dense—the culminative effect of what is left of his writing (most of the originals have been lost), is like fists drumming against one's brain.

Vespucci, on the other hand, composing his *Quatour Navigationes* (c. 1504–1505) in Portugal, did not write in the white heat of his experiences. [6] He gave us an elegant, retrospective and very persuasive view, and he was never averse to plagiarism if the accounts of other people's voyages could enhance his own. Vespucci invented a colonizer's America, and the reality that is ours never recovered from this literary assault and the distortions he inflicted upon it. The fiction of a "virgin land" inhabited by savages, at once a racist one and a contradiction, remains with us to this day. Amerigo was undoubtedly a Florentine dilettante, but he was also an extraordinarily clever one. Why would he otherwise have changed his Christian name after his voyages to the Americas?

There is a mountain range in Nicaragua called the Sierra Amerrique, and a group of Indians called Los Amerriques. These mountains stretch between Juigalpa and Libertad in the province of Chontales, and they separate Lake Nicaragua from the Mosquito Coast. The Amerriques had, since pre-Columbian times, always been in contact with the area around Cape Gracias a Dios, and the whole length of the

Mosquito Coast.[7] In 1502, Columbus visited this coast at Carriai and Carambaru. In 1497, Vespucci landed at Cape Gracias a Dios, and in 1505 sailed along the Mosquito Coast. Both navigators must certainly have heard the word *Amerrique* from the Indians over and over again during those voyages.

After the initial greetings and the limping exchange of pleasantries, it was a tradition with explorers like Columbus and Vespucci—they confirm this repeatedly in their writings—to ask the Indians where gold could be found. For, as Cortés confessed, they all suffered from a disease that only gold could cure. The alluvial gravels of the Sierra Amerrique had yielded gold for the Indians from time immemorial. They used gold, the sun's sweat, to create objects of surpassing beauty. It was a good metal for sculpture. Beyond that it had little value in itself until it was touched by man's creative genius. By capturing light on the burnished surfaces that metal workers and sculptors created through the use of fire, gold could link people to the sun, moon and stars, and both the act of creative labor and the object created became touched by magic, mystery and beauty. Sometimes they indented pieces of raw gold, and putting them in a sack full of sand, allowed the sea or a running stream to sculpt and polish them, and so through these processes the objects, man, Nature and the gods could become one.

For the colonizer gold meant money, personal and national aggrandizement and power over others. In their burgeoning capitalist system, gold could buy a place in the very Throne Room of the Kingdom of Heaven for the most despicable sinner. And in particular, once this sinner made the right propitiatory noises to the Almighty and gave generously to the Church, he could be assured of absolution from any crime committed against the colonized. "I came for gold, not to till the land," Cortés had declared. He was noted for his occasional outbursts of brutal frankness about himself and his countrymen. Their lust for gold was such that the Indians declared that the colonizer could even rape the sun to rob it of its miraculous sweat.

For Columbus and Vespucci, therefore, the words *Amerrique* and *gold* had become synonymous. After his visits to the Mosquito Coast—he made the last one in 1505—Vespucci changed his Christian name from Alberigo to Amerigo. In the Archives of Toledo, a letter from Vespucci to the Cardinal dated 9 December 1508, is signed Amerrigo with the double "r" as in the Indian Amerrique.[8] And between 1508 and 1512, the year in which Vespucci died, at least two other signatures with the Christian name Amerrigo were recorded.

Robbing peoples and countries of their indigenous names was one of the cruel games that colonizers played with the colonized. Names are like magic markers in the long and labyrinthine streams of racial memory, for racial memories are rivers leading to the sea where the memory of mankind is stored. To rob people or countries of their name is to set in motion a psychic disturbance which can in turn create a permanent crisis of identity. As if to underline this fact, the theft of an important placename from the heartland of the Americas and the claim that it was a dilettante's Christian name robs the original name of its elemental meaning. Dr. A. Le Plongeon, a nineteenth-century scholar from Mérida (Yucatán), in a letter to the French Professor Jules Marcou dated 10 December 1881, wrote:

> The name *America* or *Amerrique* in the Mayan language means a country of perpetually strong wind, or the Land of the Wind, and sometimes the suffix "-ique," "-ik" and "-ika" can mean not only wind or air but also a spirit that breathes, life itself. [9]

We must, therefore, reclaim the name of our America and give it once again its primordial meaning, land of the wind, the fountainhead of life and movement.

In the Mayan genesis myth, the Popol Vuh, Wind stands at the centre of creation. As the story unfolds, we are told that it was manifested to the gods:

> That at dawn man should appear. So they decided on the creation and the growth of trees and bees and the birth of life and the creation of man. This was resolved in the darkness and in the night by the Heart of Heaven called Hurricane. [10]

On the rocky eastern slopes of the Sierra Amerrique the wind pounds like giant fists upon the gates of time demanding to be recognized.

Asturias's novel *Strong Wind* [11] resurrects this symbol of the wind in a Guatemalan setting that is near to the Sierra Amerrique. In this novel Hurricane, the Heart of Heaven, the Mayan and Carib god, unleashed its avenging wrath upon the huge banana plantations owned by an overseas concern that was remarkably like the United Fruit Company. Other Caribbean writers, English-speaking ones, had written about hurricanes. There was John Hearne, [12] and Edgar Mittelholzer; [13] but their hurricanes had no roots in America's mythological archetypes; the British did not encourage this kind of thing in their stultified colonial educational systems. Hearne can be excused. The Jamaican indigenous connection was absolutely severed by ethnocide, but Mittelholzer came from a country where the Amerindian still lives in the forests of the Guyana hinterland and in the forests of our flesh and blood. In *Strong Wind*, Asturias reunites myth, magic, man, creative labor and the elements. His American characters with the exception of Stoner, the hero, are slightly unreal; and Stoner is real because he became indigenized. He fought with and for the people and in the process became their brother and no longer their master. So, by the time Stoner and his wife were killed, it was a death outside the pale of the Judeo-Christian tradition; rather it was one that the god Hurricane demanded so that an act of expiation could be immortalized.

Hearne and Mittelholzer's hurricanes are depicted with a kind of clinical detachment. Their strong wind seems anglicized when compared to Asturias's Amerindianized one.

The similarity between Columbus' life and that of the colonials he ultimately helped to bring into being ends the moment he himself became a colonizer. The Atlantic crossing created profound psychological changes in those who made it. If all the cultural baggage dumped in the Middle Passage during the five centuries of the Columbian era were to be dredged up, it would need a new planet to house it.

Having survived the crossing, Columbus and his sailors announced to their Indian hosts that they had come "from Heaven." [14] It was something of a contradiction, Las Casas remarked cryptically, to have come from Heaven and to be so overcome with a lust for gold. As a dying Cuban *cacique* was to reveal, the colonizer gave Heaven a bad name in the eyes of the colonized. In 1509, the self-proclaimed "men from Heaven" [15] had turned their attention to the beautiful island of Cuba. One of the principal *caciques* there, hearing in advance of their coming, carried out a propitiatory ceremony of drowning all the gold he and his subjects possessed. He was convinced that since gold was the only real god the Spanish worshipped, if this god was thrown away, perhaps he and his people would be spared. The invaders, incensed by this act of sacrilege, had the *cacique* burnt alive. When he was in the midst of the flames a Franciscan Friar of great piety, holding a cross before him, promised the *cacique* eternal life if he would embrace the Christian faith and hell and damnation if he didn't. With the fire burning slowly to prolong the torture, the Friar, as best as he could, tried to explain some half a hundred doctrines of the Christian faith. The *cacique*, in the midst of his discomfort, enquired if Heaven was open to all Spaniards:

> "Some who were good can hope to be admitted there," the Friar replied. "Then," declared the *cacique*, "since I would prefer not to share Heaven with such cruel company, if you'd swear that none of your people will go to hell, hell would be the perfect place for me." [16]

We are, in fact, re-examining the roots of our Columbian exile because as an Amerindian proverb says, those who forget the past will relive it again and again. If we neglect to complete this task of re-examination, then the contradictions between our psychological and actual exile, an induced state of intellectual amnesia and a conscious awareness of what was, what is, and what is to be done, is liable to lead us into a labyrinth of metaphysics. For our intention must be not merely to analyse the world, our world, but to change it. Only by changing our world can we inherit it, and only by inheriting it can we end our internal and external exile.

The first European settlement in the Americas was established in Marien, one of the five Kingdoms on the island of Bohío which the Spaniards renamed Hispaniola. The settlement was called La Navidad. Guacanagari, the ruler of Marien, had treated the Spaniards with great hospitality on their arrival. When the *Santa María* was wrecked on Christmas Day 1492, because Juan de la Cosa and a group of Basque shipmates had disobeyed Columbus' orders and tried to save their own skins, the Admiral himself wrote that at sunrise on 26 December, this same Guacanagari came aboard the *Niña*:

> and said that he would give him all that he had, and that he had given the Christians who were ashore two very big houses, and would give more if necessary. . . . "To such extent," says the Admiral, "are they loyal and without greed for the property of others, and that King was virtuous above all." [17]

Las Casas revealed the fate that befell Guacanagari barely a decade later:

> The Spaniards pursued this Chief with peculiar bitterness and forced him to abandon his Kingdom . . . he died of fatigue and sorrow. Those of his people who were not fortunate enough to be killed suffered countless pains in slavery. [18]

After a warm and hospitable reception, Columbus repaid his Amerindian hosts by enslaving them hardly a year later. The Atlantic slave trade began when under Columbus' sponsorship, a shipload of five hundred Indians was dispatched to Spain in 1493.

The absence of greed for the property of others is definitely not a quality that has surfaced in the hearts of colonizers during the five centuries of the Columbian era.

After the five Kingdoms of Hispaniola and their estimated three million inhabitants were erased, the peoples of Jamaica and Puerto Rico were next in line for their journey to oblivion. By 1540, these two islands which between them had a population of six hundred thousand, could boast of having hardly 200 of their original inhabitants alive. The population figures are those of Las Casas and, naturally, apologists for the colonizer have often warned us that his figures should be doubted. But who should be believed, the initiators, sponsors and apologists of ethnocide, or one who fought for its victims for sixty-eight of his ninety-two years? The silences and the empty spaces which remained in the wake of this early example of a final solution, bore eloquent testimony to the enormity of the crime. Even if the figures are incorrect we might well ask where then are the indigenous peoples of the Caribbean today? Why don't they come forward and speak for themselves? I have penetrated into those profound silences which remain in the aftermath of ethnocide, for it is not only a crime of past centuries, it lives on today. In vast areas of the Guyana highlands west of the Pakaraimas and south of the Akarai, the Amerindian peoples are still being exterminated and their land is still being violated by usurpers. There are islands of silence in those vast spaces which leave a more terrible impression on the mind than screams of the dying. In those profound silences, the Mayan Popol Vuh is no longer a genesis myth, but a prophecy, for it began like this:

> This is the story of how everything was in suspense, everything becalmed, wrapped in silence, everything immobile, silent and empty in the vastness of the sky. [19]

As one penetrates into those brooding spaces, one feels the pain and suffering of the dead Amerindian hosts, and at that moment one begins to realize that the real dead are the sowers of death, not its victims; at that moment one understands the unwritten histories of the victims intuitively and enters into the heart of their suffering. One feels their anguish in the same way that an amputee feels a persistent ache in the limb he has lost; and at that moment one also becomes the inheritor of the dauntless courage and the humanity of the victims, and at that moment suffering is no longer suffering, and death is no longer death. Perhaps it is at that moment, too, that one sees the beginning of the end of exile. But before one deals with the cure one must diagnose the ailment. The history of our exile is a dismal one of ethnocide, slavery, indentured labor, racism, colonialism and more recently neo-colonialism. Everywhere that we touch the earth in this hemisphere and seek to establish roots, the roots are bound to invade the graves of the innocent dead. For, after the Indian was sent on his journey to oblivion, the colonizer established new colonies of the dead—slaves from Africa, indentured labour from India, China, Java, Madeira and once again Africa, and along with these the permanent human flotsam in

Capitalism's Kingdom of Chance, the unemployed, the hungry, the sick who belong to no special race, color or creed, they are numbers in statistical tables, raw material for academics to pontificate upon. To define this situation today in simplistic clichés about black, brown or white power is to induce a kind of intellectual euphoria in which the mind becomes anesthetized with half-truths. One has to excavate the answers from the abyss of one's self and one's mutilated society.

I had pointed out earlier that the Caribbean writer was, poised between limbo and nothingness, like the middle man in Akan classical drama, but we, in fact, Caribbeanized the role and became not so much a figure in the middle of Furies and benign spirits, but an honorary marginal person. The writer is, therefore, islanded in the midst of marginal tides of sorrow, despair, hope, whirlpools of anxiety, cataracts of rage. He is the most articulate member of the marginal class; articulate, that is, with the written word. There are others of his class who speak to the mind's ear with music—the calypso, reggae, the folk-song—and who speak with immediacy and a sensuous ease to a much vaster audience. The marginal class is a creation of the "system" in the Caribbean. The system sustained itself for centuries, by ensuring that at all times there would be a large reservoir of cheap labor. Expatriate manipulators, while controlling vast acreages of land, brought only a fraction of what they controlled into productive use; they also exercised absolute controls over all other important means of production, distribution and exchange by an economic and cosmetic sleight-of-hand, which makes it appear as if the local surrogates were the real bosses, which they never were, and, under the present system, will never become. The economic base of the marginal class is, therefore, like mud on the Guyana coast. The tides carpet beaches with this mud for a season and then roll it up and move it elsewhere.

After centuries in the wilderness the first law of the marginals is that of survival. To the middle class, which has only recently left the shiftless and insecure world of marginality, the marginal class appears to be truly menacing, a breeding ground for symbols of terror.

The middle class, and particularly the most recent recruits to its ranks, haunted by the spectre of the marginal class, tries almost in a fury to shut itself behind ramparts of philistinism and iron bars. A regular job, a bicycle and a collar and tie used to be the symbols of emancipation from the marginals, but now the symbols have become more expensive and they are a shirtjack, a car, and the third symbol which is optional, is what Andrew Salkey described as "a waggon wheel Afro."[20] When the Black Power gesticulation promised to be safe, social and definitely not socialist, the most unlikely people began to decorate themselves with its exotic accoutrements. But, as soon as it began to crystallize into a class struggle, the middle class abandoned it and hitched their wagon-wheels once more to old tried-and-true neo-colonialist symbols. One of our distinguished literary colleagues made the profound pontifical declaration that it lacked intellectual content. But the Caribbean writer, whether he likes it or not, is an honorary marginal person, and it is from the constantly shifting islands of marginality that he makes his sallies into the world, into the wider indifference of Britain, the United States, Canada, France or wherever the rumor-gram noises it abroad that the pastures are greener.

When the colonizer exterminated the indigenous inhabitants in many regions of the Americas, he severed connections with a vast network of secret tributaries that led into the mainstream of the memory of mankind. The total reservoir of memory was seriously impoverished by this loss. The colonizer, reaching into the cultural reserves he believed he had brought with him, discovered that these were soon exhausted, leaving him with psychic voids that could not be filled. The cultural baggage he had dumped in the Middle Passage could not be salvaged. In any event, it was mostly the culturally deprived who immigrated to the Americas, so that from the start they had set out with depleted stocks. Of all the major groups that came to the Americas during the initial three hundred years of the Columbian era, the African alone understood the profound need to create a fusion of his culture with that of his Indian host:

> The African brought with him, regardless of the mosaic of cultural groups from which he derived, a built-in ethic which bound him first, as a stranger in a strange land, to study and respect the host culture before he established elements of his own. This gave the children of the African diaspora a means of surviving anywhere in the human world and they did not need guns and superior weapons in order to do this. When the African arrived in the New World, he knew that the colonizer who had brought him there was a usurper who had seized the land of the Indians, desecrated the graves and the altars of their ancestors, and sent countless of the ones who had welcomed him to the Forest of the Long Night. It was clear to the slaves from Africa, that in order to escape the terrible retribution that was certain to overtake their masters, they had to make peace with both the living and the dead in this new land. . . . The African had to recreate his vision of himself in the universe often being violently uprooted . . . to have seen himself only through his master's eyes and to have even appeared to be an accomplice in his obnoxious deeds, would have left him with a permanent heritage of self-hatred, distorted self-images and guilt. In order to reconstruct his onto-

logical system, the African was compelled by the logic of his own cultural past, to establish relations with his Indian host independent of the white man. [21]

It was fortunate for us all in this hemisphere that the African began once more to make his appearance in the New World from around 1502. It was also a matter of profound cultural significance that the African had come to the Americas in pre-Columbian times. But within two decades of his arrival in the Columbian era, there were rebellions in Hispaniola, Puerto Rico, Cuba, Jamaica and Mexico, in which Africans and Indians joined forces against a common enemy.

Herrera tells us that the Wolofs of San Juan de Puerto Rico "walked rebelliously through the land," [22] and that no sooner had they set foot in the Indies, than they "began to disaffect the Indians." [23] The Wolofs could, thereafter, only move from one island to another with special permission from the Viceroy.

The humane and civilized African example of cultural accommodation which runs counter to the bigotry of the white settler mentality, has largely been ignored by both our historians and the colonizers. And yet in dealing with questions of cultural roots, alienation and identity in the Americas, it is an example that cannot be overlooked.

At a time when independence, that is, an anthem, a flag and a color on the map, brings into sharper focus questions of national identity and liberation, the Caribbean writer is faced with harsh choices. The end of his marginal status is now in sight. As an honorary member of the marginal class he has both consciously and unconsciously internalized the mounting chaos that is pushing this class inexorably, not into revolution but revolutionary situations. Their ranks have been swelled by unemployed graduates from high schools and universities, by preachers of cults and fads, by crooks, pushers, choke-and-rob practitioners, political louts and bouncers, by instant prophets and trans-Atlantic Gurus; their dress, their speech, their music, the mumbo-jumbo they invent and discard seasonally are all imaginative forms of protest; they are often unsure of what they are for, but are absolutely certain of what they're against: the corrupt, bullying, pompous, dishonest, cruel, incompetent and often mindless regimes under which they live.

Elements from the marginal class have taken to the streets again and again during the past decade. Their most dramatic street scenes were acted out in Trinidad in 1969. "The revolution has started!" some of the more naive had cried out. But these street demonstrations could best be described by two lines from a Robert Burns poem, for they were "like the Borealis race, that flits e'er you can point its place. . . ."

Yet, one should not dismiss the street demonstrations of the marginals lightly. In every instance they attracted elements from the working class and a minority of the intelligentsia. These elements went back to bear the brunt of the repression that followed, to become more politicized and to move the struggle to a higher level.

The Caribbean writer, during this period, played the role of the middle man in the Akan classical theatre to such perfection that scholars researching African survivals would have been delighted.

Some went into hiding, others wore the gaudy costumes and transformed the slogans into academic canons. If occasionally their denunciations of white imperialism sounded too emotional, they ended by declaring that Marx was irrelevant, long live Fanon.* Others played a cunning counter-revolutionary role. The honorary marginal is a supreme mimic and in addition to this quality can perform a literary ventriloquism. He can imitate his colonial master so perfectly that the master hears himself speaking through the servant. This servant has a phonal apparatus inside his head that those who behold it marvel at its sensitivity.

The colonial intellectual passes through three stages. At the first stage, he is an imitator, devoted to the idea of showing the colonizer that he has learnt all his cultural catechisms well and is ready to be accepted as an honorary white man. He is a creature who lives as though he were constantly under the scrutiny of a disapproving colonizer's eye. He is even careful about the way in which he talks in his sleep. At the second stage, our colonial has grown bold enough to be disgruntled. He has grown cunning enough to understand that Uncle Tomming from the heart is no longer in fashion; he, therefore, assumes postures of protest. The language that he has come to know better than the colonizer himself is used like a stick to beat the man, but the beating is handed out guardedly. The intention is more to make noise than to inflict pain. It is, in essence, a protest inspired by petulance, a signal to the colonizer, a plea for recognition, a cry from the emptiness of the creole soul which says: accept me as an honorary white man and I will commit new and unspeakable treacheries against my own.

The third stage is one of unequivocal adherence to the cause of liberation: one that challenges the Caribbean writer to take sides with the sufferers and not their exploiters, local and expatriate; with the have nots, not the have gots; with the scorned, the rejected, not those lapping

---

* Franz Fanon wrote *The Wretched of the Earth* and *Black Skins White Masks*. (Editor's note)

the fat of the years. Once the writer has made the choice he is on the road to the end of exile, the road to hope, the Freedom road, the road to the new day where

> with morning bursting
> like pale lightnings from our eyes
> together side by side
> we'll burst asunder
> pale ramparts of Heaven
> with bare hands and bare feet
> to pluck wild orchids
> of ultimate release. [24]

The Caribbean writer is a person from the sun. "Sun's in my blood today," Seymour writes in his very fine poem, [25] unconsciously entering into regions of African myth which tells of how Nyankopon, the Sky-God, shoots a particle of the sun's fire into the bloodstream of the child, thus bringing the blood to life. In the Caribbean world-view, the sun is a dialectical entity: it is creative and destructive, it gives life and takes it away. Anancy, the West African folk archetype in whose name all fables were told, is shaped like a gadwal, a sun-wheel, a mathematically perfect calendar. Anancy was also the victim of an encounter with the Wax Girl. The story goes that Anancy lost his perfect shape after his encounter.

Among the Hausas [of Africa], the rainbow was called the spider's bow. This shows how close Anancy was to the divinities from heaven. And his bow which had the shape of a snake was called the god of rains and storms.

In the Caribbean, Anancy lost his contacts with divinities and is known exclusively as a trickster.

The European, settling in the tropical world in the Columbian era, brought Medieval fantasies with him of the equatorial region being a land of fire, and when this turned out to be untrue, he invented the myth that only dark-skinned people could do strenuous manual labor in the sun. White workers in Cuba, and those thousands of miles away in tropical Australia, and white peasants in the Caribbean have proved this to be the fiction that it is, but the myth persists; and the myth is now embraced not only by its originators but also by its victims. The creoles will still declare unblushingly that their constitutions are too delicate for them to attempt strenuous manual labor in the sun; that only blacks or coolies are fit for that kind of thing. Exile from the sun, therefore, begins in the creole mind. It is the result of a plot hatched by parents who are mesmerized by colonial fantasies of class and color escape. These parents begin telling children as soon as the amniotic fluid is washed from their eyes, that the only hope for them is to go abroad, away from the sun. The sun must, in this sick creole imagination, always be kept at a distance. The sun darkens the complexion and threatens to hurl the creole back into the ranks of the blacks and coolies which he had only recently abandoned.

The title of Sam Selvon's novel *A Brighter Sun* [26] suggests an unconscious desire to move closer to his peasant origins, not to the distant lands of pale sunlight, but to the regions where it is brightest. Going away from the tropics, one loses one's place in the sun. What follows is a psychic unbalance from which one seldom recovers.

But creating distances between oneself and the tropical sun was not only a question of removing one's physical presence from an equatorial to a temperate region; the colonized could also do it as part of a conditioned/psychological reflex. The colonial person rooted in the parasitical economic relationships and the schizoid cultural ones he had had with the mother country, could in his imagination be at home and overseas, in the furnace heat of his brighter sun and in pale winter sunshine at the same time. The arch-colonial still locks himself up in warm, heavy clothing in the equatorial sun and will swear that he feels no discomfort; on certain ceremonial occasions, the neo-colonial ladies and gentlemen even wear gloves. But the creole, from the beginning of his emergence as a middle man in the Columbian era—the word *creole* originally meant "bred in the house" so that the creole stood between the field slave and the master—has been forever trying to sever his connections with the dark hinterlands under the sun. His journeys have been outward bound ones, towards the "superior" culture of the colonizer and away from the "inferior" one of the colonized. The very communication networks that vein neo-colonial territories are like tracings from the creole mind and the psyche of the colonized—all roads lead outward towards overseas cultural and spiritual meccas. The situation, though, remains a dialectical one at its core. There have always been important, living cultural and spiritual bases outside the ethos of the creole's facile borrowings and spurious imitations. Both urban and rural groups, who were rejected by the colonizer and the creole alike, incorporated rich and enduring cultural survivals into the fabric of their daily life, transforming them and keeping them alive at the same time.

The Caribbean writer and artist, if he must end his exile, is compelled by the exigencies of history to move back and forth from the heart of those cultural survivals and others into whatever regions of the twentieth century the island, the continent or the cosmos his imagination encompasses; and, in roaming across the ages of man in this blood-stained hemisphere, he must penetrate into the unfathomable silences where a part of the Amerindian past is entombed, he must gnaw at the bones of universal griefs, and the reservoir of compassion in his heart for the dispossessed must be limitless.

An Acewayo droger once told me of the journeys he took in and out of the regions of his mind. The band across his forehead, and the harness strapped under his armpits distributed the hundred and twenty-five pounds he carried in his wareshi so that by thrusting his head forward he could walk at a steady, rhythmic, shuffle from day-clear to sunset. We were averaging twenty-five miles a day in the mountainous Potaro district.

"How do you manage?" I asked, thinking of the thirty pounds I was carrying and the way it seemed to double itself after every ten miles. After a long pause he replied:

> It's like this, skipper, most of the time you see me walking here, carrying this big load, I'm not here at all . . . is only a shadow here, the substance is back home in Aquero, hunting agouti or deer or labba, playing with my children, catching a gaff, listening to the Old Ones speak, talking to the Ancestors or to God. You can ask me then how come I can be two places at the same time, I will tell you the secret: the pressure of this wareshi on my brain makes it easy for me to send my mind away . . . At the start I feel like a drunken man, there's a singing inside my head, my body feels heavy and the wareshi feels like a mountain on my back. Then all of a sudden everything gets lighter and lighter until I feel like a silk-cotton blossom floating on wind. Once I reach this stage, I can walk from here to the Forest of the Long Night without feeling any weariness.

The Acewayo droger had remained for most of his life outside the awful grinding inevitability of linear time that the Columbian era had imposed upon his people. The Amerindian induction into the remorseless cycles of time of the European calendar had been traumatic. In 1493, Columbus ordered that every able-bodied Amerindian in Marien, one of the five Kingdoms of Hispaniola, should, within a specified time, pay the Spanish Crown a tribute of a hawk's bill full of gold. Those who failed were enslaved, mutilated or put to death. This was also the Amerindian's introduction to a cruel system in which forced labor of the colonized would produce wealth for the colonizer. Labor and the colonizer's timeclock became the totems heralding a new age for the Amerindian and the African. For both of these peoples, time had been something one felt like a pulse or a heartbeat. Time for them was finite. In their cosmologies, past time went back as far as the genesis of their races; it was a link between the living and their ancestors; present time merely spanned the seasons of each day, while future time covered the shortest span of all, it was restricted to the inevitable future and little else. This was how it had always been with the black and brown Men of Corn—one could live in the midst of infinities of stasis, of no time—and when one chose, one could then generate new time. In order to turn the Men of Corn into Natives of Capitalism the colonizer committed unspeakable atrocities of ethnocide and the enslavement of millions. He then attempted to remove all traces of his crime. He did it with the same cunning the authorities had used after the massacre of workers in the public square in García Márquez's novel *A Hundred Years of Solitude.* [27] In the ghoulish silence and the emptiness that came in the wake of the massacre, even the stones could not speak after they were washed clean of the bloodstains.

Having shattered forever the Afro-Amerindian concepts of time, the colonizer created a new time which he chained inexorably to his own future expectations, and time became money.

In order to illuminate the dialectic of pre-Columbian time and time in the Columbian era, a few Caribbean writers had to unlock secrets of lost centuries. They used rivers as the symbol of their journeys into the past.

In my *Black Midas*, Aron Smart had said about his grandparents that "they felt time like a river in their blood." [28]

An early Wilson Harris poem had described the journey of one of his mythical characters:

Down Rivers of his Night
Where he must drown to banish fear. [29]

This orphic journey was re-enacted later in the search for the *Palace of the Peacock.* [30]

In Alejo Carpentier's *The Lost Steps,* [31] the hero travels into primordial hinterlands up one of the great rivers of South America, traversing millenniums in his orphic journey. Carpentier went far afield from his island home to find a setting for his hero's wanderings. He needed a continent.

Edouard Glissant chose a river in Martinique as the symbol of his search for roots and a genuine identity in his novel *La Lézarde.* [32]

What was interesting about the droger's psychological escape route is that it led inwards. It never occurred to him to move beyond the frontiers of home and the forest. Glissant's river *la lézarde* however, takes us inland to its source and from the secret spring where it rises to the sea. For on an island your cosmos of the imagination begins with the sea.

In the search for an identity—one of the major themes in Caribbean writing—the impulse is either to move inward towards some undiscovered heartland as in Carpentier's *The Lost Steps*, Glissant's *La Lézarde*, Reid's *Newday*,[33] Asturias's *Hombres de maíz*,[34] Harris's *Palace of the Peacock* and my own *Black Midas*; or outward towards the meccas of the colonizer as in Lamming's *The Emigrants* and *Natives of My Person*, and Clarke's *Survivors of the Crossing* and *The Meeting Point*.[35] These novels are works I have chosen from what has now become an impressive array. They are, therefore, by no means the only ones that illustrate the dichotomy of the inward and the outward vision in Caribbean writing.

Salkey's *Come Home, Malcolm Heartland* is a novel about a Caribbean exile preparing to return home. Having explored the outward vision to its utmost limits, the hero is escaping the wide indifference of decades abroad to return to a spiritual Sleepy Hollow.

The hero of Carpentier's *The Lost Steps* is a Euro-American musicologist and composer. In his search for an identity he first goes to Europe but does not find the illusory Europe that his father had brought him up to revere. His disillusionment is complete when he realizes that a psychic uprootment had taken place when his ancestors abandoned the Old Country. But in America as a white settler, he also had to seek out and find the inner sanctuaries of a spiritual heartland that racist fantasies, a strident and spurious nationalism, and a spate of colonizer's myths had unconsciously prevented him from exploring. But he was also an artist surrounded by dilettantes and colonial cultists of art with a capital "A." After a chance encounter with the curator of a museum, he sets out from New York on an expedition to find the first musical instruments that man created in the Americas. He is delayed for a while in a South American city where, from the relative safety of a tourist hotel, he watches a palace revolt flare up only to be extinguished. His journey continues over mountains as close to heaven as a man can hope to be without leaving the earth. A steep descent brings him to tropical lowlands, the main setting of his search for an American and a human identity. In a few weeks he journeys to the upper reaches of the great river and, in the millenniums he traverses during this small span of time, his journey becomes one of self-discovery—the discovery of a new American self which was hidden in primordial rainforest fastnesses; the roots of the Amerindian psyche and the Amerindian person; the inner spiritual sanctum of the Men of Corn; the point from which they began their migrations outwards. In this remote world where linear time as he knew it had become meaningless, the hero is, he believes at first, reborn.

But this was a romantic illusion. He goes back to the world of the twentieth century, his spirit refurbished, the scales scraped away from his eyes; when he tries to return to the Eden he thought he had rediscovered, the steps are lost. Yet, he had gathered unto himself an immense creative power in that trespass into prehistory and back. He returned to the sisyphian tasks of the artist, chastened and reformed, knowing that he had to cross not only past centuries but to venture into future ones. In Glissant's *La Lézarde* the search for an identity follows the course of a river to its source, and the spring from which it rises is enclosed by an old colonial stone house. The river takes us into the heartland of a country. Glissant introduces us to a journey of discovery with a poem:

"What is this country?" he asked
And the answer was:
"First weigh every word,
make the acquaintance of every sorrow." [36]

The author's *lézarde* is really a river of life which runs through both a physical and spiritual landscape. As the river makes its way to the sea, one can feel the people stirring, the land awakening and the people, the land, the river, the sky coming together in a miraculous unity. And during the long season of a people's consciousness ripening, the author poses a question that goes to the heart of the dream to end the feeling of homelessness at home. "Can we," he asks, "give a name to any parcel of earth before the man and woman who inhabit it have arisen?" [37]

La Lézarde illuminates the psychological landscape it traverses like flashes of lightning. Its symbols are revealed to us like the vast array of different species of flora and fauna secreted away in a rain forest. The river brings clarity to the apparent chaos; it is linked to geological time; it existed before man did; it flows into an expectation of countless seasons. It is like Alegría's *The Golden Serpent*, [38] a Peruvian river that threads its way through the life of a people and one that becomes a timeless symbol of a people's fight for freedom. The river is a perfect symbol of man's seminal connection with life and being. The interior landscapes of Harris's novels are veined with dreaming rivers of life, death and seasons of eternity.

Pia and Makunaima, the Children of the Sun, are the oldest and most universal culture heroes in this hemisphere. From Patagonia to the edge of the Canadian Barrens, the same story was told by the Amerindians from time immemorial. It is the story of how these twins were born and how their two greatest feats were to bring fire to man, and to tame the rivers by placing gigantic rocks and boulders across them. An Amerindian poem sings about

> The white sun
> raping dark rivers
> the white sun
> biting like a Vaquero's ship
> the white sun singing, singing
> singing the songs of the dead
> the white sun
> a burning requiem
> but the cool night must come. [39]

In this song-poem the seminal anthropomorphic symbols—the sun, the dark interior river, the songs of the dead, the night—are united. The river rises in hinterlands of silence and flows to the clamorous sea and on the way its tributaries reach into the flesh of the land like so many capillaries. The river can be the symbol of the exile journeying outwards or the exile coming home.

"All men return to the hills finally," the Roger Mais poem had declared. [40] His hills, both real and symbolical, were an oasis where the writer and artist went to gather strength, to heal the wounds inflicted by the philistines at home and racists abroad. From the hills one moves outward, towards the sea. Both the consciousness of the sea and the absence of this consciousness are an interesting psychological phenomenon in the Caribbean. The dream that emerges in Caribbean writing is one of crossing the sea or of contemplating its moods, never of conquering it. The Caribs and the Europeans were conquerors of the sea, creators of sagas; their imaginations were forever encompassing new horizons of turbulent water. But for the new Caribbean man the sea was a capricious and often dangerous moat between stepping stones of islands and continents. The sea, which Lamming describes in great detail in *Natives of My Person*, is perceived as though from a great distance; it is something not only separating continents and islands, but suspended between them. It is a weightless, static sea, like the one described in the Mayan genesis myth, the Popol Vuh rather than a heaving, turbulent reality.

In an earlier novel, Lamming's emigrants cross the Atlantic and are barely aware of this ocean's existence. But in their conversations it is clear that they're carrying enduring memories of the smell of their earth and the dreams of their people with them. The journey by sea is an interlude between home and the Caribbean communities islanded abroad. Clarke's "survivors of the crossing" also erase the reality of the ocean they crossed from their minds. In *The Meeting Point*, the emigrants have moved to air travel and are more at ease. Perhaps we all carry deep in our unconscious minds the traumatic memory of the ancestral crossing in the Columbian and slave era. In Salkey's *Come Home, Malcolm*

Heartland, the Caribbean Janus astride two worlds is about to abandon one of the two and return home regardless of the philistines, the areas of mindlessness that he must invade and conquer, the malice waiting to ambush him and the deep awareness that a part of him had died during the decades abroad in the emptiness, the racial scorn, the endless encounters with real and imagined acts of discrimination he had had to endure. Malcolm Heartland also knows that the home to which he is returning is innocent of many social and political resonances for which he had developed an inner ear. Heartland dies both a real and symbolical death before he takes the plunge. But there are Heartlands at home who survived both crossings, the one to the meccas of the colonizer and the other home to the secret heartlands where the waters of the River of Life began their flow. Perhaps the finest evocation of this return home to slowly awakening Sleepy Hollows perched on top of a people's volcanic discontents can be found in Mervyn Morris's poetry. This poetry is uncompromisingly honest, sensitive, and it penetrates the heart of the discontents that centuries of exile and cultural alienation gave birth to.

"All people have a right to share the waters of the River of Life and to drink with their own cups, but our cups have been broken," laments the Carib poem-hymn. The writer, artist, musician, is directly involved in the creative process of reshaping the broken cups. But as an Asian writer had said from a Republic perched on the Roof of the World in the Soviet Far East, "Art and Literature are like lightning, and lightning can never be timid."

Therefore, while we shape exquisite new cups we must, side by side with the disinherited millions of the Third World, confront those who would deny us our fair share of the Waters of the River of Life, for it was at the source of those waters that the exile of the Caribbean writer began and it is there that his exile will end.

Notes

1. C.L.R. James, from a talk given at Princeton University in 1972.

2. Richard B. Moore, *Caribis, "Cannibals," and Human Relations* (New York: Afro-American Institute, Pathway Publishers, 1972); and in his article on the same theme, "Carib 'Cannibalism': A study in Anthropological Stereotyping," *Caribbean Studies* 13, no. 3 (October 1973): 117–35.

3. Roberto Retamar, "Caliban," *Massachusetts Review* (1973).

4. S. Morison, *Admiral of the Ocean Sea* (Boston: Little, Brown and Co., 1942), I: 62.

5. Ibid., pp. 62–63.

6. J. Marcou, "L'Origine du nom d'Amérique," *Bulletin of the American Geographical Society* (Paris), no. 4 (1888): 12.

7. Ibid., p. 8.

8. Ibid., p. 79.

9. Ibid., p. 6.

10. S. Paz, "Popol Vuh." Unpublished translation, 1972.

11. M. A. Asturias, *Strong Wind* (New York: Dell Publishing Co., Laurel Edition, 1968).

12. John Hearne, *Autumn Equinox* (London: Faber and Faber, 1960).

13. Edgar Mittelholzer, *Of Trees and the Sea* (London: Secker and Warburg, 1954).

14. Morison, *Admiral of the Ocean Sea*, I: 371.

15. Ibid.

16. J. Thatcher, *Christopher Columbus* (New York: G. Putnam and Sons, 1903), I: 128.

17. Ibid., p. 125.

18. Morison, *Admiral of the Ocean Sea*, I: 390–91.

19. Paz, "Popol Vuh."

20. Andrew Salkey, *Come Home, Malcolm Heartland* (London: Hutchinson and Co. Ltd., 1976).

21. Jan Carew, "The Fusions of African and Amerindian Cultures." Unpublished.

22. L. Weiner, *Africa and the Discovery of America* (Philadelphia: Innes and Sons, 1920), I: 158.

23. Ibid.

24. Jan Carew, "Poem," 1956.

25. Arthur Seymour, "The Sun's in my Blood," *Kyk-over-al* (Guyana), 1952.

26. Samuel Selvon, *A Brighter Sun* (London: MacGibbon and Kee Ltd., 1954).

27. Gabriel García Márquez, *A Hundred Years of Solitude* (London: Jonathan Cape, 1970).

28. Jan Carew, *Black Midas* (London: Secker and Warburg Ltd., 1958), p. 10.

29. Wilson Harris, "Rivers of His Night," *Kyk-over-al* (Guyana), 1952.

30. Wilson Harris, *Palace of the Peacock* (London: Faber and Faber, 1960).

31. Alejo Carpentier, *The Lost Steps* (New York: Alfred A. Knopf, Inc., 1956).

32. Edouard Glissant, *The Ripening (La Lézarde)*, Tr. F. Frenage (New York: Brazilier, 1959).

33. Vic Reid, *Newday* (Jamaica: Sangster's Book Stores and Heinemann, 1970).

34. Miguel Ángel Asturias, *Hombres de maíz* (Buenos Aires: Lozada, 1949).

35. George Lamming, *The Emigrants* (New York: Holt, Rinehart and Winston Co., 1955); and *Natives of My Person* (New York: Holt, Rinehart and Winston Co., 1972). Also Austin Clarke, *Survivors of the Crossing* (Toronto: McClelland and Stewart, 1965), and *The Meeting Point* (Boston: Little, Brown and Co., 1967).

36. Glissant, *La Lézarde*, Frontispiece.

37. Ibid., p. 18.

38. Ciro Alegría, *The Golden Serpent*, Tr. Harriet de Onís (New York & Toronto: Farrar and Rinehart, 1943).

39. Jan Carew, Unpublished poem, 1952.

40. Roger Mais, Unpublished poem, 1949.

*

DISCUSSION QUESTIONS AND ACTIVITIES

Paz

1. In his article "Mexico and the United States," Octavio Paz searches for national identity in our U.S. and Mexican histories. Trace the dictatorship of Porfirio Díaz back to its roots in Spanish Catholicism.

2. Read several periodicals that focus on international and hemispheric news. Find examples of articles on Mexico and its politics that reflect Spanish centralism.

3. Why can our political system tolerate dissent while authoritarian regimes cannot?

4. Compare U.S. and Mexican holidays. What is celebrated? What do holidays show about the respective countries?

5. Paz refers frequently to the influence of the Enlightenment and Reformation on the U.S. and Spain. Prepare a report on these two historical periods and what they represented.

6. A well-known novel by William Faulkner is *The Plumed Serpent*. After reading the novel, describe how it relates to Paz's discussion of the Mexican Indian.

7. Research the life of Emiliano Zapata and the peasant revolt he led. Present your material orally. If possible, arrange to see the film classic, *Viva Zapata!*, starring Marlon Brando. How do the facts of Zapata's life correspond with the filmic representation of the man and the events? (The film is usually found in video rental stores.)

8. Read anthropologist Oscar Lewis's *Five Families* or *The Children of Sanchez*—the latter is widely read and praised by the critics. Identify the cultural values implicit in the works and how they differ, if at all, from the values of U.S. culture.

9. Paz comments on "the evils of the West" in the last four paragraphs of his article. Organize a debate, with representatives on each side of the issue: those in support of his position, those opposed to it.

Berger

10. In Peter Berger's "A Tale of Two Moralities," what are the differences between Manuela's situation in her village and in the city of Acapulco?

11. Networks and support groups have an important function in both Mexican and U.S. society. Show how they are structured in Manuela's Mexican village and Acapulco and then compare them with the U.S. version of networks with which you are familiar.

12. Draw a family tree representing Manuela's extended family. Interview several acquaintances representing more than a single generational point of view. Find out whether they move within the nuclear family or the extended family. If the latter, what is the extent of obligation felt toward family members?

13. Form two teams and debate the two moralities that Manuela faces: one group defends collective solidarity; the other, personal autonomy and advancement.

14. View the film *El Norte*, directed by Gregory Nava. In it, a brother and sister from a village in Guatemala undertake a voyage north. Discuss the similarities and differences in the lives of the protagonists of the Berger narrative and the film.

Zurcher and Meadow

15. Read and discuss Ernest Hemingway's *Death in the Afternoon* in relation to the Zurcher-Meadow article.

16. Do you agree with the authors' description of the role of the father and mother in the U.S.? Are there variations that you are familiar with, including in your own family?

17. Do you ever use the term *macho*? If so, when and with what meaning? Where have you seen or heard the term used elsewhere? Does its meaning differ from the one the authors ascribe to the word?

18. What is the difference between a *matador* and a *toreador*? In the shift from the use of the first term to the second, what changes are implied in power relationships, according to Zurcher and Meadow?

19. What are some other sports that can be analyzed in this manner? What common American sports can serve as a metaphor for some of our values? Select one of them and develop your analysis.

20. Has baseball been replaced by football as the U.S. national sport? Defend your response. Compare the hours of media coverage of the two sports on cable and network television during a one-week period by looking at past television guides. Form a team so that each member can check advertising on television over a five-day period, two hours a day, to

see how frequently sports figures appear in advertisements. Which sports are represented?

21. Adopt an animal rights position in a debate for and against bull-fighting.

22. At several points in the Zurcher-Meadow article, the authors talk about roles we play in our lives. Interview a non-U.S., Spanish-speaking person to see how he or she defines the role of son or daughter, friend, teacher, student, employee, and employer. What are the role expectations? Do your definitions differ? How?

Sunshine

23. One of the unifying themes that Catherine Sunshine identifies in her article is the African roots of the Afro-Latin culture common to the Caribbean nations. To discover this common heritage, find recordings of music for *la bomba* and *la plena*, the *salsa* style and the *merengue*. The composer/musician Paul Simon has recently brought contemporary music of Africa and Latin America to the U.S. Listen to these recordings and identify common musical themes and styles.

Carew

24. The author of "The Caribbean Writer and Exile" corrects several myths about the Carib Indians and the discovery and colonization of the Caribbean by Columbus and those who followed. Enumerate them.

25. Read other accounts of the colonization of the Caribbean. Compare them in tone and content with Carew's version. If there is a difference in rhetorical style, what is its effect?

26. View *Spain in the New World: The Discovery of America* (13 min., VHS, Films for the Humanities). It is based on the same journals of Columbus that Carew discusses. What is the narrative point of view in the video? How does it differ from the representation Carew gives of the work?

27. Research some of the Mayan genesis myths and other legends. What are their common features?

28. What do you feel are the three most important points made in the Carew article?

Latin America

JOHN P. FIEG and JOHN G. BLAIR

Colombia

(Though Colombia and the U.S. are hemispheric neighbors, visitors to each country have noted their contrasting behavior patterns and rhythm of daily life.)

Though they are hemispheric neighbors and cultural cousins, Colombia and the United States have chosen decidedly different drummers to set the tempo for their respective life styles.

Accustomed to the cordiality and conviviality which a more leisurely pace affords at home, the Colombian is suddenly forced to march to an unfamiliar staccato beat when he arrives in the U.S.A.

"Emotionally we find America different—a little cold. Americans don't seem to care about other people. In Colombia we are more dependent on one another," a Colombian woman said.

"If a friend asks me to stay with her children in Colombia because the maid is gone, I will be right there even if I have other things to do. Your own life comes first in the U.S.; in Colombia it is completely reversed," she added.

Since the elaborate Colombian greeting involves shaking hands and asking questions about family and friends, the Colombian is dismayed when the American says a hurried "Hi" and is on his way.

From John P. Fieg and John G. Blair, *There Is a Difference* (Washington, D.C.: Meridian House International, 1989), 41–48, by permission of the publisher.

"At the beginning this was terrible for me. I didn't know what to do with my hand, for I would extend it to shake hands and find myself grasping the air. We thought, 'These people are so cold.' It is difficult if you stay in the U.S. only a short time," commented another Colombian woman.

"Your life is so planned; everything is step by step. We are not so regimented. You are very punctual. Your watch always works. In Colombia people don't look at their watches so often," said the first woman, who recalled how her brother had asked to be *awakened* at 8 o'clock for an 8 a.m. appointment.

This difference in approach can in part be accounted for by the way in which work is viewed in the two societies.

"The tendency in the U.S. to think that life is only work hits you in the face. Work seems to be the one type of motivation," a Colombian said.

"The American is aggressive in his job; work becomes something essential to his life. The Colombian approach is more leisurely," added an American who had spent considerable time in Colombia.

"The American seems to be two quite different persons. He goes to church on Sunday and takes his family for a ride in the country. Then on Monday he will do anything—crush any enemy, go to any extreme," said one Colombian, adding that his experience in the U.S. had not led him to dispel this image.

Another Colombian, who had been in the U.S. twenty-two years ago, noted some changes over the years.

"I was very much impressed at that time by the efficiency of the American worker. Now I have the impression that this attitude towards work is changing for the worse. People seem tired of work," he said.

The traditional stereotype that Colombians have held of the American blends elements of the indomitable superman, the cruel exploiter, and the naive innocent. One Colombian explained why he felt the general picture formed in Colombia did not necessarily conform to the reality he found in the U.S.

"We have historically felt that the American is naive, whereas we consider ourselves to have *malicia indígena* (indigenous [shrewdness]) and a more complicated mind. We thought that English jokes were not as sophisticated and complicated as those in Spanish. But this image was formed from observing Americans in Colombia, without realizing that people are not themselves and are usually very cautious in a foreign country," he said.

The opposite view—that the American as imperialist is the root of all evil—oversimplifies the economic reality of competitive pricing in the U.S., in this man's opinion.

"Anything trivial for you can have meaning for us. If you see that a pound of bananas is five cents cheaper in one supermarket, you will buy those. Yet to produce bananas five cents cheaper, the manager of the banana consortium might have to do things harmful to our country— such as firing a labor union leader or reducing workers' pay," he explained.

Such incidents lead to charges of "imperialism," whereas in terms of the U.S. market structure this buying behavior is a perfectly legitimate example of comparative shopping.

There is a tendency in Colombia to believe that all Americans think the same, that the U.S. is a conformist society.

"Actually there are different points of view. The U.S. is less dogmatic and more open than we had thought," said one Colombian.

Many misunderstandings arise because of the difference in attitude of Colombians and Americans concerning the concept of service.

"Service people are more solicitous in Latin America. They do more; they show more feeling. You get the idea they don't want to serve you in the U.S. They just bring you a menu and a glass of ice water," said one Colombian.

"In Colombia there is more emphasis on being polite, attentive, and courteous. In the U.S. we are taught these things; but life is more agitated and brisk, and so the emphasis is not the same," added an American.

One Colombian who initially felt service in the U.S. to be as frigid as the glass of ice water placed unceremoniously in front of him gave a perceptive account of his increasing awareness of the differences in the two societies.

"With more experience I have observed that Americans are shy before service people; they don't feel comfortable being served. They accept almost anything and consider it bad manners to complain. Latins in general want to have good service and will complain more readily. To them, the service in the U.S. always lacks *adornos* (embellishment). They will say something not expected by the American waiter and thus seem to him out of order," he said.

"Americans don't want the other person to feel inferior because he is serving them; they want to place him on an equal plane. They feel it is just an accident that you are waiting on me and I am being waited on, for in the U.S. almost everybody will be in a service position sometime in his life—a waiter, waitress, gas station attendant, or taxi driver," he continued.

"In Latin America people will work as waiters and waitresses all their lives, and they are looked at as people in inferior positions," he added.

The more assertive attitude of the American service person can be unsettling to the newly arrived Colombian.

"A person in a high position in Colombia counts on having the service people under him to confirm his position. In the U.S. he feels uncomfortable because that is eliminated; there's a loss of well-being," said another Colombian, who commented on the transformation of a Colombian service person in the United States.

"A mechanic or *campesino* (peasant) in Colombia won't look you in the eye or shake your hand; he will only hold out his hand. After three months in the U.S. he will look you in the eye and give you a firm handshake. He has more self-respect; he has become more of a person," he said.

Working out the appropriate relationship with the maid can pose some formidable problems for the American family in Colombia.

"Colombians will ring a bell for the maid to come; Americans find this repugnant. They will get up and ask the maid to come or yell for her; this is obnoxious to Colombians," said an American who lived in Colombia for several years.

"The American will be concerned that the maid 'better herself,' develop a skill. So the maid ends up going to school three-fourths of the day and working only one-fourth. The Colombian will say: 'Why? A maid's a maid.' Americans tend to negotiate the salary with the maid rather than merely telling her what she will receive. Maids who work for Americans are ruined to work for Colombians," said the American.

"But it won't do any good to tell an American that treating the maid like this will make her future in Colombia more difficult, for he can't help acting this way," he added.

Problems of a different sort are encountered by Colombians when they bring a maid to the U.S. For in Colombia, even homes of poor families will have rooms for the maids, but Colombians look in vain for such rooms in American houses and apartments.

"It's very inconvenient. American houses don't have the correct room, so some families have to build a special room. Often the maid doesn't learn to speak English, so it is difficult for her to get along out in society," explained one Colombian.

"You become the servant of the maid. You have to take her to Spanish movies, find Spanish-speaking friends for her. Families end up waiting on the maids," he said.

Linguistic differences between Spanish and English reflect the more cordial, loquacious Colombian style and the pragmatic, direct American approach.

"When you are used to the rhythm of Spanish and don't know English well, English sounds brusque and curt; the intonation seems strange," a Colombian said.

"We are a lot more flowery than you are," added another Colombian. "You have the concept that time is money, that time is scarce. Time is not a free good for you. The American will say 'Hello' and get right down to business. This appears impolite to us, for we like to do business in a cordial atmosphere. Actually, in terms of American society, the American is being considerate, for he does not want to waste the time of the other person."

"You're more outspoken. You say things bluntly without caring whether or not you hurt the other person's feelings, and you expect the other person to be as blunt. The Colombian will not speak so directly and will retract his words if he sees that the other person's feelings are hurt," he said.

A Colombian dentist living in the U.S. has devised an interesting division of her use of the two languages.

"I prefer to use Spanish colloquially—it's more expressive—but technically, I prefer English," she said.

The differences in the two languages are highlighted when it comes time to write a letter, for the same content that can be put in one page in English will often take two pages in Spanish. Depending on one's cultural perspective, the letter will appear curt or verbose.

"We have to explain that people writing letters in English are not impolite but that that is simply the way to say it," said a Colombian familiar with both business worlds. "In Colombia business letters are now becoming shorter," he added.

Language differences have their humorous aspects as well. Since the "b" and "v" sounds are often indistinguishable in Spanish, a failure to make the distinction required in English led to the following comment from a Colombian student of English: "My consonants are all right, but I'm having trouble with my bowels."

English dialogues studiously memorized in Colombia can prove inadequate when it comes time to put them to use in the U.S.

"We were taught to say 'Coca-Cola,' only to find that in the U.S. everyone says 'Coke.' We learned to order a 'hamburger' but weren't prepared for 'What do you want on it?' spoken so rapidly that we could not understand it. Even if we had understood, we still would not have known what to answer, for it was only later that we noticed the onions, tomatoes, catsup, etc.," said one Colombian.

A seemingly simple thing like the distance between speakers can interfere with effective communication.

"The American will stand at least a yard away from you, creating a cold atmosphere. The Colombian will stand right beside you and give you a pat on the back; it's a more cordial approach," said one Colombian.

To the American, however, the "cordial" Colombian manner will appear overpowering, and it is not uncommon to find a Colombian backing an American across the room—each speaker trying to establish the proper conversational distance.

A "generation gap" can develop between Colombian parents and their children when the family moves to the U.S., for as the teenagers seek the freedom enjoyed by their American counterparts, the parents will be striving to keep their customs.

"Discipline within the family is much stronger in Colombia than in the U.S. for both boys and girls. The first thing you notice here is trying to adjust to new standards of more freedom, especially for girls," said a Colombian father who had lived several years in the U.S.

The traditional system of chaperonage and *visitas de novio* (boy visiting the girl in her house) have recently been replaced by dating in some Colombian circles.

"We have the concept of dating, especially within the high-income groups, but this is rather new and has not yet extended to most of the population," explained one Colombian man.

A Colombian woman, however, thought it was unrealistic for parents to think they could "protect" their children from American mores by sending them back to Bogotá.

"Youth at home are onto marijuana, and kids are asking, 'Why should I cut my hair?' Ten years ago you could not go out alone at night with a man, and we were never left alone with our boy friends. Now it's very much like the U.S. You can go for rides and to movies and dances alone," she said.

"*Home* life is less important, but *family* life is more important in Colombia," said one Colombian in explaining that the American spends more time at home but that family ties appear stronger in Colombia.

"The American works in the garden and repairs things around the house; he's more organized. In Colombia you arrive home late and don't do these jobs. The first time I mowed the lawn was in the U.S.," he said.

"Yet we ask ourselves, 'Since so much of life is spent together at home in the U.S., why do ties between parents and children become so weak as the children grow older?' The concept of family is broader in Colombia," he added.

"Americans seem to feel more loyalty to other organizations—the work group, sports club, university, friends—than to the family," noted another Colombian, who pointed out that the traditional extended family was also disappearing in urban areas in his country.

A streak of puritanism in the American mentality tends to prevent the carefree conviviality that marks a Colombian social event, according to an American who has spent several years in Latin America.

"In the U.S. bars are dark; they're places to hide, to escape, rooted in the idea that drinking is evil. In Latin America the atmosphere is more light and open," he said.

Yet the more straitlaced American style is not without its attractive elements.

"I admire the discipline of the American people. They respect rules of all kinds. If the street sign says, 'Don't walk,' you don't walk. Everyone respects the other person's turn in a store," said one Colombian woman.

Though the mystique of *machismo* (the masculine ideal embodying honor, romance, strength, and pride) and the male's dominant position in society have by no means completely disappeared, there have been considerable modifications—particularly among the urban elite.

"The woman's role is changing rapidly. Husbands are more liberal in letting their wives work and participate in politics," said one man.

"There is a great deal of respect for the woman, but the idea still persists that woman has certain functions and man has others. We shouldn't compete but rather be complementary; we're trying to minimize competitiveness. We haven't yet accepted the fact that a woman can manage men in the sense of an executive position," said one young Colombian man, who added that worldwide changes in the role of women had virtually eliminated *machismo* among people his age.

"The freedom of the man is greater in the rural areas. In general, it's negatively correlated with the level of income," added another Colombian.

At the same time, the *matrona*—the woman who manages her household with efficiency and discipline—is a highly respected figure in Colombian culture.

The Catholic Church, while still a prominent force in Colombian life, is no longer the final arbiter in secular matters.

"We no longer look to the Church for leadership except in religious matters, whereas we formerly considered the Church as almost a supreme court which would determine whether government action was morally right or wrong. Now the civil institutions will speak out," said one Colombian.

The concept of dealing *personally* with the highest-ranking official is deeply imbedded in Colombian thought.

"We try to deal with the most important person, even for the smallest problem. If I want a scholarship for one of my sons, I must speak with the minister himself. I would be very disappointed if I had to speak first to the man actually in charge of what I want," explained one Colombian.

Obviously the minister cannot attend to every minor matter personally, but he will see every caller for at least a minute and then send him to the one actually responsible for that particular request.

"If there is a strike in a factory, both labor and management will want to come to the President directly," the man said.

"As a government official in Colombia, I could work only in the morning. In the afternoon I had to see people; I had nobody screening. I received anybody who requested an audience. This is true of all the ministers and the President," he said.

One observant Colombian discussed the philosophical outlook toward thought and action in the two societies—how an obsession with perfection serves to impede action in Colombia while a tendency to spring immediately into action hinders a planned march to a thought-out ideal in the U.S.

"We have traditionally valued conversation and have had the *mañana* idea: We'll talk about it today and act on it tomorrow. In the U.S., you just do it. We'll sit down and wait for the perfect idea," he said.

"Colombian writing is always looking towards where Colombia is going, but if you were to ask an American, 'Where are you going?', he would probably say, 'Don't ask me; I'm just going.' In Colombia, we are always reaching out for something; we don't know quite what it is."

CARMEN GARCÍA

A Cross-Cultural Study
of Politeness Strategies:
Venezuelan and American Perspectives*

(A study comparing U.S. and Venezuelan women's use of politeness shows a connection between culturally determined rules of politeness, communication styles and, eventually, how Venezuelan and U.S. women relate to others.)

INTRODUCTION

Language has a central role in human communication and it is important that we understand all aspects of this role. In particular, implicit knowledge of the sociocultural rules of language use is essential. For native speakers of a language this occurs naturally. They share not only the syntactic and phonological rules of a language, but also common patterns of sociolinguistic behavior, that is, the knowledge of the "speech conduct that is appropriate to the various events which make up their daily existence" (Wolfson, 1983: 62). For those communicating in a foreign language, however, conscious knowledge of the sociocultural rules of use is important to interpret and produce speech appropriately. Consequently, the non-native speaker needs to learn how language functions in society "as a means of interaction and communication" (Widdowson, 1979: 10). It is particularly important for him [or] her to learn how to

---

Reprinted by permission of the author.

* Material from this article has appeared in García, C., "Disagreeing and Requesting by Venezuelans and Americans," *Linguistics and Education* 1, 3, 299–322, and García, C., "Responding to a Request by Native and Non-Native English Speakers: Deference vs. Camaraderie," (manuscript).

interpret and select an utterance in terms of: (a) the speaker's intentions; (b) the extralinguistic situational factors, such as role relationship, degree of formality, channel of communication; (c) the specific discourse function, that is, requesting, disagreeing, apologizing, etc.; and (d) the linguistic environment in which it occurs.

A person expresses him or herself in a language with a distinct communicative style. Communicative style involves patterns of speech, rhythm, structure of conversation and presentation of self based on the perceived dimensions of distance and power (Tannen, 1984). Differences in style occur because of differences in cultural backgrounds such as those of native and non-native speakers. Understanding culturally based differences in style and how they arise is of vital importance for effective cross-cultural communication.

This paper presents an analysis of the stylistic devices used by female Venezuelan Spanish speakers and female American English speakers in four situations in English: disagreeing, apologizing, requesting and responding to a request. It shows that speakers' culturally based rules of politeness and rules that govern the relationships among individuals influence their choice and sequence of stylistic devices.

In general Venezuelan Spanish speakers preferred the establishment of camaraderie with the interlocutor and consequently made more frequent use of confrontational and personal stylistic devices in their discourse (with less mitigation and more use of expressive phonology). Americans, on the other hand, preferred the establishment of deference and/or distance and used more non-confrontational and impersonal stylistic devices (more mitigation and downtoning).

The data indicate that the Venezuelans' preference for camaraderie over deference and/or distance resulted from a transfer of their previous cultural patterns and gave rise to miscommunication.

THEORETICAL BACKGROUND

The theoretical model of conversational style used in this study incorporates Tannen's work on stylistic devices, Lakoff's rules of rapport (rules that govern relationships among individuals), and Brown and Levinson's study of politeness strategies.

According to Tannen, stylistic devices are the linguistic choices speakers make within a communicational interchange to get their message across. They are characterized by being made at a "certain rate, at a certain pitch and amplitude, in certain intonation, at a certain point in interaction" (1984, p. 8) and have to be considered in the context of other devices with which they occur and in terms of the possibilities from which they are chosen. These choices mark the speakers' communicative style which then affects the interaction as a whole and the perceptions of "what is said and about the speaker who says it" (Tannen, 1984, p. 8).

Stylistic devices chosen by the participants were classified in light of Brown and Levinson's theory of politeness. Brown and Levinson's theory is based on "universal wants for negative and positive face . . ." (Scollon and Scollon, 1986: 166). Negative face is defined as "the want of 'every competent adult member' of society that his actions be unimpeded by others" (Brown and Levinson, 1978: 67), and positive face is "the want of every member that his wants be desirable to at least some others" (Brown and Levinson, 1978: 67). Following Scollon and Scollon's termi- nology we shall call negative politeness strategies "deference politeness strategies" and positive politeness strategies "solidarity politeness strategies."

For the purpose of this study deference politeness strategies were identified as those that were mitigated by either gambits or routine formulae or by the presence of agent avoiders (passive voice [*have it typed*], impersonal constructions [*could anyone type it?*], collective nouns [*everybody*], and past modality [*could, would, should*]). Solidarity polite- ness strategies, on the other hand, were identified as those that exhibited high rise intonation, present-tense modal auxiliaries (*can, will, shall*), and mentioned the agent of the action (*you*), beneficiary (*me*) and object (*it*).

METHOD
Subjects

Our analysis included twenty subjects, ten non-native and ten native speakers. The ten non-native English speakers who participated were Venezuelan females who spoke Spanish as their first language. They ranged in age from 19 to 37, had studied English for an average of 8.5 years, and had lived in the United States from six months to three years. Three were high school graduates and were currently enrolled in an English as a Foreign Language program; the other seven were graduate students and not enrolled in EFL programs. Five of the seven graduate students had bachelor's degrees and two had master's degrees. The ten native English speakers who participated were American females who spoke English as their first language. They ranged in age from 22 to 45; three were high school graduates, one of whom was enrolled in under- graduate training; six had bachelor's degrees and were in graduate school, and one had a master's degree and was pursuing a Ph.D.

Tasks

The subjects were asked to participate in four role-play interactions:

1. Responding to a complaint by an apartment superintendent. This interaction aimed at studying how Americans and Venezuelans express disagreement. The situation was described to the subjects as follows:

> Last night you were studying quietly in your apartment. This morning the apartment superintendent comes to you and says, "Good morning. Sorry to bother you but the lady downstairs from you said she couldn't sleep last night because you were playing your records too loud. I'd really appreciate it if you'd be more careful in the future.

2. Apologizing to a friend. This interaction aimed at studying how Americans and Venezuelans react when the situation calls for an apology. The introduction was as follows:

> You were invited to a friend's party last night. You told your friend you were going but you didn't. This morning he calls you.

3. Requesting that a report be typed. This interaction aimed at studying how Americans and Venezuelans formulate a request. The situation presented to the subjects was the following:

> You need to have a report typed immediately because you have to hand it in early tomorrow morning. Since you can't type, you go to a Typing Service and ask to have it done. You know their policy is that they need a week's notice.

The participant meets a receptionist who asks, "What can I do for you?"

4. Responding to a request from a friend for a ride. This interaction aimed at examining the linguistic devices used by Venezuelans and Americans when responding to a request. They could either accept or reject it. The situation was presented to the interlocutor as follows:

> Your car broke down and you need a ride to go to school. Call one of your classmates and ask her for a ride.

Subjects in turn were read the following lead-in:

> One of your classmates, who lives a few blocks away from you, calls and says her car broke down and she doesn't have a way to get to school.

These situations were chosen for their diversity. In particular, they illustrated both asymmetrical social relationships (namely authority-

offender, i.e., superintendent-leaser; and customer-server, i.e., re-
ceptionist-client) and symmetrical relationships (friend-friend and
classmate-classmate).

Given this diversity our purpose is to look for patterns of linguistic
behavior common to non-native speakers, comparing these to the
patterns of native speakers.

Role-play was selected to elicit discourse because, as Scarcella
points out, it is possible to control the conversational interchange to a
certain extent and still provide an opportunity for complete interactions.
That is, it offers the subject and the interlocutor the opportunity to start
and finish the interaction following the natural evolution of the conversation.

Prior to interacting with the subjects, the participants who played
the superintendent, receptionist, friend and classmate were given a
description of the situation as well as the opening line of the conversation. Subsequent comments by these individuals, however, were
improvised according to the subjects' responses and their own perception of the role they were playing.

DATA ANALYSIS

The 80 separate interactions were recorded on videotape, and tran-
scribed following the conventions designed by Jefferson.[1] The conversational subject matter was then examined and characterized in terms
of the stylistic devices and politeness strategies used by the native
(American) and non-native (Venezuelan) English speakers. After
completing their role-play, participants were interviewed individually in
playback sessions to get their reactions. These sessions, which also were
recorded, were in Spanish for the Venezuelans and in English for the
Americans.

FINDINGS

Our analysis of native and non-native speakers' participation in the four
situations described above showed that native speakers preferred
deference politeness strategies whereas non-native speakers preferred
solidarity politeness strategies. That is, the American women were non-
confrontational and impersonal in their disagreement, apology, request
and response to a request whereas the Venezuelan women were confrontational and personal.

Upon receiving the complaint presented by the superintendent the
Americans reacted by giving downtoned challenges, downtoned sug-

gestions, expressions of willingness to cooperate, impersonal or down-toned accusations and impersonal denials. This can be seen in the following sample.

Text [1**]	Comment
S I'm sorry to bother you this morning but the lady downstairs was complaining about the noise you were making last night and I was hoping that in the future you might be able to keep it down	
L1I uhm (0.3) I'm the only one here I REALLY don't think it was me probably— I was HOME alone last night you know just reading and I didn't even have the TV on but uhm=	
S She said it was coming from your apartment	
L1I well she's <u>probably</u> confused you know	*Downtoned* *Accusation*
there's four apartments up here and it could be any one of them	*Impersonal* *Accusation*
<u>I</u> didn't happen to hear any noise but uh <u>I usually</u> try and be quiet you know if there's any other problem	*Expression of* *Willingness* *to Cooperate*
you can let me know but I– you might want to check the other apartments and see if there was anything going on because I was because I was home alone last night and there wasn't anybody with me	*Downtoned* *Suggestion* *Impersonal Denial*
S okay	
L1I you know	
S I'll check with her again maybe she's mistaken	
L1I okay thank you	
S thank you	

** See Note for explanation of transcription marks. Abbreviations:
S = Superintendent; L1I = American Respondent.

On the other hand, the Venezuelans reacted by giving direct challenges, orders, refusals to cooperate, criticisms about the third party and strong denials. The following sample illustrates a Venezuelan's participation.

Text [†]		Comment
S	I'm sorry to bother you but the lady downstairs was complaining about the noise that you made last night and I was hoping that you might be able to keep it down in the future	
L2J	The noise? downstairs my apartment?	*Challenge*
S	yeah yeah the person downstairs was complaining about the noise in your apartment	
L2J	well that person must be <u>very</u> crazy	*Criticism about the third party*
	because I was studying very quietly here all night last night=	
	so you go back to him?	*Order*
	and see what he can say to you this time	
S	well he insists it was coming from your apartment	
L2J	well what can I do? (LF)	
S	Okay I'll see maybe it was from the apartment next door	
L2J	I don't know	
S	Okay well thank you	

[†] S = Superintendent; L2J = Venezuelan Respondent.

In similar fashion, when presented with a situation where they had to apologize to a friend for not having attended his party, the Americans continued being non-confrontational and apologetic. They expressed regret and provided general accounts, offered to redress, gave deference and produced a number of self-effacement statements. The following sample illustrates one such apology by an American to her friend.

Text ††		Comment
H	Hi XX XX!	
L1H	Mark!	
H	Yeah	
L1H	How are you?	
H	I'm fine how are you?	
L1H	I'm fine what's up?	
H	Well listen I wanted to call you because we waited for you last night at the party but you didn't show up	
L1H	Uhm	
H	I wondered what happened	
L1H	I'm really sorry Mark	*Expression of Regret*
	I'm <u>really</u> sorry	*Expression of Regret*
	I I was tired last night	*Account*
	I had a <u>lot</u> of work to do	
	and I just wasn't in the mood	
H	Mm-hmm	
L1H	but uhm (LF) nothing personal	*Expression of Deference*
	I just felt like I really shouldn't go and then I . . . uh WANTED to call and then I didn't want to call because I wasn't– I was a little depressed and I just didn't <u>feel</u> like talking and I didn't want to <u>upset</u> anybody there you know . . .	*Self-Effacement*
H	well I wish you would've come because I'm sure we would've been able to cheer you up in fact I told all my friends about you and I really wanted them to meet you	
L1H	I'm <u>really</u> sorry Mark	*Expression of Regret*
	next time=	
	we'll make it another time	*Offer to*
	Okay?	*Redress*
H	Well I'll be sure to invite you then	
L1H	Okay thanks a lot : : :	
H	Bye	
L1H	Bye	

†† H = Host; L1H = American Respondent

In contrast, while the Venezuelan subjects expressed regret and followed it with specific accounts, they were very vague and noncommital in their offer to redress and did not give deference. They were generally non-self-effacing. The only self-effacement statement made by any of the ten Venezuelans is contained in the example below. As is readily apparent, it was completely dominated by other solidarity politeness strategies that diminished its deference effect.

Text§		Comment
H	Hello xxx	
L2E	Mn-hmm?	
H	Hi this is Mark.	
L2E	Oh = Mark? hi	
H	Listen where were you last night at the party?	
L2E	Oh I'm sorry I couldn't go I just had a – too –	*Expression of Regret*
	a lot to study so . . . =	*Account*
H	You had a lot to study then huh? =	
L2E	Oh yes =	
H	well see all my friends were there and I told them so much about you and I wanted them to meet you	
L2E	oh that's ni : ce that's very nice of you but uh I just couldn't go	*Account*
H	okay well couldn't you have called to tell me that you couldn't make it	
L2E	yeah well is it an <u>invitation</u> or is it a (LF) how do you say that? are you pressing me to go some place =	*Criticism*
H	no [but I	
L2E	= I thought it was an invitation	*Criticism*
H	yeah it was an invitation but I just thought if you weren't coming then you might have called =	

L2E	yeah I could have I was planning to call you you were just a little bit too early =	*Reprimand*
H	[mm-hmm	
L2E	= to call] me	
H	okay well then maybe next time we'll get you	
L2E	yeah if it isn't if it isn't obligatory I'll come (LF)	

§ H = Host; L2E = Venezuelan Respondent

The two Americans who played the roles of superintendent and friend reacted to the other Americans more favorably than to the Venezuelans. The "superintendent" accepted the former's suggestions and expressions of willingness to cooperate and concluded the interaction with harmony. When interacting with the Venezuelans, however, he left apologizing and mitigating the complaint. Similarly, the "friend" reacted to the American women by expressing understanding and accepting their apologies and offers to redress. But, when interacting with the Venezuelans he expressed incredulousness and sarcasm.

The Venezuelans also expressed their dissatisfaction with the way the situations had evolved. They expressed discontent that the "superintendent" had started the interaction by going straight to the purpose of his visit rather than establishing an interpersonal relationship first. And throughout the interaction, they perceived that he was not maintaining the social distance that his role as superintendent called for. In other words, they viewed the superintendent as inferior rather than an equal or superior with authority over them and resented it when he acted otherwise. The Venezuelans were also dissatisfied with the friend to whom they were supposed to apologize. They perceived him as pushy and rude. In their minds, they had the prerogative to attend or not to attend the party, not an obligation as the host seemed to imply.

When receiving the request for a ride, the American subjects were non-confrontational and impersonal. They expressed willingness to cooperate, saved face for the hearer and confirmed the agreement. The following sample illustrates how one of the Americans responded to [her] friend's request for a ride.

Text [§§]	Comment
C Hi this is Carolyn I'd like to ask you a favor my car broke down and I was wondering if you could give me a ride to school tomorrow L1B Oh : : no what time do you go? C I have to be in by 9 o'clock L1B Oh (0.2) ni : : : ne? but I don't have class until te : : : n but (0.3) I see would quarter to nine be too (0.3) too late for you to leave? C Oh no that'd be great L1B that's okay? C yeah good L1B ALL RIGHT I suppose I could go earlier and maybe I'll get some work done C okay good thanks L1B Okay should I pick you up? C yeah you could = L1B okay fine? see you then C Okay [bye-bye L1B Bye]	 *Expression of* *Willingness* *to Cooperate* *Saving Face* *for the Hearer* *Confirming the* *Agreement*

[§§] C = Carolyn; L1B = American Respondent

On the other hand, the Venezuelans were more personal. They expressed their willingness to cooperate using "expressive phonology" (high rise intonation, denoting enthusiasm) and were less elaborate in confirming the agreement. The following example typifies how Venezuelans responded to the request for a ride.

Text [||||]	Comment
C Hi this is Carolyn I'd like to ask you a favor my car broke down and I was wondering if you could give me a ride to school tomorrow	

L2B	Well sure? Carolyn	*Expressing Willingness to Cooperate*
	OF COURSE I can give	*Expressing Willingness*
	you a ride?	*to Cooperate*
C	Okay great	

|||| C = Carolyn; L2B = Venezuelan Respondent

When making the request to have their paper typed, Americans typically maintained their impersonal tone. They made their request for a service in an impersonal manner and made an impersonal or downtoned request for exception. The following illustrates the approach taken by a typical American.

Text |||| ||	Comment
L1H	Hi	
R	What can I do for you?	
L1H	uh I have a report I need typed	*Impersonal Request for a Service*
R	yeah and?	
L1H	quickly (LF)	
R	well you know I'd like to help you but we need at least a week's notice	
L1H	and there's no special accommodations for having it done	*Impersonal Request for Exception*
R	well I hate to make exceptions because we're so backed up and we really need a week's notice	
L1H	do you know anyone who could do it on a shorter notice?	*Impersonal Request for a Service*
R	unfortunately no I don't know anyone around this area who could do that =	
L1H	okay	
R	– in a short time	
L1H	well maybe I can find out myself	
R	[okay	
L1H	thank you]	
R	you're welcome	

|||| |||| L1H = American Participant; R = Respondent

By contrast, Venezuelans made downtoned personal requests for the service and personal requests for exception. The following illustrates how the Venezuelans made their request.

Text #		Comment
R	Hello may I help you?	
L2I	Hello uh can can you : : : =	
R	what? =	
L2I	do me a favor please?	*Personal Request for a Service*
R	[I'm sorry?	
L2I	I need] oh you know I need some papers in uh typewriter for tomorrow-early tomorrow	
	can you do it for me? you know	*Personal Request for a Service*
	I I have many I have many troubles and uh	
R	we don't sell typewriters	
L2I	no not selling you know to pass me a work in a typewriter	*Personal Request for a Service*
R	uh you-well we do but-this is our service to type but we couldn't get it to you by tomorrow	
L2I	well maybe (0.3) if you know? I in a hurry you know [I have a lot of wo : : rk	
R	we're all in a hurry]	
L2I	can you uh just for this time? this	*Personal Request for Exception*
R	no uh it takes us a week it takes us a week and I couldn't really get it to you tomorrow we're very [busy	
L2I	may be if I help you with my work because the typewriter =	
R	well then why don't you type it?	
L2I	no it's I don't have the time you know I can shorten you (0.3) [my work	
R	how many pages is it	
L2I	well : : about : one hundred (LF)	

R	Next next week bring it in – uh	
	leave it bring it in and I'll have	
	it ready for you next week	
L2I	(WN) well (0.3) that sure?	*Personal Request*
	<u>Sure</u> you don't want to help me?	*for a Service*
R	I'm sure I can't help you	
	I don't know about the other	
	secretaries [uhm	
L2I	oh]	
R	but I know they're very busy	
	a hundred pages that's that's	
	very lengthy	
L2I	well maybe fifty? (LF)	
R	what kind of paper are you writing?	
L2I	(LF) okay? (LF) okay so you don't	*Personal Request*
	want to uh	*for a Service*
R	[I can't help you	
L2I	okay] you can't well thank you	

R = Respondent; L2I = Venezuelan Participant

The two Americans who played the roles of a friend requesting a ride and the receptionist again reacted favorably to the American subjects and with suspicion and impatience toward the Venezuelans. During the playback sessions the "friend" expressed the feeling that the Venezuelans had been too enthusiastic in responding to her request for a ride in that nobody would be so enthusiastic when being inconvenienced. The "receptionist" perceived the Venezuelans as pushy and insistent.

The Venezuelans' perception of the situations was not favorable either. When asked why they did not confirm more extensively the agreement to give their friend a ride, they responded that they did not deem it necessary between friends. Their presumption was that formality did not belong in that relationship. Regarding the request to have their paper typed, they did not understand the receptionist's intransigence and why she asked so many information questions. The latter in fact led them to believe that their request was going to be satisfied and not refused.

CONCLUSIONS

A major conclusion of the above analysis is that the different stylistic devices used by Americans and Venezuelans in disagreeing, requesting, responding to a request and apologizing reflect their preferred conversational styles and that these in turn are products of different cultural backgrounds.

The effects of using these different stylistic devices become quite apparent when we contrast the discomfort shown by the superintendent, classmate, host and employee in dealing with the Venezuelans alongside the rapport established with the Americans.

What may be occurring here is that the Venezuelan women perceived the appropriate relationship between themselves and the interlocutor as one of low distance (familiar) involving no (or low) power on either side. No respect was given and none was expected. Seen in terms of Scollon and Scollon (1983: 169), it could be said that the Venezuelans

> place[d] a value on emphasizing the common grounds of social interaction . . . [and by doing this they created] a system of solidarity politeness.

This contrasts sharply with the expectation by the American interlocutors who expected a different relationship, one of distance and deference. Moreover, as Scollon and Scollon point out, the expession of solidarity might even have been interpreted by the interlocutors as an expression of power, thus adding to their discomfort.

By comparison, the American women evidently deemed the situations to be of high distance, in the sense of being more formal and less familiar, where the interlocutors assumed greater power in the interaction than accorded by the Venezuelans (Scollon and Scollon, 1983: 169). The approach used by the Americans expressed itself in deference politeness strategies and in a general posture of overall deference. On playback, the American women indicated that these were indeed their attitudes.

What this led to was a result where the American participants (both subjects and interlocutors) expressed comfort with the interaction. The American subjects were able to establish harmony through their maintenance of distance and their deferential attitude towards the interlocutors in contrast to the Venezuelans who did not adopt these attitudes.

The results of this study indicate that compared to Venezuelan conversational style, American conversational style has a distinct preference for deference politeness strategies. These two groups, moreover, can be seen in terms of a continuum, since compared to the British style, as Scollon and Scollon point out, the American style actually seems to be less formal, favoring a relatively greater amount of solidarity politeness.

To some extent then, this and other studies which examine the different styles of communication used by native English speakers and non-native English speakers might be helpful to improve cross-cultural communication. For instance if non-native English speakers are of the sort examined in this study, they bring a background which emphasizes the use of solidarity politeness stategies over deference politeness strategies. Seen in this light, it is not that Venezuelans are impolite, vague or insulting and it is not that they do not have the linguistic competence in English to express deference, but rather that their sociocultural rules of language use emphasize the establishment of camaraderie in a conversational interchange rather than deference [as in] the case for Americans.

What we can say is that when communicating in a foreign language it is important for one to know how he or she is perceived and for one to have enough sociolinguistic understanding to communicate what one really wants to.

In addition, it is important to point out that we cannot make the generalization that all Spanish speakers would prefer solidarity politeness strategies any more than we can say British and American English speakers use the same deference politeness strategies.

As presented in this article the intercultural differences in what is acceptable in a given situation can lead to misunderstandings and disharmony. This implies that we might improve cross-cultural communication and avoid the creation and maintenance of stereotypes by "the cultivation of an international, interethnic, intercultural communicative style of deference politeness" (Scollon and Scollon, 1983: 186). Byrnes suggests a comon deferential standard which would not only allow the speaker to comfortably adjust his or her participation to the interlocutor but also would establish a nonthreatening basis of communication that could then be modified to a mutually acceptable level of formality by the communicative partners.

Note

The transcription marks used are:
A. No gap: "=" placed between utterances with no time gap uttered by different speakers or to link different parts of a speaker's utterance that has been carried over to another line because of an interruption;

B. Overlap: "[" used to indicate beginning of overlap; and "]", to indicate end of overlapped utterances.

C. Pause length: (0.0) measured in tenths of a second.

D. Unintelligible utterance: ( )

E. Self-interruption: "–" placed at point of interruption. An utterance was considered to be interrupted when the speaker started making an utterance and changed its content and/or form.

F. Laughter: (LF); whine (WN)

G. Intonation, prosodic quality:
"?" marks high rise; "," marks low rise; "." marks low fall.

Capital letters mark increased volume in the production of a given word or words of the utterance.

Underlining marks stress.

": : :" marks lengthened syllable; each ":" marking one "beat."

References

Brown, Penelope, and Stephen Levinson. "Universals in Language Usage: Politeness Phenomena." In Goody, Esther (ed.), *Questions and Politeness*. Cambridge: Cambridge University Press, 1978. 56–289.

Byrnes, Heidi. "Interactional Style in German and American Conversations." *Text*, 6 (1986): 189–206.

Eisenstein, Miriam. "Native Reaction to Non-native Speech: A Review of Empirical Research." *Studies in Second Language Acquisition*, vol. 5 (1983): 160–176.

———— and Jean W. Bodman. "'I Very Much Appreciate': Expressions of Gratitude by Native and Non-native Speakers of American English." *Applied Linguistics*, vol. 7 (1986): 167–185.

Fraser, Bruce. "On Apologizing." In Coulmas, Florian (ed.), *Conversational Routine, Explorations in Standardized Communication Situations and Prepatterned Speech*. The Hague: Mouton, 1981. 259–271.

———— Ellen Rintell, et al. "An Approach to Conducting Research on the Acquisition of Pragmatic Competence in a Second Language." In Larsen-Freeman, Diane (ed.), *Discourse Analysis in Second Language Research*. Massachusetts: Newbury House Publishers, Inc., 1980. 75–91.

García, Carmen. "Apologizing in English: Politeness Strategies Used by Native and Non-native Speakers." *Multilingua*, vol. 8-1 (1989): 3–20.

————. "Disagreeing and Requesting by Venezuelans and Americans." *Linguistics and Education*, vol. 1, no. 3 (1989): 299–322.

Goffman, Erving. "Relations in Public." *Microstudies of the Public Order*. Harmondsworth: Penguin, 1971.

Gumperz, John. J. *Sociocultural Knowledge in Conversational Inferences*, 28th Annual Round Table on Languages and Linguistics. Washington, D.C.: Georgetown University, 1977.

————. "The Retrieval of Sociocultural Knowledge in Communication." *Poetics Today*, 1 (1979): 273–286.

House, Juliane, and Gabriele Kasper. "Politeness Markers in English and German." In Coulmas, Florian (ed.), *Conversational Routine, Explorations in Standardized Communication Situations and Prepatterned Speech*. The Hague-Mouton Publishers, 1981. 157–185.

Jefferson, Gail. "Transcript Notation." In Atkinson, Maxwell J. and John Heritage (eds.), *Structures of Social Interaction: Studies in Conversational Analysis*. Cambridge: Cambridge University Press, 1986. ix–xvi.

Kasper, Gabriele. "Errors in Speech Act Realization and Use of Gambits." *The Canadian Modern Language Review*, 35 (1979): 395–406.

Kochman, Thomas. *Black and White Styles in Conflict*. Chicago: The University of Chicago Press, 1981.

Manes, Joan, and Nessa Wolfson. "The Compliment Formula." In Coulmas, Florian (ed.), *Conversational Routine, Explorations in Standardized Communication Situations and Prepatterned Speech*. The Hague: Mouton, 1981. 115–131.

Scarcella, Robin. "On Speaking Politely in a Second Language." In Yorio, Carlos A., Kyle Perkins, et al. (eds.), *On Tesol '79*. Washington, D.C.: TESOL, 1979. 275–287.

Scollon, Ron, and Suzanne B.K. Scollon. "Face in Interethnic Communication." In Richards, Jack C., and Richard W. Schmidt (eds.), *Language and Communication*. London: Longman, 1983. 156–188.

Tannen, Deborah. *Conversational Styles: Analyzing Talk Among Friends*. New Jersey: Ablex Publishing Corporation, 1984.

Thomas, Jenny. "Cross-Cultural Pragmatic Failure." *Applied Linguistics*, 4 (1983): 91–112.

Varonis, Evangeline Marlos, and Susan M. Gass. "Miscommunication in Native/Nonnative Conversation." *Language in Society*, 14 (1985): 327–343.

Walters, Joel. "The Perception of Politeness in English and Spanish." In Yorio, Carlos A., Kyle Perkins, et al. (eds.), *On TESOL '79: EFL Policies, Programs, Practices*. Washington, D.C.: TESOL, 1979. 275–287.

Wolfson, Nessa. "Compliments in Cross-cultural Perspective." *TESOL Quarterly*, 15 (1981): 117–124.

FERNANDO REATI

Argentine Political Violence and Artistic Representation in Films of the 1980's

(With the return of democracy to Argentina in 1983, filmmakers used a cultural code of myths, rather than a documentary-like picture of reality, to depict the horrors of the ousted military regime. The author shows how these myths are produced from the collective imagination.)

In 1976, in the midst of increasing guerrilla activity and after years of growing radicalization of industrial workers and middle class students, the armed forces of Argentina overthrew the constitutional government of Isabel Perón. This overthrow unleashed a campaign of secret political assassinations which resulted in the disappearance of tens of thousands. The period, known as *la guerra sucia* ("the dirty war") for its unconventional methods of terrorizing the population, left deep scars in the collective experience of Argentineans and in their artistic representations. In a nation where political violence had been pervasive through the years, the "dirty war" managed to shock and transform society because of the novelty of its punitive technology. It also forced intellectuals and artists to reconsider the means available to them to represent reality, in much the same way that the experience of the European Holocaust had prompted new questions about the representation of horror. It is my purpose here to briefly analyze four films produced by Argentine directors after the collapse of the military regime and the reinstatement of democracy in 1983. I will show how these films

Fernando Reati, "Argentine Political Violence and Artistic Representation in Films of the 1980's" (*Latin American Literary Review*, 17 [34], 1989), 24–39, by permission of the publisher.

deal with the new, pressing reality through the use of certain cultural codes pertaining to the society of the period. In order to do so, I will examine Luis Puenzo's 1985 *La historia oficial* [*The Official Story*], María Luisa Bemberg's 1984 *Camila*, Héctor Babenco's 1986 *Kiss of the Spider Woman* (filmed in Brazil and based on Argentine Manuel Puig's novel) and Eliseo Subiela's 1986 *Hombre mirando al sudeste* [*Man Facing Southeast*]. These are all examples of how film extracts myths and obsessions from collective experience and turns them into visual and thematic symbols, thus giving testimony of a time without necessarily resorting to a mimetic, documentary transcription of reality.

Fredric Jameson writes, in *The Political Unconscious*, that under every individual text lie collective and often unconscious political readings of reality. It'is the task of the critic, he asserts, to show how individual texts re-write "a prior historical or ideological 'subtext' [which] is not immediately present as such [. . .] but rather must itself always be (re)constructed after the fact" (81). This means that the critic must study the works not only as individual utterances but also as part of a collective voice that emerges from their sum total. A similar re-interpretive analysis can be performed on any social discourse (including that of films) by temporarily suppressing the uniqueness of the individual works in order to extract collective obsessions from them and see what they tell us about a period. As Andrew Sarris states in *Politics and Cinema*, films will thus present us with "recurring myths and fables deep within our psyches rather than transient impressions of the surface of our society" (4).

But these myths and fables are not universal—or rather, they are not *just* universal—for each specific socio-historical situation will create its own obsessions, symbolizing both personal and collective desires, fears and passions. In like manner, Argentine critic Andrés Avellaneda considers that every text addresses its audience by using society's specific cultural codes as its own organizing principle. By looking into what some of these codes are at a particular time, we will be able to organize the apparent chaos of motifs and techniques present in a number of disparate works into a pattern. Underneath the universality of certain themes and obsessions, the particular cultural codes employed by art in a given place and time will constitute a specific and unique way of dealing with reality. Furthermore, it is necessary to relate art to these cultural codes, because whereas certain symbols have a universal appeal, others can only be understood in relation to their specific social production during a given historical period and under certain circumstances. As K.R.M. Short notes in relation to the use of films as history, certain symbols are often "so deeply part of a particular social and historical context that the 'foreign observer' may be unaware of their emotive value" (28). Paul Monaco agrees when he writes that "movies offer insight into the psychic state of the time and place in which they are created," and thus they refer us to "the mental landscape at a given moment" (65, 74). That is to say, that even though we should not expect every film to carry an intended socio-political statement, we can safely assume every film to be socio-political and epochal either by including such a statement or by avoiding it. *The Official Story*, for example, will be more consciously political than the numerous light comedies produced during the military regime in Argentina. However, in terms of a historical analysis both types of cinema will exemplify the social production of meaning in their time. This is why it is necessary to analyze films—as well as novels, poems, political speeches, songs, etc.—not as individual utterances but as a repetitious collective voice which creates meaning through the reiteration and repetition of symbols.

Argentine film has often been inspired by historical events, and political history seems to provide it with endless raw material in a society always obsessed with national identity and ideological conflict. The first documentary ever produced in Buenos Aires was Eugenio Py's 1897 *La bandera argentina* [*The Argentine Flag*], where one can already see a premonitory symbol of the recurrent preoccupation with politics and national identity. As early as 1908, a local director, the Italian immigrant Mario Gallo, produced the first plot movie, *El fusilamiento de Dorrego* [*Dorrego's Execution*], drawing from a well-known incident during Argentina's post-independence civil wars (Sadoul, 434). It is evident that from early on filmmakers drew much of their inspiration from Argentine political history, as in 1910 other works followed Gallo's attempt to render the national past: *La creación del Himno* [*The Birth of the National Anthem*], *La Revolución de Mayo* [*The May Revolution*] and *La batalla de Maipú* [*The Battle of Maipú*] (Burns, 5). In subsequent decades well-known directors have also resorted to historical and political themes in their productions: Lucas Demare's *La guerra gaucha* [*The Gaucho War*], Leopoldo Torre Nilson's *El santo de la espada* [*The Saint of the Sword*] and *Guemes*, Fernando Solanas and Octavio Getino's *La hora de los hornos* [*The Hour of the Furnaces*], to name just a few. [1]

Argentine filmmakers very early became aware of the possibilities of film as a medium to convey political and historical content. This trend, which took place in most of Latin America, became particularly noticeable during the radicalization and optimism of the 1960's and early 1970's, when not only cinema but every form of art was perceived by progressive intellectuals and artists as a tool for social transformation. [2]

There was, in the cinematic production of this period, "an uncom-
promising affirmation of a national identity, which is linked to, indeed
inseparable from, the secondary themes of underdevelopment and
neocolonialism" (Wilson, 128). This was a peroid when filmmakers
regarded themselves not only in the process of representing reality but
also of transforming it through their militant and often uncompromisingly realistic films. In Argentina, this was the time of Solanas and
Getino's acclaimed 1968 *The Hour of the Furnaces*, produced and distributed through clandestine channels. The directors of this political
documentary set the tone of the ideological atmosphere of the time
when they declared the camera to be a "gun which shoots twenty-four
frames a second" (quoted in Burton, 49). The years immediately
preceding the military coup of 1976 witnessed the creation of a socially
committed cinema which explicitly focused on the politico-historical
reality of Argentina: Gerardo Vallejo's *El camino hacia la muerte del
viejo Reales* [*The Road Towards the Death of Old Man Reales*], on the life
of sugar plantation workers in the North; Jorge Cedrón's *Operación
Masacre* [*Operation Massacre*], on the clandestine execution of Peronist
activists by the military in 1956; Ricardo Wulicher's *Quebracho*, on the
exploitation of Argentine rural workers by a British company in the
1920's; Héctor Olivera's *La Patagonia rebelde* [*Rebellion in Patagonia*], on
the uprising and subsequent execution of hundreds of rural workers in
Patagonia in 1921; and Raymundo Gleyzer's *Los traidores* [*The Traitors*],
on the corrupt leadership of Peronist workers' unions in the 1970's. This
was also the time of the first threats against artists and intellectuals
by right-wing groups, which resulted in the forced exile and later the
kidnapping and disappearance of some important filmmakers and script-
writers after the 1976 coup: Raymundo Gleyzer, Diego Bonacina,
Haroldo Conti, Rodolfo Walsh. [3]

Films produced in the 1980's, after the social and ideological
transformations prompted by the "dirty war" of previous years, continue
to a great extent the tradition of rendering historical reality through art.
Recent history, as well as the question of what the writing of history
implies, is at the core of these works. Beginning with its very title, *The
Official Story* directs the public's attention to the problem of the constant
writing and re-writing of history in a country where the past still echoes,
influencing the present. The main character is a high school history
teacher who can teach everything about the events of the remote
national past but knows nothing about what happened during the
military repression of recent years. In a society where euphemism and
secrecy oftentimes replace an open look at events, and where the former

victimizers will use every means at their disposal to avoid the public condemnation of the "dirty war," a widespread mistrust of historiography and of the official versions of the past takes place. Accordingly, the film suggests that it is the role of art to express and make known the real stories that are kept hidden. By no coincidence, it is a colleague—a literature teacher and former political activist—who makes the protagonist aware of the real events that happened in the 1970's, while she would seek refuge in her traditional history textbooks. The symbol of this encounter between historiography and art takes place when the two teachers inadvertently run into each other, and he tells her: "Don't worry, literature and history always run into each other. . . ."

While *The Official Story* is an example of art re-writing history in a society denied access to the real facts, *Kiss of the Spider Woman* is a metaphor for the necessity of individuals to tell new versions of events. Molina, a homosexual imprisoned with a political activist, tells him about an old Nazi propaganda film he has seen, and in so doing he combines his memory and his own interpretation of it. The Nazi movie and its depiction of wicked Jews and corrupt Resistance fighters is an example of manipulation of facts through art, and so the activist blames Molina for not realizing that he is being deceived. However, Molina shows himself to be perfectly aware of the false official story told by the Nazi film, and by using it as a metaphor for his own search for personal fulfillment, he is in fact "re-writing" it. *Camila,* the true story of a young Buenos Aires woman who in the mid-1800's became the lover of a priest and was later executed for her daring behavior, is another example of the clash between official and alternative versions of the past. Whereas Argentine historians have traditionally been divided over the role of the Unitarian and Federal parties in post-independence Argentina, the filmmaker decides to throw a new light on the past by presenting the protagonist as a victim of *both* parties. Furthermore, she gives a new twist to Camila's story, which had been the subject of numerous prior literary versions: "Usually women are portrayed as vulnerable, innocent victims. So I decided that Camila was going to be the aggressive one and seduce the priest. That's feminism!" (quoted in Kogan, 37). Finally, *Man Facing Southeast* is also a re-writing of history as it combines the Biblical story of the Messiah with Argentine present reality through allusion and metaphor. It thus offers a new version of both the plight of Jesus and of the victims of intolerance in today's Argentina, where each gives the other a new meaning.

History and politics are thus once again at the heart of these films, as part of a tradition going back to the origins of national cinema. However, a profound change has taken place in Argentina, and correspond-ingly in its artistic representations. The four films here analyzed follow the steps of the recent Argentine novel in not resorting to a mimetic reproduction of history. As much as modern fiction distrusts the mimetic fallacy of pretending to mirror reality with words, these films avoid direct historical referentiality. Instead, they speak of recent political events by a displacement similar to that of Argentine fiction, which in the 1980's produces relatively few "realistic," testimonial novels. While recent history is present in all four movies through the use of epochal cultural codes, only one—*The Official Story*—contains direct references to the "dirty war," whereas the others present a strong symbolism by means of non-referential plot lines.

Camila is perhaps the best example of this strategy. Despite a temporal displacement—it is based on events of nineteenth-century Argentina—an audience provided with Argentine cultural codes will find numerous references to the present and translate its symbols into contemporary political allusions. Among other things, the official investigation on human rights abuses showed an unusually high number of pregnant women among the victims of political assassination in the 1970's, a fact which has left an imprint in the collective memory. Thus, when confronted with the death by firing squad of Camila and her unborn child, the Argentine viewer cannot help but think of recent history. Camila's demand that she be given a fair trial before being shot, and the subsequent denial of her request, can be read as another reference to modern political disappearances and assassinations. So does the reference to emigration in nineteenth-century Argentina as the equivalent of death, a clear reminder of the emigration of thousands during the 1970's. Finally, cruelty towards animals—a recurrent metaphor for political violence in recent Argentine fiction—is present in the film as well: Camila's father has her little kittens drowned in the sea, an obvious and chilling reminder to the Argentine viewer of the technique used by the military for the disposal of the disappeared, thousands of whom were thrown alive from helicopters into the sea.

Whereas in *Camila* the displacement is temporal, in *Man Facing Southeast* it is spatial, by making the world of a Buenos Aires psychiatric hospital an image of Argentina in the 1970's. An interpretation of Rantes—the madman who claims to come from another planet—as a symbol of the disappeared cannot be ruled out. In a country where thousands have vanished, the doctor's surprise at the report that there is one patient too many rather than the all-too-common one missing, is especially significant. Rantes, who mysteriously appears as a Christ-like figure arrived on Earth in order to save humanity, is also a symbol for those who were killed in the 1970's because they tried to transform society. Rantes claims to be not a bodily presence but a hologram, an image projected in space, which moves, talks and looks real but cannot be touched. For a society obsessed with the memory of its disappeared, the hologram metaphor is clear; as the madman tells the doctor, "you can close your eyes and yet I still exist." In the end, he dies a Christ-like death, with the film making the parallel explicit by scenes which visually resemble the crucifixion. But we are also told that Rantes dies of a heart attack caused by electroshocks, a clear allusion to the most common form of torture during the "dirty war": electric shocks.

A recurrent preoccupation in contemporary Argentina is the perception of political violence as a cyclical phenomenon. In the films, this takes the form of numerous characters reproducing dramatic events lived by their predecessors. In *Camila*, the protagonist's grandmother is imprisoned for life in a tower for having been the mistress of a former viceroy, decades earlier. Her only crime is to have associated herself with a political foe of the new revolutionary government. She embodies everything Camila will later become: a passionate woman in the midst of a repressive society, a victim of political struggles she does not fully comprehend. It is not surprising, then, to find Camila in yet another tower at the end of the story, herself a victim of the same intolerance that condemned her grandmother.

There is also a cyclical repetition in *The Official Story*, embodied by the protagonist and her daughter. Alicia's story about how her parents had died when she was a child, and how she had been told they were on a trip and would soon come back, prefigures her own dilemma in dealing with the adopted child who belongs to a young disappeared couple. The cyclical nature of the tragedy is reinforced by a visual effect: Alicia recounts how she waited for her parents, sitting in a rocking chair, unaware that they would never come back, and at the end of the film the adopted child is rocking in a chair and waiting in like manner. *Man Facing Southeast* presents the unexpected appearance of the madman as a repetition of the Biblical story. He reenacts the fate of the savior who is sacrificed by those he comes to save. When we see him perform small miracles and speak in parables to his small crowd of followers, we can foresee that he too, like his predecessor Jesus, will be condemned by an incredulous society.

The perception of political violence as a phenomenon of a cyclical nature is one of the cultural codes of the period. To view violence as a rational endeavor performed by perfectly logical people through a bureaucracy of death is another. After the Holocaust humankind was confronted with the utter rationality that lay behind the apparent irrationality of the genocide. In *On Violence*, Hannah Arendt asserts that violence is neither irrational nor animal but instead a very rational outcome of the circumstances that make it possible (63). So does John Fraser in *Violence in the Arts* when writing: "Far from being mindless, violence is usually the cutting edge of ideas and ideologies" (162). In the case of Argentina's "dirty war," society perceives the kind of "banality of evil" attributed by Arendt to the Holocaust, as well as the technologization of state repression against its own citizens. Therefore, the conflict that takes place is often one between a passionless, rational repressive apparatus on the one hand, and its victims, full of passion and human feelings, on the other. In the films, passion is often equated with the victims and reason with the outside forces that victimize them.

In *Kiss of the Spider Woman*, the homosexual must teach the activist how to have feelings in order to become a freer man: Valentín is as much a prisoner of the government as of his own extreme rationality, which is not much different from that of his enemies. In the end, a certain measure of freedom is gained by Valentín when he learns the value of passion and compassion. A similar opposition takes place in *Camila*, where the lovers embody the force of unrestrained and irrational passion against the rational needs of a political system which cannot permit the former in its midst. Rantes, who in *Man Facing Southeast* claims to have no feelings and to come from a planet of totally rational beings, surprises the psychiatrist by having an unexpected outburst of anger which proves him to be fully human. Even the protagonist's husband in *The Official Story*, a cold and cerebral man in his role as a passive accomplice to the kidnappings, in the end becomes a more rounded figure when crying over the possible loss of his adopted child. Thus, in all four films passion is equated with humanity, in opposition to what is perceived as a rational and passionless bureaucratic mechanism for the victimization of individuals.

Enclosed space is another recurrent paradigm both in Argentine film and fiction of the 1980's. In the novels not only prisons, boarding schools, hospitals and other similar institutions serve as metaphors for the constrainment of the human body, but additionally tunnels, subways, trains, bedrooms, pyramids and closets are symbolic spaces which manifest an obsession with psychological asphyxiation. This responds not only to a widespread perception of the country under military rule as a gigantic prison from which there is no escape, but particularly to the very tangible existence of hundreds of secret detention places—army bases, police stations, concentration camps—from which it was very unlikely one could emerge alive. Even though these places were supposed to remain beyond public knowledge, their existence was well known through collective rumor and clandestine opposition propaganda, contributing to the widespread feeling of terror and helplessness.[4] In *Camila, Kiss of the Spider Woman* and *Man Facing Southeast*, we find characters imprisoned, locked up in towers, and kept in psychiatric hospitals. These places may not only refer to the historical reality of the secret detention camps where dissidents were tortured and killed, but also, in a broader sense, to oppression in contemporary life. Physical enclosure in these films manifests a cultural code in an Argentina where imprisonment and destruction of the dissident body is the logical outcome of other techniques of social control. There is no real escape from these places. Camila flees Buenos Aires with her priestly lover but is later captured, jailed in a tower, like her grandmother before her, and eventually executed. The homosexual in *Kiss of the Spider Woman* is released from prison by the authorities only to be used as bait to trap the activist's comrades, and is subsequently killed. Rantes is free to leave the mental institution but soon realizes there is no room for his ideas on the outside, and he has no choice but to remain in the hospital and die.

Closely associated with this obsession, there is in film as well as in fiction a recurrent visual and thematic use of the blindfold and the hood. As proved by the official report of the Commission on Human Rights Abuses, during the "dirty war" military forces in almost every case covered their victims' eyes, an action that was referred to as *tabicamiento* ("walling up"). This not only prevented the victims from recognizing their captors in the unlikely event that they were later freed, but more importantly terrorized them and rendered them psychologically helpless. The feelings of impotence and anguish produced by the blindfold are well summed-up in one of the many novels which allude to the subject, Miguel Bonasso's 1984 *Recuerdo de la muerte* [*Remembrance of Death*], based on the true story of a detainee who managed to escape from a concentration camp. This is how the main character recalls his experiences: "The whole world remains in shadows. Beyond the coarse and greasy fabric covering one's face lies a universe of threats. The comrades, the relatives, the friends are not there. The hood has suppressed all history and all future [. . .]. It not only prevents one from looking outward, it forces one to look inward" (my translation, 37). The topic of the blindfold and the hood has thus become pervasive in recent Argentine culture; the lack of vision serves as the ultimate symbol for the absence of freedom in general. In *The Official Story*, Alicia's closest friend recalls being hooded and hearing the voice of her torturer. She fears that she might one day recognize that dreaded voice in the street. This scene functions as the turning point, after which Alicia becomes aware of political reality. *Camila* alludes to the same cultural obsession by showing the protagonist blindfolded in two crucial scenes: with a white blindfold playing "Blind Man's Bluff" when she meets her priest/ lover for the first time, and with a black one when they are both executed at the end. In *Kiss of the Spider Woman*, the director incorporates the topic even though it is missing from the original novel. Thematically, the presence in the movie of a blindfolded prisoner who prompts the activist to reveal some secret information is essential for plot resolution. There is also symbolic blindfolding when the director chooses to show the prisoners in the only cell whose doors are covered with solid planks, which visually reinforce their sense of isolation from the outside world. *Man Facing Southeast* starts with a scene apparently unrelated to the main plot, where a mental patient recalls a homicide and suicide attempt: the nightmarish and almost surreal vision of two hooded figures trying to kiss while blood runs down their white hoods is but another reminder of this cultural obsession. So is a later scene where Rantes turns around the head of a small cardboard human figure used for psychological tests, as if to prevent it from seeing. [5]

What seems to unify all four films into a single voice is their confessional tone as part of a collective analysis of the past taking place in today's Argentina. In a society torn between revision or obliteration of the past, art seems to spearhead a much needed soul-searching process. Numerous intellectuals and artists have in recent years analyzed the atmosphere of collective intolerance and authoritarianism prevalent in the Argentina of the 1970's and have assumed part of the responsibility for it. Film director Fernando Solanas sums up the widespread need to revise the past when saying: [Ours] was a generation that needed to break away from the old, but [in trying to do so] we wouldn't conduct a dialogue with a political adversary, we would underestimate him and try to suppress him" (my translation, interview by Ulanovsky). [6] This explains in part the recurrent topic of confession in all four films. In *The Official Story*, Alicia's friend tells of her abduction and torture as if she were confessing it, a typical inversion by which the victim speaks of her victimization with guilt. Later on, prompted by her friend's revelations, Alicia shares her own fears and guilt with a priest. Finally, in order to obtain the truth in relation to her adopted child, she must elicit a confession from her husband, since he is the only one who knows the girl's true origin. *Camila* also revolves around confessions. The protagonist reveals her erotic dreams to her confessor and lover-to-be, who in turn confesses his lust to his Superior and later on his guilt in front of a crucifix. In the end, both lovers confess in jail before dying. The biblical symbolism of *Man Facing Southeast* also calls for this recurrent image when the madmen line up at night to confess to Rantes, whom they take for the Savior. *Kiss of the Spider Woman* in turn is a prolonged mutual confession between the two men imprisoned together, where each opens up his heart to the other and reveals his most intimate fears, flaws and desires.

So what is it that Argentine society is confessing through the recurrent cultural obsessions of these films, as well as through novels, poems and songs? In the face of political violence, society seems to question its identity, responsibilities and past Manichaeanism and authoritarianism. Violence fractures personal and collective identity and forces an ontological transformation where old assumptions are shattered. If the Holocaust prompted George Steiner to speak of a "post-Auschwitz *homo sapiens*" (163), it is also possible to conceive of a "post-dirty-war Argentinian" who needs to redefine himself or herself. Ernesto Sábato, well-known novelist and President of the Commission on Human Rights Abuses, summed up a national feeling when he declared, after the investigation: "I am not the same person I used to be. We saw too much horror" (my translation, interview by Aulicino). The questioning of one's identity becomes a collective obsession manifested in the films by persistent doubts about who the characters really are. The protagonist of *Man Facing Southeast* is three different persons in one: an alien from another planet, according to himself; a madman, according to society; and Jesus, according to the other patients. It is by no coincidence that Rantes has no recorded fingerprints in the police files, a most unusual situation in a country where every citizen must at all times carry a card with photographs and fingerprints for identification purposes. When told by the psychiatrist that his fingerprints will be taken in order to find out who he really is, Rantes answers: "If my prints should match someone who's dead, don't be scared," an allusion to the anonymous victims of the 1970's, whose identities were suppressed. The question of personal identity becomes even more pressing in *The Official Story*, where Alicia's obsessive search revolves around the true identity of her adopted child. The priest of *Camila* is forced to choose between his old self as a member of the Church and his new self as Camila's lover, under an assumed name. And *Kiss of the Spider Woman* is a painful search for identity on the part of both characters, where the homosexual must find his political self as much as the heterosexual must find the feminine aspect locked within his personality.

One of many forms this obsession takes both in fiction and in film is the use of photographs to signal the absence or presence of a memory of people's past. In *The Official Story*, the grandmother of the child adopted by the protagonist only possesses a handful of pictures as a reminder of the disappeared parents' plight. The photographs are both a symbol of a past that refuses to fade away and an element that triggers a possible resolution in the future. In effect, they reveal the true identity of the disappeared in a literal as well as a metaphorical way: when the protagonist is shown old pictures of the child's parents, she is confronted with the striking physical resemblance between the child and the young couple in the pictures. The scene where the grandmother produces the handful of photographs is thus a revelation and a turning point after which the protagonist's life is changed forever, since she now knows where the child came from. It should be noted that there are two previous moments of revelation which also contribute to the protagonist's progressive transformation, and that both of them are related to photographs. The first is when her students post pictures on the blackboard of children abducted with their parents during the "dirty war." The second consists of her witnessing a demonstration by mothers of the disappeared, who carry large photographs of the victims of state terrorism. In another film, *Man Facing Southeast*, a mysterious photo with one half missing is the clue to the madman's unresolved past. The psychiatrist needs to find out who or what was represented in the missing part next to Rantes—his father? another person?—in order to find a solution to the riddle of Rantes' identity. In this case the search ends with the protagonist's refusal to speak. [7]

An all-encompassing cultural code seems to tinge all four films, in agreement with the main obsession of Argentine society today: the need for a non-Manichean, non-authoritarian interpretation of reality. Artists and intellectuals, not satisfied with explaining the motivations of those who committed the crimes in the 1970's, attempt to explain the social milieu which made those crimes possible. It does not suffice to blame the Other without recognizing traits of the Other in the Self. Numerous recent studies stress the so-called "seeds of intolerance" already present in Argentina before the "dirty war," not as something foreign to its social fabric but as an intimate part of it. As sociologist Juan Corradi writes, when there is official violence and authoritarianism there is also "a proliferation of micro-despotisms" at all levels of society (119). [8] In film, there is a recurrent question about individual and collective responsibility for society's flaws. *Camila* takes a non-traditional stand in relation to the historical events surrounding the young woman's death. By suggesting that both the Federal and the Unitarian parties were responsible for Camila's tragic fate in the past century, and by placing part of the blame on her father's personal ambitions, the film forces the Argentine audience to review its own attitudes and political sympathies during the 1970's. Individual responsibility is also at stake in *The Official Story*, because Alicia is guilty of having chosen not to know the real events by never questioning the true origin of her adopted child. Valentín, the revolutionary in *Kiss of the Spider Woman*, is also guilty of reproducing the same oppressive sexuality he criticizes in his jailers. As he acknowledges at one point, "I am not any different from them." Individual responsibility is also at the center of *Man Facing Southeast*, where the doctor, calling himself a revisited Pontius Pilate, may be able to wash his hands but not his conscience for Rantes' death.

In conclusion, these films, by their use of symbols and obsessions borrowed from Argentine cultural codes, participate in an ongoing process of reconstruction and reinterpretation of the recent past. The Argentine directors analyzed here know that society does not demand from them a mimetic reproduction of reality. However, they seem to be equally aware of the fact that every aesthetic or artistic production is, in Jameson's words, "an ideological act in its own right, with the function of inventing imaginary or formal 'solutions' to unresolvable social contradictions" (79). Thus, they intuitively or consciously attempt to contribute to the understanding of Argentine political reality by organizing the chaos of collective experience in their artistic representations.

Notes

1. On the subject of films of socio-historical content before the 1940's in Argentina, see E. Bradford Burns' "National Identity in Argentine Films." Among others, Burns mentions Alcides Greca's 1917 film *El último malón* [*The Last Indian Attack*], based on a 1904 Indian uprising, as well as numerous early works on the subject of the "gaucho," the symbol par excellence of Argentine identity: *La nobleza gaucha* [*Gaucho Virtue*] of 1915, *Campo ajuera* [*Remote Land*] of 1919, *La gaucha* [*The Gaucho Girl*] of 1912. etc.

2. On this period of Latin American political film see, among others, David Wilson, "Aspects of Latin American Political Cinema"; John Mossier, "Currents in Latin American Film"; Julianne Burton, "The Camera as 'Gun': Two Decades of Culture and Resistance in Latin America"; and E. Bradford Burns, "The Latin American Film, Realism, and the Historian."

3. On the Argentine cinema of the 1970's, see the corresponding section in Alfonso Gumucio Dagron's *Cine, censura y exilio en América Latina*, 11–46. Also, Steven Kovacs' "Screening the Movies in Argentina," for an explanation of the brief period of liberalization after 1973, when Octavio Getino was appointed Chair of the Film Qualification Board.

4. This is also part of the new punitive technology I have mentioned before. In order to ensure optimum results, the repressive apparatus had to act in secrecy while letting the population know enough of what was happening so as to keep society in a state of constant terror. At the same time, in order to avoid international and domestic pressure it was necessary to conduct the interrogations and killings in clandestine centers whose existence was not acknowledged

by the State. In the sentencing of the ex-commanders-in-chief accused of human rights abuses in 1985, under the constitutional government of Dr. Alfonsín, the prosecution stated that a repressive network of more than 300 centers functioned in "the most absolute clandestinity; in order to do so, the kidnappers had to conceal their identities and conduct their raids preferably at night, the victims had to remain in total solitary confinement with their eyes blindfolded, and all government officials, relatives or acquaintances had to be denied knowledge of the existence of the kidnapped victim as well as of the supposed places of detention" (my translation; *El Diario del Juicio* II, No. 36 [1986]: 16).

5. As Mario Cesareo points out in an article on the Argentine novel of the period, power relations are manifested through the body. Therefore, repression and social control are symbolized by the suppression or obstruction of those parts through which the body communicates with the world: eyes, ears, mouth. As Cesareo notes, deafness, muteness, blindness, paralysis and mutilation are recurrent metaphors in this literature. The use of the blindfold in the films serves the same metaphorical purpose. The closing scene of Adolfo Aristarain's 1983 film *Tiempo de revancha* [*Time for Revenge*] [viscerally illustrates the consequences of such repression]. The protagonist of this thriller, filmed shortly before the final collapse of the military regime, pretends to become mute as a result of a job-related accident in order to claim some insurance money. But when the bosses try to expose the hoax and prove that he can indeed talk, he must resort to a desperate action in order to avoid detection: he [cuts] his tongue off with a razor. This is a clear allusion to self-censorship and self-imposed silence in Argentina after seven years of political terror, when the retreat into the secluded domain of private life became a survival technique.

6. It is therefore interesting to compare Solanas' statements after the "dirty war" to his previous concept of the "camera as a gun" in the late 1960's and early 1970's. Writing in 1978 with *The Hour of the Furnaces* in mind, Julianne Burton notes that "Fernando Solanas and Octavio Getino have subscribed to the same over-simplified Manichaeism. They argue that only two forms of culture compete in the neo-colonial situation: that of the 'rulers' and that of the 'nation' " (58). This is obviously no longer true in the 1980's, when most artists and intellectuals are willing to accept that politico-historical reality is more ambiguous and subject to multiple interpretations than previously thought. In the case of Solanas, one should compare the documentary realism and overtly propagandistic purpose of his 1968 *The Hour of the Furnaces*, to the dream-like surrealism of his latest movies, *Sur* [*South*] and *El exilio de Gardel* [*Gardel's Exile*].

7. It should be noted that in numerous fictional pieces of the period, photographs as well as letters are symbols of identity and personal freedom. Their absence or their being taken away often represent the loss of control over one's own life and history. In Daniel Moyano's novel *El vuelo del tigre* (1981), a small town becomes an allegory of Argentina in the 1970's when mysterious invaders occupy homes and force townspeople to radically transform their lives. Among other oppressive measures adopted, every photo and letter must be surrendered to the invaders, who thus control the people's language and memory

of the past. A similar situation arises in Enrique Medina's short story "Los intrusos," from the volume *Los asesinos* (1984), where another family's privacy is invaded by a stranger who also forces them to give him all [their] photos, letters, books, musical records, old newspapers and magazines, in order to deprive them of their own identity. In Carlos Gorostiza's novel *Los cuartos oscuros* (1976), the protagonist is a photographer whose camera is taken away when he is imprisoned in order to prevent him from recording reality; he manages to survive by using his eyes and his memory as a secret camera which will reveal the real events one day.

8. In this respect, a new film being produced by the young director Carlos Sorín, *Eternas sonrisas de New Jersey* [*Eternal Smiles from New Jersey*], seems to be one more example of the metaphorical analysis of authoritarianism in Argentine society. In the film, a dentist is sent to Patagonia on a medical crusade aimed at improving dental health among the local population. Eventually he becomes a fanatic and ends up viewing cavities and bacteria as incarnations of Evil that must be eliminated by any means. When interviewed about his project, Sorín notes: "He, like every fanatic, strives for perfection, he wants to defeat corruption" (my translation, interview by Ulanovsky). There is here an obvious allusion to the presence of Manichean discourses in Argentina, with the fanatical dentist as a telling metaphor for the ideological crusaders of the 1970's. The metaphor of society as a sick organism in need of a radical cure is typical of a repressive discourse which speaks of removing sick cells from the social body, amputating unhealthy limbs, restoring social health and eliminating the subversive virus. Not coincidentally, the same organicist metaphor appears in the motivations of Miguel Paulino Tato, appointed head of the board in charge of film censorship in 1974. Although still under the constitutional government of Isabel Perón, Tato already embodied the ideology that would permeate the military regime after 1976, as can be seen in his declarations referring to cinema: "Well-exercised censorship is hygienic and highly beneficial, like surgery. Let us *cure and disinfect unhealthy pictures and root out the harmful tumors that make movies sick and contaminate the spectators"* (my emphasis; quoted in Kovacs, 20).

Works Cited

Arendt, Hannah. *On Violence*. New York: Harcourt, Brace & World, Inc., 1969, 1970.

Aulicino, Jorge Ricardo. Interview with Ernesto Sábato. "Sobre el Nobel y la literatura." *Clarín Cultura y Nación* (28 agosto 1986): 3.

Avellaneda, Andrés. *El habla de la ideología. Modos de réplica literaria en la Argentina contemporánea*. Buenos Aires: Editorial Sudamericana, 1983.

Bonasso, Miguel. *Recuerdo de la muerte*. Buenos Aires: Bruguera, 1984.

Burns, E. Bradford. "National Identity in Argentine Films." *Americas* Vol. 27, Nos. 11–12 (November–December 1975): 4–10.

_____. "The Latin American Film, Realism, and the Historian." *The History Teacher* Vol. VI, No. 4 (August 1973): 69–74.

Burton, Julianne. "The Camera as 'Gun': Two Decades of Culture and Resistance in Latin America." *Latin American Perspectives* Vol. V, No. 1, Issue 16 (Winter 1978): 49–76.

Cesareo, Mario. "Cuerpo humano e historia en la novela del Proceso." *Fascismo y experiencia literaria: reflexiones para una recanonización*. Ed. Hernán Vidal. Minneapolis: Institute for the Study of Ideologies and Literature, 1985. 501–31.

Corradi, Juan E. "The Culture of Fear in Civil Society." *From Military Rule to Liberal Democracy in Argentina*. Ed. Mónica Peralta-Ramos and Carlos H. Waisman. Boulder and London: Westview Press, 1987. 113–29.

Fraser, John. *Violence in the Arts*. 1974; Cambridge: Cambridge University Press, 1976.

Gumucio Dagron, Alfonso. *Cine, censura y exilio en América Latina*. La Paz, Bolivia: Ediciones film/historia, 1979.

Jameson, Fredric. *The Political Unconscious: Narrative as a Socially Symbolic Act*. Ithaca, New York: Cornell University Press, 1981.

Kogan, Marcela. "Overcoming Insecurities." *Americas* Vol. 37, No. 5 (September–October 1985): 37–39.

Kovacs, Steven. "Screening the Movies in Argentina." *New Boston Review* Vol 3, No. 3 (December 1977): 19–21.

Monaco, Paul. "Movies and National Consciousness: Germany and France in the 1920s." *Feature Films as History*. Ed. K.R.M. Short. Knoxville: The University of Tennessee Press. 62–75.

Mossier, John. "Currents in Latin American Film." *Americas* Vol. 30, No. 5 (May 1978): 2–8.

Sadoul, Georges. *Histoire du cinema*. Paris: Librarie Flammarion, 1962.

Sarris, Andrew. *Politics and Cinema*. New York: Columbia University Press, 1978.

Steiner, George. *Language and Silence: Essays on Language, Literature, and the Inhuman*. New York: Atheneum, 1967.

Ulanovsky, Carlos. Interview with Fernando Solanas. "Un filme es una angustia que se vive con el cuerpo." *Clarín Edición Internacional* (2–8 mayo 1988): 10–11.

Wilson, David. "Aspects of Latin American Political Cinema." *Sight and Sound* Vol. 41, No. 3 (Summer 1972): 127–131.

MANUEL ALCIDES JOFRÉ

Culture, Art, and Literature in Chile: 1973–1985

(Cultural productions, from music and painting to theater and literature, are part of a society's worldview. The author shows the effects of an authoritarian government on recent cultural developments in Chile.)

Chile has been under military authoritarian rule since 1973. During this time, new cultural expressions, both rich and complex, have appeared. Now, after 15 years, these developments can be evaluated from a broad perspective[1] and a synthesis can be offered. The present work is an interdisciplinary approach that examines some aspects of high, formal, or learned culture. In Chile, as in any other national case, cultural production implies a specific, professional, and autonomous field. The results of this research are presented and organized in different artistic areas that are to be understood as relatively autonomous fields within a larger social and cultural context. Each artistic area exhibits characteristic modes of production, exchange, and consumption of specific meanings.[2]

Culture is understood here as a continuous production of meaning by means of human activity. The symbolic levels of any society are constituted by a set of semiautonomous cultural fields that are nevertheless in interaction with each other. The actual agents of these cultural

Manuel Alcides Jofré, "Culture, Art, and Literature in Chile: 1973–1985" (*Latin American Perspectives*, Issue 61, Vol. 16, No. 2, Spring 1989), 70–95, © Latin American Perspectives, reprinted by permission of Sage Publications, Inc.

areas are the intellectuals who set in motion diverse institutions by means of communicational processes in which cultural and aesthetic signs are produced, exchanged, and consumed.[3]

Consequently, culture is defined here as a multidimensional phenomenon, as a way of life of a people, and as complex communication processes. There is no social experience outside the universe or domain of culture. Each national culture is a system of signifying systems made up of several social codes containing already accumulated data. This polyphony of sign systems organizes the world for people. Culture, the collective self of a community, its social identity, is in a constant process of articulation and disarticulation. It functions as a multiple structure, a dynamic polyglotism in which each field (theater, painting, music, fiction, poetry) contains different modes of cultural and artistic production. Such is the case in today's Chilean social formation.[4]

Chilean culture (like other national cultures) comprises social practices, worldviews, material objects, and linguistic signs. These are components of society's power blocs, or condensations of collective wills, the essential infrastructure of politics. These social practices, worldviews, objects, or words are not part of closed static discourses. They are in a permanent state of instability, in constant processes of exchange and reorganization.

This notion of culture does not coincide with any particular apparatus, industry, or field. Culture is the whole set of signifying practices and products that convey meaning to a total society, for culture is nothing but society signifying. All social actors are active agents. Culture pervades the totality of a social formation and becomes synonymous with it (see Catalán and Rivera, 1983: 9). Art is an essential dimension of social life; thus artistic praxis is, too, a cultural practice. Art, or any one of its specific fields (painting, poetry, theater, or music), is a system within culture, and it consists of a specific mode of creating an aesthetic reality, which can also be read in reference to its context.

THE NATIONAL AND CULTURAL CONTEXT

Within this framework, Chilean cultural and artistic structural changes refer, first, to the authoritarian experiment of "national refoundation," under the initial impulse of neoliberalism, whereby the market confronts politics, and, second, to a national security theory that sees citizens' opposition as subversion.

From a cultural standpoint, the military regime has attempted to reorganize everyday life by halting the democratic development of culture. Plural and public expressions were officially eliminated from the outset. Then, some sectorized cultural conflicts emerged and expanded, and the worldviews that had been defeated, controlled, and repressed, reemerged and reestablished themselves once again. These interactions or responses, generally referred to as resistance or alternative culture, are made up of popular, highbrow, and ideological culture (see Jofré, 1984b). The new symbolic spaces, as they are called in Chile, perform the function of reconnecting with the historical past. Spaces of creation, re-creation, and communication represent strategies of diverse social groups. Gradually during the 1980s, patterns of competition and consensus have been reintroduced within the cultural arena.

In today's Chile, antagonistic views about Chilean society coexist as everyday cultural life has become more diversified. Historical, democratic, and cultural pasts cannot be continuously negated. Simultaneously, Chilean culture has tried to overcome the strong political and ideological influence that has characterized it. Torn between the economicist logic of the marketplace and the authoritarian logic of exclusion, Chilean culture and art have become part of a process whereby political and cultural spaces must be conquered as part of the struggle for hegemony. Since Chilean culture has been admittedly politicized since its origins, it has become a central case for the study of the relationship between cultural production and political praxis. The vicissitudes of repression in Chile, which might be due to political authoritarian policies, could also be related to new right-wing or neoliberal policies, which have deeply affected the different phases of recent cultural developments.

The regime's cultural policies have stemmed from its centralized position in command of the state apparatus. Regardless of the name assigned to the factions in power, they all belong to one side of the political spectrum. As part of the power bloc, they constitute the center. In contrast, democratic culture is a term that designates all those other cultural strategies that confront and challenge the official and centralist authoritarian view and constitute the margins or periphery.

Another taxonomy frequently used here for describing artistic and cultural experiences is the understanding of Chilean society as intersected by different types of circuits, which are usually termed macrocircuits or microcircuits. Microcircuits are those that correspond to the local community level, and generally this level consists of the cultural expressions of the dispossessed. Microcircuits are unofficial, informal, and nonprofessional cultural and artistic activities that integrate popular culture. On the other hand, macrocircuits tend to be institutionalized, formal, learned, and official. Macrocircuits correspond to national art and cultural activities, are professional in origin, and tend to convey formal and elite culture through official channels.

Chilean art and culture are also seen here as unitarian structures, organized in different strata such as learned, mass, and popular culture. Learned culture is a formal, aristocratic, elitarian, or highbrow culture that reflects what the upper social groups think they are or would like to be. Mass culture is a mesocratic and modern culture that tends to correspond to intermediate social sectors, such as the Chilean middle class. Chilean mass culture is fed by the so-called cultural industry (in the Frankfurt School terms), and by the transnational cultural industries. These two cultural levels have been maintained and developed by the economic, political, and cultural policies put into practice by the military regime. The third cultural stratum is popular culture. In North American terminology, popular culture corresponds to mass culture. In Chile, popular culture is created by marginal cultural groups, mainly at the amateur level, although according to some understandings the concept could also apply to professional activities competing with the officially organized cultural and artistic circuits in Chile (see Jofré, 1986b: 2–3). Popular culture is definitely associated with the left-wing worldview. The term *populism*, which is not used here, could, however, be applied to some parts of cultural policies developed both by the military regime and by the opposition parties.[5]

CHANGES IN THE SOCIAL COMMUNICATION PROCESSES

It is evident to anyone who lived in Chile before 1973 that drastic social changes have occurred during the last 15 years. For many, life has become restricted to the intimate world of family and home. The evident fragmentation of Chilean society has led to permanent distrust. Self-repression, disciplinary hierarchies, traumas, torture, and death have certainly taken their toll.

Chileans have changed their public behavior. Today in the streets, few groups can be seen; there is almost no loud conversation on buses; the volume of discourse in public places has been lowered; and body language has become more restricted. What really has been reduced is everybody's social aura, that psychological space within which one travels wherever one goes. Chileans project themselves differently now. Everything is kept inside. They walk with their heads down, arms held closely to the body, self-centered, looking furtively around them, or simply looking out. Fixed patterns of social behavior have been imposed. Appearance becomes more important than reality. The only truth is defined by the one-way vertical and official monologue of coercive power.

In Chile, communicational space contains a restricted public space and a plurality of voices who interpret society and try to enforce collective identities; some of those actors do not have access to the emission of public communication. The macrocircuits of communication (television, press, radio) only reproduce the official discourse. On the other hand, at the level of local communication (microcircuits), both the government and the opposition have developed projects. [6]

Before 1973, Chilean communicational systems allowed for differences of opinion. The authoritarian regime changed that, first, via economic transformation and, second, through the alteration of the national communication apparatus. The alteration of the communication system started with the reduction and transfer of private independent and leftist modes of communication to the authoritarian state. The social sectors that defended democracy were expelled from the public space and were placed under permanent observation. The communication circuit has been watched over and controlled, as has the information conveyed. During six years, from 1977 to 1983, all printed material was censored. Only recently have books been released from this rule. In any case, all artistic and communication processes have been affected by censorship and self-censorship.

The "refoundation" of capitalism in Chile brought with it a liberal market economy. This violent global change disarticulated the previous social discourse as the market became the determining force. Communication processes not only advertise consumer products but convey consumer values that contribute to social integration by creating pseudo-subjects. Another new element in the communication circuits is the prevalence of entertainment, usually provided by canned programs obtained from the transnational entertainment corporations. The functions of the public "structure of reception" have also been modified as a result of the increasing numbers of TV and radio receivers; demand for the press has contracted. Newspapers have attempted to counteract by adding different supplements every day of the week, directed to specialized audiences. Artistic transformations in the Chilean social space have affected both professional and amateur levels. These changes imply both continuities and ruptures. The artistic world was modified by the new authoritarian order in three different ways: by eliminating agents physically, by changing working conditions, and by allowing or forbidding certain forms or contents in the artistic messages.

The history of culture in Chile goes through phases as it responds to changes in situations. After the initial disarticulation and atomization, culture began to be used as an organic, politically cohesive strategy by both the oppressor and the oppressed. The defeated and subordinated groups opened up some organic spaces with unquestioned legitimacy, such as occurred in the case of those belonging to the Chilean Catholic church.

Among the change[s] that resulted from the new global situation, of special importance was the institutional dismantling of the state. University departments and degree studies in music, fine arts, theater, literature, and other disciplines were reduced; in some cases, they entirely disappeared. Artistic activities and products were then forced to turn to the market, where private institutions could choose and contribute to artists. This movement toward privatization accompanied new government policies and institutions, among them artistic projects within state ministries, museums, and city halls. The determining influence of the market has also been seen in the rearticulation of the cultural industry, especially in the predominance given to television, where hegemonic control rests in the hands of the state, and increased advertising is now to be found in all forms of communication.

Under the new conditions, social discourses initially became very private, turning public only after 1976. The artistic languages became symbolic, alluding to the objective in unexplicit ways. Symbols were also widely used (by artists such as Neruda and Violeta Parra) as a means of identification. However, the official culture of the regime has always been dominant over the alternative democratic culture. For instance, there has been no response by either side to the new rearticulation of Chilean cultural levels, where former marginal products have now become central, as is the case of mass culture.

Within this framework of culture and communications, several systems of artistic practice in Chile, such as music, visual arts, theater, and literature, will now be examined in detail as examples of contemporary modes of cultural production in Chile.

Music

The formative role of the state in Chilean musical activities came to an end in 1973. Folklore (both country and urban) diminished; there has been no growth of classical music. The cultural industry has disseminated mostly commercial popular music, initially designed for international consumption. Functional music and background music (for advertising) took over shopping malls, radio, and TV spots. Radio programs took on a magazine format through the presentation of musical patterns in which the entertainment function prevailed. The Chilean music industry reproduced the cheapest products offered by the transnational cultural industries. They now reproduce American billboards [hits]. During the years of the apparent economic boom, an expansion of musical shows ensued. Usually the celebrity sold more than the product. Finally, populist attempts to deal with music were carried out by two govenment-controlled stations: the state-owned Radio Colo Colo and Channel 11 (belonging to the University of Chile). [7]

An important phenomenon has been *el canto nuevo*. Young musicians and songwriters joined the survivors of *la nueva canción*, the former generation of artists. Their musical creation is related to the immediate past, for they appear as symbols of the previous period. Canto nuevo's musical texts have been political and ideological. In universities and *poblaciones* (shantytowns) it became one of the few modes of expression. In fact, canto nuevo fortified the historical memory, strengthened collective identity, and created a new musical circuit.

From the aesthetic point of view, however, the canto nuevo has made a very small contribution: its music points to continuity, with late and slow renewal, and a weak folkloric base. It consists of new songs, but not new languages. Symbolic lyrics predominate and the songs rarely sound very professional. Nevertheless, canto nuevo has appealed to a new generation of young people who did not know the pre-1973 experience. A few musicians have returned from exile, and some pre-1973 music is only now being reedited for the public market.

Canto nuevo members have participated in solidarity gatherings, where they have experienced various modes of repression. From 1980 on, canto nuevo has undergone a period of crisis. Most of its musicians retain an amateur status; they are culturally marginalized and receive very little income. Many groups have disappeared. The members have divided into two groups. One that includes popular singers is linked to the *canto poblacional*—rooted in the poor suburbs. It stresses the political and the ideological. The second, which appeals to a broader spectrum, has tried to include all dimensions of human life by defining art as a means of transforming the real.

Another important musical phenomenon has been the revival of the other type of noncommercial popular music—the new rock, also called "rock latino," which until recently did not have very much diffusion. It is very diverse and synthetic: it is nurtured by rock, Andean, electronic, classical, Latin American, and aboriginal music, as well as pop, jazz, and, in particular, Argentinean Latin rock. It is eminently musical. Most of the groups associated with this musical form convey a cosmic vision of humans and the world and propose an internal revolution and a universal harmony. They tend to escape from contingency with their totalizing attitude. Some musicians are engaged in constant creative experiments, while others are literally turned into celebrities or repeat only fixed musical patterns. Recently, the new Chilean rock or progressive music has fallen prey to commercialism under the manipulation of the media and the music industry.

Visual Arts

This is an artistic medium that has had some permanency during the last 10 years. Although there have been more than 300 visual exhibitions since 1974, not much sculpture has been seen. The official government policies have legitimized grandiose performing art (opera and ballet from abroad), nationalist, enterprise art (privatization of culture, also called *mecenazgo*), and populist art. The vanguard that has provoked the rupture with the past has sponsored *acciones de arte* (art happenings), the use of multimedia, audiovisual materials, and video, and the use of found objects as an art form, and, furthermore, has also made a contribution through theoretical and critical essays that analyze their own artistic discourse. [8]

The closing down of departments of visual arts in the universities caused the disappearance of a generation of painters and art critics. Only years later have galleries reemerged. Gradually, new groups have been formed with interdisciplinary inputs. First, allegoric or symbolic art was developed. Later, the art galleries exhibited documentary or testimonial art. Some exhibitions were part of human rights campaigns for the *desaparecidos* (those that had disappeared, kidnapped by the regime). The production of art was also collectivized and new performance art emerged.

The activity of Chilean visual artists was realized first in private workshops (ateliers). Initially, the official policies of government-controlled institutions organized an unending chain of retrospective incursions devoted to foreign artists and to nineteenth-century Chilean painters, because none of them were politically contentious. During the first years of the authoritarian regime, the practice of the visual arts was divided along two lines: first, institutional work connected with the public exhibition circuit, displaying traditional techniques, formalist in character, and without an accompanying theory; and second, the vanguard visual work done outside the established institutions, using experimental techniques, and transgressing the established order of artistic systems and media. The opening up of new artistic avenues has been accomplished by rejecting "picturality." The new theoretical preoccupation is broad: it works with landscape signs, cultural "common places," or "clichés."

In 1977, documentary and symbolic art, together with art galleries and some seminal exhibitions, reached a peak. Photography became more and more important. The human body was used as artistic support. By the end of the 1970s, the encounter between the visual arts in exile and those inside Chile took place. The artistic vanguard complemented itself with new specialized publications and self-critical workshops. Since 1980 the use of video has been steadily growing. However, the artistic panorama is not homogeneous or unidirectional: while traditional official art has emphasized continuity, the marginal artistic vanguard has provoked a healthy rupture with the past. The determinacy of the market has also had an impact on the visual arts during this period, resulting in the flow of artists into the advertising business.

Theater

The authoritarian regime has profoundly affected theater activities in Chile. Theater schools and companies were closed down at the universities. The first years were marked by subsistence and institutional disarticulation. Theater activities subsidized by the state were extremely centralized, and characterized by authoritarian modes of theatrical production. References to contemporary Chile were suppressed. A new audience for old French and Peninsular Spanish repertory theater was recruited from among high school students. This evasion of Chilean reality and the autochthonous theatrical creation was accomplished through the prevailing logic of censorship and self-censorship. Other dynamics were also in operation: the need to finance the activities (economic logic), the need to revise creative and aesthetic philosophy, and the organic-institutional problem. [9]

Independent theater grew gradually during this period as part of the commercial circuit. The repertoire consisted mostly of children's theater, comedies, and "cafe-concerts" (shows in coffee houses). Another independent trend attempted to maintain the university tradition by presenting classical and modern foreign theater; meanwhile, a new kind of theater emerged in places such as concentration camps and university student festivals. A new type of theater appeared in both universities and poblaciones, the aesthetic and cultural codes of which were not formalized in society. These theater groups originated under some organizational umbrella, such as *agrupaciones culturales* (cultural associations) or the Catholic church. The language of these plays relates to the social movement that has reconstituted itself through cultural activities such as these.

During the late seventies, Chilean theater again turned its attention to Chile. While the official government-controlled theater presented a patriotic theater, the independent commercial theater introduced the musical comedy; the "canned theater" mimicked U.S. productions. This official mass culture came to an end at the beginning of the eighties as the economic crisis became more acute.

New theater groups were also formed. Their reconstitution was slower at the amateur level. Semiprofessional groups were associated with binational institutes (Chilean-British, Chilean-French) or with independent institutions. The plays of the national independent theater inquired into Chilean reality. Most of those performing groups were part of a cultural movement linked to professional theater during the early seventies. The most creative groups presented both foreign contemporary theater and Chilean authors.

One of the most important theater genres presented during the last 10 years in Chile has been the testimonial theater of contingencies. A large number of plays belong to this type. Many of them are inspired by real people, and they are related to the culture of the popular movement. Popular and democratic values are positively portrayed. These plays, however, have not exposed the conflict between the two antagonistic forces. Rather, tensions are shown in the interior of the groups that suffer the effects. Nevertheless, these plays looked for a transforming effect in the consciousness and practice of the audience. In these works the future of hope is usually based on the characters' solidarity, and the positive model of society is always the *estado de compromiso* (the liberal democratic state).

Yet another type of theater has attempted the uncovering of authoritarian logic. These plays, fewer in number, have focused on the dominating political sectors with the purpose of rejecting the latter's kind of worldview and practice. From time to time, popular characters reproducing the authoritarian ideology, permeated by competition, dogmatism, consumptionism, and individualism, have been shown. Some other kinds of theater were also cultivated: a theater that documented Chilean history, and a theater questioning current social myths.

In the 1973–1987 period, Chilean theater acquired a new function. This was essential for the emergence of the alternative cultural movement, which agglutinated the fragmented popular movement. The importance of contingency in all these plays agrees with the channel of diffusion used: mainly the local noncommercial community. Their main function was to provide a sphere of convergence for the identity of sectors that shared the same worldview. The actors became the voice of those without a voice (as did other cultural and artistic activities); they expressed social groups other than themselves. Some of the plays were quite successful. Two of them attracted more than 50,000 spectators. However, in the end, this theater did not have a mass circuit, and it did not expand. Its aesthetic message suggested more than it stated.

The amateur theater has been in an almost permanent state of crisis. Reconstitution was slower here. The method used (an external leader) has been criticized. Problems were many: censorship and self-censorship, closed channels, limited repertoire, lack of theaters, narrow audiences, and a brief institutional history. What still remains in church and cultural theater groups is collective creation, improvisation, and the tendency to resort to narrative texts with a certain message.

In the last years the lines between the official and nonofficial have become blurred as critical theater has also become commercially successful. Characters are polarized by tensions from two opposing worlds. The purpose is not only to denounce but to analyze these events.

The search for a theatrical language that can overcome censorship and self-censorship is still valid today. The role of the playwright has been reevaluated and contacts with the social base have been stressed. Historical perspective has been added to the works, alongside a critical retrospective view. The theme of torture and repression has also emerged more publicly. There is an awareness that too much critical theater underlines its own marginality. The logic of exclusion, finance, and censorship has also pushed actors into the mainstream cultural industry: TV advertising and *telenovelas* (soap operas).

Literature

The physiognomy of Chilean literature has been altered, too. At least two new generations of writers have emerged in the Chilean literary world. The writing process has had to face the problem of authoritarian state legality that has affected Chilean literary discourse. Numerous literary agents left the country, and their writing practice abroad plus their products have formed a broad corpus known as Chilean literature in exile (see my analysis in Jofré, 1986a). In Chile, editorial houses, publishing institutions, and the processes of distribution have also changed. Books of Chilean literature can be seen as part of mass culture and are sold in newsstands. National circuits are not the same as they were 16 years ago: there is now an official version of Chilean literature, new literary competitions and prizes have been founded; the process of consumption of books in Chile is now profoundly determined by the economic and political situation.

Literature and other cultural and artistic praxis in Chile today can be official or alternative, a monologue or a dialogue, vertical or horizontal, controlling or marginal, authoritarian or democratic. Like other ideological activities, literary production is part of worldviews and social practices projected by the diverse power blocs generated within Chilean society (see Jofré, 1985a).

During the first years certain books and writers were officially erased and forbidden. Bookstores went bankrupt, censorship restrictions were applied to all imported books, and a heavy tax (20 percent) was levied on books. Literary activities were undertaken by young writers at literary workshops in universities, cultural groups, or cultural centers in poblaciones. The hardships of political life were recorded and assembled in many of these literary texts, from concentration camps to student literary festivals.

The high cost of printing contributed to the development of artisanlike modes of production and distribution. Realist tendencies diminished. The testimonial genre was publicly allowed only for the supporters of the official regime. Literary texts were very experimental, with frequent use of techniques for conveying a sense of the unreal. Time and space became ambiguous. Some of this public literature escaped from historicity; it was used commercially for success in the market. As in the other cultural and artistic spheres, a symbolic, connotative, and hermetic language appeared, producing metaphorical texts, in code.

For Chilean literature it was impossible and forbidden to represent all social groups and sectors of the nation. Individual aspects such as identity problems, the importance of the self, the predominance of soliloquy were often emphasized. The role of denouncing the situation in Chile through its literature was assumed by using techniques of indirect reference through absence, and by presenting a fragment that pointed to the totality. There are many texts already written that cannot be published yet; many anonymous texts have circulated, many others have been self-published. The sum total of these literary changes is usually referred to as the transformation of the literary genre system. Some literary currents such as structuralism or deconstruction have influenced literary creation (in emphasizing, for instance, the formal aspects of the work or the worldview conveyed).

After 1973, the book was no longer a social good, and Chilean publishing companies[10] were no longer subsidized: it became the logic of the market that predominated. Book censorship has been notoriously strict; from the beginning, the military regime showed an antibook attitude, as evidenced by public book burnings. The modern conception of capitalism considers the book both as an eternal essence and as a piece of disposable merchandise, a product for the market.

Poetry

The new poets and writers in Chile have been more strongly influenced by historical circumstances than by literary traditions, because the relationships with the two previous generations [were] violently ruptured in 1973, as many poets had to flee the country. Three areas can be distinguished within the domain of poetry: (1) the resistance poetry, underground, with an explicit role of denunciation, very political, ideological and partisan, usually linked to the repressed political parties; (2) public poetry, controlled by book censorship and affected by psychological and ideological self-censorship; a poetry connected with the lyric sentiment of Neruda, Mistral, de Rokha, or Huidobro, it constitutes the new poetics that have emerged in the last 15 years; (3) the official poetry of the regime; sometimes with a lordlike manner, it usually focuses on the subjective world or on the external appearance of reality.

The young poets of the new vanguard have engaged in theory and practice, in writing and reflection, in a prevailing state of isolation that they have gradually overcome by moving into the public arena. They usually start from artisanlike products and microcircuits, such as solitary poetry readings. To the degraded capitalist project of "refoundation," they have opposed Utopia, some universal space of freedom. They have seen their poetry books as graphic material, and understood the white space of the page and the typography itself as indispensable elements of meaning. They have insisted on a critical vision of reality, and on reflecting about their own poetic labor and language. [11]

Fiction

New, young short-story writers who have resorted to symbolic language emerged during this period. Some of the tales, while having the structure of a short story, contain testimonial or autobiographical material. Quite clearly, the language is now more elaborated, assuming new forms. Children and teenagers play a role of a protagonist in many of today's brief narratives. Sexuality and adventure are the topics most frequently treated, although life outside Chile is another constant theme. Short stories explore moments of imbalance, counter-positioning ways of life, and the parameters between repression, self-repression, and liberation.

There are many grotesque and violent moments, scenes of transgression and punishment, instances of domination. In these short stories, different narrative viewpoints introduce a polyphonic reality, a change in the focus of the narration that now centers on one character or another, or literary mechanisms that relativize one's own perception of the real (Jofré, 1984a, 1984b).

A good number of novels (almost 150) have been published in Chile in the last 15 years. However, there exist few literary awards for novelists. The novel today is marked by the presence or absence of reference to contemporary Chilean history. It has also been marked by the use of symbolic, metaphoric, and indirect language. Some fragments in the long narratives that have been produced have been quite explicit in terms of contextual reading, thus establishing the limit between censorship and self-censorship, which has been important. The end result has been a few very powerful, very polyphonic novels with numerous voices and with a multiplicity of perspectives. The processes of Chilean society appear in the concrete destiny of the characters. Very often, the characters themselves represent social forces.

In all these novels there is a central conflict related to the kind of world portrayed. Some novels, referring more explicitly to the context, tend to show processes of conflict being developed in conjunction with the image of Chilean society at a certain point in time. Often, the meaning given to the world by the narrator is predominant. Chaotic social forces are shown as acting upon the characters' actions. This Chilean novel, in a sense, proclaims the need of context for the reading of any message. The main theme is power and the effect of power in the characters' evolution and the processes of change. In these novels, historic and social determinations intertwine with existential and psychological motivation (see Jofré, 1985b).

The structure of the most representative novels of this period is very up-to-date. Although they present conflicts, they do not impose solutions. All the techniques of the contemporary novel are used, as these novels depict their own point of departure: spaces in which the established social structure is being successfully challenged by vital transformations of a new order. Chilean contemporary novels are a synthesis of the rational and the irrational by pointing outward, to the context. Generally, these novels offer a particular account of reality, which is succeeded by a new account, which then changes and relativizes the previous one. Generally, too, they contain juxtapositions of stories, a reality composed of echoes and resonances, in which the unreal expands, and in which indeterminacy provokes the borders between appearance and reality to become confused. Imagination in its plenitude is legitimized by these novels, in paradoxical conjunction with the fundamental conflicts between different conceptions of history.

Testimony

This nonfiction narrative, usually taking the form of accounts by witnesses, has clearly reached artistic status as a literary genre, if judged by recent contributions. Testimonies are personal accounts that assume a diversity of narrative structures: in first or third person, or in the form of an interview. Testimonial writing is one way of representing through language the present circumstances; it engages the reader in its denouncement of the situation and its appeal for changes (Jofré, 1982b).

Before 1973, the growth of testimonial literature was apparent; afterward, it almost disappeared. The testimony from dominant groups in control was promoted and published, while the testimony from the oppressed groups was suppressed. Strengthened in authoritarian regimes, literary testimony contributes not only to the revitalization of realism, but to the reconstitution of the social subject, as it retrieves the historical memory of a people. [12]

Most testimonies written in Chile have not been able to circulate publicly. Many of them refer to human rights, the disappearance of political prisoners, and deaths caused by the dominating forces. They look into the people's social consciousness by bringing history into literature, and literary mechanism back into reality. Testimonies circulating in Chile tend to be always more informative than aesthetic. They usually have an instrumental character. They convey events and ideas by always referring to Chilean reality. Historical laws and social movements can be appreciated in the characters. Ideological statements come from the author-narrator. This testimonial discourse completes Chilean history and unveils its most crucial moments.

Literary Criticism

The events of 1973 cut short the theoretical and practical renewal of Chilean literary criticism. At universities, literary researchers and professors were eliminated; many left the country for foreign universities. The first year saw the narrowing of the ideological-cultural universe. Public space, where literary criticism develops, was restricted and administered by the authorities. The result was that Chilean literary criticism has been reduced and isolated; the critical renewal has been disarticulated; simplified patterns of imminent analysis remain. The role and functions of the reader ("reception criticism") are not considered.

Sociohistoric methods are excluded, while the relationship of the literary work of art with its context and with other artistic or cultural productions is not considered. All the fruitful interdisciplinary approaches have disappeared. Methods of literary analysis dating from the late sixties are still being discussed as though they are the latest contribution (see Subercaseaux, 1982).

Naive and impressionistic criticism, unable to question its own foundations, predominates today. New contributions are regarded with suspicion. Literary theories are seen from purely ideological perspectives. Isolated attempts to overcome this situation have appeared only in the last few years, always in the direction of structuralism and formalism. Only the literary criticism that supports official views has access to print. Some critics have moved toward media advertising, shaped by the cultural industry: a new public circuit emerged, linked to television and the media, and to the cultural celebrities of the regime. This sector, which dominates literary culture, has been able to create a nonfiction narrative for mass consumption; modern best-sellers are created for and by the market. Official literary criticism appears in the traditional and business-oriented press. The criticism exercised here is aesthetic-ideological and tends to exclude Latin American authors and Chilean literature in exile. On the opposite side, research projects involving sociological, semiotic, and reception-oriented criticism are being developed outside the universities in the alternative microcircuits.

CULTURAL POLICIES

Dominant culture and art is organized by the discourses and meanings of the dominant power bloc. The dominant discourse has been governmental, public, and official. Discourses and effective policies have flowed from both the state and public areas. Authoritarianism did not have only one central and coherent cultural and artistic policy; there were several emitting centers or agencies. Since 1973 each moment was made up of diverse policies and discourses, and by contrasting them all it is possible to detect a logic of exclusion that has had the effect of negating a wide social sector. The policies have rendered a marked trend toward prevailing market logic and the concept of an elite culture for the upper social groups while favoring a populist art for the masses.

Official art and cultural policies originated in different traditions: available from the beginning was traditional nationalism, in combination with Catholic integralism, neoliberal thought, and authoritarianism. Immediately after 1973, the official public culture had more identity, more homogeneity, and the consensus was based upon the exclusion of a certain sector. Chauvinism was rampant, reacting against the relationship between art and life, between art and politics. In their view, culture should not be degraded.

Dominant art and culture also had to deal with the lack of freedom of expression and censorship. Some intellectuals of the right formulated the policies while others implemented them. Some centers were more discursive than factual, others more factual than discursive. Clearly, there was a division of labor, but there was no centralized cultural policy of authoritarianism. Thus the cultural arena—which is society's meaning—was left as a field in dispute. The authoritarian state funded certain activities, in particular national propaganda campaigns, while some government institutions with large funds and resources carried out top-down communication to the social base. This phenomenon was coupled with the mass and populist project (television and radio) tending to agglutinate a social movement of support for the authoritarian government.

An examination of the disparate legislation approved during the period demonstrates the overlapping of different conceptions of culture: elite art and culture, mass art and culture, the logic of war in culture and art. The permissive logic of pre-1973 changed into a repressive logic that either prohibited opposition showings and gatherings of artistic and cultural character, or else obstructed them in other ways. According to this authoritarian legislation, art and culture could not be protected anymore. With the market requirement for self-financing, art and culture also acquired an especially heavy system of taxation. The authoritarian government retained the right to decide what was culture and what was art.

The communication policy of authoritarianism has always been very active. Although this is a repressive regime, it displays a liberal image of itself, whereby the government has tried to convince people that they are protagonists in the process of community development. There was a separation between an ideal discourse on communication and the real universe of government policies. These policies view a sector of the population as adversaries and as candidates for social integration. At the macromedia level, the government controls the national television and radio networks. It also expands its worldview through a wide spectrum of sectoral micromedia (local bulletins, newsletters, brochures). The remainder of radio and press is controlled by right-wing private groups.

State cultural policies have been studied by Chilean social and humanities specialists reorganized in new groupings after the military coup. They first assessed the national situation in the period 1976–1980 and then carried out research on specific areas such as the process of institutionalization and the changes that took place during the so-called modernization. Later, authoritarian cultural policies were examined and democratic ones were proposed. [13]

Cultural policies in Chile correspond to state action in the cultural-artistic field. Before the eighties, the previous emphasis was on the dynamics of repression and control, or on the atomistic logic of the market. The new authoritarian state and the dominant social bloc that emerged in 1973 saw the cultural situation as part of a more general hegemonical model that proposed the so-called refoundation of Chilean society. According to this perspective, culture was in an intimate relationship with other areas of society. Thus art and culture are seen by the authoritarian government as activities related to general policies—an integral part of the authoritarian model imposed on the society by the state.

New cultural policies have affected two basic dimensions of cultural activities: first, everyday life (multiple microcircuits of interpersonal communication) and, second, the public domain (where symbolic goods are produced, distributed, and consumed as social values). In the first instance, the cultural policy of the authoritarian government can be seen as a project of depolitization that includes the closure of public space, massive and selective repression, the destruction of mechanisms for representation and participation, and the exclusion of groups and individuals.

Specific cultural policies have been manifested in interventions within different cultural fields, articulated with more general state policies. At this level, some degree of contradiction occurred. However, these cultural policies mobilized agents, conveyed discourses, proposed goals, established norms, developed programs, and channeled resources. In this way, they have unfolded the positive dimension of the regime. [14] These cultural policies constitute a way of representing and reorganizing culture for the state and the bloc in power, and although the gesture of the regime is always expressed in negations, it has also founded and created a new cultural institutionality that will have very profound repercussions in Chile.

In order to disclose their rationale as evidenced in the official discourse, it is necessary to first analyze the principal ideological matrices of the military regime. If one studies the official symbolic range, a diversity of discourses that form the spectrum of official cultural policies may be perceived. There is no presence of a single paradigm with a protagonist role to provide unity and coherence. Thus this situation includes contradictions among the different discourses on culture. This is a complex ideological-institutional frame needing structuring. Some of the ideological referents used in cementing the new dominant bloc are the national security doctrine, the nationalistic tendencies, and the neoliberal thought, which together originated three fundamental discursive matrices. First, the totalitarian and militant cultural project of "national foundation" expanded during the first years of the authoritarian regime. Second, the highbrow conceptions about culture developed with conservative, elitist, and enlightened characteristics. And third, commercial and "recreational" cultural production resulted from cultural industry and mass culture.

As has been said, there has been no solidification or consolidation of a global cultural model, and the unifying and common aspect of all official cultural tendencies has been their opposition to and negation of the cultural modes existing in Chile before 1973. From the official point of view, the Chilean left was accused of decadence of culture, politization of art, cultural infiltration, and totalitarian conscientization.

The events of 1973 allowed for an offensive of the old cultural discourses that had been displaced from the Chilean cultural scene. They agreed in opposing the radicalized politization of culture. This reactionary response of the regime is always present when dealing with the opposite cultural pole, that of the dissident and the excluded. Although there is agreement regarding the rejection, there is no consensus for the construction of a single official cultural pattern. Evidence for this argument is the defeat of the nationalistic foundational project: the obvious consequence is a complex process of conflicts among cultural policies trying to gain hegemony.

The nationalistic foundational discourse can be considered a state cultural project with authoritarian roots, expressed by three tendencies, with great affinity between them. First, this geopolitical conception of culture is supported by the doctrine of national security developed within the military in Latin America during the sixties. This conception emerged from the military regime during its first years in power. Second, the regime draws from Catholic traditionalism (with its Hispanic roots) transmitted since the thirties by political and academic circles of the Chilean conservative right wing and closely related to the professional *gremios* (trade unions). Third, and more marginally to the right, the cultural nationalist conception connects the regime's cultural project with the Ibañez populist political experience.

Groups rallying behind that cultural conception were the military, scholars, intellectuals, and professionals. At the institutional level, some state agencies and cultural agents were used to organize the new official social movement (National Secretariat for Women, National Secretary of Youth, Neighborhood Centers, and the regime-sponsored mothers' centers—CEMA Chile), along with some writers and folk artists. This material and institutional network represents the hegemonic cultural tendency during the first years of this period.

The main characteristics of the nationalistic foundational discourse include those listed here. (1) National identity is considered as an immutable essence, culture as a spiritual expression, and norms for collective identity as metaphysical and telluric. (2) The state is perceived as the representative of the national essence—the only institution able to interpret the national being. (3) The "Marxist cancer" is viewed as a threat to the essential values of the fatherland. Culture is seen as a preferred field for Marxism, where it uses a progressive façade to aid in the formation of a network of people and institutions. Salvation is thought to rely on the state's ability to extirpate the root of the infection in the moral body of the fatherland, in search of values from Western Christianity and "Chilenity." (4) All politicians—who by their very essence supposedly comply in the destruction of national culture—are rejected. National decadence is supposedly due to the lack of geo-political understanding by elites too open to foreign values, the loss of national unity due to antagonistic social schemes, and the rejection of history and national heroes. (5) The need to restore the national essence links culture to geopolitical goals and to fighting both the external and the internal enemy. (6) Hegemonical cultural strategies determine the need to act on different circuits. High culture is privileged as part of the notion of cultural heritage, and it is understood to be against foreign intellectual elites. (7) Finally, mass culture is seen from a Goebbels-like perspective, as mere propaganda apparatuses.

GLOBAL PROCESSES

1973 marks the end of an era of multiple discourses. Later, the official speech was the governing discourse that repeated itself in the reduced public space. The predominance of individual social relations meant a loss of collective identity, where authoritarianism could expand its already crystallized discourse. Since 1973, Chile has experienced the blocking of creativity by means of repressive bureaucratic control. The extension of the culture market brought inequality, elitism, a change in the Chilean cultural world, and a crisis in the collective identity. Less art and more mass culture was the result. Something that was marginal became central. Culture and art were invaded by the state. Now the national identity rests on the mass culture. This was a rearticulation of cultural levels. Mass culture in Chile followed the commercial populist logic. National television provided the state with a discourse of national identity that created "common sense" and a common referent for Chilean society. In the last years, television has gained hegemony over the other media. Mass communication is accomplished without social participation; the narrowing of freedom of access to the market of the senses is coupled with a deepening inequality of access to culture. [15]

It is clear that since 1973 there has been a diminishing of ideological-cultural agents, spaces, and products. The dominant group saw the subaltern groups as potential consumers and adversaries. Although Chilean governments have always used some kind of propaganda, the new situation implied a complete rearticulation of ideological functions. Later, when coercive force diminished, mass culture expanded. Artistic legitimation (first accomplished through mechanisms proper to each discipline) is now accomplished by the market, by the consumer.

Three spaces or circuits for art and culture could be distinguished in Chile. First is the mass communication market, which grew extraordinarily during the last decade, distributing foreign products, excluding Chilean works, and attracting professionals and artists to the cultural industry circuit. Second is the circuit of professional art—traditionally developed within the state—now receiving political and market sanctions. Experimental art almost completely disappeared. The public arena showed a predominance of foreign works and artists. The social processes through which cultural identities had been generated were halted; social processes of cultural synthesis were also obstacled. The third type of artistic and cultural circuit was the local community, the amateur, folkloric expressions—all of those productions that Chilean social and human scientists consider as popular culture. In opposition to dominant trends, this was an emerging culture characterized by a logic of expression that elaborated alternative discourses to the dominant authoritarianism. The closing down of the public space opened up other spaces in society, rich in meanings, where a wide range of artistic activities were presented. These were places of encounter, confrontation, and dialogue that made a decisive contribution to the reconstruction of the social fabric through the recovery of both the everyday world and the political utopia.

In the late seventies, a cultural and social movement, critical and dissenting, crystallized. This occurred as part of the rearticulation of learned, popular, and mass circuits, and this transformation in artistic processes has had a certain relationship with the available media. A consideration of the nonofficial media will show that the dissidents hold and control only one macromedium: those belonging to the Catholic church. There were some opposition magazines that particularly emphasized artistic and cultural activities, and a network of micromedia, but none of these could be regarded as alternative communication. And they too have been affected by the policies of exclusion and repression in which the means of communication are controlled only by the power bloc.

Nonofficial artistic and cultural groups have provided a democratic space for poetry, songs, theater, dances, craftsmanship, and visual arts. All these artistic and cultural activities were loaded with symbolic functions: they had a ritual and cathartic character, and they reanimated a social project by aestheticizing the political discourse and politicizing artistic activity. The culmination of this process was the artistic festival, the cultural event. All of these practices—somewhat isolated and spontaneous at first—achieved a considerable degree of organic coherence during the late seventies. First, the *peñas* (folk coffee houses) appeared, then the academic interdisciplinary centers, a small sound and recording and cassette tape industry, later workshops, and finally organizations of young musicians, writers, actors, and visual artists.

This was a cultural movement represented by two fronts: university students and young people in the poblaciones. Subsistence was very difficult in these circuits of grassroots social animation. Relationships between political people and artists were not easy either. This was an informal circuit closed upon itself. It did not expand. It did not bring in new audiences. In time, this cultural front became politicized. The political calendar was faithfully celebrated, and some "popular liberation" occurred in the collective creations, in the diffusion of works, plays, songs, and poems. The political role of denunciation was always present. In opposition to the social atomization that followed the military coup, independent cultural and artistic action provided an alternative social reconstruction through ideological and symbolic identities. During the early eighties, the number of participants in the cultural groups declined, and then they began to grow again. Cultural groups, at least at the microcircuit level, helped to constitute voices different from the official society. The relationship between the artist and the social base has now been questioned in the light of the separation of professional and amateur artists in the poblaciones and grassroots organizations.

CONCLUSIONS

An evaluation of the cultural processes of the last 15 years leaves a positive balance for the goal of establishing an alternative cultural project. Undoubtedly, the national, hegemonic culture has begun to erode. Two phenomena can account for this. In the first place, the dominant strategies to paralyze the global processes of cultural synthesis have failed due to ideological and hegemonic weaknesses on the part of the regime. An important factor here has been the existing friction between different cultural and artistic projects of the dominant sector, such as the conflict between the logic of the marketplace and the logic of exclusion and control. Second, as intellectuals were expelled from the state and public arenas, the ground became favorable to the increasingly organic project of the reconstitution of a common alternative discourse. The altered national culture and identity began to be replaced by microcultures. The amateur movement developed with the social base. These local discourses have attempted to counteract the public and official government discourse conveyed through the mass media. However, even though the contradiction between the logic of the marketplace and the political logic of exclusion has resulted in favor of the development of alternative spaces of production and diffusion, the relationship between those alternative circuits and the mass media has been problematic. Some alternative artists have moved into the public commercial space—a case in point is the canto nuevo. The visual arts vanguard has won first prizes in official competitions. Popular culture is gaining more space in the mass media. As the lines between official and alternative cultural activities become increasingly blurred at the level of the logic of the marketplace, the real possibilities of transforming the global situation fall well beyond the scope of cultural practices.

Notes

1. This monograph is part of a broader research project, "The Making of Chilean Culture: Literature, Arts and the Media," which was possible thanks to the funding provided by the Social Sciences and Social Sciences and Humanities Research Council of Canada. This research is affiliated with the "Chile Project," developed by the Center for Research on Latin America and the Caribbean (CERLAC), York University, Toronto, Canada. In Chile, this research project was housed at the Centro de Indagación y Expresión Cultural y Artística, CENECA, and affiliated with the Latin American Faculty of Social Sciences, FLACSO-CHILE. CENECA is the main research center in Chile dedicated to the popular and mass cultures as well as artistic processes and social communication systems.

2. This study is based upon personal observations, collective discussions, interdisciplinary readings, and systematic research. It is also both a first-hand account and a bibliographical review. Unfortunately, Chilean literature and art of exile had to be excluded, and there is no examination of the period 1970–1973.

It this article I attempt to define the main cultural and artistic characteristics of several important Chilean cultural fields. Special attention is given to the main cultural tendencies and not to the names of specific intellectuals, artists, and cultural producers. Here, I have chosen to write a cultural history of the recent years in Chile without personal names. Because of space considerations, the editors have deemed it necessary to reduce some sections (poetry, for example).

3. I have developed in detail the history and uses of the concept of culture as framework for my research in Chile (see Jofré, 1982a: 42).

4. Some of these ideas have been developed by Brunner (1981, 1985, and in *Chile vive*, 1987: 15–21).

5. Unfortunately, some important problems related to the Chilean ideological structure cannot be treated extensively here. Hegemonic discourses, authoritarian in nature, are of course ideological. The same is applicable to the alternative worldviews presented by the opposition. This article does not restrict the concept of ideological practices to class consciousness, although the Chilean political and cultural experience tends to identify group interest and ideological vision (see Jofré, 1982a, 1982b).

6. Two works by Giselle Munizaga have been used in this section (1981, 1983). Her most recent work is in *Chile vive* (1987: 102–109).

7. In this section I have also used information from Anny Rivera (1984) and Francisco Cruz (1983). Important studies in this field are by Carlos Catalán (1980) and Valerio Fuenzalida (1985). Two recent works in this field are by Ricardo García (in *Chile vive*, 1987: 151–154) and González Rodríguez (in *Chile vive*, 1987: 155–159).

8. Valuable information about visual arts in Chile came from different talks offered in Santiago by Francisco Brugnoli (see also Aquiló, 1983). Very important critical essays on the Chilean visual artists have been published by Nelly Richard (in *Chile vive*, 1987: 79–87). Refer also to Milán Ivelic (in *Chile vive*, 1987: 52–65), Alberto Peñez (in *Chile vive*, 1987: 66–78), and Mario Fonseca (in *Chile vive*, 1987: 33–40).

9. Some of the most fruitful research at CENECA has been carried out in theater. A good summary is by María de la Luz Hurtado and Carlos Ochsenius (1983: 1–53); a diversity of opinions can be seen in their work (1980). See also María de la Luz Hurtado and María Elena Moreno (1982) and José Luis Olivari et al. (1985). Hurtado's most recent work is in *Chile vive* (1987: 135–150).

10. Research on the Chilean publishing industry has been done by Bernardo Subercaseaux (1984a). See also the proceedings from a conference on the subject, edited by Subercaseaux (1986), and his (1984b) work.

11. Unfortunately, for reasons of space, the editors of this issue had to cut the author's section on poetry. On this subject the author had recommended readings in Noméz (1980), Cociña (1985), and Zurita (1983). For critical writings on contemporary poetry, see Bianchi (1983a, 1983b, and in *Chile vive*, 1987: 92–96); see also Jofré, 1987.

12. Latin American and Chilean testimony has been studied by Jorge Narváez (1983) and Subercaseaux (in *Chile vive*, 1987: 97–101).

13. Concerning the regime's cultural policies and the new democratic cultural proposals, see Hurtado (1985), Paulina Gutiérrez et al. (1985), Suber-

caseaux (1986), Robert A. White (1985), and Brunner (1985).

14. Some of the ideas discussed here come from Carlos Catalán and Giselle Munizaga (1986).

15. For this last section, several works were consulted. See Díaz (1982), Rivera (1983), Ochsenius (1983), and Gutiérrez (1983).

References

Aquiló, Osvaldo. "Propuestas neovanguardistas en la plástica chilena: antecedentes y contexto." Santiago: CENECA, 1983.

Bianchi, Soledad. *Entre la lluvia y el arcoiris*. Rotterdam: Ediciones del Instituto para el Nuevo Chile, 1983(a).

_____. "Un mapa por completar: la joven poesía chilena." Santiago: CENECA, 1983(b).

Brunner, José Joaquín. *La cultura autoritaria en Chile*. Santiago: FLACSO, 1981.

_____. *Políticas culturales para la democracia*. Santiago: CENECA, 1985.

Catalán, Carlos. "El canto popular en los canales de difusión." Santiago: CENECA, 1980.

Catalán, Carlos, and Giselle Munizaga. "Políticas culturales estatales bajo el autoritarismo en Chile." Santiago: CENECA, 1986.

Catalán, Carlos, and Anny Rivera. "Notas para una política cultural-artística." Santiago, 1983.

Chile vive. Madrid: Ministerio de Cultura, 1987.

Cociña, Carlos. "La nueva vanguardia poética chilena." Santiago: CENECA, 1985.

Cruz, Francisco. *Música popular no comercial en Chile*. Santiago, CENECA, 1983.

Díaz, Eugenio. "Legislación cultural durante el autoritarismo." Santiago: CENECA, 1982.

Fuenzalida, Valerio. "La industria fonográfica chilena." Santiago: CENECA, 1985.

Gutiérrez, Paulina. "Agupaciones culturales: una reflexión sobre las relaciones entre cultura y política." Santiago: CENECA, 1983.

Gutiérrez, Paulina, Giselle Munizaga, and Alfredo Riquelme. "Sistema de comunicación en Chile: Proposiciones interpretativas y perspectivas democráticas." Santiago: CENECA, 1985.

Hurtado, María de la Luz. "Bases para una discusión de políticas comunicacionales en Chile." Santiago: CENECA, 1985.

Hurtado, María de la Luz, and María Elena Moreno. *El público del teatro independiente*. Santiago: CENECA, 1982.

Hurtado, María de la Luz, and Carlos Ochsenius. "Transformaciones del teatro chileno en la década del 70," in *Teatro chileno de la crisis institucional 1973–1980, antología crítica*. Minneapolis: University of Minnesota and CENECA, 1983. 1–53.

Jofré, Manuel Alcides. *El concepto de cultura*. Santiago: CENECA, 1982(a).

_____. "Cuentistas chilenos de hoy." *Taller de Letras* (Santiago) 12 (1984 [a]): 41–46.

_____ . "El hombre en la literatura y cultura de Chile hoy." *Ecce Homo* (Santiago) 3 (1984[b]): 137–148.

_____ . "La novela chilena: 1974–1984." Santiago: CENECA, 1985(a).

_____ . "La novela en Chile: 1973–1983," in *Literature and Ideologies.* Minneapolis: Institute for the Study of Ideologies and Literature, 1985(b). 332–384.

_____ . "Literatura chilena de testimonio," in *Repression and Liberation in Latin America.* Toronto: CALACS and CERLACE, 1982(b). 53–65.

_____ . *Literatura chilena por el mundo.* Santiago: CENECA, 1986(a).

_____ . "Popular education: urban youth organizations in Chile." *CUSO Bulletin* 1 (1986[b]): 2–3.

_____ . "La voz de los 80: poesía joven chilena." *Espíritu del Valle* (Santiago) 2 (1987): 17–26.

Munizaga, Giselle. "Políticas de comunicación bajo regímenes autoritarios: el caso de Chile." Santiago: CENECA, 1981.

_____ . "Algunas problematizaciones en torno al tema de la democratización de las comunicaciones." Santiago: CENECA, 1983.

Narváez, Jorge. "El testimonio: 1972–1982; transformaciones en el sistema literario." Santiago: CENECA, 1983.

Nómez, Naín. "La poesía chilena actual: poesía vigilada y vigilante," in *Primer cuaderno de ensayo chileno.* Ottawa: Ediciones Cordillera, 1980. 14–28.

Ochsenius, Carlos. "Agrupaciones culturales populares bajo el autoritarismo: esbozo de periodización: 1973–1982." Santiago: CENECA, 1983.

Olivari, José Luis, Carlos Ochsenius, and Enrique Bello. *Documentos sobre una experiencia de teatro con campesinos huilliches.* Santiago: CENECA, 1985.

Rivera, Anny. *Transformaciones culturales y movimiento artístico en el orden autoritario.* Santiago: CENECA, 1983.

_____ . "Transformaciones de la industria musical en Chile." Santiago: CENECA, 1984.

Subercaseaux, Bernardo. "Transformaciones de la crítica literaria en Chile: 1960–1982." Santiago: CENECA, 1982.

_____ . *La industria editorial y el libro en Chile (1930–1984).* Santiago: CENECA, 1984(a).

_____ . "Notas sobre autoritarismo y lectura en Chile." Santiago: CENECA, 1984(b).

_____ . "El debate sobre políticas culturales y democracia" Santiago: CENECA, 1986.

Subercaseaux, Bernardo (ed.). *El libro en Chile, presente y futuro.* Santiago: Centro de Estudios del Desarrollo (CED) and CENECA, 1986.

White, Robert A. "Políticas nacionales de comunicación y cultura." Santiago: CENECA, 1985.

Zurita, Raúl. "Literatura, lenguaje y sociedad (1973–1983)." Santiago CENECA, 1983.

✳

DISCUSSION QUESTIONS AND ACTIVITIES

Fieg and Blair

1. Demonstrate the "traditional stereotypes" the Colombians hold of the American (superman, exploiter, naive innocent) by finding examples in the press, television, and film.

2. Colombians note that life in the U.S. is faster, more agitated and brisk. Demonstrate or disprove this observation by keeping a daily schedule for a week, entering what you are doing throughout the day and evening. What do you discover? Ask a friend to carry out the same activity. What differences or similarities do you note when comparing your schedules?

3. In matters of language, Fieg and Blair are told by Colombians that Spanish "is a lot more flowery." Find examples of this drawn from Spanish language books you have read or studied.

4. Compare an English and a Spanish business letter. What differences and similarities do you note?

5. The Fieg and Blair article does not deal with the contemporary reality of Colombia, that is, the Medellín drug cartel and their terrorist acts to destabilize the Colombian government. Research current developments in the crisis in newspapers and periodicals and present your findings.

García

6. Professor García bases her analysis on videotaped role plays. Form a small group and invite an international student or visitor that you know to join you in a similar role play. Write the scenario you want to test (turn down an invitation, apply for a job, etc.), videotape the conversation of the role players, and analyze the tape in order to identify differences in communication styles.

7. The Venezuelan women appear to define several roles differently than Americans. Read the text again and, working with a group, construct a definition of the term " friend," of the tenant/landlord roles, and of that of a customer dealing with service personnel. How do U.S. expectations for these roles differ from those of Venezuelans?

Reati

8. View one of the several films mentioned in the Reati article. *Kiss of the Spider Woman*, for example, played widely in the U.S. and should be available at local video rental stores. If you are unable to view any of the films, using the reference section of the library, find several reviews of *Kiss of the Spider Woman* in newspapers and periodicals. What elements of the film are the critics most interested in? How frequently and in what manner do the critics allude to political realities in Argentina?

9. A number of Argentine film directors created a new cultural code or discourse to deal with the trauma of their history. Can the same be said about other national cultures? In the U.S., for example, the Vietnam War was a traumatizing political and military event (although of a much different nature than what occurred in Argentina). View a series of film representations of the Vietnam War (*The Deer Hunter, Apocalypse Now, Full Metal Jacket, Coming Home, Born on the Fourth of July*). What are the symbols, myths, and discourses that emerge to represent the event?

10. View one of the following documentaries: *Las Madres: The Mothers of the Plaza de Mayo* (1986, Directors: Susan Muñoz and Lourdes Portillo, 64 minutes, subtitled). The film documents the present-day campaign to discover the whereabouts of the missing and to get those responsible for the torture and murder prosecuted. *Colors of Hope* (Amnesty International, 20 min., VHS, 1985, narrated by Meryl Streep). The video tells the story of an Argentine family's incredible ability to maintain hope and closeness in the face of torture and anguish during their years as political prisoners.

Identify what themes found in Reati's article are also found in the documentaries. What new information, theme, or perspective is brought to the subject of Argentine political violence?

Jofré

11. Discuss U.S. rap music using Jofré's definition of popular art. What is the function of rap music? (If you are unfamiliar with the content of some of the major rap recordings, listen to some tapes.)

12. The question of censorship is not limited to authoritarian regimes like Chile. In 1990 the National Endowment of the Arts (NEA) was widely accused of censorship by refusing to fund certain artistic proposals that it felt were pornographic. The most celebrated case related to

an exhibition of the work of Robert Mapplethorpe. Trace the lines of the debate in the press and periodicals. Once you have the facts, write a series of questions you would ask the director of the NEA regarding freedom of expression and public responsibility.

13. Jofré introduces several terms around which he organizes his discussion. Choose five of those terms and define them.

14. What three questions, issues, or problems would you like to discuss to have a better understanding of the Jofré article?

15. The last two articles in this section deal with creative production and political repression in Argentina and Chile. What parallels are there in the two situations?

Spanish-Speaking Communities
in the U.S.

*

WALKER CONNOR

Who Are the Mexican-Americans?:
A Note on Comparability

(Many mainstream Anglo-Saxon Americans fail to differentiate between the several Spanish-speaking populations in the U.S. When key terms like nation and ethnic group are defined, we can begin to appreciate and respect the diversity of these groups.)

The validity of comparative analyses concerned with the attitudes and behavior of peoples has all too often been undermined by (1) the improper use of key terms, such as *nation* and *ethnic group*, (2) the failure to differentiate whether the group under study is living within or without its ethnic homeland, and (3) the failure to differentiate the country in which the group under study is living, according to whether it is a *nation-state, multination-state,* or *immigrant state*. A few words concerning each of these pitfalls may therefore be advisable.

NATIONS AND ETHNIC GROUPS

In its pristine sense, *nation* refers to a group who share a myth of common descent. It derives from the past participle of the Latin verb *nasci* ("to be born"). Hence the Latin noun *nationem*, which connoted breed or race. The myth, of course, need not be grounded in fact. Thus, an old European saw defines the nation as "a group of people united by

From Walker Connor, ed., *Mexican-Americans in Cultural Perspective* (Washington, D.C.: The Urban Institute Press, 1985), 3–28, by permission of the publisher.

The author is indebted to Arturo Muñoz for an informed and informative critique of an early draft of this paper.

a common error about their ancestry and a common dislike of their neighbors."

Unfortunately the term *nation* is habitually misused as a synonym for (1) a state (consider the League of Nations or the United Nations) or (2) the population or citizenry of a state without regard to its ethno-national composition (consider the widely used expression "the British nation," despite the fact that the British people are composed, inter alia, of the Cornish, English, Manx, Scottish, and Welsh nations). "The American nation," whether used in reference to the country called the United States or to the polygenetic citizenry of that country, is also a misnomer.

The term *ethnic group* has also been fatally compromised. Sociologists use the term loosely to describe any minority, whether of a religious, linguistic, national, or still other variety. Thus, one dictionary of sociology defines ethnic group as "a group with a common cultural tradition and a sense of identity which exists as a sub-group of a larger society."[1] Historically, however, the term was derived from the Greek word *ethnos*, which, like *nationem*, conveyed the notion of an ancestrally related group. Consonant with this etymology, Max Weber defined *ethnic groups* as "those human groups that entertain a subjective belief in their common descent. . . . This belief must be important for the propagation of group formation; conversely, it does not matter whether an objective blood relationship exists. Ethnic membership (*Gemeinsamkeit*) differs from the kinship group precisely by being a presumed identity."[2]

An evident danger associated with the tendency to ignore this pristine meaning of ethnic group and to use it as an umbrella term to cover nearly any type of minority is that the term's application to a series of generically unrelated groups will cause the unwary to assume that all groups can be considered essentially the same for comparative purposes. Thus, while the 1980 U.S. census professed to use *ethnic group* in its pristine sense of an ancestrally related people, it is evident that this definition was not honored in practice.[3] State citizenry rather than kinship was reflected in such entries as Belgian, Swiss, Iranian, Lebanese, Ethiopian, Ghanian, Nigerian, Asian Indian, Indonesian, Pakistani, and Jamaican. Interspersed with such identities were true ethnonational categories, such as Czech and Slovak (rather than Czechoslovakian) and English, Manx, Scottish, and Welsh (rather than British).[4]

A second peril in grouping such vitally different phenomena under a single rubric of ethnic groups is that the analyst will be lulled into assuming as fact that which may most demand questioning. Thus, the census would appear to signify that all Belgians consider themselves to be blood-related in the same way that all Czechs and all Slovaks (but not all Czechoslovaks) do.[5] Mexican-Americans were also listed as an ethnic group in the census, and they are quite regularly described and treated as such in the scholarly literature.[6] But again, this categorization may preempt the potentially vital question: are Mexican-Americans agreed that they constitute an ancestrally related group?[7]

A group's perception of itself as a kinship group possesses important ramifications for its attitudes and behavior. Commencing with Napoleon, an array of political leaders has demonstrated appreciation of the strategic value of appealing to ethnopsychology as a means of mobilizing the masses. Thus Bismarck, when exhorting the people, over the heads of their several princes, to unite into a single state, urged all Germans to "think with your blood." And Marxist-Leninists also have not hesitated to appeal to blood links as a technique of mass mobilization, as witness Mao Tse-tung's 1931 attempt to appear as the defender of the great Han (Chinese) family: "Brothers! Sisters! Can we allow the reactionary rule to connive freely with imperialism to carve us up like sheep? Can we watch our land being forcefully taken away by Japanese imperialism? Can we silently watch our own brothers being whipped, killed, and slaughtered? Can we unfeelingly watch our sisters being molested, insulted, and raped? No! No! Ten thousand times no!"[8]

And in 1937 the Central Committee of the Chinese Communist Party addressed "all fathers, brothers, aunts, and sisters" as follows: "We know that in order to transform this glorious future into a new China, independent, free, and happy, all our fellow countrymen, every single zealous descendent of Huang-ti [the legendary first emperor of China] must determinedly and relentlessly participate in the struggle. . . ."[9]

Through such speeches and common allusions to themselves as the protectors of "our race and nation," Mao's movement successfully transferred the Hans' loyalty to itself.

A shared sense of ancestral ties can also become intermeshed in foreign policy and raise the issue of divided loyalties if important segments of the group are separated by political borders. Hitler's appeals in the name of the *Volksdeutsch* to all Germans living within Austria, the Sudetenland, and Poland are well known. More recently, Albania has claimed the right to act as the protector of Albanians within Yugoslavia on the ground that "the same mother that gave birth to us gave birth to the Albanians in Kosovo, Montenegro, and Macedonia"; China has proclaimed its right to Taiwan on the ground that "the people of Taiwan are our kith and kin"; and Kim Il Sung has declared the need to unify Korea in order to bring about the "integration of our race."[10] But again, whether such appeals are addressed to an internal or external audience, people's receptivity to them is conditional upon the existence or nonexistence of a sense of consanguinity.

HOMELANDS

As illustrated in ethnographic atlases, most of the populated land masses of the world are divided into ethnic homelands—territories whose names reflect a particular people. Armenia, Catalonia, Croatia, Finland, Iboland, Kurdistan (literally "land of the Kurds"), Nagaland, Pakhtunistan, Pol(e)land, Scotland, Somaliland, Swaziland, Uzbekistan, and Zululand constitute but a small sampling. To the people who have lent their name to the area, the homeland is much more than territory. The reverential, emotional attachment is reflected in such widely used descriptions as the native land, the fatherland, this sacred soil, the ancestral land, this hallowed place, the motherland, this blessed plot, land of our fathers, land where our fathers died, and, not least, the *home*land.

As concisely summed up in the nineteenth-century German phrase *Blut und Boden*, blood and soil become mixed in popular perceptions. Members of the homeland people are convinced that they possess an inalienable and exclusive proprietary title to the homeland. Nonmembers of the homeland may be tolerated or even encouraged as sojourners (consider the guest workers in Germany, for example), but they remain an alien presence in the eyes of the more indigenous element. The cry of "alien, go home!" can be raised at any time and can be aimed at compatriots as readily as at foreigners. To cite a few of the many current examples, the call of "Russian, go home!" has been heard in Estonia, Lithuania, and Uzbekistan; "Punjabi, go home!" in Baluchistan and Sind; "Frenchman, go home!" in Corsica; "Han, go home!" in (East) Turkestan; "Albanian, go home!" in Slovenia and Serbia; "Persian, Arab, and Turk, go home!" in Kurdistan; "Bengali, go home!" in Assam; "Castilian, go home!" in Euzkadi (Basqueland); and "Ethiopian, go home!" in both Tigre and the Ogaden district of Somaliland.

A people's sense of a plenary claim to a homeland is, of course, more dependent upon sentient than actual history, more dependent upon myth and popular perception than upon fact. In some cases, two peoples may possess conflicting claims to the same homeland. What to Israelis is "the homeland of the Jews" is part of Arabdom in Arab perceptions. Moreover, a relatively few generations may suffice to give rise to the *Blut und Boden* linkage. Thus the case of the Parti Quebecois for cultural and political autonomy—sloganized as *Maîtres Chez Nous*

("Masters in our Home")—rests upon a primal sense of homeland rendered no less powerful by the fact that no Frenchman had resided in the region prior to the sixteenth century.

The patterns of attitudes and behaviors of people living within their homeland are significantly different from those of people living outside. An impressive number of studies conducted within the multihomeland Soviet Union confirm patterns observed elsewhere. The Soviets have discovered that residence within or without the homeland exerts a perceptible influence upon, inter alia, willingness to learn a second language, willingness to enter into interethnic marriage, the choice of ethnonational identity on the part of children of interethnic marriages, and attitudes toward members of other ethnonational groups.[11] Residents of the homeland manifest greater hostility toward other groups and greater resistance to acculturation and assimilation.

Nation-States, Multinational States, and Immigrant States

Although scholars commonly refer to all states as nation-states, the true nation-state, as its name implies, is that relatively rare phenomenon of a country that demonstrates a very high level of homogeneity from an ethnonational viewpoint—that is, a situation in which a nation (in the pristine sense of an ancestrally related people) has its own state. Contemporary examples of nation-states include Japan (99.4 percent Japanese), Poland (98 percent Polish), and Sweden (93 percent Swedish). In these cases, political and ethnonational borders closely coincide. In some instances, however, although a state might be quite homogeneous and therefore qualify as a nation-state, the homeland extends well beyond its borders. Such situations, referred to as irredentist, frequently give rise to a clamor for unifying the homeland.[12]

Easily the most common type of state is the multinational variety, whose population consists of at least two significant elements with different ethnonational backgrounds. As in the case of India and Nigeria, it may contain scores. The borders of a multinational state may coincide fairly closely with an ethnic homeland if the state's heterogeneity is due to the immigration of a nonhomeland people (Sri Lanka is an illustration). Far more typically, however, the multinational state contains several, or segments of several, homelands. Iran, for example, contains all of Persia and segments of Arabdom, Azerbaijan, Baluchistan, Kurdistan, and Turkmenia. The Soviet Union contains several homelands in their entirety (for example, Estonia, Ukraine, and Georgia), and segments of several others (Azerbaijan, Turkmenia, and Tadzhikistan).

The immigrant state is the rarest form of polity. It is a state essentially devoid of homelands, with a highly variegated population in terms of ethnonational ancestry. It is not disqualified if a small fraction of its area is composed of homelands within which dwell a small percentage of the population. The United States, for example, is clearly an immigrant state, despite the presence of American Indian and Eskimo homelands.

When analogizing concerning group behavior, it is dangerous to cross the dividing lines separating nation-states, multinational states, and immigrant states. Failure to distinguish the experiences of the immigrant state from the other two classifications has been a particularly common and pernicious practice. Many reputable scholars have erroneously drawn upon the history of acculturation and assimilation of immigrant groups within the United States as a guide to the path that peoples ensconced in their own homelands within a multinational state could be anticipated to follow. Thus, they conclude that since Germans, Poles, and the like have become "Americans," Walloons and Flemings can be expected to become "Belgians," and Ibos and Hausa-Fulani to become "Nigerians." [13]

Such analogies are deficient on a number of grounds. The immigrant society, as noted, is a nonhomeland state, and the complex of attitudes and behavior of the population toward newcomers, although falling far short of "the Golden Rule," is qualitatively different from that of homeland peoples. There may be resistance to immigration, but it is not suckled by a broadly held, intuitive sense of a prehistoric and exclusive claim to the land. As set forth in the lyrics to a popular folk song, this land may indeed be "my land," but it is also true, as the lyrics add forthwith, that "this land is your land." Given the officially and popularly endorsed image of the society as "a nation of immigrants," the exclusion of individuals from any activity on the basis of ethnic heritage would necessarily undermine the society's most cherished self-held image. Thus, slavery and its aftermath, "Jim Crowism," being diametrically opposed to this image, had either to trigger the implosion of the image or to be vanquished by it. Neither could indefinitely coexist with the image; nor could various nativist movements, the application of prejudicial national origin quotas to immigrants, and Oriental exclusion acts.

The influence of the immigrant society's self-held image of a people composed of several strains is not restricted to the reception accorded to immigrants. It pertains as well to the attitudes of newcomers toward acculturation and assimilation. It is one thing, for example, for a member of the Korean minority in Japan to contemplate Nipponization and quite another for a Korean-American to contemplate Americanization. The latter can be undertaken with one's emotional memory bank intact, because the new identity is ethnically neutral. Americanization does not require one to deny or hide his or her ancestry. There is nothing inconsistent between Americanization and pre-American national ancestry. The same cannot be said for Nipponization. Moreover, as Milton Yinger notes in his chapter in [Walker Connor, ed., *Mexican-Americans in Cultural Perspective*], Americanization is a graduated process, a continuum characterized by "more-or-less" rather than "either-or." The far more traumatic, clear-cut decision of the above example to *either* retain one's identity as Korean *or* to attempt to assume the identity of a Nipponese need not be faced. Indeed, Americanization for most affected people has been more the result of a barely perceived daily process than the result of a premeditated decision.

IMPLICATIONS FOR THE COMPARATIVE STUDY OF MEXICAN-AMERICANS

It is apparent from the foregoing that there are at least two analytical frameworks within which the Mexican-American community might be placed. First, Mexican-Americans might be viewed as a geographic extension of a Mexican nation, separated from the larger segment by the U.S.-Mexican border. In such case, the framework will be global, with the analyst drawing on the experiences of several peoples in Africa and Eurasia who are similarly divided among two or more states. Second, the Mexican-American community might be viewed as an immigrant ethnic element within the framework of the United States, with analogies drawn from the experiences of German-Americans, French Canadian Americans, and the like. The two approaches need not be mutually exclusive. When properly conditioned by an appreciation of the unique features of the Mexican-American community (and this community's variance from each of these ideal models is substantial), both approaches promise added insight concerning the Mexican-American community. . . . However, the relative validity of either approach will be materially affected by the group's ethnonational self-perception.

A Mexican Nation?

As noted, the first approach would conceptualize the Mexican-Americans as an extension of the Mexican nation. But this presupposes the existence of a Mexican nation, a presupposition that requires examination.

Mexico is a mestizo-state, that is to say, a state in which people of joint European-Indian ancestry form the politically dominant element. The mestizo-states of Latin America have traditionally posed severe problems of classification and analysis to those engaged in the comparative study of ethnonationalism. If the ethnonational image that is commonly endorsed and propagated today by the governments of these states were to approximate the self-held view of their entire populations, these states would merit classification as nation-states. According to the image, a new breed or race has come forth from the melding of the European (a near synonym for Castilian) and the Indian, a breed that is not less self-perceptively homogeneous because of its antecedents than is, say, the English nation because of its Angle, Briton, Norman, and Saxon inputs. Thus throughout Latin America what is celebrated in the United States as Columbus Day is honored as *El Día de la Raza*, "the Day of the Race," or advent day for the mestizo race. [14]

The image of its populace propagated by a mestizo-state's government is therefore one in which the various indigenous Indian peoples have been fused with one another and with lesser numbers of Spanish people to form a basically undifferentiated whole. The image further maintains that from this homogeneous base has evolved a nation that is coterminous with the state—that is, a Guatemalan, Peruvian, or Mexican nation. [15]

The image of a Mexican nation is blemished by a number of contrary considerations, however. To begin with, there is a serious question concerning the degree to which the indigenous peoples have surrendered earlier ethnonational identities to a Mexican *mestizaje*. Estimates of the percentage of Mexico's population represented by Indians, in contradistinction to mestizos, range from 5 to 44 percent. [16] A popular source describes the ethnic composition of Mexico as 10 percent Caucasian, 55 percent mestizo, and 29 percent American Indian. [17] Whatever the correct figure, the number of Indians is certainly substantial.

It is also certain that the Indians remain the objects of severe discrimination. Contrary to the myth of *la raza cósmica* as the happy commingling of two equally esteemed ethnic stalks, the Indian is popularly perceived and treated as a lower species. As one anthropologist who has done field work among the Indians of Mexico has noted: "Generally speaking, Ladinos [mestizos] consider Indians as inferior beings, or children from whom it is proper to demand subordination and obedience. They believe that they themselves represent the 'superior culture'—another *raza* (race). Until recently only Ladinos were permitted to mount a horse. . . . Intermarriage between Ladinos and

Indians is likewise exceptional and looked upon with great disgust."[18]

In the words of another scholar: "The Indian is someone who is denied recognition as a full member of the human community, one who is thought to be naturally inferior."[19] Still another observes, "The Indio identity is strongly stigmatized as 'backwards' and 'inferior.' "[20]

Many Mexican mestizos have in fact come to deny that *la raza* incorporates any Indian blood. As one observer concluded from his field interviews and observations: "Originally, the term 'Mestizo' was used to refer to the Hispanized Indians or those of Spanish and Indian blood, or 'mixed blood.' But now the Mestizos claim, sometimes too vehemently, that they have no hereditary connections with Indian ancestors. . . . This claim is often expressed by their use of the label *raza blanca* (white race) to refer to themselves."[21]

And a handbook on Mexico notes that mestizo culture "values 'white blood' and deprecates Indian ancestry."[22] It adds: "Perceived racial difference is the oldest and most tenacious element affecting interethnic relationships. In some ways it is also the most pervasive. Rural ladinos and mestizos distinguish themselves from their Indian neighbors through ascribed superiority of race, blood, and genealogy. They attribute certain superior cultural qualities to their white race and blood, and they undervalue the Indian's dark skin and alleged mixture of races. Mestizos perceive cultural differences as a consequence of natural inferiority on the part of the Indian, and from the Indian point of view they represent distinctions that are natural and indelible, based on biological heredity."[23]

With Indian blood and heritage held in such low esteem, visible gradations of admixture become important within the mestizo group itself. Not just Indians, but mestizos with more evident Indian characteristics, become the target of prejudice.[24] This tendency toward further self-differentiation provides a constant reminder to its members that the mestizo community is not per se a homogeneous, ancestrally related national group.

In this setting of "us-them" cleavage between mestizo and Indian, the Indian communities within Mexico cause that country to more closely resemble a multinational state than a nation-state. And in passing, it is worth noting that in a series of other mestizo-states, Indian peoples have been adopting an increasingly assertive political stance. Antimestizo sentiments on the part of Indian peoples are already a key element in the guerrilla struggles within Guatemala and Peru, and threaten to become so within Bolivia, Ecuador, and other Latin

American states.[25] Thus, the so-called mestizo-states are experiencing the same challenges to their legitimacy as are multinational states elsewhere.

Such popular repugnance toward Indians and things that are Indian would at least superficially appear to be in sharp contrast to the official *indigenista* policies of several mestizo-states. In theory, *indigenismo* stresses the Indian stalk of the mestizo's twin heritage. And in the form of anthropological and archeological museums, the graphic arts (particularly murals and statuary), and the restoration of ancient ruins, pre-Columbian indigenous culture has indeed been promoted by a number of governments. However, far from fostering the society's adoption of Indian culture or even fostering a system of cultural pluralism, *indigenista* policies have sought the hastened integration and acculturation of the Indian peoples into the mestizo culture. The motto of Mexico's National Indian Institute, *Redimir al indio es integrar la patria* ("To redeem the Indian is to integrate the Fatherland"), is a case in point. What is intended by the Indian's redemption is his "civilizing" or Hispanization, as has been made clear by the institute's director:

> The purpose is still integration and in no way to develop in [the Indians] an ethnic consciousness that separates them from the rest of the nation. . . . The indigenous societies—rural and isolated within their self-sufficient economy and technological backwardness—try to conserve modes of life which they consider acceptable, but which constitute an obstacle to the integration of a common nationality and nation. . . . If the regional and parochial populations of Mexico do not share in a national consciousness, the changes which they experience as the inevitable consequence of their contact with modern culture could bring them—as has happened in the nations we mention—to the organization of a panindian movement that could lead them to the formation of a second nationality. As such a goal is contrary to goals of national formation the education for integration carried out among the Indian population should complement the education of the dominant population.[26]

Indigenismo therefore becomes a euphemism for acculturation and assimilation of the Indians. As one scholar has noted with regard to Peru: "*Indigenismo* is an ideology for *Mestizos*."[27] Whereas colonial powers were often accused of pitting one ethnonational group against another as part of a strategy of divide and rule, this stratagem of trying to convince the Indian peoples that they are part of a larger cosmic race might be termed a strategy of unite and rule. But, as noted, the growth of

Indian consciousness and movements strongly suggests that this strategy is not succeeding and that Mexico, as other mestizo states generally, is taking on the coloration of a multinational entity. [28]

Yet another body of evidence that blurs the image of the Mexican people as sharing a strong sense of nationhood and as perceiving the Mexican state as the political expression of that nation consists of attitudinal surveys that disclose a remarkable lack of identification among the Mexican people with the Mexican state and its political institutions. One such study disclosed that more than one-third of the population was not at all affected by the Mexican state apparatus and only a tenth considered themselves as participants in the system. [29] Moreover, in Almond and Verba's highly publicized comparative study, fully two-thirds of the respondents stated that the central government had no effect whatsoever upon their daily life. [30] As was generally true of all of the case studies in the Almond and Verba book, the ethnic factor was simply ignored, but it can safely be assumed that the Indian peoples are among the most alienated. [31]

A portrait of Mexico as a nation-state would therefore be a highly overdrawn one. Some unknown percentage of mestizos unquestionably do consider themselves part of a Mexican nation in the sense of an ancestrally related group. But the Indian component certainly does not. Nor do a large but incalculable percentage of mestizos who are dissuaded from identifying themselves with a Mexican nation because of commonly encountered denigration of their ethnic roots. By definition, such attitudes characterize a *trans*national, not an *intra*national relationship. An inkling of the growing significance of interethnic relations within Mexico was offered by the current president of Mexico during the 1982 presidential campaign when, in a "first" for Mexican leaders, he publicly acknowledged that Mexico was a multinational state. [32] His action suggested that dissension among the Indian peoples had become too pronounced to be any longer hidden or ignored.

A Homeland People?

Refocusing on our primary concern—those people of Mexican background living north of the U.S.-Mexican border—raises the question of the degree to which Mexican-Americans perceive of themselves as living within an extension of the Mexican homeland. There are two quite different, although not contradictory, cases that are made for such a transborder homeland. One is mythological in nature, holding that what is now the southwestern United States was once *Aztlán*, the legendary original homeland of the ancient Aztecs. Belief that a particular territory constituted the original cradle of one's people is the more powerful for being mythical and unprovable, and the militant Chicano movement of the late 1960s and early 1970s made liberal use of this emotion-laden term when attempting to raise ethnic consciousness among Mexican-Americans. [33]

The other justification for declaring the region part of a Mexican homeland involves the fact that people from Mexico began to settle in the area in the late sixteenth century and were there before the coming of "Americans." It is probably not important that the only numerically large settlement before the U.S. annexation had been in what is now New Mexico and that many of the early settlers subsequently moved south of the newly established border. [34] Nor is it of vital significance that these early Mexican settlements testify that Mexicans were not native to the area and that the area could therefore not be their homeland. [35] Perceptions are again the key, and some Mexican-Americans perceive that they have a plenary right to the land because it was part of their heritage before it was wrested away by the invaders. [36]

Mexican-Americans are, of course, intently aware of this aspect of the region's history. Daily reminders of previous Mexican ownership abound in the plentiful presence of Spanish place names (El Paso, Los Angeles, San Antonio), Spanish names for the region's outstanding natural phenomena (Sierra Nevada Mountains, Colorado River), and examples of early Spanish and Mexican architecture. This knowledge that the region was once Mexican has a psychological dimension, inspiring a special sense of a historically derived right to live in the region, a right that immigrants from an overseas ancestral homeland cannot feel (such as those of Swedish descent living within Minnesota, with its plethora of names derived from the American Indians for places and natural phenomena). One manifestation of this feeling among Mexican-Americans is the popular eschewing of the adjective *illegal* to refer to those who have crossed the border without U.S. authorization. Whereas the expression *illegal immigrants* is most commonly used by others, Mexican-Americans have tended to describe such migrants as merely *undocumented.*

Despite this special historic connection, however, there is ample evidence that most Mexican-Americans do not feel that they possess a plenary and exclusive right to this territory, which has been described above as the hallmark of a homeland people. Separatist sentiments and cries of "Anglos, go home!" have been rare and have failed to elicit broad support. Even the militantly ethnonational party *La Raza Unida,* which realized some highly localized electoral successes in the early 1970s, projected its goals within a continuing U.S. framework. As a position paper noted, the party "must symbolize the creation of a nation within a nation, a spiritual unification for effective action of all persons of Mexican descent in the United States."[37] The concept of national self-determination was part of the party's program but, as described by two students of the party's history, it was "self-determination interpreted not as secession from the United States but as the gaining of control of existing institutions and the creation of new ones where necessary."[38]

As noted earlier, studies conducted in a number of other societies establish that residence within the homeland tends to buttress the maintenance of ethnonational identity. But group self-identification studies establish that most people who, or whose ancestors, came to the United States from present-day Mexico do not consider themselves to be Mexican. In three careful surveys carried out in the mid-1970s, respondents were asked the most appropriate group designation for themselves. The *combined totals* for those replying Mexican, Mexicano, or Chicano were only 16 percent, 28.5 percent, and 31 percent of all interviewees in the respective surveys.[39] All other respondents identified themselves either as Mexican-American or by a group nomenclature that contained no reference whatsoever to Mexican background. Similarly, when offered the opportunity in the 1980 census to designate themselves as "Mexican, Mexican-American, [or] Chicano," nearly 1.25 million people living within the five states that are commonly considered to constitute the homeland (Arizona, California, Colorado, New Mexico, and Texas) opted instead for a category ("Spanish/Hispanic") which denied any hint of Mexican ancestry.[40]

The matter of group self-referent is extremely important, for research has established that employing *American* as part of one's group name is a good index of behavior. Those who use it are more apt to have a positive view toward integration into the society and a more positive view toward other ethnic groups.[41] In other words, use of the term *Mexican-American* is correlated with behavior and attitudes that are the opposite of those that comparative studies have found associated with residence in a homeland. And, again, most of the community under study refer to themselves as Mexican-Americans, while a substantial number reject all reference to a Mexican heritage.

Even the percentage figures for that small fraction who identify themselves as Mexican or Mexicano may not necessarily possess ethnonational overtones but may be analogous to Ibos or Hausas identifying themselves as Nigerian when outside of the country, or persons of Flemish or Walloon background reporting themselves as Belgian in the U.S. census. In this context it is pertinent to note that when asked to choose from a list of attributes those aspects of the Mexican heritage they would like to preserve in their children, only 5 percent of the respondents in Los Angeles and only 3 percent in San Antonio selected "identity as Mexican" and only 2 percent and 1 percent, respectively, selected "patriotism, Mexican nationalism."[42] Moreover, employing a substantial data base, John Garcia has determined that more than half of the U.S. minority who describe themselves as "Mexican" (56.2 percent) and three-quarters of those identifying themselves as "Mexicano" (74.6 percent) were born south of the U.S.-Mexican border.[43] And newly arrived members of any group would be those most expected to describe themselves as German, Chinese, Mexican, or what have you.[44]

Data on intermarriage further attest to the weakness of a homeland psychology. Comparative studies, as noted, disclose a resistance to intermarriage on the part of those living within a homeland. But a 1965–66 survey found that 82 percent of Mexican-Americans living within San Antonio and 88 percent living within Los Angeles did not frown upon intermarriage. The credence of these figures is lent powerful support by increasingly high rates of group intermarriage. Geography and urban or rural domicile exert great influence, but the rate of intermarriage in nearly every locale, and most assuredly the rate for Mexican-Americans as a whole, is well above that normally associated with an endogamous group. For example, in San Antonio the percentage of exogamous marriages among Mexican-Americans progressively increased from 17 percent in 1940–55 to 27 percent in 1973; in Albuquerque, the percentage went from 22 percent in 1945 to 48 percent in 1967;[45] in Los Angeles the exogamy rate jumped from 17 percent in 1924–33 to 40 percent in 1963 and has remained slightly above 50 percent in California as a whole for the past two decades.[46] As with other groups in the United States, studies of Mexican-Americans show that exogamy increases significantly with each subsequent generation. Given the fact that the Mexican-American community has a large percentage of new arrivals and that the influx continues, these rates of exogamy become even more striking.[47]

The pattern may be duplicated with regard to language maintenance. Basing his study on language use in Los Angeles, David Lopez has concluded that when the impact of continuing mass migration is controlled for, the rate of attrition in language maintenance is comparable to the attrition rate experienced by earlier European immigrants: "The inescapable conclusion is that were it not for new arrivals from Mexico, Spanish would disappear from Los Angeles nearly as rapidly as most European immigrant languages vanished from cities in the East."[48] Minimally, it can be said that the intermarriage and language maintenance patterns of Mexican-Americans do not reflect those associated with homeland peoples.

Yet another indication of a lack of consciousness of homeland is the increasing tendency for Mexican-Americans to disperse widely outside the five states that are generally described as comprising the homeland. The numerical size of the California and Texas components, which alone account for 26 percent of all Mexican-Americans, tends to hide the scope of this diffusion. Today, Mexican-Americans in Illinois alone more than double the number in either Colorado or New Mexico and roughly equal the numbers in Arizona. There are now important pockets of Mexican-Americans in such geographically dispersed states as Michigan, Washington, Florida, Indiana, and Kansas. At the time of the 1980 census, more than a million Mexican-Americans (15 percent of the total) were living outside of the five southwestern states, and the trend was definitely in the direction of greater dispersal.[49]

A final consideration concerning the image of a homeland people concerns the views that Mexican-Americans hold toward further immigration across the U.S.-Mexican border. In fact, these attitudes show little deviation from those of the U.S. populace as a whole. According to Gallup, 75 percent of people of Hispanic descent agree that the hiring of undocumented workers should be decreed an illegal act, and precisely the same percentage support a proposal requiring citizens and legal (documented) residents to carry internal "passports" that would have to be presented as a prerequisite for employment.[50] The corresponding figures for the entire population were 79 percent and 66 percent. Another poll recorded that 60 percent of all Hispanics within the United States and 66 percent of those Hispanics holding U.S. citizenship were in favor of "penalties and fines for employers who hire illegal aliens."[51] Spokesmen for Mexican-American organizations have generally lobbied against such legislation, but a 1984 poll indicated that even the leaders of the Mexican-American community were badly split on the issue, with 40 percent favoring sanctions against employers of undocumented migrants.[52]

Overall, then, the data show that Mexican-Americans do not broadly conceptualize themselves as a homeland people. Mexican-Americans are unquestionably aware that the southwestern United States was once part of Mexico, and this awareness tends to lead to a feeling that people from Mexico consequently possess a claim to the land—a claim that, because of its longer history, is superior to any claim that could be made by someone of English, German, or Irish descent. But judging by their attitudes and behavior, most Mexican-Americans perceive this claim more in chronological and historic-legal terms than in the spiritual-mythological terms of an ancestrally created linkage between blood and soil.[53] While even the former type of claim has psychological and emotional dimensions, the data demonstrate that it is vitally different from the latter in the patterns of attitudes and behavior to which it gives rise.

A much smaller percentage of Mexican-Americans, some incalculable fraction of that minority of the community who identify themselves as Mexican or Mexicano, do conceive of themselves as an extension of a Mexican nation. In addition, an unknown percentage of the undocumented migrants unquestionably think of themselves as Mexican. The undocumented element represents a not insignificant consideration. Given the present U.S. government's estimate of some 3.5 to 6 million undocumented aliens, these people possibly account for from 37 to 51 percent of all people of Mexican background currently within the United States.[54] (If the sometimes-encountered figure of 12 million undocumented aliens were used, they would account for two-thirds of the total Mexican-American population.)[55] Nevertheless, no evidence was encountered to contradict the conclusion of Rodolfo de la Garza that "though they feel strong cultural ties to Mexico, Chicanos overall feel almost no political attachment to Mexico."[56]

An Ethnic Community within the U.S. Context?

Aside from that fraction of Mexican-Americans who consider themselves a homeland people, can one comparatively treat the remainder as equivalent to other ethnically defined immigrant groups, such as the Polish-Americans? Polish-Americans, of course, conceptualize themselves as ancestrally related. By contrast, many people who are treated in the literature as Mexican-Americans emphatically deny any Mexican ancestry, insisting that they are of purely Spanish (by which is usually meant Castilian) ancestry. Many of these people trace their history back to the earlier settler families in the Southwest. Apparently vexed by this renunciation of Mexican ancestry, a number of writers have taken pains to establish that only a small handful of families can legitimately make such a claim. But this type of criticism again ignores the fact that in matters of group identity, it is the perception and not the fact that shapes attitudes and behavior. If people delude themselves into believing that they are not of Mexican descent, they will be deaf to calls in its name.

The 1980 census indicates that the number of people shunning a claim to Mexican ancestry is quite substantial. In addition to the categories of "Mexican, Mexican-American, Chicano" and "Spanish/

Hispanic," the census made allowance for people to declare themselves Argentinean, Bolivian, Chilean, Colombian, Costa Rican, Cuban, Dominican, Ecuadoran, Guatemalan, Honduran, Nicaraguan, Panamanian, Peruvian, Puerto Rican, Salvadoran, Spaniard, Uruguayan, and Venezuelan. It is therefore safe to assume that those who opted for the "Spanish/Hispanic" category were largely those who are customarily grouped statistically with Mexican-Americans but who prefer to stress a pure Spanish, non-Mexican heritage. As indicated in Table 1, those who spurned the offered category of "Mexican, Mexican-American, [or] Chicano" in favor of "Spanish/Hispanic" accounted for more than 15 percent of those customarily grouped with Mexican-Americans. More than 500,000 "Hispanics" in California alone denied any Mexican ancestry. In Colorado, those who chose "Spanish/Hispanic" were nearly as numerous as those indicating a Mexican background. And in New Mexico, Hispanics denying Mexican roots substantially outnumbered those who acknowledged them.

It can further be assumed that many people who chose the "Mexican, Mexican-American, Chicano" category were indicating thereby a country of ancestral origin, rather than an ethnonational unit. It has been shown that Mexico does not contain an ethnically homogeneous population and that, from a combination of choice and rebuff, Indians and dark-skinned mestizos have maintained a sense of identity distinct from that of the dominant group. Not surprisingly, these same considerations play a role north of the border.[57] One is seriously handicapped in pursuing this matter, however, by an almost total absence of data, for, as Carlos Arce has noted, "The function and impact of color and race [read ancestry] among Chicanos has been seriously neglected."[58] There is, for example, no firm basis for estimating the number of Indians among the Mexican-American community. One commonly cited set of figures holds that Mexican-Americans are 40

Table 1. Ancestral Self-Referent in the 1980 Census

State	Mexican, Mexican-American, Chicano	Spanish/Hispanic	Ratio of First Column to Second Column
Arizona	368,259	48,495	0.13
California	3,361,773	539,285	0.16
Colorado	160,548	154,396	0.96
New Mexico	153,960	281,189	1.82
Texas	2,495,035	221,568	0.09
Totals	6,539,575	1,224,933	0.19

percent full-blooded Indians, 55 percent mestizos, and 5 percent people of purely European ancestry, but the basis for these figures is not clear.[59] Arce adds that the class profile and geographic source of migrants make it likely that the percentage of American Indians among the Mexican-American community is larger than that among the population of Mexico: "The overwhelmingly lower class, rural, Central Mexican origin of Chicanos suggests that Mexicans in the United States are more likely to be of Indian than European ancestry, or if they are *mestizos* (part Indian, part European), to be genotypically more Indian than Mexicans south of the border." [60]

In any case, it is not figures indicating ancestry but rather figures indicating perceptions of ancestry that are required. Moreover, treating the Mexican-American community as a triad composed of Castilians, mestizos, and Indians does not do justice to the community's complexity, for *Indian* is itself a transethnic category. In bemoaning the lack of key data concerning the various identities of Mexican-American peoples, one source has cogently noted: "Another facet of which there are curious hints in many interviews is the symbolic significance of particular Indian strains. Being part Tarahumara is very different in meaning from being part Tarrascan, just as Hopi is from Sioux. These differences in meaning would be more strongly felt in Indian-conscious Mexico, of course, than in the United States. But it is also a matter of special interest in the United States among a population whose legal 'whiteness' is symbolically important." [61]

Future research will therefore presumably confirm that sociopolitically important divisions predicated upon perceptions of ancestry exist at the intra-Indian level of the Mexican-American community.

Although it is therefore oversimplified, the tripartite division into Castilian, mestizo, and Indian does reflect the dominant self-held view of the key divisions within the Mexican-American community. The low regard in which Indian blood is held is evident in the aforementioned tendency of large numbers to hold fervently to a fictional, purely Castilian account of their ancestry.

Quite inadvertently, the militant Chicano movement of the late 1960s and early 1970s provided a hint of the social distance between the larger community and those of predominantly Indian heritage. In an attempt to propagate a single ethnonational identity among all Mexican-Americans, the movement emphasized the Indian roots common to the entire community. Aspects of its campaign included (1) the popularization of the group self-referent *Chicano* (formerly considered a pejorative); (2) appeals to a separate and unifying consciousness on the basis of a presumed difference in skin pigmentation between the dominant society and the community ("brown power," the brown berets); (3) the dichotomous division of the society into "us" and "them," all "them" being regularly described as "Anglos"; and (4) the development of a common sense of nationhood by the ubiquitous venerating of *La Raza*. In his not unsympathetic account of the Chicano movement, Edward Murguia describes the impact of the movement upon its converts as follows:

> Expressions of antagonism toward Anglos as well as toward anglicized Mexican Americans are heard. There is an attempt by those in the movement to become very Mexican. One begins to speak Spanish more and more on every occasion that presents itself. On purpose, one begins to eat tortillas, enchiladas, tamales and beans very often. One becomes very racially and culturally aware of what others in the decolonization movement are doing. One begins to pay attention to the struggles of *La Raza* as an oppressed people in the United States nationally, regionally and locally. Instead of the more "güero" (light-skinned) Mexican Americans being favored, the more Indian physical type is favored. Instead of wishing that they looked more güero, those in the movement find themselves wishing that they looked more Indian. [62]

Here, then, was a call to unity predicated upon Indianness. But the Chicano movement's star, which never shined very brightly, soon went into eclipse. Its party, *La Raza Unida*, was never able, despite great effort, to acquire even one-third of the necessary 66,000 registrants to qualify as a legally recognized political party in California. [63] And the group designation of Chicano is still far more popular among those who write about the Mexican-Americans than it is within that community. [64] In John Garcia's survey of Mexican-Americans, only 4 percent described themselves as Chicano, and in a survey in Denver undertaken by Nicholas Lovrich and Otwin Marenin, only 10 percent did so. [65] In sum, appeals to an Indian heritage failed to elicit broad support. [66]

The failure of the Chicano label, or any other group self-designation, to find broad favor casts yet another shadow across the image of the Mexican-Americans as a single ethnic community. Upon first introduction to the Mexican-American literature, the comparativist is struck by what has been aptly termed "the Battle of the Name." [67] Surveys document that the designations American and Americano, Chicano, Hispano, Latin-American, Latino, Mexican and Mexicano, Mexican-American, Spanish, Spanish-American, and Spanish-speaking all have their devotees. Because choice of name indicates the ancestral family to which one feels one belongs—or from which one wishes to clearly disassociate oneself—the battle of names has been waged with great fervor and has often prevented cooperative action among organizations.[68] One finds nothing remotely comparable among Armenian, Croatian, German, Irish, Japanese, and Ukrainian-Americans, each of whom is defined by a collective sense of common ancestry.

TWO FRAMEWORKS

Mexican-Americans therefore represent a far more heterogeneous people than their common grouping under a single rubric would suggest. This heterogeneity possesses substantive implications for comparative analysis. To the degree that Mexican-Americans consider themselves part of an uninterrupted homeland people, they can be placed within a global framework and validly contrasted with transborder ethnic groups. To the degree that Mexican-Americans consider themselves an ancestrally related immigrant group, they can be validly contrasted with other such groups in the United States. . . . But what should not be lost sight of is that there are many people, commonly grouped under the collective title of Mexican-Americans, who do not share in either perception.

Notes

1. George Theodorson and Achilles Theodorson, *A Modern Dictionary of Sociology* (New York: Thomas Y. Crowell Co., 1969), p. 135. A similar definition is offered by H. S. Morris, under the entry "Ethnic Groups" in *The International Encyclopedia of the Social Sciences* (New York: Macmillan and Free Press, 1968).

2. Max Weber, *Economy and Society*, vol. 1, Guenther Roth and Claus Wittich, eds. (New York: Bedminster Press, 1968), p. 389. Elsewhere (p. 395), Weber made clear the close relationship he perceived between the nation and the ethnic group: "The concept of 'nationality' (or 'nations') shares with that of the 'people' (*Volk*)—in the 'ethnic' sense—the vague connotation that whatever is felt to be distinctively common must derive from common descent."

3. See U.S. Department of Commerce, Bureau of the Census, *1980 Census of Population: Ancestry of the Population by States: 1980*, Supplementary Report PC80-S1-10 (Washington, D.C.: U.S. Government Printing Office, April 1983), p. 1 and particularly footnote 1: "In this report, the terms 'ancestry' and 'origin' (and ancestry group and ethnic group) are used interchangeably."

4. The confusion was guaranteed by the instructions to the respondents for answering the question, "What is this person's ancestry?" The instructions read, "Print the ancestry group with which the person *identifies*. Ancestry (or origin or descent) may be viewed as the nationality group, the lineage, or the country in

which the person or the person's parents or ancestors were born before their arrival in the United States," ibid., p. 9. Given the complex multiethnic composition of most countries, this encouragement to substitute country for ancestry was certain to invalidate the results.

5. Belgium, of course, has been riven by ethnonational rivalry between its Flemish and Walloon components.

6. The census first inquired, "Is this person of Spanish/Hispanic origin or descent?" If answered affirmatively, the respondent had a choice of answers, one of which was "Yes, Mexican, Mexican-American, Chicano." U.S. Department of Commerce, *1980 Census: Ancestry.*

7. The question is addressed below.

8. Mao Tse-tung, *Selected Works of Mao Tse-tung*, vol. 3 (Peking: Foreign Languages Press, 1975), p. 38.

9. Conrad Brandt, Benjamin Schwartz, and John Fairbank, *A Documentary History of Chinese Communism* (London: Allen and Unwin, 1952), pp. 245–47.

10. See Robert King, *Minorities under Communism* (Cambridge, Mass.: Harvard University Press, 1973), p. 144; *New York Times*, September 1, 1975; and *Atlas* (February 1976), p. 19.

11. For a review of Soviet studies, see Walker Connor, *The National Question in Marxist-Leninist Theory and Strategy* (Princeton: Princeton University Press, 1984), chapter 11.

12. The desire of the Somali Democratic Republic to incorporate those parts of Somaliland currently within Djibouti, Ethiopia, and Kenya is a current case in point.

13. Karl Deutsch and Alfred Cobban are among the better known scholars to have fallen prey to this faulty analogy. For details, see Walker Connor, "Self-Determination: The New Phase," *World Politics*, vol. 20 (October 1967), pp. 30–53; and "Nation-Building or Nation-Destroying?" *World Politics*, vol. 24 (April 1972), pp. 319–55.

14. The principal inspiration for the notion of a new race was a book written by José Vasconcelos, *La Raza Cósmica* (Barcelona: Agencia Mundial de Librería, 1925). For a sympathetic account of Vasconcelos's ideas on the new race, see John Haddox, *Vasconcelos of Mexico* (Austin: University of Texas Press, 1967), pp. 53–71. For highly critical accounts, see Carlos Rangel, *The Latin Americans: Their Love-Hate Relationship with the United States* (New York: Harcourt Brace Jovanovich, 1976), particularly pp. 91–99; and Leo Grebler, Joan Moore, and Ralph Guzman, *The Mexican-American People* (New York: Free Press, 1970), pp. 379–80.

15. See, for example, the speech of Ríos Montt, former president of Guatemala, in *Foreign Broadcast Information Service*, vol. 26 (July 1982), p. P8: "We Guatemalans . . . are a dark-skinned people. We are not Anglo-Saxons. . . . Ours is an Indian country. This is our nation. . . . Our Indian is more of a man

when he works more, when he can do his job better, when he can do two jobs better. We should learn to be his kind of man, a Guatemalan man, not a gringo or Russian but Guatemalan."

16. See *Area Handbook for Mexico*, 2d ed., Department of the Army Pamphlet 550-79 (Washington, D.C.: U.S. Government Printing Office, 1975), p. 88. A major contributing element to the broad range of estimates is that contrary to the conceptualization of the mestizo as a new cosmic race, mestizo often has more of a cultural than an ethnonational basis. Indigenous peoples have become mestizos over time by adopting the Spanish language, non-Indian garb, and possibly a Spanish surname. The reverse procedure is also possible.

17. *The World Almanac and Book of Facts 1983* (New York: Newspaper Enterprise Associations, 1982), p. 544.

18. Henning Siverts, "Ethnic Stability and Boundary Dynamics in Southern Mexico," in Fredrik Barth, ed., *Ethnic Groups and Boundaries: The Social Organization of Culture Differences* (London: George Allen and Unwin, 1970), p. 110.

19. Julian Pitt-Rivers, "Race in Latin America: The Concept of 'Raza'," *European Journal of Sociology*, vol. 14 (1973), pp. 12–30. Reprinted in John Stone, ed., *Race, Ethnicity, and Social Change* (North Scituate, Mass.: Duxbury Press, 1977). The citation can be found on p. 320.

20. Edwin Almirol, "Economic Strategies and Ethnic Alternatives," *Human Relations*, vol. 31 (1978), p. 368.

21. Ibid., p. 364.

22. *Area Handbook for Mexico*, p. 103. This fixation with blood recalls a much older obsession of Spaniards with what was once termed *limpieza de sangre* (purity of blood). It was popularized during the period of the Inquisition to differentiate the faithful from the infidel Moors and Jews. It was later employed in the New World to differentiate those of pure Spanish (Castilian) ancestry from those with American Indian background. Its more recent adoption (in content, if not in name) by members of a cosmic race, defined as an admixture of two races, in order to deny any ancestral connection to one of the two constituent races is indeed a paradox, but the sort of psychological paradox with which issues involving ethnonational identity abound.

23. *Ibid.*, p. 104. For two other accounts of the prejudice practiced by Mexican mestizos toward Indian compatriots, see Pablo Gonzales Casanova, *Democracy in Mexico* (London: Oxford University Press, 1970), pp. 94–103; and Rodolfo Stavenhagen, *Between Underdevelopment and Revolution: A Latin American Perspective* (New Delhi: Abhinav Publications, 1981), particularly p. 65. Given all the evidence and numerous accounts of the ubiquity of this discrimination, the glancing references to it in the case study of Mexico found in José Domínguez et al., *Enhancing Global Human Rights* (New York: McGraw-Hill, 1979) on pp. 69–71 and 83–84 are surprisingly meager.

24. See, for example, Joan Moore, *Mexican Americans*, 2d ed. (Englewood Cliffs, N.J.: Prentice Hall, 1976), p. 114: "(Thus the myth of 'pure blood' was not invented in the United States.) Mexicans of mixed Spanish-Indian blood or of pure Indian ancestry have long suffered from discrimination and exploitation in their own country." A mestizo with strong Indian features is apt to be sarcastically referred to as an *indio revestido*, (a "redressed Indian"), that is to say, one who has simply changed his clothes but cannot thereby hide his non-Latino Indianness.

25. The Maoist *Sendero Luminoso* (Shining Path) movement within Peru is Indian (Quechuan) based. For the proclamation of a movement dedicated to the obliteration of the Bolivian-Peruvian-Ecuadorian borders and the establishment of a state along the geographic lines of the old Inca Empire, see *Keesing's Contemporary Archives* (1982), p. 31308. Demands for increased autonomy have recently been pressed by a number of Indian peoples within Panama, and separatist/autonomous aspirations on the part of the Miskito Indians have become an important element in the Nicaragua saga. In the literature that these movements have spawned, the Day of the Race is termed "the Day of Misfortune."

26. The statements were made by Gonzalo Aguirre Beltrán during 1972 and 1973 and are cited in Alicia Barabas and Miguel Bartolomé, *Hydraulic Development and Ethnocide: The Mazatec and Chinantec People of Oaxaca, Mexico* (Copenhagen: International Work Group for Indigenous Affairs, 1973), IWGIA Document 15, pp. 16–17.

27. François Bourricaud, as cited by Pitt-Rivers, "Race in Latin America," p. 323. See also Stavenhagen, *Between Underdevelopment and Revolution*, particularly p. 67.

28. See Rodolfo Stavenhagen, "Indian Ethnic Movements and State Policies in Latin America," paper prepared for the VII World Conference of the World Future Studies Federation, Stockholm, Sweden, June 6–8, 1982.

29. *Area Handbook for Mexico*, p. 226.

30. Gabriel Almond and Sidney Verba, *The Civic Culture* (Boston: Little, Brown & Co., 1965), p. 46.

31. A recent criticism of the Almond and Verba work states that, if anything, the study painted a more homogeneous picture of Mexico than was warranted because its sample did not reflect "the pronounced differences among regions in that country in terms of economic development, land-tenure patterns, occupational structure, *ethnicity*, religiosity, political participation, relationship with the federal government, and other dimensions." See Ann Craig and Wayne Cornelius, "Political Culture in Mexico: Continuities and Revisionist Interpretations," in Gabriel Almond and Sidney Verba, eds., *The Civic Culture Revisited* (Boston: Little, Brown & Co., 1980), p. 337 (emphasis added).

32. Stavenhagen, "Indian Ethnic Movements," p. 12. At the time this article was written, the president of Mexico was Miguel de la Madrid. The current

president of Mexico is Carlos Salinas de Gortari. His Institutional Revolutionary Party, of which Mr. de la Madrid was also a member, has ruled without interruption since 1929. (ed.)

33. Its use extended to entitling a journal *Aztlán*.

34. The most commonly employed estimates hold that at the time of U.S. annexation, there were approximately 60,000 Mexicans in present-day New Mexico, but only 7,500 in California, 5,000 in Texas, and 1,000 in Arizona. These statistics are customarily based upon those first offered by Carey McWilliams, *North from Mexico* (Philadelphia: J.B. Lippincott, 1949).

35. The approximately 70,000 Mexican settlers were outnumbered by some 120,000 American Indians of the area. See Moore, *Mexican Americans*, p. 12.

36. Steiner, for example, states flatly that the Mexican-Americans are native to the area: "One of the distinguishing characteristics of the Mexican American people is that it is one of the two indigenous minorities; the other being the American Indians. The saying is: We did not come to America, America came to us!" See Stan Steiner, *The Mexican Americans* (London: Minority Rights Group, 1979), p. 14. One author has suggested that the area was not so much conquered as it was lost through neglect. He draws on an extensive body of primary and secondary literature to conclude that Mexico City's disinterest caused the people dwelling in the area to perceive the United States as a more responsive alternative. See David Weber, *The Mexican Frontier, 1821–1846: The American Southwest under Mexico* (Albuquerque: University of New Mexico Press, 1982).

37. Cited in Carlos Muñoz and Mario Barrera, "La Raza Unida Party and the Chicano Student Movement in California," *Social Science Journal*, vol. 19 (April 1982), p. 113.

38. Ibid., p. 111. For additional avowals that the Chicano movement, including La Raza Unida party, was integrationist, see Fred Cervantes, "Chicanos as a Post-Colonial Minority: Some Questions Concerning the Adequacy of the Paradigm of Internal Colonialism," pp. 129, 130, 131, and 132; and Tatcho Mindiola, "Marxism and the Chicano Movement: Preliminary Remarks," pp. 179 and 185; both in Reynaldo F. Macías, ed., *Perspectivas en Chicano Studies I* (Los Angeles: National Association of Chicano Social Science, 1975). Both writers note that there were those who were unhappy with this integrationist posture.

39. In the same order: Philip Lampe, "Ethnic Self-Referent and the Assimilation of Mexican Americans," *Journal of Comparative Sociology*, vol. 19 (September–December 1978), p. 262; John Garcia, "Yo Soy Mexicano . . .: Self-Identity and Sociodemographic Correlates," *Social Science Quarterly*, vol. 62 (March 1981), p. 90; and Nicholas Lovrich and Otwin Marenin, "A Comparison of Black and Mexican American Voters in Denver," *Western Political Quarterly*, vol. 29 (June 1976), p. 291. Geographic differences and differences in the questions (specific categories versus free choice) skew the results.

40. Department of Commerce, *1980 Census: Ancestry*, p. 9 and table 3

pp. 28 et seq. For additional comment on these "Spanish/Hispanics," see the discussion below under the heading "An Ethnic Community within the U.S. Context?"

41. Lampe, "Ethnic Self-Referent," particularly p. 267. The difference in attitudinal patterns is not just between those who identify themselves as Mexican-American and those who identify themselves as Mexican or Mexicano. Some rather sharp differences can be found between self-identified "Mexican-Americans" and "Chicanos." As Lampe has more recently reported: "Finally, differences have been found to exist between those who self-identify as Mexican Americans and those who self-identify as Chicanos, with the latter exhibiting significantly more anti-Anglo feelings and antiestablishment orientation in addition to greater anger, hostility and militancy." Philip Lampe, "Ethnic Labels: Naming or Name Calling?" *Ethnic and Racial Studies*, vol. 5 (October 1982), p. 546.

42. Grebler et al., *Mexican-American People*, p. 384. "Spanish language" (51 percent and 32 percent) was the most popular choice, followed by "manners and customs" (33 percent and 38 percent). Significantly, 15 percent and 28 percent stated that they wish to preserve nothing of the Mexican heritage in their children. The interviews were conducted during 1965 and 1966. In 1972 Ambrecht and Pachon reinterviewed 51 of the original 759 respondents in the Los Angeles area. See Biliana Ambrecht and Harry Pachon, "Ethnic Political Mobilization in a Mexican American Community: An Exploratory Study of East Los Angeles 1965–1972," *Western Political Quarterly*, vol. 27 (September 1974), p. 508. They found an increase in what they termed "Mexican identity, culture, pride" (21 percent). However, given (1) the small sample, (2) the addition of culture and pride to "identity as Mexican," and (3) the failure to include the category of "patriotism, Mexican nationalism," there appears to be a lack of comparability between the two studies.

43. Garcia, "Yo Soy Mexicano," p. 92. By contrast, 94.3 percent of those identifying themselves as Mexican-American and 99.1 percent of those selecting "Other Spanish" were born in the United States. Those replying *Chicano* were also overwhelmingly U.S.-born (96.3 percent). However, those identifying themselves as Chicanos accounted for the smallest percentage of the total sample (4.0 percent, as contrasted with 20.1 percent responding *Mexican* and 4.4 percent responding *Mexicano*). Moreover, there is a close association between Chicano identity and membership in La Raza Unida party, and, as we have seen, that party, although militantly ethnonational, defined its goals within a U.S. context.

44. Given the high percentages of foreign born among those reporting themselves as Mexican or Mexicano, it is also probable that the sample contains a number of undocumented migrants who consider their stay in the United States as temporary. Studies of undocumented workers and data gathered by the U.S. Immigration Service record a great deal of circular migration between the two countries.

45. A subsequent study in 1971 indicated a sharp drop to (the still very high rate of) 39 percent. However, as later studies in other Mexican-American communities have indicated, the 1971–73 period represented a deviation from the norm. This was a period of intense Chicano militancy, particularly among those of marrying age. On this point, see Alverado Valdez, "Recent Increases in Intermarriage by Mexican American Males: Bexar County, Texas, from 1971 to 1980," *Social Science Quarterly*, vol. 64 (March 1984), p. 139.

46. For a helpful summary of the findings of a number of intermarriage studies, see Edward Murguia, *Chicano Intermarriage: A Theoretical and Empirical Study* (San Antonio: Trinity University Press, 1982), pp. 48–49. The lowest figures recorded have been for Hidalgo County in Texas, a nonmetropolitan area in a state with a traditionally higher level of intergroup tensions than California or New Mexico. However, even here exogamous marriages nearly doubled from 5 to 9 percent during the 1960s. For a recent study of intermarriage not covered by the table in Murguia, see Valdez, "Recent Increases in Intermarriage."

47. For comments on the impact of generation, see Grebler et al., *Mexican-American People*, pp. 409–10. Murguia, *Chicano Intermarriage*, detects some leveling off in the rate of intermarriage, but this perception is seemingly due to a disregard for the closely interrelated phenomena of intergenerational differences and the continuing huge influx of first-generation immigrants.

48. David Lopez, "Chicano Language Loyalty in an Urban Setting," *Sociology and Social Research*, vol. 62 (January 1978), p. 276.

49. All the figures would be altered if those who described themselves in the 1980 census as "Spanish/Hispanic" were included in the calculations.

50. *New York Times*, November 15, 1983. Although the report did not further break down "respondents of Hispanic descent" in the 1980 census, Mexican-Americans accounted for nearly three-quarters (72 percent) of all people of Hispanic background who furnished a country of origin for themselves or their ancestors. (Extrapolated from Department of Commerce, *1980 Census: Ancestry*, p. 14.)

51. See the letter by the executive director of the Federation for American Immigration Reform, in "Letters to the Editor," *New York Times*, May 7, 1984.

52. *Wall Street Journal*, June 11, 1984.

53. Thus, some of the more publicized and bitter episodes arising from ancient claims to the land by Mexican-Americans have been predicated upon the legality of centuries-old land grants from the Spanish and Mexican authorities, rather than upon claims to a homeland. See, for example, the article entitled "Ethnic Tensions Rise in New Mexico after Arson," *New York Times*, July 16, 1982.

54. For a statement by Attorney General William French Smith to the effect that during 1983 an additional 500,000 illegal aliens were expected to join the 3.5 to 6.0 million already here, see the *Christian Science Monitor*, March 1, 1983.

55. These estimates are based on the assumption that Mexican-Americans account for the lion's share of undocumented immigrants. It is also based upon an assumption of some 5.5 million Mexican-Americans who are citizens or documented residents. The latter figure was derived by subtracting the 2,074,000 illegal immigrants who were counted in the 1980 census from the census figure of 7,692,619 Mexican-Americans. For the source of the 2,047,000 figure, see "Estimates of Aliens Baffle U.S.," *New York Times*, June 19, 1983. Again, these calculations do not consider those who identified themselves as "Spanish/Hispanic" in the 1980 census.

56. Rodolfo de la Garza, "Chicano-Mexican Relations: A Framework for Research," *Social Science Quarterly*, vol. 63 (March 1982), p. 121; see also his "Chicanos and U.S. Foreign Policy: The Future of Chicano-Mexican Relations," *Western Political Quarterly*, vol. 33 (December 1980), pp. 571–82.

57. For an excellent treatment of this issue, see chapter 16, "Ethnic Perceptions and Relations: Ingroup and Outgroup" in Grebler et al., *Mexican-American People*.

58. Carlos Arce, "A Reconsideration of Chicano Culture and Identity," *Daedelus*, vol. 110 (Spring 1981), p. 180.

59. These figures were first used by Jack Forbes, "Mexican-Americans," in John Burma, ed., *Mexican-Americans in the United States* (Cambridge, Mass.: Schenkman Publishing Co., 1970), p. 15. The 5 percent European figure would be greatly out of line with the number reporting themselves "Spanish/Hispanic" in the 1980 census. For a related article by the same author, see Jack Forbes, "Race and Color in Mexican-American Problems," *Journal of Human Relations*, vol. 16 (1968), pp. 55–68.

60. Arce, "A Reconsideration of Chicano Culture," p. 180.

61. Grebler et al., *Mexican-American People*, pp. 381–82. In correspondence with this writer, Arturo Muñoz wrote that he has encountered numerous people on either side of the U.S.–Mexican border who took great pride in claiming descent from the Yaqui Indians, a formerly warlike people from northern Mexico.

62. Edward Murguia, *Assimilation, Colonialism and the Mexican American People*, Monograph Series 1 (Austin: University of Texas Center for Mexican American Studies, 1975), p. 85. Stoddard succinctly describes how some Mexican-Americans who were formerly "reluctant to openly proclaim their Indian heritage" suddenly began to emphasize it. See Ellwyn Stoddard, *Mexican Americans* (New York: Random House, 1973), pp. 60ff.

63. Muñoz and Barrera, "The Raza Unida Party," pp. 112 and 115.

64. The movement received its primary impetus from intellectuals and university students, which may help to account for its lack of mass support in the barrios.

65. Garcia, "Yo Soy Mexicano," p. 90; and Lovrich and Marenin, "A Comparison of Black and Mexican American Voters," p. 291. In their dangerously small sample taken in Los Angeles, Ambrecht and Pachon ("Ethnic Political Mobilization," p. 571) found that only 2 percent of Spanish-speaking and 2 percent of English-speaking Mexican-Americans referred to themselves as "Chicano." Given the prejudice toward Indianness to which I earlier alluded, the tendency to equate Chicano with Indian may partially explain the finding of Miller that those who chose the self-referent of "Mexican-American" felt a strong dislike both for the appellation of Chicano and for those who self-consciously bore it. See M. V. Miller, "Mexican Americans, Chicanos and Others: Ethnic Self-Identification and Selected Social Attitudes of Rural Texas Youths," *Rural Sociology*, vol. 41 (Summer 1976), pp. 234–37.

66. "Indianness" possessed serious handicaps as a focus for common identity among Mexican-Americans. In addition to encountering the prejudice toward Indianness that infects many members of the community, it also faced the previously mentioned hurdle that common Indianness is itself a transethnic category. Several earlier trans-Indian movements within Mexico had floundered on the unwillingness of various Indian peoples to cooperate. (See, for example, Sivers, "Ethnic Stability and Boundary Dynamics," p. 116.)

The significance that American Indians ascribe to their national (usually described as tribal) identity was demonstrated in a study of intertribal relations in [the] southwestern United States. It found that each of the region's five major "tribes" felt a greater animosity toward some other Indian people than it did toward "the white man." See Joe Fagan and Randall Anderson, "Intertribal Attitudes among Native American Youth," *Social Science Quarterly*, vol. 54 (June 1973), pp. 117–31. This study would suggest that attempts to get American Indians to impute greater significance to racial divisions than to ethnic divisions is doomed to disappointment. Indeed, the racial perceptions of American Indians are quite complex. In the 1980 census, 1.9 million people claimed to be totally American Indian and 4.8 million people claimed partial American Indian ancestry. But on the racial question, only 1.4 million respondents circled "Indian (Amer.)." The remainder circled "White." (See U.S. Department of Commerce, *1980 Census: Ancestry*, pp. 9 and 14.) Emphasizing "brownness," as did the Chicano movement, may have therefore triggered more perplexity than emotion.

67. Grebler et al., *Mexican-American People*, p. 385.

68. Stoddard, *Mexican Americans*, p. 64; Garcia, "Yo Soy Mexicano," p. 89; Lampe, "Ethnic Self-Referent," p. 259; and Grebler et al., *Mexican-American People*, pp. 385–87. In his chapter in [Walker Connor, ed., *Mexican-Americans in Cultural Perspective*], Rodolfo de la Garza cites a study suggesting that differences in class between earlier and more recently arrived immigrants from Mexico are viewed as more important than a sense of shared cultural characteristics. Such an ordering is much more typical of an international than an intranational situation.

M. EILEEN HANSEN and
ROBBIE W. PEGUESE, Editors

The Culture Capsule: A Device for Improving Cross-Cultural Understanding

(The culture capsule involves members of at least two cultures in a situation of conflict. Of the two scenarios the authors present, both are set in the U.S. The first involves a Puerto Rican mother and the local school teachers, the second, a Colombian mother and her Anglo landlord.)

Features of the Culture Capsule*

The Intercultural Relations and Ethnic Studies Institute's (IRES) perception of the culture capsule is similar to that of the anthropologist's view of the culture construct. Therefore, the degree to which the culture capsule represents a relatively static piece or capsule of culture with specific spatial and temporal dimensions, determines a measure of its validity and its limitations.

The intention of the culture capsule is to portray or identify a specific cultural feature that is identified with a particular ethnic group. The culture capsule in reality involves members of at least two cultures in a situation of conflict: it is, then, by definition bicultural. A culture capsule must accurately reflect the ways in which a specific value or attitude of a culture is conveyed by individuals of that culture through language and behavior. Essential to the teaching/learning dimension of

From Eliane Condon, ed. *The Culture Capsule: A Device for Improving Cross-Cultural Understanding* (New Jersey: Intercultural Relations and Ethnic Studies Institute, Rutgers University, 1975), 1–34, by permission of the publisher.

* Adapted from a monograph prepared by Dr. E. C. Condon, Director of the IRES Institute, Rutgers University, and a paper written by Robert Berkowitz.

the culture capsule is the focus on a particular value or attitude so that ambiguous factors are excluded.

What is a "culture capsule"? A culture capsule is an instructional device consisting of a conversation, or descriptive narrative, in which certain specific cultural features identified with a selected group of people are deliberately constructed for the purpose of analysis.

What is the purpose of a culture capsule? A culture capsule serves to highlight the values, opinions and attitudes which are common to a group of people, as well as to describe the ways in which such information is conveyed by individuals through behavior or speech.

Its purposes are:

1. To teach cultural understanding.

2. To teach cultural differences (cultural pluralism).

3. To teach points of interference in cross-cultural communication.

4. To teach skills in cross-cultural communication, i.e., to sensitize people to the kinds of cultural differences which may cause intercultural conflict and to assist people in devising effective means of conflict resolution.

What is the format of the culture capsule? A culture capsule may consist of a dialogue or skit illustrating a typical cultural interaction between typical members of the selected group in a typical everyday situation. It may also consist of a cultural "problem-solving" presentation in which all the ingredients of a situation are presented, but no solution is included. Or it may consist of a description of a cultural incident occurring in the selected group.

In addition, the capsule may be presented in written form, on tape, or on videotape, or it may be simply dramatized . . . by selected [participants] in a role-playing situation.

How should a culture capsule be used? It should be used to teach cultural understanding, cultural differences, points of interference in cross-cultural communication, and skills in cross-cultural communication, on a step-by-step basis.

What are the components of a culture capsule?

1. The selected culture setting.

2. The culture topic and a description of the situation, background explanation, and basic principles.

3. The type of [participants] for whom the cultural information is intended.

4. A set of "cultural" behavioral objectives.
5. Illustrations of cultural features, symbols, beliefs, attitudes, and the like, to be presented.
6. Presentation:
    The characters
    The dialogue
    The audio-visual materials
    Other realia
7. Cultural items to be elicited from the students (in keeping with their level of sophistication).
8. Suggested questions for discussions:
    a. Related to the physical factors of the situation (time, place, etc.).
    b. Related to the human factors of the situation (socioeconomic, ethnic, and the like).
    c. Related to the expression of "hidden" values, beliefs, and the like, through behavior (gestures, actions, etc.) or speech (style of delivery, choice of words, etc.).
9. *Optional*: alternate methods of presentation and activities.

CULTURE CAPSULE A: REGISTRATION AND FRUSTRATION **

Introduction (Description of the Situation). A Puerto Rican mother and her English-speaking sister meet the secretary, principal, nurse, and staff of a mainland school in the course of seeking to register the mother's second-grade son for school. The scene occurs on the day after the time set aside for school registration.

Purpose	To demonstrate the kind of conflict which is possible between two groups of people where each group is of a different cultural background.
	To emphasize the need for an awareness of cultural differences and the need for adequate resolution of those conflicts which arise from these differences.

** Adapted from a culture capsule written by Florence Brenner, Orlando Castro, Ester Connelly, Mike Da Mato, Betty Dodd, Anna Lopez, Carmen Matteo, and Kathy Zucker; edited by M. Eileen Hansen and Robbie W. Peguese.

Re-state the social situation	A Puerto Rican mother seeks to enroll her young son in a mainland school which he has not attended before. The mother is unable to communicate in English although she is accompanied by a sister who can.
Student level for whom intended	This activity is designed for adult learners of various ethnic backgrounds, adult educators on all levels, as well as for adults in specific categories, such as immigrants or aliens seeking citizenship, adults involved in personnel training, and persons in ESL classes.
Relevance and usefulness in adaptation	Intended for adults representing a variety of cultural backgrounds or persons who work with individuals having diverse cultural orientations, this culture capsule has particular adaptive possibilities for educators or other types of personnel working in schools that are located in bicultural / bilingual communities.
	The exercise may also be adapted for basic English classes or ESL (English as a second language) courses.
Background explanation and basic principles relating to language and culture	The primary situation of conflict in this capsule relates not so much to the language barrier (Spanish-speaking vs. English-speaking) since the mother's sister is able to communicate in both languages but to certain conflicts in cultural orientation.
	The significant social situation relates basically to differences in cultural perspective concerning the absence of the son's registration papers.
	Moreover, a cultural conflict also exists in regard to the attitudes expressed concerning the mother's younger son and the fact that he was not enrolled in kindergarten.
	Essentially, then, two situations presented in this capsule could give rise to cross-cultural conflict. In Puerto Rico the use of the mother's last name and the father's last name as the child's last name is normative in contrast to the use of only the father's name on the mainland.
	In Puerto Rico, the lack of formal structure in admitting students to school is not unusual. Nor is the apparently protective nature of the mother who prefers to keep her child with her rather than send him to kindergarten.

Behavioral objectives
: As a result of participating in the presentation of this dialogue (as active participant or observer), students will:

— Have a greater awareness of the problems faced by Hispanic people entering an American institution such as the school with its orientation for procedures, rules, and regulations.

— Become cognizant of Hispanic attitudes towards their young children and become aware of Hispanic customs concerning, last names.

— Anticipate the cultural conflicts that may arise when people of a different culture come together in institutional situations such as this one.

Presentation of dialogue

Place:	Local mainland [U.S.] school
Characters:	Mrs. Pérez—mother
	Mrs. Martínez—sister, interpreter
	Salazar López Pérez—7 yrs. old
	Guillermo Pérez Pérez—5 yrs. old
	Ms. Starkle—principal
	Miss Hoffman—school secretary
	Kathy—clerk
	Miss Holland—school nurse

Miss Hoffman:	Yes, what can I do for you?
Mrs. Martínez:	Good morning, she wants to register the boy.
Miss Hoffman:	Good, do they speak English?
Mrs. Martínez:	No.
Kathy:	Terrific!
Miss Hoffman:	O.K. What is the boy's name?

(Mrs. Pérez speaks in Spanish and Mrs. Martínez translates. Their dialogue is presented in Mrs. Martínez's words.)

Mrs. Martínez:	Salazar López Pérez.
Miss Hoffman:	(Writes) Salazar Pérez.
Mrs. Martínez:	No, Salazar López Pérez.
Miss Hoffman:	O.K., then, Salazar López Pérez. Where are his transfers? What grade is he in?
Mrs. Martínez:	We don't have papers, but he's supposed to be in second grade.

Miss Hoffman:	How do I know that? You *have* to have his papers.
Ms. Starkle:	(Enters.) What is going on in here, a circus? I suppose you know I haven't gotten my coffee yet today. What are you doing?
Miss Hoffman:	*These people* . . .
Ms. Starkle:	Now look, you people have got to have papers. Miss Holland, come here, these people don't have their papers.
Mrs. Martínez:	I didn't think it was so important. We have them at home, and he is in second grade because he was in first grade last year.
Miss Holland:	But how about his shots? He might have just about any disease. And who is this child? He looks old enough to be in school. Isn't he cute?
Ms. Starkle:	What is wrong with this kid? Is he retarded?
Mrs. Martínez:	He is okay.
Ms. Starkle:	Are you going to send the other one?
Mrs. Martínez:	No, he is only 5 and . . .
Ms. Starkle:	He is only 5! Why all the kids in kindergarten are 5. He's got to come.
Mrs. Martínez:	No, he's too young. He should be with his mother.
Ms. Starkle:	He'd be better off in school. We'd take better care of him and he'd learn about other children.
Miss Holland:	And we'd feed him well.
Ms. Starkle:	What's the matter? Don't you want him to be an American?
Mrs. Martínez:	He's not coming to school. We might as well all go home.
Ms. Starkle:	(Wearily) No, no, put this kid in Mrs. Hibble's class and forget it.
Salazar:	Miss Hibble!?

A unique quality associated with the use of the culture capsule is its flexibility in actual presentation. It is suggested that the participants in a given training session act out the dialogue with persons from the dominant and minority cultures. This will enable the participants to gain better understanding of the other person's position and should elicit more meaningful analysis and interpretation.

Debriefing   *Analysis* of the presentation may be made in terms of its reality and authenticity, its ability to provide insight into situations of conflict where the conflict is based upon cultural differences, and its ability to provide a base for conflict resolution.

The following questions may be considered:

1. What difficulty did the name cause?
2. Why were the papers so important to the secretary and not to the parent?
3. Why did the mother not want her five-year-old child in school?
4. Why did this cause a conflict with the school personnel?
5. How could this situation have been reconciled?

Activities or   ... Role play this dialogue by reversing the ethnic
alternative   background of the performers and determine if sen-
methods   sitivity toward the conflict situation is increased by the reversal of roles.

... Rewrite the dialogue assuming much greater understanding on the part of the school personnel of those cultural attributes associated with the Puerto Rican culture. Role play and analyze.

... Rewrite the dialogue using other ethnic groups. Role play and analyze.

... Prepare dialogues based on other conflict situations. Role play and analyze these alternative dialogues.

Evaluation   Adequate analysis of the culture capsule should fulfill the requirements of evaluation though more formal oral and written evaluation is possible. Particular points of interest include the objectives of the culture capsule, identification of points of cultural interference, validity of the script, authenticity of the character representation, and the reliability of the alternative models of presentation.

CULTURE CAPSULE B: NO VACANCY! †

Introduction (Description of the situation). A Colombian family of four has recently moved to New Jersey where it is successful in finding a suitable apartment. Three months after moving into the apartment, several relatives find it necessary to move into the apartment also. This increases the number of persons in the apartment to four adults and four children. Because the owner of the apartment building has received several complaints from neighbors, he confronts the tenants of this apartment threatening possible eviction should the second family fail to vacate the premises.

Purpose	To illustrate that in instances where people of different cultural backgrounds are involved, a particular culture trait—though in some sense universal for all cultures—also may be exhibited differently for each culture. And where these differences occur, interaction (communication) may be affected adversely.
	This exercise is designed to explore the nature of this interaction . . . , and to reveal alternate patterns of behavior which will enhance communication.
Re-state the social situation	A conflict situation arises when a Colombian family which has relocated in New Jersey, USA, responds to the needs of relatives who need a place to stay. In conflict are Colombian and American values regarding space allocation for habitation and conceptions of responsibility to the extended family.
Student level for whom intended	This activity is especially suitable for educators and other types of adult personnel that come in contact with persons of a different cultural background. Other types of personnel would include employers (to improve employer-employee relations) and employees (to improve employee-customer relations).
Relevance and usefulness in adaptation	This exercise has tremendous adaptability for many types of adult personnel. It could be used to enhance employer-employee relations, employee-customer relations, or community relationships. In these instances,

† Adapted from a culture capsule written by Yolan Arlett, John Cooke, Joe Crawford, Rae Ann Kitson, Marilyn Rosenberg, Mila Salazar, Gonzalo Velez, and Vinnie Vellico; edited by M. Eileen Hansen and Robbie W. Peguese.

the exercise performs a human relations function.

Obviously, the activity may be adapted for ESL [English as a Second Language] and basic English classes, particularly for adult learners.

Background explanation and basic principles relating to language and culture

Normative patterns of housing habitation (number of persons per room) vary from culture to culture.

Personal commitments seem to take precedence over legal ones in some cultures; legal considerations take priority over personal commitments in the dominant American culture.

Persons of some cultures, as perhaps with people of Colombian origin, seem to possess a stronger sense of responsibility to one's extended family than others, whose sense of responsibility tends to be limited to the nuclear family.

Behavioral objectives

As a result of participating in the presentation of this dialogue participants will:

— Increase their awareness of cultural differences— realize that people of different cultures may possess different cultural traits.

— Tend to investigate their tendencies toward an ethnocentric interpretation of people's behavior and develop instead a more tolerant and understanding position.

— Have a greater understanding of the Colombian value of maintaining a personal commitment to their extended families, as in this case, even at the expense of rejecting the American value relating to space allocation in habitation.

— Become more aware of how behavior based upon this value may result in conflict with the value associated with the dominant (American) society.

Presentation of dialogue

Place:	At the door of Mrs. Ortes's apartment
Characters:	Mrs. Ortes
	Landlord
Landlord:	(Knocks on apartment door and woman opens it.) Hello. How are you today?
Mrs. Ortes:	(She is surprised by his visit.) Fine, thank you.
Landlord:	When you and your husband signed a

	lease for this apartment, you said that you had two children.
Mrs. Ortes:	Yes.
Landlord:	I have received many complaints from your neighbors who say that there are eight people living here, four adults and four children. Is this true?
Mrs. Ortes:	My sister's husband lost his job and they have no money. So they have to stay with us until he finds another job. What's wrong with that?
Landlord:	Lady, you don't seem to understand that we have health laws in this country. Eight people cannot live in a two-bedroom apartment.
Mrs. Ortes:	But they have no place to live. You don't understand—she's my sister.
Landlord:	(Getting louder) I don't care who she is. We have laws. It's against the fire code.
Mrs. Ortes:	When my sister's husband finds a job, they will get their own apartment.
Landlord:	(Getting very angry) Lady, there are sanitation codes. Eight people can't use one bathroom. And where do you all sleep? In shifts? I'm giving you one week—seven days—to get them out of here. Either that or I will have the sheriff evict all of you.
Mrs. Ortes:	Please. They have no money.
Landlord:	I said seven days or you're all out. (He leaves.)

Analysis

1. Why have the neighbors complained?
2. From the woman's point of view, what is the most important consideration in this situation?
3. What is the landlord's prime consideration?
4. How do these conflicting cultural considerations cause a problem?

Activities or alternative methods

... Rewrite this dialogue so that the landlord demonstrates some understanding of Mrs. Ortes' situation. Is this revised script realistic or possible?

... Write other scripts which center about conflict caused as a result of cultural difference. Role play these scripts and analyze. Reverse roles and analyze.

Evaluation   Analyze the original capsule and the alternative forms prepared by the students:

Were the objectives of the capsule clearly fulfilled?

Exactly what cultural differences or points of interference are highlighted?

Is the cultural interaction authentic? Are the characters typical? Do the characters play realistic roles? What attitudes, values, opinions, etc., are displayed in the actual speech or in the body language of the characters?

SHIRLEY BRICE HEATH

Language Policies: Patterns of Retention and Maintenance

(An ongoing debate in the U.S. and Mexico deals with bilingualism and whether to support minority languages. What are the needs and responsibilities of those who speak minority languages on the one hand and the interests of national, state, and local governments on the other?)

For centuries, the mystery of why some people keep their native tongue while others give it up to learn another language has intrigued poets, philosophers, politicians, and pedagogues. Actually, throughout most of the world, the established pattern of language learning is an additive one—individuals keep their native tongue while learning a second language, or even several other languages. Countries with an Anglo-Saxon heritage, however, tend toward a replacement pattern—that is, individuals give up their mother tongue when they learn English.

Cultural and societal forces in the United Kingdom and the United States, in particular, have pushed nonnative English speakers who have come to these countries as immigrants, refugees, or migrant workers to learn English so that they might move into the work force and achieve acceptance in the society beyond their own communities. In modern times, no official national-level policies mandate English; the status of English has been achieved in these countries without official declaration or the help of an official language academy. For speakers of other languages, the primary mandate for English has come from societal forces working on an individual's desire to secure education and employ-

From Walker Connor, ed., *Mexican-Americans in Cultural Perspective* (Washington, D.C.: The Urban Institute Press, 1985), 259–282.

ment, move into English-speaking social circles, and negotiate daily interactions with the bureaucratic and commercial mainstream.[1]

The United States today is an extremely complex laboratory in which to examine language policies—whether at the national, state, or local level. Truisms often used to describe the path of upward mobility and assimilation for past non-English-speaking groups in the United States have little support from careful historical examinations of immigrant groups in the United States. Moreover, social scientists studying the current context find that they can no longer speak of socioeconomic opportunities for immigrant groups only in the context of rapid industrialization in urban regions and other broad patterns of national economic growth.

Social scientists can no longer consider national economies as isolates; as part of the global economy, they are interdependent, and the economic conditions of one country affect another. Because of the nature of the single world economic system, development and underdevelopment of countries are not autonomous processes but two parts of the same whole. Within the United States (or any other highly industrialized country), migrants and other unskilled workers are part of the whole that includes skilled workers and executive management. Substantial changes in one sector of this work force can have ramifications not only locally but throughout the country and the world economy.

In the past two decades the role of U.S. manufacturing, agribusiness, and industry in the world economic system has greatly altered traditional patterns of cultural and linguistic adjustment for non-English-speaking immigrants or migrants. Generalizations across all nonnative English speakers remain as laden with myths as they have always been, and "conclusions" about language policy for any unit of analysis above the community level are likely to be untestable and subject to charges that they fail to represent the dynamic and diverse natures of these groups. Quantitative attempts to measure national or regional trends can be seriously questioned by qualitative research at the local level. Such research attempts to describe change over time in the context of local economic and social circumstances responding to international and national economic trends. Not only is rapid geographic mobility a reality for many individual families of nonnative English-speaking groups, but also the geographic movement of agribusiness and manufacturing groups has increased in an era of changing state tax laws and improved circumstances in regions of the United States that are not unionized.

In addition, variation across and within immigrant groups with respect to prior education, social class backgrounds, and familiarity with urban industrialized life is complicated by the fact that this variation occurs not only across language groups, as has been the case in the past, but within language groups as well. Among Spanish speakers, the differences are vast. Puerto Ricans, Cubans, Mexican-Americans, and newcomers from South America and Central America have extremely diverse attitudes toward their own language and the role of language in their adaptation to life within the United States.

This [discussion] focuses on immigrants and migrants who have come to the United States from Mexico since the 1960s and considers the contexts of their linguistic and cultural adaptation. These contexts are (1) the national language policies of Mexico and the United States toward people who do not speak the majority language, (2) the socioeconomic conditions of migration and initial settlement in the United States, and (3) the community and family situations that prevail for these newcomers.

In this paper, I maintain that research examining the responses of these migrants to U.S. language policies will benefit from a distinction between *language maintenance* and *language retention*. The former term refers to federal or state *policies toward a language-minority group* that are aimed at helping the group retain its own language. The latter term refers to those *conditions, behaviors, and values within a language group* that enable it to retain its own language. Language retention may evolve in response to local socioeconomic circumstances and may be largely beyond the awareness of minority speakers; nevertheless, some portions of language-minority communities may consciously promote opportunities, institutions, and ideological supports for retaining the minority language. Because language retention takes place at the community level, research that examines how, when, why, to what extent, and in what forms minority-language groups retain their mother tongues must also be community- and family-based. I conclude with suggestions for such research and sketch the types of findings that may be expected.

A COMPARISON OF LANGUAGE POLICIES IN MEXICO AND THE UNITED STATES

The term *language policies* usually refers to the decisions of an authority regarding the appropriate language(s) for carrying out the political, economic, legal, and educational affairs of a country as a whole or of regions within the country. The people who formulate such policies seek to achieve other goals: national unification; modernization; mass education; or reduction of institutional disruption in courts, markets, and military services. Policymakers usually designate the people who are to implement policies as well as those who are to carry out the language research and preparation of materials necessary for the policies to be put into effect.

Throughout world history, institutions such as nation-states, churches, and schools have formed and implemented language policies. Ancient literature describes decisions made by military conquerors to preserve and cultivate some languages while condemning other forms of a language or entire languages as "barbaric." Since human social groups began, the practice by those in power of restraining, prohibiting, or ignoring one or more languages or forms of language while cultivating, spreading, and promoting others has served the dual purposes of separating and unifying peoples.

In the modern world, most nation-states establish language policy through their constitutions and implement their plans for language change through their educational systems. A country may declare one language or language variety to be the official one in which laws are published and affairs of the government are conducted. A country may select one language or language variety for secondary or higher education, while another language or languages are mandated for use in the lower schools. A state may ignore all languages other than the official choice, or give other languages ceremonial or symbolic recognition, or support the use of other languages for certain functions or specific populations. Until the nineteenth century, imperial powers generally issued language policies in the name of religious conversion or the building of an empire. The leadership of nation-states of the nineteenth and twentieth centuries proclaimed language policies to strengthen national unity or to reconcile internal dissent among rival language groups.

In the cases just described, most of the language groups have remained relatively stable geographically, and conquerors or new national boundaries have brought new language policies. The twentieth century has, however, brought to international attention the timeless pattern of populations migrating in search of a new homeland, improved economic opportunities, or freedom from religious or political persecution. Since World War II, many such migrants have been workers moving from developing countries to highly industrialized countries in search of wage labor. Thus the imbalance of industrial development among countries has produced groups around the world who have become migrant workers or "guestworkers" in other countries, sometimes through contractual arrangements between the countries and sometimes without formal international agreements. Policymakers have had to consider language policies for these groups. Educational decisions, as well as rulings on citizenship, work permits, and property ownership, have included language choice.

Whereas in earlier decades of the twentieth century, host countries seemed to assume these migrants would learn the language of the society in which they worked, some countries in the 1970s and 1980s began to consider it in their best interest to promote maintenance of the guest-workers' native tongues. Ethnic revivalism and reexaminations of human rights have also helped push politicians and educators to consider the responsibilities of the state for *language maintenance*, policy-backed efforts to enable a group to keep its own language.

Different groups have, however, had very different goals for these maintenance efforts. Some language minorities have judged state tolerance—and even promotion—of their native tongue an asset and have increased the number of their ethnic language schools and other ethnic institutions. Especially in periods of declining national economic productivity, language maintenance has also been a way to encourage guestworkers or migrants to keep their identity tied to their homelands. Countries wishing to cut back on social welfare to segments of their population have wanted to support conditions that might facilitate the return of migrant workers to their countries of origin.

In short, authorities, more often than not, have generated language policies to direct changes within the population. Thus language is inevitably an instrument of control to bring about religious, political, or socioeconomic shifts for individuals and groups. Some countries for-malize their national language policies. Other countries have brought about changes in language without nation-level policies, through alterations in socioeconomic conditions, ideological pressures, and policies related to immigration, naturalization, and employment. Mexico and the United States provide contrasting approaches to language policies; the colonial and early national assumptions about language differed greatly, as have twentieth-century economic conditions and programs of social change for language minorities.

Mexican Language Policies

Mexico is a country with a legacy of a linguistically diverse indigenous population. Throughout much of its colonial history, the majority of people in Mexico spoke one or more of nearly 240 different Indian languages. By the nineteenth century, Spanish was dominant in some areas, but the size of the country and the multitude of indigenous languages presented special problems. The subsequent history of the country has been heavily shaped by the legacy of colonial language policies. Today, though the majority of citizens speak Spanish, many small indigenous groups retain their mother tongues. For four centuries, Mexico has been a testing ground for a struggle between the indigenous and the Castilian or Hispanic languages. [2]

Colonial members of religious orders in Mexico saw Castilian as the common tongue that would provide an effective bond of communication between Indians and the clergy and at the same time expedite the conversion of the Indians. The Spanish crown maintained that Christianization meant Castilianization and counted on religion as the national symbol behind which the citizens of New Spain would rally. In the seventeenth century, when King Charles II attempted to unify the citizens of New Spain behind shared cultural values that extended beyond religion, he raised the Spanish language to a position of highest priority in a massive program of Hispanization. He also promoted an increasing amount of social and cultural contact between Spaniards and Indians. Following independence and throughout the nineteenth century, Mexican political leaders embraced the idea of a new society in Mexico that would be dependent on the "Mexican" point of view. Embedded in the definition of the Mexican individual and the Mexican nation was the desire to unify dissimilar peoples into a new nation.

The crisis of the Mexican Revolution in the early twentieth century stimulated a renewal of interest in indigenism in Mexico's history. The unity of revolutionary Mexico depended on taking the best of the Indian past and incorporating it in the Mexican identity. Increasingly during the twentieth century, however, *indigenismo* has been a tension-ridden movement. In the first years after the revolution, political leaders feared the struggle between the nationalistic and the particularistic in Mexico's culture would create isolated enclaves of Indian-tongue speakers locked away from socioeconomic and political participation in the society as a whole. Officials promoted Spanish instruction in rural schools and other means of incorporating the indigenous populations into the national culture.

What has followed—as industrial and urban expansion has attracted more and more rural migrants, including Indians, to Mexico City—has been a commercial focus on the cultural habits and group identification of indigenous groups. Indian craft centers have become modern-day sweatshops of tourist-focused commercial interests. For many, Castilianization has meant movement to the periphery of economic opportunities; many of the indigenous have left their self-sustaining agricultural and market activities to become incorporated only at the bottom rungs of the Mexican national labor force. Individuals and organizations sensitive to indigenous interests continue to face a dilemma. Should they promote assimilation of all groups through the adoption of Spanish as the single Mexican linguistic standard and Hispanic as the national cultural norm, or should they work to maintain indigenous linguistic and cultural values for Indian groups so the latter can retain both a secure sense of control over their own identity and links with their historical roots?

In recent decades, the Mexican government has seen promotion of the indigenous languages as a way to keep Indians involved in productivity, often agricultural, in their own regions. Migration to the cities of Mexico since the late 1960s has become a major problem, as industrialization and urbanization have not brought socioeconomic equality. As the government has sought to increase agricultural productivity and the distribution of manufacturing outside the major cities, some maintenance of indigenous languages is seen as facilitating these goals.

Language policies for the indigenous vary greatly from region to region in Mexico today. In areas such as Chiapas, the indigenous languages are used through the secondary level of public schools; in other areas, such as the Yucatan and Oaxaca, indigenous languages are used only when necessary as a transition to learning to read, write, and speak Spanish. Beyond language differences, the Indian groups have different cultural systems, patterns of language socialization, and attitudes toward their languages. Yet many Mexicans, especially those in the north of Mexico and in the major urban areas, are relatively unaware of the remaining Indian languages and cultures.

The country's indigenous heritage is most evident in its massive archeological riches and its colonial church buildings, which are a synthesis of Castilian and Indian art forms. Many Mexicans do not know that in regions such as Oaxaca and the Yucatan, their fellow citizens must make a choice of one language over another or learn at least one other language to participate as merchants in regional markets. Despite a past in which policymakers, colonial and national, devoted considerable attention to language policies, the majority of Mexicans today view Spanish as the only national language of Mexico and know little of regional and community-level decisions regarding other languages.

U.S. Language Policies

This "linguacentric" notion that the language in widespread use is the only language of the country is shared by Mexico's northern neighbor, the United States. Following the Anglo-Saxon tradition of considering language choice the responsibility of the individual, the United States has maintained the English legal custom of not regulating language officially or of denying personal liberties in language through federal policies. In spite of several efforts in the colonial and early national periods to establish an academy of language to formulate policies and standards of language use, the United States consistently turned down such proposals from both political officials and citizens. Since the nineteenth century some states and local communities have tried to promote a monolingual tradition and to emphasize standard English as the mark of reason, ethics, and aesthetics, but the federal government has formulated no official language policy.

American society has in large part regarded the public school as the institution to create a unified conforming citizenry. Throughout U.S. educational history, training institutions, publishing houses, and professional organizations have supported the public schools' efforts to organize the linguistic and cultural knowledge and behavior of America's young. Standard English as the "right" language has become both a fundamental instrument and a required symbol of knowledge and character.[3]

With the Bilingual Education Act of 1968, federal legislators recognized the educational role of languages other than English for language-minority groups. The act promoted the use of the mother tongue of language-minority students in the early elementary years to facilitate the transition of these students to improved academic performance in English. By acquiring early cognitive development for academic skills in the mother tongue, students were expected to be able to move on to higher-order skills in English.

In the 1970–74 *Lau vs. Nichols* case, Chinese-speaking students in San Francisco argued that they did not receive an equal educational opportunity in schools where they could not understand the language of instruction. The Supreme Court ruled that under state-imposed standards that required school attendance, mandated use of the English language, and required fluency in English as a prerequisite to high school graduation, the Chinese students were not receiving equal treatment under Title VI of the 1964 Civil Rights Act. The *Lau* regulations that followed this decision greatly affected educational policies for all language minorities, but especially for Spanish speakers.

In California, in other southwestern states, in Florida, and in New York, Hispanics challenged the use of bilingual education as a transitional aid to enable students to replace Spanish with English. These Hispanic groups urged involvement by the federal government in helping language-minority communities maintain their language. The decade from 1974 to 1984 was marked by struggles between those who saw the government's role as simply promoting Spanish sufficiently to instill early academic skills and those urging extended used of Spanish for higher levels of schooling and for a wider range of economic opportunities outside the immediate Spanish-speaking neighborhood. The latter groups increasingly have called for language policies that would establish bilingual education not as a path of transition to English for native Spanish speakers, but as a program to help Spanish speakers maintain and spread their language by increasing opportunities for its use in work places, the courts, and social services agencies. [4]

Such policies would constitute a sharp break in the historical pattern of U.S. language policies. Observers of American society since de Tocqueville have noted the tendency of its citizens toward conformity; traditionally, people who have taken advantage of opportunities of either geographic or socioeconomic mobility have asked in their new surroundings, "What is expected of us ?" Institutions of education, work, and leisure have in the past answered that the language that is expected is English. Despite the lack of a federal policy, local and state institutions have created practices limiting access to higher-level jobs to those who speak standard English.

One observer has assessed the U.S. failure to enact a specific language policy as "one of history's little ironies" and has suggested that "no polyglot empire of the old world has dared to be as ruthless in imposing a single language upon its whole population as was the liberal republic dedicated to the proposition that all men are created equal." Throughout U.S. history, in the absence of federal compulsion, socioeconomic forces have created an indirect compulsion, both on a community and individual level, for learning English. However, close examination of current socioeconomic conditions and community and family responses by Mexican-Americans suggests that migrants may increasingly be retaining Spanish while capturing at least some of the economic gains that motivated their migrations north. This community-level retention can, however, proceed without any maintenance efforts from the federal polity. [5]

THE CHOICE OF LANGUAGE AMONG MEXICAN-AMERICANS

Since their earliest experiences in territory that is now the United States, people of Mexican origin have responded in a variety of ways to choice of language. They have been in what is now the United States longer than any group besides the American Indians, and they have thus faced numerous types of challenges—military, economic, social, and legal. As individuals and as groups, they have met extremely varied circumstances in which to consider the role of the Spanish language as an essential part of the way they identify themselves.

The Indians of the American Southwest had their first contact with European culture from Spanish speakers; early waves of settlers from Mexico spread Spanish in the Southwest before the arrival of English. Until well into the nineteenth century, California and the American Southwest were the Spanish borderlands, but in the late 1800s the Hispanic presence in these areas dropped considerably. In the 1900s, however, economic conditions motivated Mexican immigration. Drawn both to the rapid development of the Southwest after World War I and to agricultural opportunities, especially in Texas and California, in the post-World War II period, Mexican-Americans settled first in the West and Southwest; but, since the 1960s, they have found homes in every state of the Union and a wide variety of occupations. [6]

Language and Socioeconomic Opportunities

Conditions for employment and community building for migrants from Mexico in recent decades differ greatly from those of earlier immigrants from Mexico as well as differing from those of other immigrant groups. In the American Southwest before the latter half of the nineteenth century, many of the settlers from Mexico became landowners. They created economic niches for themselves, and in New Mexico, families of Mexican origin were able to influence state politics and to create legislation that recognized the Hispanic presence in the region.

Later Mexican immigrants turned to mining, sheep herding, and agriculture. In the first half of the twentieth century, they were the backbone of migrant work forces in cotton, fruit, and vegetable production. Unlike many other immigrants prior to the mid-twentieth century who came initially to urban ghettos, most Mexicans prior to the 1960s moved to the cities only after experience in rural life within the United States.

Some European immigrants rapidly learned English, while others remained in transitional immigrant enclaves in which they could continue to use their mother tongues in much of their daily world. In American cities, immigrants in the late nineteenth and early twentieth centuries settled in ghettos from which young and middle-aged men went daily to find factory work. The women and the elderly remained behind to establish small neighborhood businesses and to build family and community bonds; on the whole, the latter continued to use their mother tongues. In cities such as Cleveland, New York, and San Francisco, the children of immigrants attended bilingual schools; in other cities where the immigrant groups were not so large, the children went to schools where only English was used and learned to aspire to economic and social niches that depended upon the primary use of English.

Although the foreign-language presses and radio stations, community religious organizations, and even private schools that offered instruction in the mother tongue kept languages other than English alive for some families, most members of the younger generation set aside their mother tongues in favor of English. Work outside their own community demanded English, and the earning power gained outside those communities made subsequent generations want better housing, improved schools, and more distance between them and the lower-status groups that took their places in the ghetto. As second- and third-generation immigrants moved to the suburbs, they often brought only English with them for use within their families as well as in their leisure and work activities. [7]

The socioeconomic contexts into which migrants of Mexican origin have come since the 1960s stand in sharp contrast to those of earlier European immigrants whose labor was needed in the rapid industrialization of the late nineteenth and early twentieth centuries and in the manufacturing booms surrounding World War I and World War II. Although the popular media still frequently identify them as being primarily concentrated in agricultural labor, Mexican-Americans have rapidly moved out of agriculture into other occupations. In 1978, less than 7 percent of the documented Mexican-origin population worked in farm-related occupations, and only 19 percent lived in rural areas.

In recent decades, Mexican-Americans have participated heavily in rural-to-urban migration as agricultural labor markets have contracted and urban areas have offered increased opportunities for employment. The extraordinarily rapid growth of agribusiness, light industry, and the garment industry in the 1960s and 1970s, and of the electronics industry and service occupations (especially in hotels and fast-food establishments) in the 1980s, has provided wage-earning positions in and around cities across the United States. In many work places, the foremen or bosses speak Spanish, and the majority of production line workers can communicate with both co-workers and middle management in Spanish. [8]

For some workers, early experience in manufacturing was acquired in Spanish. Mexico's export-processing zone, located in northern Mexico and devoted primarily to garment and electronics manufacturing, in the

1970s provided initial wage labor experience to many unskilled workers who subsequently migrated across the border to similar jobs in the United States. These industries in Mexico and in the United States pay low wages and heavily discourage any attempts at organization by workers for higher wages or improved conditions. Approximately 90 percent of the laborers have been women, whose low socioeconomic position has been supported by an infrastructure within Mexico linked to multinational business interests within the United States.[9]

Once settled in the United States, recent migrants of Mexican origin have established large communities of Spanish speakers—communities large enough to support small businesses of sufficient variety to meet a majority of the needs of community members. Merchants and service personnel in these community businesses find their native language a business asset.[10]

Language in Community and Family Life

For Mexican migrants, these relatively recently established communities are often the first buffers for adjustment to life in a new homeland. As long as ensuing waves of newcomers were compatible in class, educational background, and regional allegiances, established migrants have taken in the newly arrived migrants, often taking risks to protect undocumented workers. For the most part, however, the recent waves of Mexican migrants have not been able to depend on those of Mexican origin who came in past centuries and earlier decades of the twentieth century to take them in. The earlier immigrants have been so long established that they have left the communities of their first arrival and settled in mixed communities or in suburban neighborhoods away from opportunities for low-income work. Thus in the steady flow of migrants since the 1960s, the people who have been there to assist the new arrivals have been relative newcomers themselves.[11]

Within a community in which the majority of members are still trying to find their way in school and work places beyond the neighborhood while others have settled into retailing within the community, the key support institution for newcomers is the extended family household, which may be a residential unit or a nonresidential support network. The family itself is a tight nexus of emotional support and primary identification, even under strong influences from acculturating forces. Mexican-Americans maintain relatively large local kinship networks with high rates of reciprocity. Kinship ties of the extended family contribute both to the relative geographic stability of Mexican-American families and to the tendency of those families who do move to consider kinship ties in selecting new locations.

COMMUNITY-LEVEL RESEARCH AGENDA

Social science researchers and policymakers know very little about patterns of language use in the homes, communities, and work places of these recent Mexican migrants. The avalanche of sociological, economic, and political writings on Mexican-Americans since World War II contains few examinations of cultural habits and ways of using language in local communities. Information is needed regarding shifts in language and culture patterns when early twentieth-century Mexican immigrants moved from rural to urban environments and changed from agricultural to industrial work settings. For comparison, scholars need detailed descriptions of language use in those communities that have accommodated the repeated waves of migrants since the 1960s.

To be sure, one cannot easily generalize patterns of behavior or expressions of attitudes by people of Mexican origin in one region to any other region or determine whether trends reflected at a given time represent a temporary change or long-term patterns. The relatively few studies that focus on language suggest that the only generalization that accurately encompasses language and culture patterns for this population is that one cannot generalize. Families and communities reflect wide diversities of cultural habits, language acquisition patterns, and values related to language uses. Much of this diversity existed in Mexico, and within the United States it has been both accentuated and leveled by the regional, economic, and socioreligious conditions into which the diverse migrants came.

Within studies of language use among Mexican-origin populations, the major topics are language attitudes, school testing and teaching patterns, and code switching (the alternating use of two languages in a single discourse). Almost no research treats language change in coordination with socioeconomic change for specific communities over time. We do not know (1) the extent to which communication networks remain stable linguistically over time or (2) the values members of such networks hold toward the retention of Mexican Spanish (as contrasted with a variety of Spanish which includes many anglicisms), or their beliefs about the correlation between learning English and adopting other behaviors viewed as alien to those of the local community. [12]

Both bilingual education and efforts since the late 1960s to accommodate more Spanish speakers in public services, medical centers, and law courts have prompted some studies of community attitudes. However, these studies have not systematically analyzed the correlation of behavior patterns with particular attitudes. Existing research is thus insufficient for determining predictable patterns of response to school language policies. Some groups strongly favor using Spanish in the elementary grades and involving parents extensively in school activities; others would leave to the schools the choice of language policies; still others are apathetic and believe it would be inappropriate or impractical for them to play a role in making decisions about language use in school. Neither socioeconomic level nor length of residence in the United States correlates consistently with any of the most frequent community responses noted above. Clearly, factors that account for these differences in community links to the schools with respect to language have yet to be identified and compared across communities. [13]

Patterns of valuation of Spanish by institutions closely linked to communities and families, such as the church, are also almost completely unresearched. The relatively few studies available suggest that Mexican-Americans have faced "decades of isolation" from positions of leadership in the Catholic church. Only during the 1960s did volunteer organizations run by Mexican-Americans in Spanish for the benefit of Spanish speakers develop, and as these groups have been taken over by the institutional church, the trend has been to increase the use of English and to reinstate traditional structural patterns of Anglo dominance.

Traditional mutual aid and civic societies, ranging from the relatively conservative Sociedad Progresista Mexicana to the League of United Latin American Citizens (LULAC), have rarely held language policies to be centrally important in their business operations. Providing ballots and government publications in Spanish has helped special-interest groups and local political figures bring some Spanish-only speakers into political participation. Yet political leaders from Mexican-American communities who reach regional, state, or federal offices do not take up language issues as a central concern; instead, they bring language into debate under broader concerns, such as improved education, protection of jobs for Spanish speakers, and adherence to federal funding guidelines in public agencies. Protestant groups, such as Jehovah's Witnesses, have been strongly influential in some communities of Mexican origin, and their members have encouraged the learning of English and the practice of reading and writing skills by parents and children. [14]

The language practices and policies of labor unions and specific work settings managed by Mexican-Americans have been described relatively infrequently. Here again, generalization is difficult because practices differ from region to region, as well as from group to group. The United Farm Workers, organized by César Chávez in the 1960s, initially used primarily Spanish, but by the 1980s, its leaders used Spanish or English, according to the audience they were addressing. The Alianza por Pueblo in California has generally carried out its business in English.

Some branches of the Mexican-American Political Association (MAPA) —such as that in San Jose, California, which was led in the 1980s by Fernando Chávez (son of César Chávez)—handled many of their affairs in Spanish, while other branches preferred English. COPE, a branch of the AFL-CIO in San Jose, has primarily used English in its activities and published materials.

One description of nondocumented kitchen workers done in the early 1980s in a restaurant with Mexican-American (English-dominant) waitresses and Anglo clientele indicated ways in which the Mexican-American waitresses helped kitchen workers acquire English on the job. It also documented reasons these workers gave for viewing English as necessary for their move up to becoming waiters. The study suggests that these workers will "enter an indefinite period of varying forms of coordinate and compound bilingualism." [15]

Community-level research on patterns of language retention and responses to language maintenance policies by language-minority communities around the world repeatedly stresses the importance of the links between these communities and the larger society. For communities of Mexicans who recently arrived in the United States, only the most tentative suggestions concerning the nature of these links can be offered. Links to mainstream institutions such as the school, the work place, and government bureaucracies apparently depend on individual family initiatives or small groups of significant friends.

Despite the availability of Spanish-language newspapers, sources of mainstream institutional information remain primarily oral and family-based. They are therefore so short-lived as to limit possibilities of building habitual cultural patterns of initial contact, clarification of job demands, and follow-up with appropriate paperwork. Spanish remains for many of the adults in these families the primary language, although their children may use English at school, among their peers, and sometimes with their parents. However, institutional links to English, aside from the schools, seem to be minimal even for young people; they have few opportunities to hear or use the formal, standard English required for school success and job placement above the bottom socioeconomic level. [16]

Almost the only economic niche above this lowest socioeconomic level which has been identified primarily with Mexican-Americans in the past two decades is the business of bilingual education. Many immigrants from past decades who have risen in class status and become local elites have moved into positions of influence in education following the Bilingual Education Act of 1968. Their increased number and their influence in education have depended on the continuation of bilingual education. Calls for language maintenance and more supports for language retention from within communities have come largely from this relatively new middle class of educators. Many of these educators have left their old communities and may find it difficult to accept the eagerness of new arrivals who want to learn English and to become "American." Mexican-American educators may unwittingly promote bilingual education for their own institutional and professional goals as well as for the practical needs and personal goals of recent arrivals. [17]

Conscious language retention efforts by the recent Mexican migrants themselves have not been documented; thus they cannot be compared with the methods and goals of their middle-class spokesmen. Some recent migrants seem to see English as the determinant not of their own future but of their children's future in a different community and a different set of jobs. Many migrants who speak minimal English, however, achieve entry into unskilled jobs that provide relatively steady hourly wages. No matter how ruthlessly they are exploited in industry and agriculture by U.S. standards, the wages and social service benefits, combined with the educational opportunities for their children, are a considerable gain over their economic chances in Mexico. The crisis of the Mexican economy after 1981 accentuated this view among migrants who increasingly traveled back and forth to visit family members in Mexico and sometimes bought land there to help family and friends and to give themselves and their children a tangible tie to the homeland.

Aside from a focus on groups, such as the church and labor unions, which directly serve Mexican-American communities and on conditions that help determine self-identification, researchers interested in language retention must also look carefully at patterns of language socialization within families. How do families of recent migrants use Spanish or English at home, and do these uses prepare the young to handle school tasks and communication with the wider society? Some recent research studying mothers' habits of socializing their children to language use details methods of telling stories, asking for clarification, giving directions, and scolding or praising. This research shows that these parents do not provide extended explanations to children, nor do they give direct instructions and model clarification questions. Instead, much verbal instruction is indirect and children are expected to learn through observation and modeling. Several discourse forms that are critical to academic success and skilled jobs (such as sustained accounts on a single topic, punctuated by mention of secondary authorities or reference to written sources) are rare.

Although children and adults may read and write at home, their uses of literacy skills are primarily practical (writing letters and completing forms) or confirmational (reading religious materials or preparing for rites of passage, such as the fifteenth birthday). Numerous types of skills that schools require, such as responding to requests for labels of items and events and literate-based information about these, are not called for in language uses at home or in the community.[18]

For the migrants of the past two decades, families represent their only "tightly coupled" institutions. Other institutions, such as the church, voluntary associations, the school, and the work place, appear to be only "loosely coupled" and to offer almost no occasions to supplement the language socialization of the home. Thus, many children of migrants do not become familiar with or have occasions to practice language uses such as focused questioning, sustained oral and written discussion, and extended descriptions of sequential actions. The family remains the primary source of opportunities to use oral and written language, as well as the major source of future self-identification.

Individuals who wish to improve their language skills have to look beyond the family. However, there appear to be no cultural or linguistic institutions ready to help in this regard. Those who do try to extend themselves beyond the family may find few daily interactive learning situations in which they can practice formal discourse and acquire language styles necessary for ensuring job opportunities in semiskilled or skilled domains. In short, the language forms that can translate into capital in moderately skilled or highly skilled jobs are often unavailable for recent migrants in settings other than the school. Opportunities to practice there are insufficient to enable children to acquire a firm footing in standard English skills, particularly when children start school without basic English-language socialization patterns.[19]

CONCLUSIONS

The majority of the American populace seems to believe that the United States still holds out the American dream to newcomers from Mexico. Yet the continuing movement back and forth across the border, the purposeful isolation of some of these communities, and the maintenance of intangible and tangible links to Mexico indicate that in recent decades not all people of Mexican origin have adopted this dream as their goal. Most Americans believe that the driving force behind language shift is individual enterprise, and that the society at large need not take much responsibility for facilitating or easing this shift. They believe that people who seek upward social mobility, profitable participation in a labor market, and steady work in modern factories will choose English and that schools will help them make that choice.

Economic conditions in the 1980s, however, have altered this pattern in many regions of the country. Certain sectors of the work force in industrial production and manufacturing and in service occupations for restaurants, hotels, and office buildings may achieve relatively high wages, but remain cut off from the upward mobility that would integrate them with English-only speakers. In some industries, the increased use of computers is making available more jobs at the lowest levels, while creating a greater gap between these unskilled workers and the semi-skilled workers above them.

In the mid-1980s, many people of Mexican origin are able to retain their own language because of the supportive nature of their extended family in both the United States and Mexico, their divided sense of community between their residence in the United States and their "home" in Mexico, and the current availability of economic opportunities that do not demand English. Spokesmen for bilingual education may find it useful to consider these conditions for language retention and evidence that the educational policies of the federal government and other public service organizations could support the immigrants' maintenance of Spanish by facilitating its spread. (Language spread is the increase over time in the proportion of a communication network that adopts a given language or language variety for a given communicative function.) Federal or state government sponsorship of rules requiring Spanish in social services, legal affairs, medical establishments, and other institutions serving the general public would increase the communicative functions of Spanish beyond those of face-to-face interactions among intimates within their own homes and friendships or retail networks. People advocating such spread want to make Spanish, along with English, a language that links the mainstream institutions and the Mexican-American communities. [20]

The diverse conditions of persons of Mexican origin who have come to the United States in recent decades and the variation in their subsequent path of adaptation to American life limit the value of generalizations across communities and regions. Community-based research is needed to answer some key questions regarding language retention and maintenance. What are the conditions—social, economic, cultural, and religious—that support language as an instrument of change? Do internal group factors lead groups to retain their language in spite of strong historical and broad societal forces which promote English? Are federal, state, or local policy pressures toward language shift more likely to succeed with some groups of migrants or immigrants than with other groups? A series of carefully conducted community studies in different regions of the United States could provide answers to these questions and help develop a theory accounting for ways in which language uses and the values associated with language held by local groups are connected with socioeconomic conditions brought into play by the global and national economies.

Notes

1. The legal background of language policies in the United States is explored by Arnold Leibowitz in *Educational Policy and Political Acceptance: The Imposition of English as the Language of Instruction in American Schools* (Arlington, Va.: Center for Applied Linguistics, 1971); and "Language and the Law: The Exercise of Power through Official Designation of Language," in William M. O'Barr and Jean F. O'Barr, eds., *Language and Politics* (The Hague: Mouton, 1976). For a discussion of recent bilingual education legislation in the context of U.S. legal history on language-related matters, see Shirley Brice Heath and Frederick Mandabach, "Language Status Decisions and the Law in the United States," in Juan Cobarrubias and Joshua A. Fishman, eds., *Progress in Language Planning: International Perspectives* (The Hague: Mouton, 1983).

2. The history of language policies in Mexico is given in Shirley Brice Heath, *Telling Tongues: Language Policy in Mexico, Colony to Nation* (New York: Teachers College Press, 1972).

3. Attempts to establish a national language academy are traced in Shirley Brice Heath, "A National Language Academy: Debate in the New Nation," *International Journal of the Sociology of Language*, vol. 11 (1976), pp. 9–44. Reviews of the role of standard English in the shaping of Americans' self-identification may be found in Harvey A. Daniels, *Famous Last Words: The American Language Crisis Reconsidered* (Carbondale: Southern Illinois University Press, 1983); and Shirley Brice Heath, "Standard English: Biography of a Symbol," in Timothy Shopen and Joseph Williams, eds., *Standards and Dialects in English* (Cambridge, Mass.: Winthrop Publishers, Inc., 1972). A historical review of American attitudes toward language is given by Edward Finegan, *Attitudes toward English Usage: The History of a War of Words* (New York: Teachers College Press, 1980). Charles A. Ferguson, "National Attitudes toward Language Planning," in James E. Alatis and G. Richard Tucker, eds., *Georgetown University Round Table on Languages and Linguistics* (Washington, D.C.: Georgetown University Press, 1979), describes language attitudes of Americans in contrast to those of other countries which engage in direct language planning. Heinz Kloss, *The American Bilingual Tradition* (Rowley, Mass.: Newbury House, 1977) sets the language attitude of Americans in historical perspective and suggests that in earlier eras local conditions favored a "bilingual tradition."

4. Susan Schneider, *Revolution, Reaction or Reform: The 1974 Bilingual Education Act* (New York: Las Americas Publishing Co., 1977) provides the history of lobbying efforts and legislative debates surrounding bilingual education between 1966 and 1974. Gary Keller and Joshua A. Fishman, eds., *Bilingual*

Education for American Hispanics (New York: Teachers College Press, 1981) fill in some details of the subsequent history of bilingual education. Articles in *Aztlán* and the *Bilingual Review* during the late 1970s and throughout the 1980s provide further evidence of the trend toward maintenance arguments by Hispanics, as do the documentary records of organizations such as the Center for Hispanic Leadership in Boulder, Colorado.

5. Gerald Johnson in *Our English Heritage* (Philadelphia: J.B. Lippincott, 1949), pp. 118–19, noted the irony of the absence of language policy in the United States. Einar Haugen, *Language Conflict and Language Planning: The Case of Modern Norwegian* (Cambridge, Mass.: Harvard University Press, 1966), identified the focus on the individual as a key factor in U.S. attitudes toward language policies for immigrant groups.

6. A useful brief history of "colonial Spanish," that [was] brought by the earliest Spanish immigrants to the Southwest, is given by Jerry R. Craddock, "New World Spanish," in Charles A. Ferguson and Shirley Brice Heath, eds., *Language in the USA* (Cambridge, England: Cambridge University Press, 1981).

7. The classic treatment of language among immigrant groups in the United States is Joshua A. Fishman, *Language Loyalty in the United States* (The Hague: Mouton, 1966); this volume contains individual chapters detailing the patterns of language retention of the major immigrant groups. Several chapters in Margaret A. Lourie and Nancy Faires Conklin, eds., *A Pluralistic Nation: The Language Issue in the United States* (Rowley, Mass.: Newbury House, 1978) provide useful updates on those groups covered by Fishman a decade earlier. Other updated information for some of these groups is in Charles A. Ferguson and Shirley Brice Heath, eds., *Language in the USA* (Cambridge, England: Cambridge University Press, 1981). Bilingual schools are discussed in Shirley Brice Heath, "English in our Language Heritage," in Charles A. Ferguson and Shirley Brice Heath, eds., *Language in the USA* and in *The American Bilingual Tradition*. The role of language-related ethnic community schools, as well as other non-English language resources such as the immigrant press and radio, is examined in Joshua A. Fishman, *Non-English Language Resources of the United States* (Final Report to Research Section, International Studies Branch, Department of Education, 1982). Structural and occupational adaptive patterns of European immigrant groups since 1880 are detailed in Stanley Lieberson, *A Piece of the Pie: Blacks and White Immigrants Since 1880* (Berkeley: University of California Press, 1980).

8. The movement by Mexican-Americans out of the migrant stream in the United States and the rapid recent movement away from agricultural labor by this group is detailed by M. Wells, "Emigrants from the Migrant Stream: Environments and Incentives in Relocation," *Aztlán*, vol. 7 (1982), pp. 165–90.

9. Researchers at the Center for Mexican American Studies, University of California, San Diego, have described the export-processing zone phenomenon and have linked its existence to international economic forces. See M.P. Fernandez-Kelly, *For We Are Sold, I and My People: Women and Industry in Mexico's Frontier* (Albany: State University of New York, 1983).

10. Trends of employment patterns in Southern California are detailed in reports (1982–84) of the Center for Mexican American Studies, University of California, San Diego. For a discussion of the role of small businesses in another recent immigrant group, see Edna Bonacich, Ivan Light, and Charles Coy Wong, "Small Business among Koreans in Los Angeles," in Emma Gee, ed., *Counterpoint: Perspectives on Asian America* (Los Angeles: University of California Asian American Studies Center, 1976). Sympathetic and graphic portrayals of daily life in Mexican-American communities in the Southwest in the 1960s appear in Stanley Steiner, *La Raza: The Mexican Americans* (New York: Harper & Row, 1970), especially chap. 11.

11. A comparison of kinship ties in the support networks of Mexican-Americans and Anglo-Americans is given in S.E. Keefe, "Personal Communities in the City: Support Networks among Mexican Americans and Anglo Americans," *Urban Anthropology*, vol. 9, pp. 51–74; and S.E. Keefe, Amado Padilla, and M.L. Carlos, "The Mexican-American Extended Family as an Emotional Support System," *Human Organization*, vol. 38, pp. 144–52. Compare these reports with that of J. Sena-Rivera, "Extended Kinship in the United States: Competing Models and the Case of La Familia Chicana," *Journal of Marriage and the Family*, vol. 41, pp. 121–29. The pattern in the United States of using personal networks in the adjustment to life in a new area is consistent with patterns described within Mexico as well. Both D.L. Kincaid, "Community Networks: Locus of Control among Migrants in the Periphery of Mexico City," Ph.D. dissertation, Michigan State University, 1972; and F.J. Morrett-Lopez, "Community Networks among Marginals in Mexico City," Ph.D. dissertation, Stanford University, 1979, describe communication networks among recent migrants to Mexico City. In both studies, newcomers depend on personal links to achieve stability. Morrett-Lopez reports the unexpected result, however, that the most stable links are those which are reciprocal and spatially proximate; actual kinship ties are negatively related to the stability of these networks.

12. A historical survey of Spanish language and educational policy in California that suggests the types of diversities current communities may present with respect to language decisions is provided by Alexander Sapiens, "Spanish in California: A Historical Perspective," *Journal of Communication*, vol. 29 (Spring 1979), pp. 72–83. A survey of research on Mexican-Americans' language attitudes is given by Miguel A. Carranza, "Attitudinal Research on Hispanic Language Varieties," in Ellen Bouchard Ryan and Howard Giles, eds., *Attitudes towards Language Variation: Social and Applied Contexts* (London: Edward Arnold, 1982). See Fernando Penalosa, *Introduction to the Sociology of Language* (Rowley, Mass.: Newbury House, 1981), for a general discussion of the social and economic factors affecting attitude formation among Spanish speakers in the United States. A recent study of the repertoire of Mexican-Americans' language varieties is reported in Lucia Elias-Oliveras, "Language in a Chicano Community," *Working Papers in Sociolinguistics*, no. 30 (Austin, Texas: Southwest Educational Development Laboratory). A collection of essays on regional varieties of Spanish, with some discussion of their acceptance by educators, is

Eduardo Hernandez-Chavez, Andrew D. Cohen, and Anthony F. Beltramo, eds., *El Lenguaje de los Chicanos: Regional and Social Characteristics of Language Used by Mexican Americans* (Washington, D.C.: Center for Applied Linguistics, 1975). Studies of code switching as well as school testing and teaching trends are discussed by authors included in R.P. Duran, ed., *Latino Language and Communicative Behavior* (Norwood, N.J.: Ablex, 1981). For an early analysis of patterns of teacher interactions with Mexican-American students, see U.S. Commission on Civil Rights, *Teachers and Students: Differences in Teacher Interaction with Mexican American and Anglo Students*, Report 5, Mexican American Education Study (Washington, D.C.: Government Printing Office, 1973). David Lopez, in "Chicano Language Loyalty in an Urban Setting," *Sociology and Social Research*, vol. 62 (1978), pp. 267–78, warns against overgeneralizing studies done in one region to populations of Mexican-Americans in other areas.

13. Guadalupe Valdes, a longtime researcher in the courts of New Mexico, reports her findings and recommendations for future research in "Language Needs of Hispanic Minorities in the Criminal Justice System: A Research Agenda," unpublished report, July 1982. Cynthia Prince, "The Use of Spanish in a San Jose Medical Clinic," Ph.D. dissertation, Stanford University, 1984, describes interpreting services in a clinic that serves a largely Spanish-speaking population. Two Puerto Rican neighborhoods and their interactions with bilingual schools are described by Alicia Pousada, "Community Participation in Bilingual Education: The Puerto Rican Community of East Harlem," Ph.D. dissertation, University of Pennsylvania, 1984. Pousada also summarizes the literature on Hispanic communities' participation in bilingual education programs since the late 1960s. She finds in the two communities of her study that the overwhelming majority of residents maintain at least passive skills in Spanish and that community members carry "a strong conviction that bilingual programs are one of the best ways to foster bilingualism among the youth of the community" (p. 345).

14. Most accounts of Chicano life in the Catholic church are either highly journalistic or strongly biased in their presentation of facts. A. Soto, "The Chicano and the Church in Northern California," Ph.D. dissertation, University of California, Berkeley, 1978, provides a thorough study of the leadership opportunities offered Chicanos in one region.

15. For a description of labor and political groups in the 1960s, see Steiner, *La Raza: The Mexican Americans*, chap. 14. The author characterizes one branch of MAPA as "middle-class," and calls attention to the diverse ways different branches represent themselves. Jose Limon, in "Language, Mexican Immigration, and the 'Human Connection': A Perspective from the Ethnography of Communication" working paper, 1982, gives one of the few detailed descriptions of Mexican-Americans' language use in a work setting and predictions for future trends (p. 17).

16. Ralph Fasold, "Language Maintenance and Shift," in R. Fasold, ed., *Sociolinguistics and Society*, forthcoming, describes the role of links between

immigrant communities and mainstream institutions in bringing about a language shift.

17. R. Romo, *East Los Angeles: History of a Barrio* (Austin: University of Texas Press, 1983), portrays the desires of different waves of residents to become "American." See also H. Romo, "Sra. Mercedes: A Mexican Immigrant Parent," in *Working Papers in Sociolinguistics*, no. 86 (Austin, Texas: Southwest Educational Development Laboratory, 1981). R. Stavenhagen, *Sociología y Subdesarrollo* (Mexico City: Ed. Nuestro Tiempo, 1971); and Pablo Gonzalez Casanova, *Sociología de la Explotación* (Mexico: Siglo XXI, 1969), describe the tendency of formerly exploited groups to develop a stratified hierarchy that brings to the top people who become exploiters of those of their own group left below them in the social structure. B. B. Khleif, "Ethnicity and Language in Understanding the New Nationalism: The North Atlantic Region," *International Journal of Comparative Sociology*, vol. 23 (1980), pp. 114–21, compares ethnic revival movements and suggests their interdependence with changes in the world economy in the 1970s. See also E. Allardt, *Implications of the Ethnic Revival in Modern, Industrialized Society, Commentationes Scientiarum Socialium* (Helsinki: Societas Scientiarum Fennica, 1979), on the role of language in new self-identification of ethnic groups.

18. For a review of the literature on patterns of language acquisition among children in Mexican-American families, see Davida Desmond, "Language in a Mexican American Community," Ph.D. dissertation, Stanford University, forthcoming. Desmond also provides an ethnography of communication in an immigrant community, which is in the same research tradition as the work of John Attinasi, P. Pedraza, S. Poplack, and A. Pousada, *Intergenerational Perspectives on Bilingualism: From Community to Classroom* (New York: Language Policy Task Force, Center for Puerto Rican Studies, 1982). Luis Laosa has identified several mainstream oral language patterns, such as questioning, verbally explicating directions, and offering repeated praise, which are not used in Mexican-American families; instead these families stress modeling, visual cues, and directives; see "Maternal Teaching Strategies and Cognitive Styles in Chicano Families," *Journal of Educational Psychology*, vol. 72 (1980), pp. 45–54. For further evidence of differences in general discourse forms, see C. Briggs, "Communicative Hegemony in Fieldwork," *Semiotics*, forthcoming. Further evidence of the strong links between home language use and performance in outside institutions such as the school is given by David P. Dolson, "The Influence of Various Home Bilingual Environments on the Academic Achievement, Language Development, and Psychosocial Adjustment of Fifth and Sixth Grade Hispanic Students," Ph.D. dissertation, University of San Francisco, 1984. In this study, students from families who have retained Spanish as the dominant home language outperformed students from homes where a switch to English has occurred on five of ten scholastic measures.

19. The terms "loosely coupled" and "tightly coupled" are drawn from the research on organizational systems of K. E. Weick, "Educational Organizations

as Loosely Coupled Systems," *Administrative Science Quarterly*, vol. 21 (1976), pp. 1–19. The characteristic patterns of reading and writing in bureaucratic institutions and the ways in which these control clients' access to goods and services are described in Roger Fowler, Bob Hodge, Gunther Kress, and Tony Trew, *Language and Control* (London: Routledge & Kegan Paul, 1979).

20. David E. Lopez, *Language Maintenance and Shift in the United States Today: The Basic Patterns and their Social Implications. Vol. III: Hispanics and Portuguese* (Los Alamitos, Calif.: National Center for Bilingual Research, 1982), points out that, according to national data collected in 1976, Mexican-Americans have "considerable intergenerational maintenance" and there is "a strong indication that Mexican Americans are more language retentive than other groups" (p. 50). National statistics show that approximately 30 percent of all U.S.-born Mexican-Americans retain Spanish as the language of the home; yet, Lopez cautions that considerable differences exist across regions of the United States as well as among Mexican-American communities, and that "our knowledge of the variation . . . is still very crude," p. 50. It is ironic that in 1947–48, George Barker, in *Social Functions of Language in a Mexican-American Community*, Anthropological Papers of the University of Arizona, no. 22 (Tucson: University of Arizona Press, 1972: first published in 1947), reported a study that could be a basic model of the kind of community-level research currently called for on language retention among Mexican-Americans; yet other scholars have not followed and expanded this pioneer study. In Tucson, Arizona, Barker, an anthropologist, studied the uses of Spanish and English among Mexican-Americans and concluded: "In a bilingual minority group in process of cultural change the functions originally performed by the ancestral language are divided between two or more languages, with the result that each language comes to be identified with certain specific fields of interpersonal relations. Thus for each individual, language takes on symbolic values which vary according to the individual's social experience. The character of this experience, in turn, depends on, first, the position of the minority group in the general community; second, the relation of the individual to the bilingual group; and, third, the relation of the individual to the general community," p. 45. Barker studied the uses of Spanish and English in the home and community, as well as in the social and work relations of members of a small Mexican-American community in Tucson in the mid-1940s. He concluded his study by calling for further research examining the retention and spread of Spanish at the community level, and he suggested (p. 47) that the study of language in use could provide "the basis for a new and widely applicable method of sociological analysis." Robert Cooper, ed., *Language Spread: Studies in Diffusion and Social Change* (Bloomington: Indiana University Press, 1982) provides case studies of the spread of languages to new speakers or new functions and a theoretical statement about conditions that facilitate either type of spread.

CARLOS G. VELEZ-I.

The Nonconsenting Sterilization of Mexican Women in Los Angeles:
Issues of psychocultural rupture and legal redress in paternalistic behavioral environments

(Medical and legal ethics are at risk in a case that began at the Los Angeles Medical Center and continued in a subsequent jury trial. The reader learns about the stresses affecting minority groups and the majority in a pluralistic society.)

.

In late September 1977, I received a telephone call from a lawyer who represented a civil suit against one of the major metropolitan hospitals in Los Angeles for allegedly permitting sterilization procedures to be conducted on nonconsenting "Chicana"[1] women. The lawyer and I agreed to meet. On November 1, 1977, the two attorneys and I discussed the effects of alleged unconsented sterilization procedures that had been conducted on ten Mexican women in Los Angeles, California. I had heard comments regarding the case in other contexts but had not paid a great deal of attention, since from my own personal bias this sort of institutional behavior was not unexpected. Both lawyers presented the case from the perspective that ten Chicanas had been sterilized without their consent. They asked for my assessment of possible cultural and social ramifications of such practices on the ten women.

I replied that I could not offer an informed judgment without analyzing the case and the women. However, I felt able to venture an opinion, an educated one at best. I suggested that quite a variable response could be expected dependent on the behavioral contexts in which these women had been a part, their cultural histories, and their

Form Margarita B. Melville, ed., *Twice a Minority: Mexican-American Women* (St. Louis: Mosby Co., 1980), 235–248, by permission of the author.

present support networks. Furthermore, at that time, I postulated, and it must be emphasized that it was merely a postulate, the following: If the women had been born in Mexico in rural contexts or in the United States in equivalent circumstance, then sterilization could have severe psychocultural and social results even beyond those expected of other women in the United States. Also, I suggested that the degree of damage could vary with the background of the women. Thus, if the women were urban Chicanas and part of lower-class sectors, their reaction could also be severe, but perhaps their social beings may not be as importantly related to the potential for bearing children. In either context, the severity of a nonconsenting sterilization on the women would be dependent on a variety of exogenous and endogenous variables including class, ethnic maintenance, social networks, work experience, and the psychological well-being of each woman prior to the sterilization procedure.

The lawyers then asked me if I would be willing to serve as a consultant on the case in order to test the postulates that I had suggested. I explained that I could not entertain any a priori conclusions in regard to the women, but that I would be willing to undertake a basic field study of the individuals involved and the circumstances of their sterilization. From the data I would submit an informed opinion of the effects, if any, of the surgery. Consequently, I agreed to serve as a consulting cultural anthropologist for their clients, with the stipulation that whatever conclusions I reached would have to be validated by empirical findings.

THE CULTURAL STRATEGIES OF THE WOMEN

From November 1, 1977, through May 30, 1978, the field studies of these women and their families were designed to gather accurate data that would "place" them in relation to a heterogeneous Mexican population. The studies sought to establish the "subcultural strategies" that these women shared within the cultural boundaries of the Mexican/Chicano population in the Southwestern United States. Using participant observation, unstructured interviews, and questionnaires, it was determined that in fact the women shared subcultural rural Mexican strategies that were adaptive in urban contexts. These findings even surprised the lawyers who themselves had not quite known what to make of the reactions that these women had expressed in regard to the sterilizations.

The data showed that nine of the ten women were born in small rural communities such as *rancherías* or *ejidos* [2] and had been socialized in such environments through the age of 14. In Mexico, these women had fulfilled agricultural chores from milking cows to planting and sowing corn. The one woman who had not been born in a rural Mexican setting was born in Dallas, Texas, but had adopted equivalent strategies in Mexican barrios. We can infer that their socialization experiences from early ages were strictly divided according to sex. Also, among other adaptive patterns, they learned high values on childbearing and strict divisions of labor.

In such social environments, fictive kinship, extended familial networks, and dense friendship networks assisted emotional survival. In urban Los Angeles such extensive and intensive networks had been generated by all of the women and their spouses. Thus, *compadrazgo* relations were shared by all the women. All ten women prior to sterilization had extensive fictive kinship ties for the four traditional occasions in which such ties are generated: baptism, confirmation, communion, and marriage. For some of the women who had four children, *compadres* and *comadres* alone had numbered eighteen persons. Five of the ten women had maintained extended generational ties so that a three-generational tier was valued and experienced.

In addition, the mean number of children in the women's families of orientation was 7.5 and in their spouses' families of orientation it was 9.5. Thus, not only were they from large families, but these consanguineous relatives could be regarded as possible network supports. Visitations between consanguinities [were] intensive, and Sundays were generally the days in which the gathering of both fictive, consanguineous, and ascending generational relations would meet for commensal activities or for the celebration of birthdays or feast days. Another means of network expansion was that generated through *amistad* (friendship). Their functions were not only primarily affectionate but also material. The males assisted each other and reciprocated repair and construction work, the women visited and exchanged information, and in all, they formed borrowing and lending networks for household goods. In addition, all of the women and/or their spouses had participated with their families in *tandas* or revolving credit associations.

Such consanguineous, fictive, and *amistad* relationships had been identified as rewarding or not, based on *sentido familiar* (familial sentiment). That is, persons who did not generally reciprocate in exchange relations within these various networks were considered to be lacking in *sentido familiar*. This *sentido familiar* had as its basis, however, two core elements as organizing principles: first, marriage and children mark adulthood and responsibility; and second, as a social corollary for the first principle, is the internalization of the social identity of *una mujer* and *un hombre*. For the women in the case, although having had ritual markers through *quinceañera* (debut) to announce the passage from adolescence to adulthood, in fact adulthood was defined once marriage had taken place and children had been procreated. Without such circumstances and regardless of statuses gathered in other contexts such as professional standing or educational achievement, a female was not considered privy to the councils of discussion among women on such topics as sex, behavior of men, or topics of seriousness such as death, and other aspects of the life cycle. It is interesting to note that as long as one of the female lawyers in this case was not married, she in fact had no access to the discussions these women shared regarding their marital difficulties experienced as the aftermath of the sterilization procedures. It was not until the lawyer married that she gained access to their discussions.

While marriage marks entry into adulthood, as a ritual it also legitimizes sexual intercourse for the specific purpose of propagating children. While all of the women were Roman Catholics, it was not only specific Church doctrine to which they pointed as the rationalization of this central principle. Rather, they adhered to a belief that sexual relations were the mechanisms for bearing children and not for the distinct pleasure of the male and female. Thus, the potential for bearing children and concomitantly the potential for siring children were given expression in the belief that sexual relations were primarily for the propagation of progeny. This potentiality quotient was the main vehicle by which continuity of all relations could be assured through *sentido familiar*. As long as children were likely to be born, reciprocal relations were likely to be generated, and the various social networks in which these women and their spouses participated could be assured of continuation.

The social corollary of the first organizing principle that defines adulthood through marriage and children is that the social identities of the women, and in part [those] of the males who were their spouses, were measured not just by the potential for bearing and siring children but by their actual manifestation. The actual manifestation of childbearing for these women of this subcultural strategy was the means by which their adult status was reinforced and articulated within the domestic group. There these women received prestige and were recognized as valued adults because of the potential and ability to bear children, a potential and ability that was reinforced by the continued presence of small children in the household. To be *una mujer* was to have children. During the various network activities previously described, the private domestic value of the women's social identity as *una mujer* was assured by the adult female members of those various networks. Constant references during social intercourse about the ages of the children of the women present, the short spacing between children in order to ensure maximal peer relations and caretaker roles available, and in fact the various household duties assigned to females during such network activities as cooking, serving, washing dishes, and feeding children contributed to a total domestic social identity.

For males, on the other hand, prestige among cohorts and within the network activities was indirectly associated with the potential for siring children. This potential took a slightly different political avenue for men because it was also used as the measure of political control over the female within the domestic household. Within the networks, a pregnant woman was the symbolic presentation of the male ability to control her social existence within the domestic household. Therefore, *un hombre* was able to control *una mujer* through impregnation. In addition, *un hombre* was assured continued existence through his progeny, since they bore his name. They assured also the efficacy of the various social networks to which he belonged. As will be seen, for males this control of the female and of her continued social existence was one of the central social principles that was greatly compromised as the aftermath of sterilization.

For the most part, then, social identity of these women was closely associated to the domestic group but more importantly to the potential for bearing children and the potential for their spouses to sire children as domestic group political leaders. Certainly, within the domestic group activities, such relations were expressed in the division of labor not only of the spouses but in the division of labor of their children. For the most part, male children had distinct responsibilities from that of female children, with the latter primarily fulfilling caretaker household duties including feeding and caring for younger brothers and sisters. For the most part, male siblings were assigned protective roles, regardless of age, and tasks unassociated with the household. Gardening, collection of garbage, and permissive explorations were largely in the hands of male siblings. When asked at one point during the course of the work as to why none of the male children were observed participating in kitchen tasks, the general response from the women was that their husbands did not want them to be *maricones* (effeminates).

For the most part, then, such qualitative findings pointed to a subcultural rural Mexican strategy for both spouses, since all husbands had been born in small towns in Mexico except for one spouse who was born in rural Imperial Valley in California. Certainly the composition of their past networks had been very much in keeping with traditional means of support and help. They had generated fictive kinship, *amistad* relations, maintained intragenerational solidarity, and planned for large numbers of children.

The socioeconomic characteristics indicate the following: at time of sterilization the mean age of these women was 32.6 years with a range of 24 to 39 years; they had 3.6 mean number of children and a mean income of $9,500 per year, which was the median family income for that of the total United States population; a mean education of 8.5 years which is only 0.6 years below that of the median Mexican females in the United States; and stable housing and employment characteristics. In no way could a "culture of poverty" be suggested as the core of behavioral principles.

THE HOSPITAL AS THE BEHAVIORAL ENVIRONMENT:[3] THE CONTEXT OF STERILIZATION

Within the confines of a public hospital these Mexican women were selected for nonconsenting sterilizations. In part, such an abuse is greatest in public hospitals, such as the Medical Center* in which the sterilizations of these women occurred, because these are institutions where the poor are regarded as practice cases for medical students. Interns gain status by the number of operations they perform, so it is unlikely that they would turn down the surgical opportunities that a dependently oppressed minority represents. According to one source, a doctor told a group of physicians training at a Southern California county hospital as part of their entry into obstetrics:

> I want you to ask every one of the girls if she wants her tubes tied, regardless of how old she is. Remember, every one who says yes to getting her tubes tied means two tubes (practice) for some resident or intern and less work for some poor son-of-a-bitch next year. (Kennard 1974: 66)

In addition, there is a general neomalthusian ideology that permeates the medical profession. Dr. H. Curtis Wood, Jr., a medical consultant and past president of the Association for Voluntary Sterilization, indicated this point of view:

---

* The public hospital in which the sterilizations were carried out will be referred to as the "Medical Center."

People pollute, and too many people crowded too close together cause many of our social and economic problems. These in turn are aggravated by involuntary and irresponsible parenthood. As physicians, we have obligations to the society of which we are a part. The welfare mess, as it has been called, cries out for solutions, one of which is fertility control (Wood 1973).

At the Medical Center where the ten women were sterilized, Dr. Bernard Rosenfeld, co-author of a Ralph Nader Health Research Group study on surgical sterilization and one-time Ob/Gyn resident at the Center stated:

Surgical teaching programs are having increasing difficulty in finding patients because they have traditionally had to rely upon the availability of indigents. With the increase of third party payments (insurance), the number of indigents has decreased, causing the medical center to resort to 'selling' and various forms of coercing patients into consenting to surgery.

I estimate that while I was at the Medical Center, between 20 to 30 percent of the doctors pushed sterilization on women who either did not understand what was happening to them or who had not been given the facts regarding their options (Interview quoted in Siggins 1977).

Another "insider" also commented on the coercive practices at the Medical Center at the time that the sterilizations of the ten women were taking place:

I saw various forms of actual physical abuses used to force women in labor to consent to sterilization. There were incidences of slapping by doctors and nurses. A syringe of pain-reliever would be shown to a woman in labor and she would be told 'we will give you this and stop the pain if you will sign' (Benker, press conference 1975).

THE CASE IN POINT: THE STERILIZATION OF MEXICAN WOMEN IN THE LOS ANGELES MEDICAL CENTER

The evidence illustrates practices by the Medical Center staff (nurses and doctors) to pressure these women into signing consent forms during intensive labor stages by withholding medication, not soliciting consent for sterilization, or not informing the patients of the permanency of such procedures. In addition, some husbands were pressured to sign consent forms for their wives without their knowledge. Even though there were no medical indications for such procedures to be performed, consent was obtained from the husbands after their wives had refused to sign the consent forms. There was even a recorded refusal by one woman to submit to sterilization, which appears on her medical chart at 5:00 A.M.; after having been given Demerol, consent forms appear to have been signed by 6:28 A.M.—the time at which the surgical procedures were performed. One woman was told falsely that a tubal ligation was necessary because the state of California did not allow more than three cesarean sections. Her third child was to be born in this manner as had her two previous children. According to her physician, conception of a fourth child had to be avoided since this one would also have to be delivered by cesarean section.

It is a remarkable fact that among the ten women, four did not learn of the sterilization procedures until after they had sought birth control devices. One woman did not become aware that such a procedure had been performed until 4 years later during a medical examination.

In each case the Medical Center reflects the basic characteristics of a paternalistic behavioral environment. In fact, a stay in any hospital exposes an individual to a condition of passivity and impotence not often replicated easily in other environments, except perhaps in judicial contexts. Certainly, in each woman's case, the consent of sterilization was not informed because of the unusual pressures applied and the specific physical conditions most of the women were suffering. Furthermore, their lack of knowledge regarding the irreversibility of the procedures, the sedated condition of some of the women who did sign, and the total lack of written consent of three of the women all point to a "neutralization" of the women as human beings and the objectification of the practice as a necessary one because of population rationalizations, surgical practice procedures for the interns, or for the "social good" of the patient. Such practices led to the rupture of subcultural strategies, the fracture of social networks, and the psychological generation of acute depression as the following section describes.

THE STATE AND STRESS OF THE SUBCULTURAL SYSTEMS OF THE STERILIZED WOMEN

From the knowledge gained of the manner in which the social and cultural systems had worked before sterilization, it was then necessary to ascertain the "state" of the sociocultural systems after sterilization. On a social level, it was discovered that most of the women had gone through a process of social disengagement, beginning with the husband-wife dyadic relationship. Two of the husbands remained highly supportive of their spouses and no appreciable damage seemed to have resulted in their relationship. One of the two husbands, however, compensated for the loss of his wife's ability to procreate by showering her with gifts at most inopportune times. The other remained a saddened, but not bitter, male who counseled his wife and was extremely supportive of her. The other eight relationships to different degrees suffered irreparable damage. Three couples filed for divorce prior to the completion of the judicial procedures on July 7, 1978. The other five relationships were marked largely by jealousy, suspicion, and in two cases, physical violence and abuse. Jealousy and suspicion arose in three of the husbands because of the change they perceived in their political control over their wives' sexuality. Basically, they feared that their wives would avail themselves of the sterile state, or that other males would make overtures toward their wives once their sterile state was revealed. In this regard, their wives' social identity had changed from respectable woman to possible libertine.

The relationships between mothers and children for eight of ten women shifted as well. Physical punishment of children had increased to the point that, in at least five of the cases, children sought to remove themselves from their mother's presence at every opportunity. Children themselves had begun to express anger to their own siblings so that sibling conflict had also increased. Aggression between mothers and their children and between siblings shifted the qualitative relationship from affection and nurturance to that of fear and violent reaction.

In all cases fictive and *amistad* relations suffered and visitations that germinated such relations decreased dramatically. Saints' days, parties, fiestas, and Sunday exchanges have been largely avoided by all the women through withdrawal from fictive and *amistad* relations. For the most part, the women agreed that it was less painful to withdraw from these relationships than to answer questions regarding either the sterilizations or the reason why more children have not been sired since the last born were at this time at least 4 years old. To inquiries about future pregnancies, the retort that they were "guarding against pregnancies" was short-ranged. Such questions were exceedingly painful since, of the ten women, five had already chosen names for their future progeny. For the most part, these were names of paternal or maternal grandparents.

Consanguineous relations were also affected. Six of the women did not share the fact that they had been sterilized with immediate siblings and in three of the cases with their own mothers. This denial of course could only take place if social relations were themselves withdrawn by the women in order to avoid the topic altogether. In addition, this also meant that their spouses' consanguineous relatives were also avoided so that this provided another source of conflict between husbands and wives. Such conflict became so endemic that in three of the relationships the husbands lost their employment, two became alcoholics, and one left the family and has not been seen for 4 years from the date of the sterilization.

The degree of cultural disruption has been immense. The basis of social identity and self-image has been largely eliminated for all of the women. In the place of the culturally constituted social definition of self, a substitution of what can be termed the "mula (mule) syndrome" has been generated. The "mula syndrome" refers to the cultural redefinition of the women as "unnatural," "insufficient," or "incomplete women" for they are no longer of domestic value. One woman expressed her situation: "I can no longer be a companion to my husband." Cultural symbols of self-worth were negated and in their place symbols of self-deprecation and self-blame took hold. Of course, these led to feelings of guilt, shame, worthlessness, and self-blame. They blame themselves for what has occurred and are blamed in part by some of the husbands for not resisting sterilization; they then turn in anger against themselves. This situation has been expressed in an acutely vivid dream content. One woman dreamt she found herself traveling to Mexico without her children and on arrival becoming embarrassed when asked by relatives where they were. Another has nightmares in which her children have been stolen, killed, and eaten by unidentified figures. Others have dreamt of finding themselves alone with dead persons, or totally alone and lost without their children or husband, while others recall seeing their children drowning in lakes.

The sense of personality loss and worthlessness, all part of the grief reaction to the sterilization procedures, led to acute depression. For each woman her sense of continuity with the past had been fractured, her sense of self-worth had been shattered, self-blame had been internalized, and a new social identity of impotence had been generated. Each woman in fact is now stigmatized. The sterilization procedures stand as visible and permanent marks of humiliation that they can never remove. The greater the effort at denial, the greater the anger and self-hate generated. The greater the anger and self-hate, the greater the necessity of expression on themselves or on others. The greater the expression, the greater the increase in conflict, social disengagement, and cultural disruption. The final effect was acute depression.

These findings and the verified hypotheses were presented in a court of law as part of the evidence in behalf of a law suit these women had filed in federal court. As will be seen, it is ironic that the very evidence used to illustrate the damages done to the social and cultural systems of these women was, in fact, partially used by the court to rationalize a decision against them.

MADRIGAL VERSUS QUILLIGAN: THE TRIAL AS A BEHAVIORAL ENVIRONMENT

On May 31, 1978, a civil suit for damages began in the United States District Court of the Central District of California. The complaint was entitled *Dolores Madrigal, et al., Plaintiff, versus E.J. Quilligan, et al.* The action was brought against Dr. E.J. Quilligan, chairman of Medical Center's Department of Obstetrics and Gynecology, and eleven other doctors on behalf of the ten women previously mentioned. In order to appreciate the final outcome of the suit, however, we should recall the central contention that "paternalistic behavioral environments" foster differential treatment of Mexicans when the efficient conditions are present. The trial will be treated as such a behavioral environment and the efficient conditions articulated.

The courtroom was very much like most in that spaces were defined in proper domains for the judge, the plaintiff's attorneys, and the defendants' attorneys. Since the trial was a nonjury type, the focus of all the attention by the attorneys on both sides was on the judge. Neither the trial per se nor the judicial arguments will be detailed, since both are much beyond the scope of this work. Instead, the contrasts within the confines of the trial will be addressed in order to understand the behavioral environment within the total context of the social question involved.

These contrasts are most immediately apparent in the attorneys. The plaintiffs' two Chicano lawyers came from the local poverty legal centers who represented their interests. Of the two plaintiffs' lawyers, the male was a 35-year-old person who had graduated well at the top of his class a few years previously. He was legally blind from a childhood disease so that the enormously thick glasses accentuated and distorted his dark brown eyes. For the most part this soft-spoken, medium-sized, and slightly pudgy man shuffled as he moved between the plaintiffs' table and the podium that sat squarely in the middle of the room facing the judge's panelled bench. The other lawyer was a recently graduated Chicana from the same poverty legal center and, like the other lawyer, had been working on the case for 4 years. Dark, thin, and well-dressed, the young female lawyer moved assertively between the plaintiffs' table and the podium. She spoke with clear, clipped, and slightly accented diction. They differed little from the ten plaintiffs in court, except for variance in quality of dress.

In opposition, the defendants' lawyers were the best that money could buy for this sort of civil action. Both the male and female lawyer were from one of the more prestigious Beverly Hills law firms and both seemed quite relaxed in their roles in the courtroom. She moved assertively and quickly from the defendants' table even though she was about 30 pounds overweight. This well-dressed, articulate, and quite polysyllabic Anglo woman did not, in fact, actually present any of the defendants nor did she cross-examine witnesses. Instead, she was largely responsible for making legal motions, registering legal requests, and seemed to assist her partner. He was like his fair-haired counterpart, fiftyish, well-groomed, articulate, and quite polysyllabic without the stuttering that seemed to mark the presentations of the plaintiffs' lawyers. Both in hue and in presentation of themselves, there were obvious contrasts that seemed to divide the courtroom into the Mexican side and the Anglo side. The judge seemed to sit in the middle, or so it seemed.

The judge, the Honorable Jesse W. Curtis, a white-haired 70-year-old person, seemed like the stereotype of the paternalistic figure commanding the courtroom. Firm-jawed, angular faced, with piercing blue eyes set beneath profuse eyebrows that moved in unison in mostly frowns, this Nixon-appointed judge to the federal bench was known by reputation as largely a conservative judge who lived aboard his yacht in Newport Beach, one of the most prestigious areas in Southern California. He and the defendants' lawyers were obvious analogues and stark contrasts to the plaintiffs and their lawyers. The judge did not in fact sit in the middle.

For two and a half weeks the plaintiffs' lawyers presented evidence that under duress, after hours of being in labor, and under medication the plaintiffs could not have given informed consent. Dr. Don Sloan, an internationally known gynecologist and obstetrician, testified that given the circumstances surrounding the sterilization procedures none of the women could have provided informed consent. Each woman in turn provided her testimony in Spanish in which the context of her sterilization was detailed. A handwriting expert examined the signatures of those women who had signed consent forms and concluded that in fact each woman had been suffering great distress and stress at the time. Dr. Terry Kuper, the plaintiffs' psychiatrist, presented his evidence of the effects of the sterilization procedures on each woman and concluded that to different degrees each woman had suffered irreparable psychological damage and that long periods of psychotherapy would have to be undertaken by each one. I offered the data discovered in this work in much the same manner and development, except initially the judge was not going to permit my testimony. When Judge Curtis was made aware of my impending testimony, he remarked from the bench that he did not see what an anthropologist was going to say that would have any bearing on damages and that if I were getting paid, my testimony would not be worth a "plugged nickel." He concluded that after all, "We all know that Mexicans love their families." Nevertheless, I was able to present the data contained and except for minor cross-examination, no opposing expert was presented to refute my testimony. Of interest to note, however, were the concluding questions that Judge Curtis addressed to me that would be of significance in the final opinion.

After having concluded my testimony, the Judge asked me how long I had spent on the case. I answered that I had spent 450 hours of time between field work, creating the instrument, selecting the control groups, and ascertaining what the effects had been on the women's sociocultural systems. He then asked me if I would have undertaken the study in any other manner. I responded that I would not have since "... as an anthropologist to have done otherwise would not have been worth a hill of beans." He repeated the same question again, slightly rephrased, and I answered that professional ethics would have prevented me from coming to the conclusions that I did unless I rigorously followed the methodology I had used. The judge thanked me and I stepped down.

The defense presented no rebuttal of expert witnesses and did not cross-examine the plaintiffs. Instead, they called each one of the doctors in question and from the plaintiffs' medical files commented on the medical procedures contained therein. At no time did any of the doctors recall any of the women, but they all asserted that their "custom and practice" was not to perform a sterilization unless a woman had consented and understood what she was doing. When cross-examined as to whether they spoke Spanish well enough to detail the procedures, they responded generally that they knew enough "obstetrics Spanish" to get them by. When pressed for details about the individual women, they all answered that they could not recall them as patients since they were so many.

The final decision was handed down June 30 before Judge Curtis left for a lengthy Scandinavian vacation. It stated rather succinctly that the judgment was entered for the defendants. The women lost, but the judge's rationalization is interesting and informative because it, in fact, verifies the theoretical position that underlies this exposition—that in paternalistic environments in which Mexicans are differentially treated in a negative manner, the "ideology of cultural differences" will be used as a rationalization for the structural and asymmetrical characteristics of the environments.

The Judge's remarks are as follows:

Communication breakdown

This case is essentially the result of a breakdown in communications between the patients and the doctors. All plaintiffs are Spanish-speaking women whose ability to understand and speak English is limited. This fact is generally understood by the staff at the Medical Center and most members have acquired enough familiarity with the language to get by. There is also an interpreter available whose services are used when thought to be necessary. But even with these precautions, misunderstandings are bound to occur.

Furthermore, the cultural background of these particular women has contributed to the problem in a subtle but significant way. According to the plaintiff's anthropological expert, they are members of a traditional Mexican rural subculture, a relatively narrow spectrum of Mexican people living in this country whose lifestyle and cultural background derive from the lifestyle and culture of small rural communities in Mexico. He further testified that a cultural trait which is very prominent with this group is an extreme dependence upon family. Most come from large families and wish to have large families for their own comfort and support. Furthermore, the status of a woman and her husband within that group depends largely upon the woman's ability to produce children. If for any reason she cannot, she is considered an incomplete woman and is apt to suffer a disruption of her relationship with her family and husband. When faced with a decision of whether or not to be sterilized, the decision process is a much more traumatic event with her than it would be with a typical patient and, consequently, she would require greater explanation, more patient advice, and greater care in interpreting her consent than persons not members of such a subculture would require.

But this need for such deliberate treatment is not readily apparent. The anthropological expert testified that he would not have known that these women possessed these traits had he not conducted tests and a study which required some 450 hours of time. He further stated that a determination by him based on any less time would not have been worth "beans." It is not surprising therefore that the staff of a busy metropolitan hospital which has neither the time nor the staff to make such esoteric studies would be unaware of these atypical cultural traits.

It is against this backdrop therefore that we must analyze the conduct of the doctors who treated the plaintiffs in this case.

Doctors' custom and practice

Since these operations occurred between 1971 and 1974 and were performed by the doctors operating in a busy obstetrics ward, it is not surprising that none of the doctors have any independent recollection of the events leading up to the operations. They all testified, however, that it was their custom and practice not to suggest a sterilization unless a patient asked for it or there were medical complications which would require the doctor, in the exercise of prudent medical procedures, to make such suggestion. They further testified that it was their practice when a patient requested sterilization to explain its irreversible result and they stated that they would not perform the operation unless they were certain in their own mind that the patient understood the nature of the operation and was requesting the procedure. The weight to be given to such testimony and the inferences to be drawn therefrom will be determined in the light of all the testimony relating to each doctor's conduct.[4]

The Judge's final opinion also excluded the testimony by the hand-writing expert, the psychiatrist on the case, and refuted the testimony by Dr. Sloan, the gynecologist and obstetrician, by saying that his statements "... completely defy common sense." Why they do so, he did not explain. His conclusion, however, is quite enlightening in that he admits that in fact all of the women had suffered. He states:

This case had not been an easy one to try for it has involved social, emotional and cultural considerations of great complexity. There is no doubt but that these women have suffered severe emotional and physical stress because of these operations. One can sympathize with them for their inability to communicate clearly, but one can hardly blame the doctors for relying on these indicia of consent which appeared to be unequivocal on their face and which are in constant use in the Medical Center.

Let judgment be entered for the defendants.

Jesse W. Curtis
Senior United States District
Judge (19)

CONCLUSIONS

First, it must be obvious that within paternalistic institutionalized behavioral environments, Mexicans have a high probability of being negatively treated. Certainly the medical sterilizations and the legal judgments uphold this fact. Regardless of the overwhelming evidence to the contrary, the judge disregarded evidence and testimony presented and chose instead to consider the "custom and practice" of the doctors rather than following rules of evidence.

Second, his misuse of the anthropological data in which he identified the women as belonging to a "relatively narrow spectrum of Mexican people" was not presented as empirical evidence. Instead, this commentary was used to illustrate the "atypicality of their cultural traits." In other words, the women were so culturally different that the doctors could not have known that the sterilizations would have affected them in so adverse a manner. This belief removes the legal and moral responsibility for their actions. The "ideology of cultural differences" then is used as the very basis for an unjust and detrimental decision against a group of largely defenseless Mexican women. After all, how could the doctors have been aware that the sterilizations would have such an effect on Mexican women, since the hospital in which these operations were carried out is in the middle of the largest Mexican barrio outside Mexico City. The judge legitimized the doctors' actions and his action against the women by noting that the doctors were too busy to note these cultural differences, and even more importantly, they were so different that the doctors could not have known the effects of sterilizations unless they had carried out studies similar to the one I carried out in the case.

Third, all the work that went into the presentation of this material is still very much in the "meliorative and reformists attempts" of the well-intentioned liberal establishment. I, too, blundered and in fact was responsible for providing the judge with exactly the knowledge he needed to utilize the "ideology of cultural differences." Ironically, while fairly objective empirical findings of effect were presented, which were too overwhelming to ignore on the record, the judge's only recourse was to utilize the data against the women since it could not be refuted.

Fourth, and last, all of the activities that made up this work occurred within the confines of an industrial capitalist state in which the diversity of culture is organized and controlled by a national prism, reflecting a dominant ethnic group of Anglo-Saxon Americans. Both the sterilization of the physical ability of a group of ethnic minority women to procreate and the resultant cultural sterilization of the same group of women were, in fact, provided legitimization by the court. The decision reinforces that national prism and ensures the superordinate ethnic group of Anglo-Saxon Americans continued domination by whatever means.

Notes

1. I use the term "Chicana" to designate American-born women of Mexican heritage who are socialized within industrially structured population centers in either agricultural or urban contexts. Cultural specifics from language to belief systems are "distributed" according to class and occupational sectors. "Mexican" is the term I use to designate Mexican-born persons who are socialized within rural or urban contexts and in a possible variety of structural settings from industrial to small village "closed corporate" communities. Cultural specifics from language to belief systems are "distributed" according to class and occupational sectors. The differences between populations will be both cultural and structural; however, similarities will also be reflective of cultural specifics arising from equivalent structural conditions. The term "working-class" Mexican denotes little specifically and assumes a homogeneity of experiences that is ahistorical in content.

2. *Rancherías* are small agricultural settlements in which the population density of the residential area is equal to the area used for subsistence. *Ejidos* are communal lands assigned to a community by the Mexican federal government.

3. I utilize the concept of behavioral environment as an important construct that may be fruitful in designating those situations that promote negative differential treatment. Some environments can be considered "paternalistic" when the cultural constructs demand extreme deference articulated through a routinized and elaborate etiquette; titles of reference and superiority; a specialized argot or jargon; differentiated costumes and attire; allocated physical spaces; segregated activities; and when social relations are based on dependence asymmetry, social distance, and ascribed status differentials without vertical mobility for the client population. "Clients" are perceived as immature, childish, ignorant, and underdeveloped so that the controlling figures in the environment have political control over them and economic access that commands the allocation of valued resources, services, material goods, or information. Enforcement is based on the withdrawal or threatened withdrawal of such resources so that ultimately the roles fulfilled by "clients" vis-à-vis their "patrons" are based on "coercive" support. "Legitimate" support is based on value consensus. For a complete discussion, see Marc J. Swartz (1968).

Yet, "competitive behavioral environments" in comparison to paternalistic ones are marked by factors of achievement, affective neutrality, mobility, legitimate support, and are legalistic, representative, and "earned." The relations between participants, although hierarchical, are not passive-dependent but active-interdependent. These may be asymmetrical, but all concerned here expect change and development through participation. Competition is designed within boundaries, and conflict is defined and agreed to within parameters that do not threaten the relations between members in the environments. There is a general value consensus without coercion, and resources are allocated to those who can best meet the goals of the behavioral environment. Both "paternalistic" and "competitive" models are polar types and operationalization is still to be developed.

The basic notions of paternalistic and competitive relations are owed to Pierre Van den Berghe's two fine basic works in ethnic and race relations: *Race and Racism* (1967) and *Race and Ethnicity* (1970). In these two works, the author uses the characteristics of paternalism and competition as independent and dependent societal variables that mark the nature of the relations between dominant and subordinate groups within a developmental polar model. I contend that, regardless of larger societal developments, paternalistic and competitive behavioral environments will coexist in even the most "competitive industrialized" social contexts. In the most rational of institutionalized bureaucratic contexts, paternalistic factors may very well mark most relations between participants.

4. See Judge Jesse W. Curtis "Opinion," (No. CV 75-2057-JWC, United States Federal Court, June 30, 1978, pp. 1–19).

References

Benker, Karen. Statement made before a press conference at the Greater Los Angeles Press Club, December 6, 1975.

Curtis, Jesse W. Opinion, June 30, 1978, No. CV 75-2057-JWC: 1–19.

Kennard, Gail. "Sterilization abuse." *Essence*, October, 1974, 66ff.

Siggins, Richard V. "Coerced sterilization: a national civil conspiracy to commit genocide upon the poor?" Unpublished manuscript. Loyola University, School of Law, 1977.

Swartz, Marc J. "Introduction." In Marc J. Swartz (ed.), *Local-Level Politics*. Chicago, Illinois: Aldine Publishing Co., 1968.

Van den Berghe, Pierre (ed.). *Race and Racism: A Comparative Perspective*. New York: John Wiley & Sons, Inc., 1967.

_____ . *Race and Ethnicity*. New York: Basic Books, Inc., Publishers, 1970.

Wood, H. Curtis, Jr. "Statement of address." *Contemporary OB/GYN*. January. Quoted in Kennard "Sterilization abuse," *Essence*, October, 1973: 86.

DISCUSSION QUESTIONS AND ACTIVITIES

Conner

1. Using Walker Connor's definition of "ethnic group," identify the ethnic groups in your community or region.

2. Organize a debate where one side defends Connor's definition of ethnic group, while the other supports the more general definition that the U.S. Census Bureau and many social service organizations use.

3. Ethnic minorities in the Soviet Union are seeking a new political voice. If you need to, review the issue in the press over the past year, using library references. Do these groups meet the criteria for an ethnic group that Connor sets forth?

4. Find an ethnographic atlas at a reference library. What criteria do the editors use in organizing the atlas? Do they correspond with Connor's criteria?

5. Mexican-Americans constitute only one Spanish-speaking community within the U.S. The picture becomes more complex when one adds Spanish-speaking immigrants, documented or undocumented, from Central and Latin America. Check the most recent census for your area. What population of Spanish-speaking or other ethnic groups live in the area? What support networks for the groups are there (local foreign language newspapers, social clubs, festivals, etc.)?

6. Define transnationalism (as opposed to intranationalism).

7. Research the "militant Chicano movement" of the 1960s as documented in the national press.

8. What nuances of meaning do you find in the two terms, *undocumented immigrants* and *illegal immigrants*? Of the two terms, which do you prefer and why?

9. Chart the elections won by Hispanic candidates at the national, state, and local levels. Concentrate on Los Angeles, Florida, Texas, New Mexico, Arizona, and Colorado.

Hansen and Peguese

10. After studying the culture capsules described by Hansen et al., form a group to write and produce a culture capsule. You may want to video-

tape the incident. Before beginning the project, talk with visiting Spanish-speaking or other internationals.

Brice Heath

11. Adopt a position with respect to the bilingual education issue and prepare a defense of your position.

12. Write a first-person narrative of César Chávez and his role in the farm labor movement or Richie Valens and his career as a musician and performer.

13. If the option is available, become involved with the international population in your community: join international organizations, tutor in English, volunteer at an international visitors' center, for example.

14. Compare the Indian language policy of Mexico with the Indian language policy of the U.S. administered through the Bureau of Indian Affairs.

15. Heath raises the question of the status of minority language in the U.S., in particular the Spanish language. Find examples of a bilingual ballot, of bilingual textbooks, or other bilingual printed matter available to Spanish speakers in the U.S.

16. Find out about other national language conflicts outside the U.S.: Spanish and the Basque language in Spain, Welsh and English in Great Britain, Wolof and French in Senegal, Walloon and Flemish in Belgium, Quechua and Spanish in Peru. What policies affect their use? How politicized is the issue of ethnic languages?

Velez-I.

17. Professor Velez-I. describes an extended support network enjoyed by the Mexican-American women involved in the illegal sterilization lawsuit. Looking at U.S. society, what kinds of support networks do women have in your community? Are they composed of friends, acquaintances, or professionals? How does the type of support system we prefer reflect U.S. interpersonal styles identified by Gudykunst and Young Kim in Section I?

18. Identify the ethical issues in the case described by Velez-I.

19. Role-play the witnesses who appeared on behalf of the hospital (physicians, hospital administrator, etc.).

20. Show how the role expectations for the adult women in your community do or do not differ from those role expectations for the Mexican-American women in Los Angeles.

21. Two films have been produced about two similar incidents, one in Bolivia, *Blood of the Condor* (1969, Jorge Sanjines, 72 min.), the other in Puerto Rico, *La Operación* (1982, Ana María García, 40 min.). Arrange to view one or both of the films. Compare the incidents that occurred in the films with those described by Velez-I. What were the reasons for the sterilizations? What was the effect of the sterilizations on the women, on their spouses, on their immediate community?

SECTION V

Iberia:
The Emerging Contexts of New Spain

SALVADOR GINER

Ethnic Nationalism, Centre and Periphery in Spain

(Two of Spain's ethnic minorities, the Catalans and the Basques, are testing Spain's new parliamentary democracy and redefining the complex economic and ideological relationship between periphery and center.)

This [article] attempts to dispel some common misconceptions about the nature of Spanish "centralism" as well as about the "separatism" of some of her regions and nationalities by reflecting on the complex and in some ways contradictory relationships between centre and periphery. Some considerations of the historical aspects of the issue open the way for a brief analysis of developments after 1977. [We] . . . look behind the constitutional and political arrangements with which the new parliamentary democracy has tried to tackle the inherited problems of Spain's ethnic pluralism and diverse territorial loyalties. The "nationalities" question in Spain is then approached from a corporatist perspective, in the expectation that it will shed some light on the issue by taking into account both the new economic and ideological forces at work and the ethnic legitimation of Spain's complex polity.

CENTRE AND PERIPHERY

Any society in so far as it is a relatively well-integrated structure has a core, a centre. Such a centre is ultimately located in the realm of culture,

From Nissa Torrents and Christopher Abel, eds., *Spain: Conditional Democracy* (New York: St. Martin's Press, 1984), 78–99, by permission of the publisher. World rights granted by Croom Helm, London.

for it entails shared values and beliefs, including those which define predominant forms of inequality, power and privilege. It is often the case that the spatial, political and economic structure of the society physically expresses the existence of the centre. In turn, by constantly mirroring the periphery and answering its needs and demands, the centre reinforces the intimate union between the two. They depend on each other. They explain each other. Thus the political capitals of empire from Rome to Moscow have also been seats of government, temples of ideology, hubs of trade and communication, and places of pilgrimage. This applies equally today to the capitals of a number of well-established states and nations. Together with their immediate surroundings the capitals tend to be the moral, political and economic cores of the larger society.[1] It is possible that the world technological revolution and other contemporary factors may change this arrangement; but up to the present time this is the manner in which well-integrated, complex societies have been functioning.

There is, by contrast, a number of historically important societies which deviate from this relatively unitary pattern. They are societies suffering from acute economic disparities, not just in terms of wealth and poverty but, more significantly, in the modes of production and consumption of goods. They tend to be societies divided into salient ethnic groups and often ruled by simultaneously weak and strong political powers at the heart of the state. They are torn between centripetal and centrifugal forces and are often paralyzed and bewildered by their own internal antinomies. And yet, despite all these contradictions, some such societies are recognized as units by the immense majority of their inhabitants as well as by outsiders, for they are no mere congeries of irreconciliably different peoples. Bonds stronger than their cleavages endow them with unity. One such society is Spain.

Both the *grandeur* and the *misère* of that country, its readily recognizable tragic dimension and the equally easily identifiable tawdriness of much of its social life owe much to the tensions bred by such imbalances and contrasts. In some favourable circumstances they have stood Spaniards in good stead, for they have been significant sources of creativity and civilization. All too frequently, however, they have crippled the country and given a lack of direction to its people. Worse, they have too often become causes of civil strife and even fratricidal warfare. This [section] examines fratricidal warfare, chiefly from a political viewpoint. It looks at the problems generated by political and administrative centralism as well as the nationalist, regionalist and separatist responses elicited by centralism in the peripheral areas of the country.

The historical process of political unification and state formation in Spain differed in a number of ways from that in other Western European countries. In all of them, including Spain, there arose a central hegemonic nucleus upon which the modern state was founded. Often, that nucleus was also a nation. In Great Britain a number of peripheral nations—Ireland, Wales, Scotland—were accommodated into the English polity. The long process was painful but largely successful: only most of the Irish domain, despite considerable anglicization, severed itself from the main body politic while the rest remains at a heavy cost. Even British and other modern Western states which show discontinuities in political integration and unfinished nation-building processes exhibit a much greater degree of coalescence with their respective societies than the Spanish state does with its own.

THE POVERTY OF SPANISH CENTRALISM

Spain, we are told, was politically unified at a very early stage in modern European history. With the notable exception of Portugal, a kingdom that took longer to fall within the pale of the Spanish Crown, by the end of the fifteenth century Spain had become a single, powerful, indeed fearsome political unit, extending its influence in every conceivable direction. In fact, that influence was coterminous with Castilian foreign and overseas expansion as well as with its undisputed hegemony within the Iberian peninsula. In turn this hegemony was exercised over a loose number of political units whose respective degrees of autonomy varied considerably. Thus while recently reconquered Andalusia was directly ruled by Castile which imposed its laws, the kingdom of Aragon—itself a confederation that included sizeable overseas Mediterranean lands—was hypothetically on a par with Castile. The countries under the Spanish Crown had the same monarch, but in many ways they were foreign to each other. Catalans, for instance, were forbidden to trade with the overseas provinces of the empire until as late as 1778: the Catalans were as alien to the areas assigned to Castilian dominion as other subjects of the Spanish sovereigns—the Flemings, the Neapolitans—were.

The origins of the political formula for both union and separation are not to be found in Castile herself but in the history of the Aragonese confederation. Having inherited the formula from Ferdinand and Isabella, the Hapsburgs maintained it throughout their rule, though there were some belated attempts at the end of their dynasty to overcome divisions through the imposition of Castilian law and government in areas hitherto free from them. It was in the nature of the "universalistic imperialistic aspirations that Spain and the House of Hapsburg represented" that its government "rested entirely on local autonomy and inclined towards federative combinations." And, of course, this was also the stance taken by the Austrian branch of the dynasty. [2] The interestingly loose and in some ways resilient Hapsburg formula finally came to grief when confronted, on the one hand, with more efficient and centrally organized states and, on the other, with the tendencies towards independence of its own ethnic and political subunits. The nations of the Iberian peninsula are not, nor have they ever been, similar to those that made up the Austrian empire: their ethnic and cultural affinities run deeper than those of the mosaic-like patterns of central Europe. Nevertheless interesting parallels between the two political structures can be drawn, over and beyond the simple fact that they were once under the same sovereign and were both the embodiment of an *ordo Romano-Hispanicum* or, as the Dutch Calvinists used to say, *iugum Romano-Hispanicum.*

It is within this context that the failures and achievements of Spaniards attempting to modernize the country under the early Bourbons are better understood. Progress for them was not restricted to secularization, the improvement of the economy and the advancement of the arts and sciences. It also meant the creation of one single nation, transcending the limits and internal frontiers of the traditional kingdoms and principalities which were seen by liberals and reformers as inextricably linked to a feudal past.

The eighteenth-century revolution in Spain was, however, a notoriously truncated process. There is irony in the fact that the greatest creation of the enlightened modernizers was posthumous—the 1812 Constitution of Cádiz proclaimed by the Cortes while the country was at war with the Napoleonic invader. The relatively peaceful transition to a modern state envisaged by the 1812 Constitution did not occur. Instead there were civil war, imperial dismemberment, military *pronunciamientos*, national despondency, fiscal crises of the state, endemic dictatorships and an inability to industrialize thoroughly. The stark fact that an eighteenth-century revolution never took place in Spain meant that the country entered the period of the European industrial revolution and capitalist imperialism with a weak and inefficient state apparatus, backward patterns of privilege and inequality and only small enclaves of peripheral bourgeois industrialism.

Three salient aspects of the poverty of Spanish centralism are now addressed:

(a) The weakness of the Spanish state. In modern times Spain has usually been ruled by either reactionary or conservative governments. Radical governments have been given little or no chance to rule the country in peace and have lasted for only very few short-lived spells. The idea of right-wing rule suggests a centralized, stronghand government, as indeed has often been the case in Spain. Frequently, however, the despotic severity of the rulers was tempered by the blundering in-efficiency of their patrimonial (or dictatorial) traditionalist ways. Right-wing or reactionary rule in Spain meant the maintenance of inherited privilege in a spirit of intransigence, of ancient religious pieties and of equally ancient concepts of national identification. Spanish governments were, therefore, particularly unsuited to meet the needs of modernity in marked contrast with conservative governments elsewhere in Europe. Other conservative—even reactionary—European governments were possessed by a mentality which was more akin to the true spirit of capitalism and far less hostile to the demands and implications of industrialization. Accordingly, the task of dismantling the burdensome remnants of the past fell largely upon the radicals, i.e., diverse liberal forces in quasi-permanent opposition during the nineteenth century and the Socialists and extreme republicans in the twentieth.

The belated disentailment of Church and seigneurial lands, admini-strative reform, the creation of a system of artificially demarcated provinces, the development of a radial network of railways and roads and other far-reaching decisions were mostly inspired by the Jacobin centralism of the liberals even when they were not carried out by them. Some liberals were committed to free trade and were apprehensive about the power of the state, but others were protectionist in economic matters and relied openly on the powers of the government, thus opening the way for the rise of a new interventionism. This was based less on a rational conception of the country and its economy as a whole than on the sheer factional interests of a number of disparate segments of the upper classes which differed sharply in outlook according to region and source of income and privilege and lacked integration into a single national ruling class.

Political and administrative centralism was felt as a harsh and unbearable burden in Spain. In areas with a recognized historical identity and local law like Navarre, the Basque country and Catalonia, "liberal" centralism from Madrid was answered by an affirmation of ancient roots. This affirmation made Carlism the "separatism" of the age. It was active from 1822 until its final demise along with the Francoist dictatorship that it had helped to power in 1936. Carlism reasserted local *fueros* and time-hallowed forms of home rule in the name of a particularly virulent brand of anti-Jacobinism and a sacred fear of modernity and secularization. Carlism succeeded in the rural hinterland of those areas that spearheaded industrialization: perhaps the combination of distance from central government and proximity to the new world of industrial production gave Carlism some of its remarkable, if misplaced and misspent, force. It could be said that Carlism has not entirely died, especially in the Basque country and to a lesser extent in Catalonia, for Carlist allegiance to the land and Carlist collective emotional identifications have perhaps been redefined in terms of a local modern nationalism. Many of the early representatives of Catalan or Basque autonomism could trace their ideological and kinship ancestry to Carlism. It would be far-fetched to see contemporary Basquism and Catalanism as Carlism in a new guise, but a historical continuity between them can hardly be ignored.

The inefficiency, clumsiness and parasitism of the centralist bureaucracy underscored the essential weakness of the state over a long period. This is a well-known phenomenon which took place in several European peripheral states from czarist Russia to Italy after unification. The hostility towards central government felt by the peasants and factory workers was shared by the more advanced middle and upper classes in the small industrial enclaves who saw the central government as a remote, ignorant, alien body, that was also a necessary evil to be summoned whenever the threat of the *classes dangereuses* became too acute. For some members of the middle and upper classes the state also meant access to secure administrative and military employment and to political office. These attitudes of either adherence or rejection soon became a source of ideological identification with the larger entity of Spain or with one of its constituent nationalities or regions. Feelings of Spanish identity—through occupational opportunities—were strongest in nonindustrial parts of the country like Galicia, both Castiles and Andalusia. This identification was later to have far-reaching consequences for the character of political conflict and the elaboration of national ideologies.

(b) The intensification of within-nation differences through industrialization. It is often assumed that capitalism and industrialization, together with the growth of the modern state, give rise to a process of social convergence between the different regions of a given society. Allowances are often made for the appearance through capitalist industrialization of developed and underdeveloped regions, as well as of forms of economic dualism, and such-like. Although it is probably true that most societies become more homogeneous thanks to the combination of these powerful forces, in some, like Spain till the 1960s, precisely the opposite effects are to be detected.

The deepening of disparities through modernization are best illustrated by the case of Catalonia,[3] where the rise of a thoroughly indigenous capitalism with its corresponding class structure and mentality was followed by an equally indigenous industrialization which enhanced Catalan distinctiveness within both the Spanish and the Mediterranean framework.[4] Industrialization not only made the distinctiveness of Catalonia more acute but also generated problems that stemmed from the paradox that a politically subordinate and incompetently administered part of the country had clearly become the most vital focus of industry and progress. Ultimately the chronic limitations of Catalan capitalism—the smallness of its ethnic base, its small population, its marginal geographical position, its lack of a powerful financial structure—condemned it to a secondary position very different from comparable Mediterranean regions like Lombardy and Piedmont. Whereas in Italy the unified state was essentially a northern initiative, the unified state in Spain was already constituted on the basis of an older legal order before Catalonia came of age. The imbalances between the nationalities on the periphery and the centre came to be an endemic source of misunderstandings, mistrust and mutual exasperation.

(c) The dislocation of Spanish society. Imperfect modernization, enclave industrialization, ethnic nationalism, a weak state—all these factors accentuated the cleavages and polarities that ran through Spanish society even before they found expression in the form of modern ideologies. Yet, contrary to cliché, these opposites did not simply coalesce into two antagonistic Spains each ready—in Antonio Machado's words—to "freeze the heart" of the other. Spain was torn by a set of deeprooted antinomies that became more pronounced in modern times. Several come to mind: regions of *latifundios* in the South and of *minifundios* in the North-West; islands of bourgeois ethos in the midst of an anti-modern culture; "free-thinking" anticlericalism versus fanatical Catholicism; reactionary conservatism versus nihilistic anarchism. The rise of a financial bourgeoisie in Madrid with strong government links combined with all the features outlined in different ways to dislocate Spanish society. Whereas separatism was Catholic and traditionalist in the Basque provinces, it was largely radical and secular in Catalonia. Whereas anarchism was chiliastic in Andalusia, anarcho-syndicalism contained a potential for stable labour relations in Catalonia; socialism was strongest in the mining areas of Asturias and among the working classes elsewhere in the non-anarchist strongholds. Antinomies did not produce "two Spains" but several, for they combined severally. And the ensuing clusterings of interests and ideologies and the cleavages they created did not always correspond with a neat centre-periphery pattern.

The much criticized Second Republic made notable strides towards solving some of Spain's antinomies by initiating an agrarian reform programme and granting home-rule to Catalonia, the Basque country and Galicia. But the opponents of parliamentary democracy joined forces to destroy it.

DICTATORSHIP AND THE ETHNIC LEGITIMATION OF DEMOCRACY

It is possible to speak only imprecisely of a progressive periphery and a backward centre in Spain. The presence of a vigorous radical-liberal and socialist movement in Madrid and other cities of Castile alone invalidates an oversimplified notion of a territorial distribution of tensions. The North-South divide that so clearly applies to the Italian peninsula has never been valid for the Iberian.

The Civil War erased complexities, hesitations and nuances regarding the centre-periphery problem. Wars, rather than ideologies, are the *terribles simplificateurs* of history. In the conflict and the long dictatorship that ensued the antinomies coalesced in peripheral nationalism and further tensions between the government and local and regional sources of power. It is my contention that such a process of coalescence was based on a cultural and not only upon an economic and class distinctiveness because ethnic and cultural identities are singularly important structuring factors upon the society as a whole. Neither in Spain nor elsewhere can nationalism be reduced to the economy or any other single sphere of collective activity. It tends, instead, to be a structural component of social life.

To a considerable extent the Franco regime found its justification in its ability to suppress and extirpate all forms of autonomism and separatism by ethnic minorities. Francoism saw any form of federalism or desire for a degree of home rule as pure "separatism."[5] Separatism, in turn, was defined as the worst political sin against the sacred unity of the country. This is not the place to analyze the precise nature of the regime that took such a stance towards the ethnic minorities of Spain.[6] Suffice it to say that the conception of national unity at the expense of cultural diversity became a central and obsessive dogma of the Francoist coalition that ruled until 1977. This dogma was intimately linked to another: fanatical anticommunism. Both went hand in hand, especially in the propaganda directed against the "separatist" areas. The distortion that resulted from the Francoist identification of communism with "separatism" was accompanied by a relentless determination to uproot the national cultures that has been seen as an attempt at cultural genocide. Both efforts were made in the name of abstract Spanish culture whose timelessness and universality were continually emphasized. In fact, such a quintessential Spanish culture was an ideological rendering of what the rulers believed to be the essence of a hypothetical Castilian spirit whose language and sublime ideals constituted the epitome of the "eternal Spain." And Spain, of course, stood alone, victorious and misunderstood in a turbulent modern age. The real cultures of the non-Castilian peoples were belittled as mild, folkloric, regional deviations from the norm.

Francoism may not have been entirely fascist; but culturally it was not wide of the mark. It practised linguistic and cultural oppression with unprecedented thoroughness. Except in the special case of Navarre, whose populist, Catholic fundamentalist Carlists had also risen against the Republic, Francoism practised political centralism and anti-autonomism with single-minded efficiency. This observation leads us to a principal, though often overlooked feature of Francoism: it represented the belated emergence of a really strong modern state.

The traditional weakness of the Spanish state has been emphasized. The shortcomings of the modern Spanish state, including its failure to overcome fully its Hapsburg legacy have been indicated as one of the causes of the vigour of her ethnic nationalisms today. In other words, the much-hated "centralism" of the past must be thanked by autonomists and separatists alike for its inefficiency. With the advent of Francoism, however, we encounter for the first time a government and a state both willing and able to carry out the task of "national" homogenization.

Even under the most extreme totalitarian circumstances such a task cannot be easily accomplished. One consequence of attempts to erode communal identities and national traits can be their intensification. External threats and conflict often lead to both internal cohesion and mobilization. They may also bring classes and interest groups together which otherwise have little in common with each other or whose aims are mutually antagonistic. That is why nationalism appeals to the solidarity of the non-solidary. Thus a nascent nationalist ideology is legitimized by the persecution of a people, a language and a culture.[7]

Despite its longevity Francoism did not last long enough to achieve its aims of national "homogenization." Paradoxically it achieved the precise opposite.

Until the mid-1950s, the Francoist government concentrated upon the task of eradicating the social, cultural and economic features of "separatism." Its political features were annihilated through traditional means like the suppression of the press in the minority languages and their total ban from schools. Subsequently, Francoism reinforced existing policies with the help of state television and other efficient means of cultural penetration.[8] These policies had the unintended consequence of heightening autonomism, separatism and regionalism nearly everywhere in different degrees.

In the late 1970s regions and areas that had never considered home-rule discovered the attractions of autonomism. To some extent these attractions were the consequence of a policy carried out by the first constitutional governments to counterbalance the serious "historical" autonomist claims of Basques and Catalans. It was hoped that a semi-federalism would allay military anxieties. A more important cause of this generalized "autonomism" which seemed to affect every distinct region in Spain stemmed directly from the political order of Francoism. Under Francoism the democratic opposition was particularly powerful in the "historical" nationalities where the absence of democracy was compounded by the relentless official attack on ethnicity and collective feelings of identity, especially linguistic.[9] In those areas the demands for home-rule and democracy became analogous, if not one and the same thing. The granting of home-rule became a constant demand in every negotiation of Basques and Catalans with other opposition forces in Spain until they also became thoroughly committed to autonomism and began to identify democracy with the territorial and cultural rights of ethnic minorities. It was in this manner that the ideology of "autonomism"—this time, general home-rule for all regions—entered the consciousness of all democratic political forces in the early stages of the transition period. Until the coming of Francoism it had only done so imperfectly. Francoism therefore unintentionally created a most favourable atmosphere for "regionalism," "minority nationalism" and federalism. Before Francoism such concepts were only significant irritants for the many democrats of different political persuasions who held an essentially unitary vision of the Spanish polity.

Opposition to the dictatorship in the Basque country and Catalonia was formulated in the name of the oppressed nation as well as in terms of standard grievances against arbitrary rule and class exploitation.[10] The capacity of nationalism to overcome internal ideological and political divisions was exemplified by the Assembly of Catalonia set up in 1971. Basing its operations on a simple four-point programme (political amnesty, freedom, home-rule and democracy) the illegal Catalan Assembly succeeded in mobilizing Christians, Communists, Socialists, disgruntled Carlists and countless trade unionists, intellectuals and ordinary citizens into a vast, peaceful and highly representative movement. By contrast in the Basque country guerrilla warfare combined for a time with a popular democratic mobilization. It should not be forgotten that the advocates of political violence enjoyed for some time a degree of popularity and goodwill that was not confined to the Basque country. They appeared to many at first as freedom-fighters whose sole targets were police torturers or those—like Carrero Blanco—who were seen as primarily responsible for the dictatorship's atrocities.

One consequence of intense democratic-nationalist opposition in both the Basque country and Catalonia was that after 1977 they had to be promised a degree of political autonomy if the transition to democracy was to be achieved through agreement and consensus rather than by renewed violence and confrontation. "Political autonomy for all communities" (i.e., nationalities and regions within the Spanish state) became the key to the problem of the supposed "separatism" of two of them. Its general acceptance of "political autonomy for all communities" by all concerned became the linchpin of the complicated and far-reaching multilateral negotiations and mutual concessions which culminated in the remarkably peaceful transition from dictatorship to democracy in Spain.

ETHNICITY AND THE POLITICAL FORMULA OF THE MONARCHY

When political parties were legalized after the 1976 referendum, a massive upsurge of nationalist fervour was allowed to express itself with relative freedom. A new era had begun: new in terms not only of its articulation of the "nationalities question" but also of economic and sociostructural centre-periphery relations.

The concessions granted by the centralist establishment to the historical nationalities (i.e., those "regions" seen by it as potentially secessionist) were an essential aspect of the political formula of the new parliamentary democracy that was consolidated by the constitutional referendum. Although very substantial in the eyes of the centralist establishment which included army sectors loyal to Crown and Constitution, the concessions fell short of the aspirations of most autonomists. In exchange for these concessions the representatives of the minority nations gave assurances that they would use all possible means to avoid the fragmentation of Spain and would support the controlled extension of autonomism to other Spanish regions. Hence autonomism began to embrace old regions like Galicia with linguistic and ethnic identities that were arguably as strong as those of Catalonia or the Basque country; regions like Andalusia with a marked personality; and also provinces like La Rioja and Cantabria with more questionable historical claims to separate nationhood and without a federalist or autonomist past. Even the Madrid metropolitan region now identified with its province came to join the rush for autonomy. The traditional core regions of the Hispanic monarchy and Spanish national identity, Castile and León were to some extent encouraged to develop auto-nomism by reflection or mimetism and no doubt under the pressures of political expediency. These exchanges found their ideological for-mulation in the notion that the Spanish state is neither federalist nor unitary but *un estado de las autonomías* (state made up of autonomies). As this strange but apparently effective notion was not enough to allay the fears of the extreme civilian and military right, it was agreed in 1981 by the two main parties, the UCD and PSOE, to pass a law for the "harmonization" of the autonomies.

Clearly, the planned law for the harmonization of the autonomies [*Ley Orgánica para la Armonización de las Autonomías*] was an attempt to assuage the anxieties of *golpistas* and other centralists by circumscribing the powers and faculties of the regional governments. But that was not its most interesting aspect. Its chief characteristic was that it was wholly prepared outside parliament, in the form of an obviously corporatist pact, between the two parties which jointly presented a *fait accompli* to both legislative chambers of the Cortes. This arrangement raised questions about the exact nature of Spain's political order after 1977, its limitations, class composition and the veto powers of the military and other forces.

By October 1982 Spain had gone a long way towards *un estado de las autonomías*. With varying degrees of support most nationalities and regions—from the Canary Islands to Andalusia, from Extremadura to Aragon—obtained some form of autonomous or preautonomous government by 1981.[11] However, the harmonization law (LOAPA) loomed. Political forces that had not been party to the UCD-PSOE pact, including the Communists and the Basque and Catalan conservative nationalists, voiced their discontent. Other guarantees and safety mechanisms were put into effect. Thus sensible measures for "territorial compensation" between rich and poor regions were taken; rulings and decrees of the Catalan parliament were often overruled as unconstitu-tional by the central Constitutional Court; numerous acts of ritualistic or symbolic allegiance to the unity of the nation were obtained from the political representatives of the historical nationalities. Above all, the post of civil governor appointed by the central government was maintained while a new office of government delegate to the autonomous region was created. Serious delays arose and difficulties in the process of devolution—before and after the attempted coup of February 1981—can be seen as an effort to appease the ever-powerful right-wing and centralist establishment, and particularly its military component.

It would be wrong to infer that the political formula of the *estado de las autonomías* is a mere sham. Despite the strong reservations of many autonomists and minority separatists, the position in 1983 bears no comparsion with the recent Francoist past when no measure of home-rule was tolerated or even contemplated without direct and dangerous confrontation. Today exists the possibility of an improvement in the process of devolution, possibly towards a genuine federalism. Much can be done within the present constitutional framework in spite of a Constitution that is not federal. (It is doubtful, however, that Spain could ever resemble Germany or the United States in their respective federal arrangements, at least without the introduction of a constitutional amendment.) Not much will be achieved, it appears, until centralist forces—both on the far-right and among radical republicans—are made to yield their veto powers and put an end to their active and skilful obstruction of decentralization and home-rule.

Some countries have a national question. Spain now has a nationalities question. It tends to be cast in ethnic terms because economic disparities and different social structures are not seen in the last instance as respectable legitimizers of communal claims. However, certain adverse "material" conditions are frequently used as grounds for autonomy. For instance, rural poverty in Andalusia can be attributed by politicians and ideologues to exploitation by external agents like the state and the bourgeoisies of other regions rather than to endemic local problems. At the opposite end, economic prosperity is obliquely attributed to the virtues of Basque and Catalan national character like industriousness and a hardworking disposition and is thus made to reinforce a given nationalist programme. To a large extent ethnic nationalism continues to reflect the diverse interests of the regional economies and their different social classes. This is why the state is conceived differently by Catalan and Andalusian autonomists belonging to relatively similar social classes. Catalans want non-interference and a substantial measure of fiscal independence: their main argument is that Catalonia contributes more to the Spanish state than it receives from it. This imbalance persists, according to the Catalans, even after deducting a share of Catalan wealth redistributed to the underdeveloped areas of the country.[12] By contrast, some Andalusians would like the central government to subsidize the regional economy and its industry, help the unemployed and improve the social services. In consequence, each region has a slightly different idea of its actual mode of articulation to the state and different expectations as to its respective contribution and responsibility for national burdens, tasks and policies.

The political formula of the constitutional monarchy largely rests on a recognition of historical and ethnic identities and the rights that flow from them. With the possible exception of the planned Madrid autonomous region, Spanish regions have some claim to a regional identity. Such claims have paradoxically been exerted at a time when Spanish society has undergone unprecedented economic, social and cultural changes and when, arguably, there is more than ever a "lack of fit" between an ethnic legitimation of political structures and their corresponding economic, class and power underpinnings.

CORPORATISM, ETHNIC NATIONALISM, SOCIAL CHANGE

Spain has been transformed. It has seen massive demographic, economic, technological and cultural changes over recent decades. They seem to affect every aspect of life. They include an intense rural exodus, a decline in the demographic growth rate, rapid urbanization, industrialization, a rise in the standard of living, secularization, changes in the occupational structure, a decline in political polarization and much deradicalization of ideologies. The exceptions to these trends are significant but do not obscure their obvious presence. The country is no longer what it once was.

Often these changes have gone against the very grain of earlier structural differences. The contemporary transformation of Spain has not limited, say, Andalusia or La Mancha to agriculturalism, nor kept Basques and Catalans as the sole custodians of industrialism. New industrial centres have arisen everywhere. Madrid, Saragossa, Valladolid are now also industrial cities, though Barcelona and Bilbao continue to be wedded to industrialism. Mass tourism has changed the coastal regions of Valencia, Andalusia, the Canaries and the Balearic Islands. New occupational groups have arisen with few or no roots in the past: managers, skilled workers, engineers. A traditional sexual division of labour has been upset. The state and its welfare and social services have continued to grow relentlessly. Spain therefore resembles in many ways other Western European countries. It shares with them similar problems of inflation, recession and unemployment; and even political terrorism and, indeed, some aspects of the tension between centralism and home-rule find their parallel in other advanced societies.

When Spain finally shed the Francoist dictatorship, it joined the political order characteristic of the West founded, in some fundamental sense, upon the traditions of liberalism. But it is, to a certain extent, post-liberal, based on a technologically advanced, politically competitive and organizationally corporate society. [13] The corporate society can be characterized, on the one hand, by a measure of political pluralism, civil rights and democratic representation and, on the other, by large formal organizations at many levels: the state, first and foremost, but also trade-unions, employers' and professionals' associations, mass political parties, multinational corporations, financial institutions, welfare agencies, and so on. It is also a society where class conflict, market trends, and personal and collective social integration are constantly mediated by formal organizations or "corporations" of all kinds: they are defined, filtered and governed by them. Political power, market prices, working class demands, even religious beliefs are mediated by corporate interests and groups, from public bodies to the mass media organizations. Nationalist movements, in particular, are also mediated by them. Spain's nationalisms may appear as non-corporatist or may even stem from anticorporatist feelings, but they do not altogether escape the constraints of the new society.

Ideally the result of the semi-federal structure represented by a plurality of autonomous regions and nationalities should loosen up the inherited rigidities of old Spain, eliminate the frustrations of ethnic oppression and find a more adequate political order for the new economic realities. To some extent the *estado de las autonomías* was well-timed. The regions roughly correspond to "natural" economic regions, though the same cannot be said of the provinces which are now too small in terms of communication and planning. Yet no serious step has been taken by the central government to replace provincial units with larger ones. The central government is too jealous of its powers, too diffident of devolution, too much in the hands of civil servants whose vested interests in the old bureaucracy and suspicion of reform act as a brake upon realistic innovation. The creation of regional governments and parliaments without the simultaneous dismantling of the provincial centralist apparatus breeds bureaucratic duplication and increases taxation while fostering a confusion of jurisdictions and reinforcing corporatism. This is the opposite of what was intended, for regional authorities were set up to achieve greater popular representation, to mediate between a distant and impersonal state and its citizens and their natural communities and to disperse the powers of the state without dilution.

Administrative duplication has been compounded by the growth of one of the most characteristic features of corporatism: extra-mural politics. The project for a general law for the regulation of the auto-nomies (LOAPA) in spring 1983 was still being scrutinized by the Constitutional Court at the request of the smaller ethnic nationalist parties. The delay may indicate that the extra-mural manoeuvre to push the law through Congress was too crude to be acceptable. It is clear that the entry of ethnicity into the political arena has given rise to manoeuvres and deals that may be unconstitutional. By accepting the appeals against the LOAPA proposal the Constitutional Court has, indeed, admitted that there may be reasonable doubts about the law's constitutionality. [14]

The obstacles to a more satisfactory form of autonomy do not always come from inherited centralism. Often enough they stem from new situations created by social change in the nationalities and regions concerned. Thus the massive presence of an immigrant Spanish-speaking population in Catalonia poses serious problems to the more traditional Catalanist parties whose nationalist ideology is based on ethnicity and collective identity. Though they pin their hopes upon the cultural integration of such immigrants into a thoroughly "Catalanized" society, it is clear that such an aim cannot be easily achieved within the fore-seeable future and with the means at their disposal. (To give one single decisive example, by 1983 the mass media and education were still overwhelmingly biased towards the Spanish, rather than the Catalan, language). Some parties, like the Catalan Socialist party have found a solution to the electoral "immigrants problem" by amalgamating on a federal basis with the PSOE. This decision brought benefits in terms of power—the Socialist government formed in late 1982 contained several Catalan ministers—and electoral advantages—the Catalan Socialists managed to obtain a very sizeable part of the immigrant working-class vote.

Economic and social class change has had a significant effect upon Basque politics. In contrast with the unity of purpose before the Civil War that was embodied in the Basque Nationalist Party, today Basque nationalism is fought over by three factions: the traditional Basque con-servative nationalists; the left-wing, constitutionalist opposition (Euska-diko Ezkerra); and the independentists (Herri Batasuna) whose connections with the advocates of violence and the "armed struggle" are clear enough. A further faction consists of those parties that are federated to Spanish parties but which also support home-rule. Similar comparisons could be made for both Andalusia with its minority Andalusian Socialist Party and its majority Spanish Socialists, once again also supporters of home-rule, and the political formations in the Canary Islands, Valencia, the Balearic Islands and Galicia.

The emerging pattern is intricate. On the one hand, competing forms of nationalism confront the new social structures of their home areas, in at least two of which are included substantial numbers of new and "second generation" immigrants. On the other hand, the nationalist factions must cope with the active presence of "centralist" parties, notably the conservative Alianza Popular. Only the allegiance of a number of Spanish-wide parties (Socialist, Communist and others) to autonomism allows the present arrangement to operate smoothly. [15]

Finally, the nationalities question in Spain has to be seen as a response to more general transnational processes. Its modern origins were related to the loss of the Spanish empire, the sclerosis of the state and the failure of the industrial revolution. The peripherization of Spain within the world capitalist system spurred some local bourgeoisies to embrace the cause of regionalism and even minority nationalism. By contrast, the reverse movement, represented by Spain's economic expansion and its integration into the advanced Western community is now forcing industrial, financial and other elites to operate on a non-regional level. Both the unions and the employers' organizations (though they, like elsewhere, often possess regional bodies) now enter into discussions at a Spanish-wide level. Corporate "social compacts" between the central government, the unions and the employers have not been rare. Class and interest groups cannot afford to ignore the everyday realities of employment, income and location of manufacturing and agro-industries. These factors often work against the past: multinational corporations establish themselves in regions without prior industrial experience; formerly industrialized regions are beset by deindustrialization and unemployment; and agro-industry penetrates and transforms traditional rural structures. Banking and finance follow their own logic, often against the desires of ethnic minority politicians. [16] As the centre-periphery relations of Spain vis-à-vis the wider world have been transformed so have those within the country.

The rise of a post-modern, corporate or mass society—to use some of the imperfect, even unfair, labels often used to describe our universe—has intensified the search for collective and personal identity. Some countries have arrived at such a stage with much of their ancestral legacy undamaged by the potent solvents of early modernity. Spain is one of them. She now confronts the new, emerging society with a considerable stock of communal, ethnic consciousness. It may still stand her in good stead.

Notes

1. This paragraph reflects in part the description of a societal centre as it appears in Edward Shils' essay "Center and Periphery" of 1961, reproduced in Shils, *Center and Periphery: Essays in Macrosociology* (Chicago, 1975), pp. 3–16. My own notes look at a case which evidently differs from Shils' model in a number of ways, where societal consensus about a centre (in the cultural and political more than in the physical sense of the word) is lacking and yet an awareness about the existence of one single society is recognizably present. I am therefore looking at within-state and within-society (and more problematically within-nation) centre-periphery problems. For transnational issues of the centre-periphery issue dealing with Spain and other Southern European countries Cf. Giner "Political Economy, Legitimation and the State in Southern Europe", *British Journal of Sociology*, June 1982, pp. 172—199 and Nicos Mouzelis "Regime Instability and the States in Peripheral Capitalism: a General Theory and a Case Study of Greece", Wilson Center Working Papers, No. 79, Washington, 1980.

2. O. Hintze, *Historical Essays*, ed. F. Gilbert (New York, 1962), p. 99.

3. I have explored elsewhere in greater detail the paradox of Catalan industrialization as a factor increasing Spanish social and political heterogeneity. See Giner, *The Social Structure of Catalonia*, University of Sheffield, 1980.

4. I purposefully use the term "nation" in all its ambiguity throughout this paper in order to avoid entanglement in an issue which has become thoroughly intractable in contemporary Spain. Discussion of the term, however brief, would divert our attention from the central problems of these notes.

5. The term "separatism," as the term "nation," poses serious problems of interpretation, for strictly speaking even mild forms of autonomism mean in some sense "separation" from the central government. In this section I have opted for the equally ambiguous term "ethnic nationalism" to refer to *minority-* ethnic nationalism (and separatism). On the latter, see C.H. Williams, ed., *National Separatism* (Cardiff, 1982).

6. For my own analysis of the nature of Francoism, Giner and E. Sevilla "From Despotism to Parliamentarianism: Class Domination and Political Order in the Spanish State" in R. Scase, ed., *The State in Western Europe* (London, 1979), pp. 197–239.

7. For these propositions, G. Simmel, *Conflict and the Web of Group Affiliations* (New York, 1955), pp. 88–99.

8. Fòr the relationship between language and the polity in Spain, Juan J. Linz "Politics in a Multi-Lingual Society with a Dominant World Language: The Case of Spain" in J.G. Savard and R. Vigneault, eds., *Les états multilingues: problèmes et solutions* (Laval, Canada, 1975), pp. 367–444.

9. After this section was completed I was able to consult S. Rokkan and D.W. Yurwin, eds., *The Politics of Territorial Identity: Studies in European Regionalism* (London, 1982). It contains a short opening essay by both editors on "Centres and Peripheries in Western Europe", pp. 1–18. The centre-periphery distinction is also used by several of its co-authors. There are two essays on Spain: M. Heiberg "Urban Politics and Rural Culture: Basque Nationalism", pp. 355–88, and C.E. Díaz López, "The Politicization of Galician Cleavages", pp. 389–424. For further use of the distinction, S. Mardin "Centre-Periphery as a Concept for the Study of the Social Transformation of Turkey" in R.D. Grillo, ed., *"Nation" and "State" in Europe* (London, 1980), pp. 173–90.

10. Class grievances (particularly working-class ones) remained separate issues for a long time in regions like Valencia. Although Valencian Pan-catalanists (e.g. the PSAN party) incorporated them into their programmes in the 1970s their working-class support was problematic. By contrast a drift towards the emphasis upon class and a marked de-emphasis on nationalism could be detected among the supporters of small but strategically very significant Bandera Roja group in Catalonia (later incorporated into the Catalan Communist Party) who denounced for a while the Catalan language as "the language of the bourgeoisie" [sic] and therefore of the exploiters. On this point, Francesc Vallverdú, "El català:¿no és la llengua de la classe obrera?" in Vallverdú, ed., *La normalització linguistica a Catalunya* (Barcelona, 1981), pp. 181–94.

11. For a detailed account of the "autonomic process" in each area, containing opinion surveys, party allegiances, regional economic differences, etc., see Manuel García Ferrando, *Regionalismo y autonomismo en España, 1976–1979* (Madrid, 1982).

12. See for instance, Ramón Trias Fargas, *Introducció a l'economia de Catalunya* (Barcelona, 1972).

13. On corporatism and the corporate society, Giner "La sociogénesis de la desigualdad y la estructura de las sociedades corporativas" in *Comentario sociológico: estructura social de España*. vol. II (Madrid, 1981), pp. 719–54; a first attempt to relate corporatism to nationalism in Spain is that of Javier Rodríguez del Barrio and Eduardo Sevilla "El corporatismo como enfoque para el análisis de la cuestión nacional en la actualidad: aproximación al caso andaluz", mimeo., Universidad de Córdoba, and TEAG, Córdoba, 1982. Also S. Giner and Manuel Pérez Yruela, *La sociedad corporativa* (Madrid, 1979).

14. Editorial, "Esperando la sentencia sobre la LOAPA", *El País*, 8 April, 1983.

15. This brings up the all-important question of the fluidity of the situation, the variations in allegiance through time. By the early 1970s, for instance, Spaniards had developed a number of new ideas about national identity, state identity, and so forth. Important minorities did not think it was a nation state at all. Cf. Juan J. Linz "Early state-building and late peripheral nationalisms against the state: the case of Spain" in S.N. Eisenstadt and S. Rokkan, eds., *Building States and Nations* (London and Beverly Hills, 1973), p. 99. In the 1970s it became fashionable to refer to Spain as the *estado español* or Spanish state, especially among the Left, who appropriated this Fascist expression with alacrity. For some of us "Spain" (like Great Britain) is a national-multinational entity encompassing a number of nations and regions. Scotland is not a region, nor is Catalonia, save perhaps in a purely technical economic sense. I have called attention to this misuse of the name of Spain since 1971.

16. There are signs that certain groups, like business elites, are ready to accept the new situation and even to use it to their own advantage. According to the president of the Barcelona Chamber of Commerce, Industry and Navigation, Josep María Figueras, the solution (to Catalonia's problems) is to put the emphasis on small business and to think small which is not surprising, as Catalonia is dominated by small and medium-size business, though it continues to have the highest gross domestic product of any region. *(Per capita* income in 1980: £4,500). cf. *The Times*, 26 January, 1983, p. I, Special Report on Catalonia.

Acknowledgement: Special thanks are due to Jackie Rees who read the text critically and made some suggestions which are incorporated in it.

HENK DRIESSEN

Male Sociability and Rituals of Masculinity in Rural Andalusia

(By studying male social interactions in rural Andalusian bars, the author identifies why the bar is central to male socialization in this rural setting. We also discover how masculine display rituals are linked to contradictions between ideal and actual sex roles.)

In Mediterranean society the bar or café is a focal institution of public life, the stage *par excellence* of male sociability and consequently one of the main settings for doing fieldwork. Oddly enough, the bar has been left almost completely out of the ethnographic record of Southern Europe.[1] Anthropologists working in Latin Europe also haven't shown much systematic interest in the expressive culture of daily sociability.

To the casual observer the behavior of men in Andalusian bars will appear to be informal, easy-going, merry and boisterous. After prolonged participation and observation, however, the bar not only turns out to be more than a center where men congregate for recreation, but café manners also prove to be rather formal. I find it useful to employ *ritual* broadly as a pilot concept in the ethnographic description of daily male sociability.[2] When I use the phrase *rituals of masculinity*, I refer to formal, repetitive, stereotyped behavior that is expressive or communicative in the sense that it carries a message about male self-perception and men's image of women. This conception of ritual has been inspired by Goffman (1967) and Leach (1968). The emphasis on expression and

Henk Driessen, "Male Sociablitity and Rituals of Masculinity in Rural Andalusia" (*Anthropological Quarterly*, 56, 3 [1983]), 125–133, by permission of the publisher.

symbolic charge differentiates ritual from instrumental features of behavior. The symbolic and ritual dimension of sociability deserves special attention, since it yields considerable insight into the realities of domination and subordination as some recent studies on Mediterranean communities have shown (Brandes 1980; Silverman 1979, 1981).

In this essay the following questions will be dealt with: why is the bar so central a focus for Andalusian men, especially agricultural laborers and other lower-status males? Why do these men need to assert their masculinity in homosocial gatherings? In the conclusion I will briefly discuss recent explanations offered for this phenomenon in the expanding literature on gender identity in the Mediterranean area. I will argue that rituals of masculinity in bars and at festivities serve important male-identity functions in a society where the gap between the ideal and actual sexual division of space and labor is widening.

THE SOCIO-CULTURAL SETTING

Andalusia is a region of agro-towns and latifundia. Although most of the people who live in rural towns depend on the land for a livelihood, they hate and despise the countryside which represents to them uncivilized space of hard, dirty and backbreaking work. Everything that is highly valued—ownership of land, leisure, ambiance, education, personal autonomy, cleanliness—originates in the town.[3]

The small town in the plains of Córdoba, where I conducted fieldwork, stands on a hill approximately in the center of its large municipal territory. It is made up of a higher and lower part, corresponding to two clearly defined barrios. The *plaza* lies in between. Almost three out of four employed town-dwellers work in agriculture. Ninety percent of them are dependent on casual wages. Between this large proletariat and the local elite is a growing group of hardworking, self-employed tradesmen, lower civil servants, skilled workers, and agriculturists. The opposition between town and country, educated and working class, male and female are the major divisions of local society.

Andalusia is a strongly male-dominated society, where the relationships between the sexes are ambiguous and often antagonistic. The ideal male is tough (*duro*), strong (*fuerte*), formal (*sobrio*), autonomous and undisputed head of the household. He supports his family, guards the family honor, and is seldom at home. A woman should be virtuous, competent and docile, devoting her life to her husband and children. She is the guardian of family shame. The sexual division of labor is rigid, at least in theory. Men, regardless of class and occupation, hold that their wives should not work outside their home for an income. This image corresponds to the native conceptualization of social space. The public domain (*calle*) constitutes the world of men, while the women belong to the private domain (*casa*).

However, the reality of social class and the division of labor among the sexes contradicts this image. In the middle and upper-class families men play an active part in both the private and public domain. They not only provide for the family's income, but also control the household budget, make economic decisions and participate in child-rearing. On the other hand, it is increasingly becoming respectable for middle-class women to take prestigious white-collar jobs and join their husbands at outdoor activities at festivals and on summer weekends. [4]

In the class of agricultural day-laborers, women's labor power is of paramount importance to the maintenance of a household. Female labor in agriculture is tied to the olive, cotton and grape harvests and summer crop cultivation. Although it is a generally voiced opinion that in times of unemployment men should be hired preferentially over women, in practice employers often prefer to hire women because they earn lower wages and are "easier to handle." Moreover, women have access to alternative employment, traditionally in the domestic service sector and recently in the textile and food-processing workshops. So, it is not rare to find women in casual and permanent jobs while their father, husband, brother or son are unemployed. Among the working-class families, the wife is in charge of the household finances and the socialization of children. [5] There is close cooperation between mother and daughter, who visit each other almost daily. Because of the prominence of the mother-daughter link there is a strong tendency towards matrifocality. The insecurity of the day-laborer's contribution to the household budget and his physical self-removal from the house stress female dominance in the private realm. The tension produced by the contradiction between ideology and reality plays an important role in structuring male sociability.

PLACES AND TIMES OF MALE SOCIABILITY

Cafés are focal points in the townscape. Their presence is felt to be a necessary condition for *ambiente* (ambiance), a highly important quality of community life that derives from the assemblage of large numbers of people marked by differences in age, personality and occupation. *Ambiente* inspires local patriotism and is one of the bases for claiming urbanity. [6] There are nine *establecimientos* in the rural town I studied, all but two located on the plaza and the main traffic artery. They mark off the social center of the town and almost exclusively belong to the male domain.

Townsfolk employ the following criteria to differentiate various types of bars: location, social class and age of the clientèle, the barowner/tender's personality and reputation and the specialities he provides, the quality of the bar's interior, and the degree to which women have access.

The *casino* is clearly set off from the others in several respects. Until recently, it acted as a center of recreation and informal politics for the landed and commercial elite. It is the center of gravity of urbanity and the local shrine of civilization. In its fashionable lounge with plush armchairs, carpets and engravings, the best wines and snacks are served to gentlemen who discuss local and national politics. Workers call the casino the "fat club." It is the first establishment that opened its doors to women, though in a very restricted sense. At festivals and on summer weekends, a growing number of the local elite bring their wives to the casino to have a chat and drink in the lounge or on the pavement terrace. However, the bar and the games-room are still exclusively male realms. Adolescents rarely enter the *casino*.

There are two other places that stand out for quite different reasons. In the late 1970's a discothèque and a *whiskería* were established in the town's periphery. Both are closed to prevent people from looking in from the outside. The arrangement of the interior, subdued light and fancy music create a sexual atmosphere in both places. In the discothèque adolescents of both sexes can meet in relative privacy to engage in dancing and petting. The whiskey bar or night club is an expensive place where adult males can congregate with scantily clothed waitresses. Though men maintained that these girls could be "laid," the performances taking place in the *whiskería* can best be described as ritual seduction. After some scandals—one of them involving a group of middle-class women entering the place to fetch their husbands—the municipal council was forced to close down the whiskey bar.

A small bar attached to a grocery store on the main street is known as the snail bar for the speciality it serves. Its clientèle largely consists of young people—high school students of both sexes, engaged and newly-wed couples.

The remaining five establishments are cafés in the strict sense of the word. They all serve coffee, the usual gamut of wine, beer, *aguardiente* (cheap anisette), cognac and soft drinks and a varying number of cold and warm snacks. They all have pavement terraces from May through September. One of them is considered a traditional bar. It displays the atmosphere of a pre-Civil War *taberna* and has old-fashioned furniture.

It is mainly patronized by working-class men from the lower barrio. Another accommodates the sportsclub and is the favorite café for the medium and small landowners-operators, self-employed workers, and small bureaucrats. The atmosphere of this bar is conservative. At the corner of the plaza and the main street is a large café that attracts shopkeepers, ambulant traders, skilled workers, and civil servants. The remaining two locales are typical agricultural working-class taverns. Women seldom enter these five bars.

For a man the café is both an acceptable and obligatory place to be when he is not at work. The average Andalusian male spends most of his leisure time *en la calle* (in the street), of which bar attendance is an essential part. An adult man who withdraws himself too much from the company of bar mates must have very good reasons to do so, if he is not to be accused of anti-social and anti-masculine behavior.[7] Unemployed laborers are not supposed to stay home. Drinking, smoking and sharing is a coercive script for Andalusian men. When a man gets up in the morning, he immediately leaves his house and goes to a café to have a coffee and a glass of anisette or cognac. If he works in town or in the surroundings he will have some glasses of wine at one or two o'clock in the afternoon before going home for dinner. Self-employed, unemployed, retired and leisure-class men patronize the bars more frequently during the day. The high time of bar attendance is in the evening between seven and ten o'clock when the bars fill up with busily talking and gesticulating men who have returned from work. The atmosphere gets high-spirited. Wine, tall stories, horseplay, riddles, comments on diverse topics, but mostly on work, sex, women and football, contribute to the *ambiente*.

There is some seasonal variation in this time schedule. During the annual cycle of festivals which starts with Lent and ends with the festival of the patron saint in September, bar life goes on till midnight and for a minority till one or two o'clock in the morning. November to February is a nadir in the yearly round of bar attendance. Many day-laborers march off to neighboring provinces to work in the olive harvest and people who stay go to bed early. The town turns sad (*se pone triste*) and little or nothing happens (*no pasa na'*).

Besides daily bar attendance there are two institutionalized activities in which fellowship is celebrated, the so-called *juerga* and *perol*. Both constitute a climax of male sociability. Andalusian men believe that it is necessary for their well-being to drive away daily worries through an elaborated spree. A number of bar mates agree to have a *juerga*. In the morning they meet in their favorite bar where they start with some drinks "in order to clean their throats." Then they travel to a neighboring town—Montilla and Puente Genil are first choice for their size and ambiance, La Carlota for its *whiskerías*—where they feel more free to relax and loosen up. Hopping as many bars as possible is the essence of this outing. Nostalgia for the bachelor days when they were not yet bothered by wives, mothers-in-law, and children, sets the tone of the binge. Sometimes an interesting football match or bullfight in the cities of Córdoba and Sevilla provides an excuse for a *juerga*. In these cities a visit to the red-light district is often included. Wives accept these outings as an inevitable outlet for a man's nature.[8] The *perol* (literally "frying pan") differs from the *juerga* in various respects. It takes place in the countryside where a lamb or billy-goat is killed for a banquet prepared by the participants themselves. A larger number of men is involved and it is usually organized by the owner of a large estate. Consequently, it is often an elite affair, sometimes combined with a shooting-party.

The major communal festivities—Lent, Holy Week and the fair in honor of the patron saint—constitute another climax in male sociability. One of these festivals will be described below.

BAR ETIQUETTE

Bar attendance is a highly patterned activity and so is the behavior displayed in bars. Although on a normal day most men enter more than one café, the majority of them have a favorite which is, as a rule, close to the neighborhood where they live. A man usually starts the evening with a couple of drinks in one of the taverns but very soon finds himself in his favorite bar where he spends most of the evening with his friends and neighbors. A variation on this pattern occurs when a man happens upon an *amigo* whom he invites for some drinks in his own café. After a while the *amigo* attempts to persuade the host into coming along to his favorite bar. This pattern often gets more complicated because of the involvement of more than two men.

Social drinking in a bar is regulated by a strict etiquette. Though there are numerous ways in which a man may offer, accept and reciprocate a drink, there are some golden rules. A man attending his own café has a right and an obligation to invite anyone who is not a regular customer. In general, "established" men have a priority to initiate a round of drinks with entering persons. Strangers and guests are never allowed to buy a round.

The following scenario is enacted again and again, resulting in ritualized behavior. A man announces that he is going to "invite" (*invito yo*) the mates standing around him to a glass of wine. His companions protest in a roundabout way, the first man repeats his invitation for form's sake, gives the barkeeper a sign to fill the glasses, and after repeated demurrals everyone "yields" to the hospitality. Before the glasses are drained, a second man invites the group to another round, and the same performance is repeated. Cigarettes are offered, refused and accepted with similar decorum.

To cultivate friendship is a time-consuming and rather expensive but socially necessary activity. There are, of course, various strategies to limit exchanges. For instance, the frequently used expression *dame la espuela* or *penúltima* (give me the next to the last) conveys the wish to conclude a series of drinks and at the same time enables a man to reciprocate by claiming the last round. Both the refusal to allow other men to buy drinks as well as the constant acceptance without reciprocating are felt to be attacks on the code of equality and viewed as "ugly" (*feo*) behavior. Men who offend the bar etiquette are stigmatized as *sinvergüenzas* (shameless ones) and treated as such. Generosity among equals is a sacred café value. Although, ultimately, exchanges should be reciprocal, Andalusians abhor the principle of "on the spot" or balanced reciprocity, sharing the costs alike or paying separately. This is also considered ugly for it offends the value of fellowship. Emigrants often refer to the instrumental behavior in city cafés to illustrate the "coldness" of industrial society, which they contrast with the "warm" social climate of rural Andalusia.

Participation in the elaborate exchange circuits of drinks, cigarettes, snacks, and small talk is a prerequisite of male adult status. Since a man's face is at stake, the politics of bar hospitality sometimes gives rise to heated arguments. It is the difficult task of the bartender to mediate and take care that none of his customers lose face.

THE MALE ETHOS AND RITUALS OF MASCULINITY

The café provides an ideal scenario for showing off masculinity. In particular men standing at the counter, which is the favorite area of the bar, stage rituals of masculinity. Basic cultural notions of manliness and womanliness model their behavior.

The native terms for masculinity are *hombría, ser hombre* or *ser macho* (in rural Andalusia the anglicism/neologism *machismo* is only used in intellectual circles), which refer first and foremost to sexually aggressive behavior. The essence of *hombría* is *tener cojones*, to have balls. Virility is thought to reside in the testicles.[9] Andalusians argue that it is the testicles that make the difference between a real man and a woman who acts like a man, just like they make the difference between a bull and an ox. Hence an aggressive and fearless male is called *cojonudo* (big-balled). When a man asserts himself, he so to speak extends his genital qualities. Hence men frequently touch their privy parts in public when meeting other men or entering a café, situations in which they must assert themselves. However, being a real man (*todo un hombre*) means more than sexual aggression. It also involves the willpower and ability to defend one's interests and those of the family, which center upon honor. It has been argued that in Andalusia the stress on manliness is entirely upon sexual aggressiveness rather than upon physical toughness (cf. Gilmore & Gilmore 1979: 282). It is true that the actual use of violence is rare and that Andalusians strongly devalue fighting. However, this does not mean that physical strength is absent from hypermasculine behavior. In bars men are constantly showing off their *potential* for physical aggression; they show each other that they are capable of violence. While doing so, they prove their virility to their peers (cf. Brandes 1980: 126). This is apparent from the amount of force which is used when men slap each other on the shoulder, hit their coins on the counter, knock dominos on the tables, and order drinks with a sharp clap of their hands. It also appears from the muscle-tight clothes young men wear and the proofs of physical strength to which they take themselves. Behavior that communicates a man's potential for physical prowess is strongly ritualized. [10]

The celebration of manliness implies spending much time and money in bars, where one of the major topics is men's relationships with women. Their gender identity is defined by the following basic beliefs. Men are "by nature" superior to women. At the same time men are convinced of their inability to control themselves in the area of sex. They think it natural that a male is constantly on the hunt for women. It is the responsibility of females to control themselves, maintain their shame, and be aware of the social consequences of extra- or pre-marital liaisons. [11] However, men also feel that their superiority is under constant female attack. They fear women's sexuality, which they believe to be insatiable and socially disruptive. Women's seductive qualities, their power to emasculate and cuckold men, and their obstinacy are dangerous weapons in the battle between the sexes. So, men feel that they have to defend their masculinity from female incursions. While the ideal woman is a virgin and a mother, the messages men in cafés express about women is that they are whores. Many jokes, tall stories and songs reveal men's negative image of femininity. [12] In fact, mothers impress this image upon their sons when saying that they have to "beware of women, they are *astuta* (cunning) and *engañadora* (deceitful)."

The exchange of boastful stories about male sexual conquests, obscenities and jokes about female sexuality is intimately tied to social drinking in bars, and both make up the core of the masculinity cult. Although normally men do not drink to the point of losing self-control, it is considered masculine to get drunk once in a while. This socially accepted drunkenness is institutionalized in *juergas*, *peroles* and festivities.

Revels always consist of boozing and obscenities; they are charged with verbal and body-idiomatic allusions to sexual performances. At one of the *peroles* I attended, the owner of the estate where it was held forced one of his laborers into playing the female part in a burlesque of the coitus. He was "taken by the ass" (*tomado por culo*), an act symbolizing a double subordination, i.e., sexual in the sense of a man being feminized, and economic in the sense of an employee who has to suffer this humiliation for fear of being sacked. In fact, many practical jokes in bars, in which the victim is approached from behind, capitalize on the obsessive fear Andalusian men have for being feminized. [13]

The Holy Week is above all a high time of male sociability. The processions are prepared and staged by religious brotherhoods, which are exclusively male and organized along class lines. [14] On Ash Wednesday four of the town's seven Holy Week brotherhoods—three of working-class and one of middle-class composition—open clubhouses where in the evenings both members and nonmembers congregate, sharing wine and food. These clubhouses expand the bar circuit during Lent. The most important ritual object of a religious brotherhood is a saint's image. Among laborers female saints are most popular. The Good Friday procession starts at five o'clock in the morning. The great majority of the members who participate in the procession stayed up all night, drinking and eating in the clubhouses. When the procession begins, most participants are already in a frantic state. Fireworks, the monotonous rolling of the drums, the excessive drinking during the procession, sleeplessness, the carrying of the heavy floats through the winding and inclined streets, hoarse competitive shouts like "long live Veronica, the prettiest of all," or "La Soledad is the best," dramatize the atomsphere. The procession ends in chaos between three and four in the afternoon. Groups of drunken boys and men sing and dance. [15]

This popular interpretation of a Holy Week procession is a reversal of the official Roman Catholic precepts. Like the revels discussed above it is also a ritual of masculinity through which men re-create their self-image. To beat the drums for hours, carry the floats, drink in excess, and go without sleep, requires toughness and endurance. Men who drop out before the ritual is completed are rebuked for being weaklings. It is highly significant that women are part of the audience, proudly watching their husbands, fathers, sons, brothers and fiancés act out their masculine role. After the procession men glory in showing each other the bruises on their shoulders from carrying the floats. They have lived up to the image of virility.

The second component of the ethos that guides male sociability is *formalidad*. This value counteracts sexual and physical aggressiveness. It means self-control, the ability to stand upon one's dignity by putting a restraint upon strong emotions. Formality is exhibited most markedly by the town's elite, who hold that the public behavior of laborers lacks this quality. However, formality has undeniably permeated the ideas and behavior of the town's proletariat. While honor and masculinity entail assertive behavior, violence is rare in Andalusian agro-towns. During my fieldwork there was only one fight among adult males in the town where I lived. This observation is confirmed for a Sevillian agro-town (Gilmore 1980: 187–88). Besides the occasions described above, I rarely saw drunks in the cafés and streets of Andalusia. Yet bar performances are a critical test for self-control. Besides competitive social drinking there is another challenge to a man's dignity.

Cachondeo, a particular type of joking, is very popular in Andalusian cafés. It is playful yet aggressive in the sense that the initiator of the joke tries to get a rise out of his victim. It is important for the victim to keep his face, withstand the jest, and strike back in a cool manner. A man who loses his temper is scorned by the audience. The following examples illustrate the mechanism at work in *cachondeo*:

> A group of day-laborers is engaged in a round of drinks at the counter. A landowner walks up to them and orders a glass of wine without paying attention to the laborers. One of the workers starts a cachondeo, exclaiming: "This *tío* (fellow) is a real capitalist. He owns a lot of money but pays lousy wages. Moreover he is a fascist. They should kill off fellows like him." At once he gives his victim a friendly slap on the shoulder, playing down the aggressive tone of the jest, and starts to fool around with one of the onlookers. The landowner maintained his composure.

> In one of the bars a company of five men is playing a prohibited game of chance. At a given moment one of the onlookers hisses, "Look out, the *cabo* (the commander of the Civil Guard)," whereupon the players stop in a fright. The audience bursts into laughter.

Since *cachondeo* capitalizes so heavily upon male sensibilities, there is an inherent risk that the bounds of what is acceptable are transgressed. This is apparent from the following example:

In a café a construction worker delivers a man standing next to him a sudden push, too strong, for the victim knocks into another group and spills his glass of wine. He is furious but checks himself and does not say a word. Nodody laughs.

Andalusians call this a *broma pesa'a*, a graceless joke. This brings us to the third element of the male ethos, *gracia*. One of its meanings is the power to entertain, to evoke laughter (cf. Pitt-Rivers 1971: 189 ff.). Men have to be sociable, witty and amusing. Metaphors, funny word games, ambiguities, riddles, tall stories, and jokes are highly praised in homo-social settings. Men with *gracia* are always foci of attention in bars. A carpenter, nicknamed Curro Pistola, enjoys the reputation of making even the dead laugh with his witty pranks. Jesus, a tough construction worker, has a gift of telling stories, spontaneously put into rhyme. Gracia contributes to ambiance, a quality that is warmly cherished in the cafés of Andalusian agro-towns.

CONCLUSION

So far, I have depicted the specific pattern of male sociability and shown how a strongly male ethos influences the conduct of men in cafés. The question of why masculine display is so pronounced in homosocial settings remains to be answered. One explanation in the literature on male-female relationships in the Mediterranean area focuses on male ego-formation. It is argued that a boy growing up in a household dominated by women will develop a feminine identity in the face of his father's absence. Upon reaching adolescence, the boy finds out that his early view of male and female dominance is wrong. In reaction to his primary female identity he develops hypermasculine behavior (cf. Gilmore & Gilmore 1979). The problem with this explanation is that the evidence for the link between psychodynamic and cultural processes is thin and inconclusive. Since the primary process of personality formation is largely unconscious, it can never be made perspicuous. Consequently, verification of this explanation remains highly problematic.

Another approach analyzes male sexual identity on its own terms (cf. Brandes 1981). Ignoring the socio-economic context of relationships between the sexes, this approach fails to note that there are significant differences in the degree to which Andalusian men are preoccupied with the fundamental fact that they are men. Taking male dominance for granted, it misses the all-important point that in the agricultural pro-letariat women do challenge the economic superiority of men. An explanation that fails to contextualize the symbolic representations of male behavior can at best be partial.

I hold that the basic characteristics of male sociability cannot be adequately comprehended except in relation to the actual division of domains, tasks and power among the sexes. [16] In a society where the notion that women are inferior to men is a cultural assumption shared by both sexes, where men's ability to provide for their family is taken as axiomatic, the position and identity of day-laborers are vulnerable. When women contribute substantially to the family income through wage labor, as is the case in the rural Andalusian working class, the dividing line between male and female identity and private and public roles tends to get blurred. To prevent this the male role and self-image are reinforced in the public domain by symbols and rituals that exclude females. Day-laborers justify their absence from the house by stressing that the "home is for women and children," for the "weak" who have to be protected from the hostile world outside. Too much involvement in the matrifocal household ruins a laborer's reputation as a *macho*. [17] The marginality of day-laborers in the private and public realm helps to explain why they engage in a more intense form of bar sociability than middle and upper-class men who hold rather firm positions of power and influence. Rituals of masculinity in cafés act to mask the reality of the day-laborer's dependence upon the female members of his household and his weak economic and political position in local society. However, I would not go to the extreme of calling male dominance in Andalusia a "myth." [18] Rituals of masculinity re-create male identity. They are forceful and efficacious in the sense that they help to keep women in a subordinate position. They really work.

Notes

My gratitude goes to my Andalusian informants with whom I spent so much time in local bars, and to Anton Blok, Bill Christian and Willy Jansen for advice and inspiration. The generous comments of the journal's anonymous reviewers were particularly helpful.

1. Exceptions are Davis (1964), Photiadis (1965), and Brandes (1979). Hansen, who devoted a section of his monograph to bar culture, rightly suggested that the bar "would be a good place for field inquiry almost anywhere in Spain" (1977: 166).

2. The greater part of the evidence presented here has been collected from 1977–78 in a Cordobese township of 5,290 inhabitants.

3. See Driessen (1981) for an elaboration of these values and the role of an urban ethos in Andalusian agro-towns.

4. In the middle and upper-class families whose incomes are mainly derived from landownership and agriculture, domains and tasks are more strictly segregated according to sex than in families whose incomes come from professions outside agriculture. Men who rose to political and economic prominence in the Franco era hardly participate in bar sociability; they subscribe to a very strict code of formality.

5. Also see Luque Baena (1974) and Gilmore (1980) for the organization of Andalusian households.

6. Gilmore (1980: 203) also found this to be true for an agro-town of 8,000 in the plains of Sevilla.

7. Acceptable reasons for not attending bars are illness, mourning when a close relative has died, and extreme lack of cash.

8. Also see Gilmore (1980: 190–191) for a description of *juergas.*

9. This is a general Mediterranean conception, cf. Blok (1981). While a man is defined as possessing "balls," a woman is defined negatively, i.e., as lacking "balls."

10. More research will be needed to study the impact of state formation —the monopolization of the means of violence—on masculine behavior and the role of ritualization in the control of violent impulses.

11. Also see Aguilera (1978: 29–30) on this point. Writes Press: "Backsliding or failure to meet certain expectations are almost forgivable as 'natural' consequences of being a man" (1979: 129–130).

12. There are numerous popular flamenco verses—which men sing to men —expressing the view that women are treacherous:

El amor de la mujer
es como el de la gallina,
que en faltándole su gallo
a cualquier otro se arrima.

(A woman's love
is like a chicken's,
for when her cock is not around
she gives herself to whomever she may find.)

Quien se fía de mujeres
muy poco del mundo sabe,
que se fía de unas puertas
de que todos tienen llaves.

(He who puts faith in women
doesn't know much of life,
for he trusts doors
to which everybody owns a key.)

13. In daily usage *tomar por culo* means to make a fool of a person. It clearly expresses dominance and submission. For an interesting parallel in the verbal duelling of Turkish boys see Dundes, Leach & Ozkok (1970).

14. For a useful discussion of religious brotherhoods in Andalusia see Moreno Navarro (1974). In the late 1970s one of the town's brotherhoods decided to recruit three girls to carry ritual paraphernalia in the procession. This triggered off a heated discussion since the majority of men oppose female membership in religious brotherhoods.

15. Aguilera (1978: 104–105) describes a similar procession in the Andalusian province of Huelva.

16. More than fifteen years ago the *Anthropological Quarterly* (1967) initiated a debate on the role and position of Mediterranean women from the viewpoint of women. Since then, systematic examination of female power has shown that women do participate in the public domain, that they exert considerable influence on men through their sexuality, control over channels of information, and access to the supernatural realm (cf. Nelson 1974).

17. Anthropologists working in North-American slums and in the Carribean area have also stressed the connection between matrifocality and the cult of machismo (cf. Hannerz 1969; Wilson 1973; and Manning 1973). One is struck by the similarities in the area of male ethos and patterns of sociability.

18. See Rogers 1975 who argues that in peasant societies formal male power and prestige are balanced by informal female power and influence. This non-hierarchical power relationship is maintained by the acting out of a "myth" of male dominance (Rogers 1975: 729). Her model of male-female relationships underestimates male power in the local community and in the society at large and overstresses the importance of the private domain in the power structure of peasant societies. This is not to deny that women have considerable power chances. However, the power resources controlled by men are quite different in their scope from those controlled by women, i.e., "formal" and "informal" power are not identical nor are they interchangeable.

References Cited

Aguilera, Francisco E. *Santa Eulalia's people. Ritual Structure and Process in an Andalucian Multicommunity.* St. Paul (Minnesota): West Publishing Co., 1978.

Anthropological Quarterly. *Appearance and reality: Status and roles of women in Mediterranean societies.* 40: 3 (special issue), (1967).

Blok, Anton. "Rams and billy-goats: A key to the Mediterranean code of honor." *Man* 16 (1981): 427–440.

Brandes, Stanley H. "Drinking Patterns and Alcohol Control in a Castilian Mountain Village." *Anthropology* 3 (1979): 1–16.

_____ . *Metaphors of Masculinity: Sex and Status in Andalusian Folklore.* Philadelphia: University of Pennsylvania Press, 1980.

_____ . "Wounded Stags: Male Sexual Ideology in an Andalusian Town." In *Sexual Meanings. The Cultural Construction of Gender and Sexuality.* Sherry B. Ortner & Harriet Whitehead, eds. Cambridge: Cambridge University Press, 1981. 216–240.

Davis, John. "Passatella: An Economic Game." *The British Journal of Sociology* 15 (1964): 191–207.

Driessen, Henk. *Agro-town and Urban Ethos in Andalusia.* Nijmegen: Centrale Reprografie Katholieke Universiteit, 1981.

Dundes, Alan; Jerry W. Leach; and Bora Ozkok. "The Strategy of Turkish Boys' Verbal Duelling Rhymes." *Journal of American Folklore* 83 (1970): 325–349.

Gilmore, Margaret, and David D. Gilmore. "Machismo: A psycho-dynamic approach (Spain)." *The Journal of Psychological Anthropology* 2 (1979): 281–300.

Gilmore, David D. *The People of the Plain: Class and Community in Lower Andalusia.* New York: Columbia University Press, 1980.

Goffman, Erving. *Interaction Ritual: Essays in Face-to-Face Behavior.* Chicago: Aldine Publishing Co., 1967.

Hannerz, Ulf. *Soulside: Inquiries into Ghetto Culture and Community.* New York: Columbia University Press, 1969.

Hansen, Edward C. *Rural Catalonia under the Franco regime: The Fate of Regional Culture since the Spanish Civil War.* Cambridge: Cambridge University Press, 1977.

Leach, Edmund. "Ritual." In *International Encyclopedia of the Social Sciences.* Vol. 13. D. Sills, ed. New York: Macmillan and the Free Press, 1968. 520–526.

Luque Baena, Enrique. *Estudio antropológico social de un pueblo del Sur.* Madrid: Editorial Tecnos, 1974.

Manning, Frank. *Black Clubs in Bermuda.* Ithaca: Cornell University Press, 1973.

Moreno Navarro, Isidoro. *Las hermandades andaluzas: Una aproximación desde la antropología.* Sevilla: Publicaciones de la Universidad de Sevilla, 1974.

Nelson, Cynthia. "Public and Private Politics: Women in the Middle Eastern World." *American Ethnologist* 1 (1974): 551–565.

Photiadis, J.D. "The Position of the Coffee-house in the Social Life of the Greek Village." *Sociologia Ruralis* 5 (1965): 45–56.

Pitt-Rivers, Julian A. *The People of the Sierra.* 2nd ed. Chicago: The University of Chicago Press, 1971.

Press, Irwin. *The City as Context: Urbanism and Behavioral Constraints in Seville.* Urbana: University of Illinois Press, 1979.

Rogers, Susan C. "Female Forms of Power and the Myth of Male Dominance: A Model of Female/Male Interaction in Peasant Society. *American Ethnologist* 2 (1975): 727–757.

Silverman, Sydel. "On the Uses of History and Anthropology: The Palio of Sienna." *American Ethnologist* 6 (1979): 413–436.

————. "Rituals of Inequality: Stratification and Symbol in Central Italy." In *Social Inequality: Comparative and Developmental Approaches.* Gerald D. Berreman, ed. New York: Academic Press, 1981. 163–182.

Wilson, Peter. *Crab Antics: The Social Anthropology of English-Speaking Negro Societies of the Caribbean.* New Haven and London: Yale University Press, 1973.

STANLEY BRANDES

Women of Southern Spain:
Aspirations, Fantasies, Realities

(Drawing from his research, the author identifies the ideals of womanhood in
southern Spain and what is socially acceptable behavior for women. He then
turns to women's potential for achievement within the limits of a male-
dominated culture, and the obstacles that hinder their achievement.)

INTRODUCTION:
THE SOCIAL AND POLITICAL CONTEXT

In this paper I ask how the people of southern Spain traditionally define
ideals of womanhood. What does the good life consist of for women in
that part of the world? How can women realize their potential, according
to the parameters established by their culture, and what are the impediments to such realization? When disappointments arise, either through
failure to achieve personal aspirations or disillusionment with the
aspirations themselves, how do women react? What repercussions do
they suffer? I develop the answer to these questions with specific
reference to "Monteros," a pseudonym for an agrotown located north of
Granada. Although my remarks refer concretely to the situation that I
observed in Monteros, comparative evidence indicates that this community is hardly unique in its social-structural design and ideological
assumptions. Traditional lifestyles, not only in southern Spain but also
throughout much of the Mediterranean, have been described in terms
that echo my own findings. Except for occasional parallel evidence,

Stanley Brandes, "Women of Southern Spain: Aspirations, Fantasies, Realities" (*Anthropology* 9, 1–2 [1985]), 111–128, by permission of the author.

however, I shall confine my analysis to this one town, which I have experienced directly and therefore know best. The ethnographic present tense, which I utilize throughout much of this essay, reflects my observations during 1975–76 when the bulk of my research in southern Spain was carried out.

It should be kept in mind that I am writing a full decade after my original field material was collected. In the interim, Spain has embarked upon a new era of social relations, so that the patterns I observed are now history. What was then unimaginable has become daily occurrence. Divorce is legal. So is abortion, under certain circumstances. There is an active women's movement, and female consciousness of and rebellion against subordination to men nowadays pervades Spanish society. Through the combined influence of television, return migration, and increased travel and education, these trends have penetrated even the most remote rural areas. The Church no longer enjoys extensive control over education, and women at all levels of society have achieved considerably more independence than was the situation in 1975.

To place my work further in context, we should also recall that 1975 was the year of Francisco Franco's death. Because of political uncertainties, there was probably a more repressive atmosphere during 1975–76—the period during which I lived in Monteros—than I had ever before experienced in Spain. Political and sexual oppression often go hand in hand. Franco's Spain, for all its advances in the domain of industrial development and living standards, maintained strictly conservative policies in the realm of social relations. And Franco's demise initially accomplished next to nothing to change this situation. After all, most Spaniards, including those of Monteros, could recall the time-honored Castilian saying, *"Más vale lo malo conocido que lo bueno por conocer"*—"Bad things, already familiar, are better than good things, yet to know." Although there was much that was undesirable in Spanish society under Franco, this was the only regime that the vast majority of Spaniards had ever experienced. Necessary and desirable changes would certainly come. For the moment, however, there was no rush into that uncertain future (Brandes 1977).

Hence for a variety of reasons traditional rules governing interpersonal relations—particularly rules concerning sexual conduct and morality—continued to exert their influence. Consider the implications of a Spanish Communist Party poster issued in 1977. It promises a society that gives *"A la mujer, su importancia, y escuelas en abundancia"*—"to woman her importance, and an abundance of schools." And yet the cartoon that accompanies this text shows a crowd of men gawking at a statue of a shapely, naked female, elevated on a pedestal. Even well-meaning expressions of equality such as this betray traditional gender-related attitudes.

This, then, conveys some general feeling for the political and social atmosphere in which I collected my Monteros material. Monteros itself, located in one of the two provinces with the highest illiteracy rates in the country, was hardly in the forefront of whatever changes were going on in Spain at the time. The community is situated in an olive-producing region, in which a large proportion of the workers have been landless and have depended on uncertain daily wage labor. Like most agrotowns in Andalusia (e.g., Moreno Navarro 1972, Gilmore 1980, Driessen 1981), Monteros is a relatively complex society for its size. Its approximately seven thousand inhabitants are divided by disparities in wealth, education, occupation, and family prestige. The community also houses a small but highly visible Gypsy population, an endogamous group that lives a largely segregated life socially while participating fully in town affairs economically. Crosscutting all these social divisions is a marked psychological separation between men and women, a separation that I tried to analyze from the male point of view in *Metaphors of Masculinity* (1980).

Here I attempt to provide a glimpse into the corresponding female experience, which should serve partially to counterbalance the picture I offered in my book. To achieve thematic coherence and thoroughness, I focus on marriage, spinsterhood, and widowhood. Marriage, as we shall see, is probably the central event in the life of Monteros women. It is reasonable, then, to single out for analysis this aspect of the life course and its place in the context of Monteros gender relations and ideology as a whole.

MARRIAGE

For the women of Monteros, as perhaps for all peoples who share in the Judeo-Christian tradition (Bouwsma 1978), the good life is not a static entity. Rather, it unfolds through time, develops, and eventually realizes itself over the course of the life cycle. The good life is, in reality, a series of good lives that conform to a more or less standard sequence of desirable developmental stages. The good life, too, potentially varies according to social class and ethnic affiliation.

No matter what their social station, the women of Monteros share one overriding criterion for a fulfilling life: marriage. Marriage is the universal female goal, and the concern with getting married sometimes reaches obsessive proportions, especially as unattached girls get into their mid- and late twenties. In Monteros, people joke about this obsession. A woman quipped, for example, that when a young man eyes a young woman his reaction is, "I like her" (*"Me gusta"*), while hers is "I'm ready for marriage" (*"Ya me caso"*). Men and women in Monteros believe that females are the more eager of the two sexes to get married. As reported elsewhere (Brandes 1980:84), men think that women try to trap (*atrapar*) them into marriage, by wearing alluring makeup and clothing. Women are said to hunt (*cazar*) men for the purpose of getting married, and although many women would disagree with this characterization, there are some who claim to have been clever enough to choose and chase after their husbands, while letting their future spouses feel that they had the upper hand.

The popular stereotype is that women are downright frenetic in their attempts to trap a mate. Witness the following traditional parody of woman's conjugal ambitions, as related to me by a middle-aged Monteros widow:

> When a woman is 15–20 years old, she says to herself, "May a handsome attractive man come along" (*"Que venga un hombre guapo y atractivo"*). When she's 20–25 she says, "May a handsome man with a good profession come along" (*"Que venga un hombre guapo y con buena carrera"*). When she's 25–30, her line is "May the man have a good future" (*"Que tenga el hombre un buen porvenir"*). Between 30 and 35 she just wants "That he be a good man" (*"Que sea bueno"*). And, finally, between 35 and 40, her only wish is "May he come!" (*"¡Que venga!"*).

Here, to be sure, is a joking portrayal of marriage-hungry women. But the humor rests on the reality of females who, for their own well-being, recognize that marriage provides their best hope for leading fulfilled lives, at least within the confines of Monteros.

The belief that only married women have access to the good life, that only married women can fulfill their human potential, rests on contradictory notions of womanhood. In Monteros, as in other parts of the Mediterranean (e.g., Blok 1980, Saunders 1981), people think of women, first of all, as embodiments of evil. "Women are of the Devil," a Monteros laborer once explained to me as several of his friends listened and nodded in agreement (Brandes 1980: 76). In Monteros it is said that women "dress like serpents" (*se visten de serpientes*), their spiritual kin through the obvious association between serpents and women in the Biblical story of the Fall. Some Monteros men claim that "All women are whores," that their lust is insatiable, their seductive powers impressive, and their willingness to resist temptation virtually nonexistent. It is this aspect of womanhood—the female as whore—that provides an ideological justification for marriage. Since women are unable to control their passions, they need some sort of outside controlling force, namely husbands, to bear primary responsibility for harnessing their unlimited, potentially destructive sexual impulses.

At the same time, and apart from ideological considerations, practical day-to-day concerns make marriage the most reasonable alternative for women. Unmarried women—at least adult women, who have left the protective confines of their parental homes—are subject to the persistent advances of townsmen who fantasize that these women are all too eager to capitulate. Sometimes, as elsewhere in Andalusia (Pitt-Rivers 1971: 92) and throughout the Spanish-speaking world (Suarez-Orozco and Dundes 1984), these advances take the form of harmless *piropos*, or "traditional verbal comment[s] addressed by a man . . . to one or more females . . . in a public place" (*ibid.*: 113). Often women interpret these comments as flattering, but with equal frequency they do not. Indeed, the content of *piropos*, as Suarez-Orozco and Dundes have pointed out, can be "insulting, aggressively bold, and denigrating" (*ibid.*), so that they may be considered genuinely offensive. With marriage, a woman becomes redefined; she is off limits to men other than her husband, who is invested by society with the responsibility of safeguarding her sexual integrity. Only with matrimony can Monteros women achieve some measure of freedom from disturbing, if otherwise harmless, verbal attacks.

Women in Monteros are thought to require controlling for both their own well-being and that of society at large. Their presumed lustful nature necessitates that they be limited both spatially and socially. Spatially, the home and the workplace are the primary female domains. Women are responsible for taking care of the physical well-being of their husbands and children, and to this end oversee the cleaning, shopping, cooking, and medical needs of their families. Women, to be sure, can be found in every corner of town at any time of day. But unlike men, an unaccompanied female in a public locale must be justified according to some instrumental activity: if she enters a bar, it is to purchase wine for the evening meal; if she stands at a street corner, it is to await the van that transports workers to the olive fields for harvest. Women occasionally go to bars for drinks and indulge in leisurely walks through the town streets and plazas. But these activities are carried out mainly with their husbands who "take them out" (the verb *sacar*, "to take out," is used in this Spanish context just the way it is in English) at predictable times, generally Sundays and holidays.

The social restrictions placed on women mainly concern their permissible associations. Until marriage, Monteros women enjoy friendships with girls their own age and social class. As teenagers, girls bear major responsibility for helping their mothers at home; in addition, many young women attend to schoolwork. But in their free time they get together with other girls, often including first cousins and more distant kin as well as non-relatives, for leisure-time activities. With marriage this situation abruptly changes. A married woman's social contacts outside her home come almost exclusively from a circle of relatives. When she pays social calls, which frequently occur in the late afternoons, they are either to her natal home or to those of her female kin, be they aunts, cousins, or in-laws. Relations with friends become increasingly distant after marriage, until vestiges of the original close bond all but disappear. There is an inherent incompatibility between the concerns of married and unmarried women. Unmarried women supposedly are constantly on the lookout for mates; married women, having achieved that goal, must thereafter confine their interests to what is good for their families. Anything that removes them from, or competes with, the familial domain, including friendships with sexually vulnerable women, is considered threatening and dangerous, and must be suppressed. Hence, in addition to their spatial confinement, most women are also socially confined.

Here, however, there are exceptions, which are both salient and instructive. For one thing, upper-class women, with superior finances, education, travel experiences, and the like, usually retain close female friendships after marriage. These women relate to one another within Monteros as they do elsewhere: as equals, with shared social and cultural interests. They are guided by a basically urban industrial lifestyle, in which not only friendships among women but also friendships between married couples are defined as acceptable and desirable. Friendships are also common in Monteros among middle-class women—store clerks, government workers, and schoolteachers—who have moved into the community from outside. In Monteros, even married women who were born and raised elsewhere claim that they are never fully accepted into Monteros society, and are treated like barely tolerated strangers. The situation is all the more alienating for unmarried female outsiders, with no families to fall back upon for support. No wonder, then, that they band together for companionship and mutual reassurance.

Only by seeing these female adult friendships as exceptional can we explain what to me was initially a mystery: defamatory accusations of lesbianism. At least four pairs of female friends in Monteros are accused of sustaining homosexual relations. In two of these cases, the women are married mothers; the remainder are unmarried women in their thirties and forties, ages that place them well beyond normal marriage eligibility.

Moreover, all these women are either members of the town elite or have recently moved into Monteros from elsewhere. They therefore share one common factor: a vast social distance from the majority of working-class townspeople, among whom the rumors of their homosexuality circulate.

Whether or not these couples are really lesbians is unverifiable. What is significant is that, from the majority point of view in Monteros, adult female friendships are anomalous. They are reasonably explained only as the result of homosexuality. This is the explanation that has therefore emerged within the community. Moreover, the tremendous social distance between the victims of the rumors, on the one hand, and the perpetrators of the rumors, on the other, assures that the truth about these women will never be known. What is important, in fact, is not the accuracy of the stories but rather their use as mechanisms of social control. Through rumormongering—hardly uncommon in Spain (e.g., Freeman 1970: 88, Gilmore 1980, Murphy 1985)—working-class men and women unwittingly collaborate in controlling women, in restricting the kinds of social bonds that women can draw upon for sustenance and growth. The rumors implicitly announce that adult women who establish close friendships are likely to suffer defamatory accusations, to their own considerable detriment and that of their families. The wisest course for such women is to stay close to home and family, to avoid competing social ties, rife with the potential for grief and shame. The best policy, for the vast majority of Monteros women, is to get married and seek companionship among female kin; it is in this context that women have the best chance of leading fulfilling lives.

And yet it is not only because of social control, because of the potentially disruptive, shameful dimensions of femininity, that Monteros society defines marriage as essential. It is also that matrimony provides the opportunity for maternity. Only through the nurturant role of mother can Monteros females achieve true fulfillment. The rewards of life for women include, most importantly, rearing children, overseeing their development, and caring for their physical and emotional well-being. This is why several women I have known have suffered bouts of severe depression upon the temporary summer departure of their children to visit relatives elsewhere, and why these ephemeral losses occasionally motivate women to become pregnant. The so-called "empty-nest syndrome," familiar to developmental psychologists (e.g., Glick and Parke 1965, Rogers 1982: 197) is common among Monteros women whose children leave home. Their departure deprives mothers of the ability to serve the daily role of nurturant caretaker. It is in order to adopt this role, as well as to avoid the social and moral problems attendant upon spinsterhood, that Monteros women seek the good life in marriage. For this combination of positive and negative reasons, the vast majority of townswomen want to and actually do marry.

SPINSTERHOOD

Why, then, do some women remain single? and what are the social and psychological repercussions of spinsterhood? In Monteros, as elsewhere in Spain (e.g., Brandes 1976, Iszaeovich 1975), there are a variety of explanations for non-marriage, depending on individual circumstances. Most of the explanations, however, refer to one or another type of social stigma. Certain women, because of random vicissitudes of life, become defined out of the marriage market. They are implicitly declared unclean, defiled. Whether or not they actually wish to get married, their tarnished reputations assure that they will not.

In Monteros, as elsewhere in Mediterranean Europe (e.g., Schneider 1971, Schneider and Schneider 1976, Goody 1983), a double sex standard prevails, such that the main prerequisite to marriage for women, but not men, is virginity. Most Monteros men believe that pre-marital sex taints a woman; with the certain or presumed knowledge that a young woman has been initiated into sex, her eligibility for marriage within the community becomes severely reduced. As reported elsewhere, this experience is symbolically defiling:

> "Why," I once asked, "are you men so concerned about marrying a virgin? What difference could it possibly make if a man married a woman who was already deflowered?" My informant's response was immediate and simple. "Suppose you were thirsty and I put before you two glasses of water. And suppose, too, that I had already drunk out of one of them. Which would you choose?" I answered that I would of course choose the clean glass. "Then why should we not similarly prefer a virgin over a woman who has already been taken?" he retorted (reported in Brandes 1980: 181).

A young deflowered woman, therefore, is seen as impure, like a dirty glass of water. She makes an unfit bride. This, more than anything, is why families have to control the behavior of their daughters, in order to preserve their reputations and therefore their marital prospects. As Monteros parents remind themselves, *"El buen paño en el arco se vende"*—"Good linen, preserved in a trunk, can readily be sold." Likewise, a virtuous daughter, guarded within the confines of home, will make a fine match.

Given this prevalent ideology, it is no wonder that the primary cause for spinsterhood is tainted reputation—the presumption or actual knowledge of premarital sexual experience. For example, women who were household servants during long periods in childhood commonly find it difficult to get married. Townsmen assume that their dependent status in the homes of powerful, wealthy employers necessarily caused them to compromise themselves; this work experience is therefore sufficient in some cases to exclude women from marriage eligibility. There are also women who are known to have had sexual escapades —either one weak moment of low resistance or more long-term, publicly visible relationships. These women, too, are unable to marry within the confines of Monteros. Finally, there are young women who simply were born unlucky because they belong to families with a reputation for producing females who are *locas sexuales*—sexual crazies, or, as we would identify them, nymphomaniacs. Regardless of the actual comportment of these women, the unfortunate reputation of their families makes marriage highly improbable for them. Even if these women were to remain virgins until the wedding day, the spectre of cuckoldry would be sufficient to keep eligible bachelors away.

There are a considerable number of women, however, who have only themselves to blame for remaining unmarried—at least as far as the community at large can judge. I speak here of those who, because of financial independence or vanity, are said to have been excessively finicky in looking for mates. Some of these women, wealthy themselves, waited for richer men; others, with illusions of superiority, rejected one suitor after another until they slid past marriageable age. It is for this reason, in fact, that a Monteros proverb warns, *"La suerte de la fea/la bonita la desea"*—"The beautiful woman wants to be as lucky as the ugly one." Attractive women, it is thought, often adopt condescending attitudes that seriously impede their search for husbands. This was the case, for example, with one working-class lady, elderly at the time my fieldwork was carried out and living with a married sister and the sister's family. As if to justify her circumstances and place herself in an appropriate, fulfilling female role, this woman would introduce herself to newcomers by saying, "I'm the mother to all of them in this house."

In Monteros, no woman could ask for more. As Julian Pitt-Rivers declared long ago with regard to another southern Spanish town, "a woman in motherhood attains her full social standing" (1971: 109). For women who remain unmarried, the fantasy of motherhood accords at least a semblance of the elevated marital and maternal status that most townswomen manage to attain.

WIDOWHOOD

Apart from women who never get married and are therefore deprived of maternal fulfillment, there are those who were married but have lost their husbands. Young or old, with or without children, Monteros widows are devoid of a husband's protective guidance and control, and thereby find themselves in a potentially vulnerable position. It is partly the case, as Pitt-Rivers states, that a widow's behavior "tends to become freer as regards the other sex. Widowhood brings, for the first time, full legal and economic responsibility as well as the greater influence which she enjoys within the family" (1971: 89). But it is also true that widows are the objects of intense sexual desires and that to them are attributed considerable libidinal passions and amorous designs. For this and other reasons, widowhood automatically produces difficulties.

First of all, widows are naturally never entirely free from the ideals with which they were imbued during childhood. Matrimony; romantic love; the intact home consisting of man, wife, and children—all these goals, once realizable, now must remain abstract dreams that the widow herself can no longer hope to implement. In Monteros, as elsewhere in southern Spain (e.g., Pitt-Rivers 1971: 169–175), remarriage is infrequent and poorly regarded. Of course, in many instances here, even as in urban America, "there is a strong belief among some widows that second marriages bring nothing but trouble" (Lopata 1980: 107). And yet a variety of culturally specific reasons explain why widows in Monteros are highly unlikely ever to remarry. For one thing, widows are tainted in more or less the same way that deflowered women are prior to marriage. Hence a popular Monteros *copla*, or traditional four-line verse, states:

Con la viuda no me caso
With the widow I won't marry
Lo digo con sentimiento,
I tell you in deepest honesty,
Por no poner la mano
For I won't put my hand
Donde ya [la] puso el muerto
Where the dead man placed his.

The widow is, in a way, polluted through previous sexual contact; almost on this ground alone she makes an undesirable marriage partner.

Widow remarriage is also considered by many people in the community to be tantamount to adultery. Consider, first, the contrast with men. Men, as I have stated above, are judged by a different standard from women; flirtatious behavior and promiscuous sexuality prior to marriage are not only permitted for men, but might be said to be positively encouraged. Afterwards, it is best for men to refrain from extramarital sex; however, occasional escapades, if carried out discreetly, are thought to be normal, understandable, and forgivable. Consequently, when a widower remarries—and many do—he merely perpetuates the male role of maintaining a romantic interest in an assortment of women. Widower remarriage conforms to the ideology and expectations of masculine social behavior.

Not so for widows. Ideally a woman is supposed to have a sole man in her life, at least from the romantic and sexual point of view: her husband. In a small-town rural context such as that of Monteros, the bond between this couple is for all practical purposes eternal. The husband's death brings not a release from the marriage contract and the potential for a new union but rather tenacious adherence to the original marriage vows. Any new relationship, whether or not legalized through marriage, is virtually equivalent to adultery. The widow who establishes amorous ties or who remarries seriously threatens her own reputation as surely as she defiles the memory of her deceased husband.

In addition, as I have pointed out elsewhere (Brandes 1981: 179), people in Monteros operate on the assumption that the deceased are aware of worldly proceedings, that they know what is happening on earth. As one shopkeeper put it, "We believe that the dead person sees and exists. . . . We believe that the deceased observes." Under such circumstances, widow remarriage becomes no different from sexual looseness and cuckoldry. It is the mark of a shameless woman, unconcerned with her own and her family's reputation.

One middle-aged man, in trying to explain the absence of widow remarriage, pointed to the difficulties that this practice would pose for all parties involved once they were deceased and reached heaven. After all, if you believe that loved ones are reunited after death, inevitable problems arise from the possibility that a virtuous woman, who has ascended to heaven, might encounter not just one, but several, husbands in the afterlife. The safest course, to avoid both criticism in this world and embarrassment in the next, is for a Monteros widow to remain unmarried.

And yet merely being faithful to one's deceased spouse is rarely enough to stave off community criticism. Monteros widows—especially young widows—are likely to find themselves in a double bind. It is assumed that widows, because they have already tasted sex, possess particularly intense desires. (The situation is similar to the one portrayed by Kazantzakis in *Zorba the Greek*.) If such women become sexually active, they are automatically criticized for shameless behavior or, if the situation warrants, for wife-stealing, home-breaking, and the like. If they refrain from sexual activity, their reputations remain no less tarnished; it is simply assumed that they are seeing men on the sly. It is difficult—especially for Monteros men, who tend to project their own libidinal feelings onto the women themselves (Brandes 1980: 98–114)—to accept the idea of a celibate widow. A widow's excessive sexual appetite inevitably manifests itself in socially unacceptable ways.

In this kind of adverse environment, how do widows—particularly young widows, for whom the situation is most difficult—manage to establish rewarding personal relationships? The example of one widow, whom I shall call María, illustrates in extreme form the problems of adjustment that such women face. María was born into an old landed family which, in her father's generation, had fallen onto hard times. Despite her father's precarious circumstances, she insisted on marrying within her class; consequently, she had to wait until her late twenties, somewhat older than most townswomen of her station, to find a suitable mate. Her husband was a doctor, alcoholic, and considerably older than she. Only ten years into the marriage, and with an eight-year-old son, María was widowed.

María was an attractive, well-dressed woman, who looked and acted younger than her years. Tall and shapely, with becoming auburn hair, she was a prime candidate for local gossip. It was too much to believe that such a woman would remain faithful to her deceased husband, all the more so because of the difficulties he had caused her while alive and the uncertain financial situation he bestowed upon her with his death.

For six or seven years following the death, María spent most of her time watching television or reading, either at her own home or next door with an elderly, wealthy, spinster neighbor. Although this was socially appropriate behavior, María claims that rumors nonetheless spread during this period about her supposed romantic entanglements. She insists that the rumors were unfounded. There were three reasons, she claims, why she decided not to engage in any affairs. First there was her *educación*, or family upbringing, which operated as a strong influence against any such behavior. Second was her *formación*, or religious instruction, which specifically prohibited illicit sex. And finally, according to her reckoning, there was the practical consideration that any man she might sleep with would surely refuse ever to formalize a match. María's overt goal was to find another husband. Her chances were as slim as any widow's, but they certainly would not be enhanced through sexual involvement. Quite the opposite, even by her own reckoning.

And yet, despite this virtuous comportment, rumors continued to circulate about María's promiscuity. As discreetly as possible, she did in fact begin to see men again. She was lonesome in the company of her young son and her spinster neighbor, and needed the comfort and support that she believed a man alone could provide. Besides, townspeople accused her of going out with men anyway, so why not enjoy the pleasure of being with a man rather than simply suffer accusations for behavior maliciously and erroneously attributed to her?

Soon after she began to go out again, she fell in love with a bachelor several years younger than she. For well over a year, she would meet with him in secret trysts, always harboring the illusion that he would marry her. When it became clear that he wanted to remain unattached, and when, in fact, he left her altogether, María fell into a deep depression. Adopting the villagers' harsh, uncritical voice as her own, she suffered overwhelming guilt over the immorality of her behavior. She now perceived herself as bad, a common tramp.

The remedy for María, as for Spanish women in similar circumstances throughout the centuries, was a retreat to the Church. She began to attend Mass and take communion daily. She walked half a day into the mountains to a remote monastery, where monks provided her with a *cilicio*—a leather penitential belt shot through with hundreds of protruding nails. María wore this item night and day for three weeks, as a means of cleansing, self-imposed punishment. Religion became her solace and remedy.

Six months into this religious phase, María once again took up with men, but this time openly, promiscuously. To earn income and keep herself occupied, she had several years earlier begun a small grocery business. Travelling sales representatives provided most of her male company. Having experienced severe self-punishment, as well as cruel community gossip and semi-ostracism, she was beyond caring what anybody would think. She became hedonistic. As one might predict, however, this behavior was only temporarily satisfying. The shame that she had brought upon herself made life in Monteros increasingly difficult. The only solution was to leave. As soon as her son graduated from high school, she closed her Monteros apartment and moved to Granada, where, if she could not achieve anonymity, at least she would be free from the opprobrium of the community in which she was born and raised.

This move was hardly the spontaneous, random by-product of idiosyncratic life circumstances. When people in Monteros gossip about the (real or imaginary) scandalous behavior of young widows, they state that it would be best for everybody—widows and community alike—if these women migrated to the city. There, free from the inevitably critical public eye—the infamous *qué dirán* (what they will say) of small-town life—widows are free to fulfill their supposedly boundless sexual fantasies and desires. Given the prevalence of this kind of thinking, it is hardly surprising that María eventually moved to Granada. Although the decision was hers, the community in effect pushed her out. It perpetrated the double bind in which she found herself, and then provided the solution: migration. Life in Monteros simply holds too many contradictions for a young widow. As people there say, the best advice is to leave.

FLIGHT THROUGH FANTASY

María's flight from Monteros involved a very real restructuring of her existence. Although small-town life was difficult for her, at least her culture provided her with a solution, migration. How can married women, who fulfill their society's ideals, free themselves from restricting social controls?

Both popular ideology and practical life circumstances in Monteros support the interests of married women; single or widowed women are automatically confronted with impediments to a fulfilling life. And yet marriage, in the end, is no more than a socially acceptable bond, yielding some possibilities for the partners but closing off others. The controls that all Monteros women suffer, the restrictions on movement and behavior, are perhaps even more severe for married than for single women. If marriage confers respectability, it also produces serious constraints. It is no wonder, therefore, that many married women, frustrated by having to conform to the wishes and interests of their husbands and bound by the highly constricting rules of female comportment that are prevalent in small-town southern Spain, seek to escape through fantasy. In fact it may be the oppressive conditions under which women in Monteros live that stimulate them to artistic creativity. There is certainly no other environment in my experience that has produced so many popular poets, including women from virtually all social classes and educational levels in town.

To illustrate, I cite one such poet, a member of the town elite in her mid-fifties. By town standards she has enjoyed a fulfilling life. She married into a good family, has been prosperous enough to maintain several residences, and has reared four children who are devoted to her and of whom she can be proud. And yet her poetry expresses her fantasies of escaping, liberating herself from the social confinement to which she has been subjected throughout her otherwise ideal life.

In poem after poem she identifies herself with birds, symbols for her of freedom. Hence:

> *Me siento pájaro*
> I feel like a bird
> *Volando muy alto;*
> Flying very high;
> *Me siento un lucero*
> I feel like a shining star
> *Flotando entre nubes*
> Floating among clouds
> *(Al fin que sea cierto).*
> (In the end may it be true).

In another verse, the poetess describes an incident in which a friend asks her, half humorously, if she has swallowed a canary. Her reply:

> *El canario quien lo pilla*
> He who catches the canary
> *Lo enjaula, y yo no sé*
> Imprisons it, and I don't know how
> *Poner barreras a nadie.*
> To place bars around anybody.
> *La libertad es la vida,*
> Liberty is life,
> *Tú ya lo sabes muy bien.*
> You know it very well.

And, finally:

> *Corriendo voy placentera*
> Running with the motorcycle
> *Con la moto en la carretera.*
> Along the highway is pleasurable.
> *Corro y corro como el viento . . .*
> I run and run like the wind . . .
> *Sólo viento, sol y agua*
> Only wind, sun and water
> *Dejan mi mente tranquila;*
> Leave my mind at ease;
> *Y junto al viento yo corro*
> And I run together with the wind
> *Como pájaro que fuera*
> Like a bird who was
> *Preso y en libertad quedara.*
> Imprisoned and placed at liberty.

Our poetess's themes, in addition to the bird, include the fear of being buried in death, of being confined and encased once again. Her preference, rather, is for *"mar, aguas sin fin/ que de vida al mar inmenso/ siendo alimento de peces/desaparezca mi cuerpo"*—"the sea, endless waters/that from life to the immense sea/being fish food/my body should disappear."

In Monteros, a woman's aspirations, even if realized through years of adherence to culturally approved goals, rarely lead to a completely fulfilling existence. Women need to draw on liberating fantasies, too, to acquire the dignity and independence of which they are deprived in everyday life.

Acknowledgements

This is the written version of presentations delivered to Project Zero, Department of Education, Harvard University; the Department of Anthropology, Cornell University; and the Symposium "Women in the Mediterranean," Mills College. I am grateful to audiences at all these institutions for providing me useful commentaries.

Research was carried out in Monteros during 1975–76, 1977, and 1980 with financial assistance from the National Institute of Child Health and Human Development, the Wenner-Gren Foundation for Anthropological Research, the American Council of Learned Societies, and the Insitute of International Studies, University of California, Berkeley. I wish to thank all these agencies for the support that made this and related projects possible.

References Cited

Blok, Anton. "Montoni e becchi: un'opposizione-chiave per il codice mediterraneo dell'onore." *Quaderni di Semantica* 1 (1980): 347–362.

Brandes, Stanley. *"La Soltería*, or Why People Remain Single in Rural Spain." *Journal of Anthropological Research* 32 (1976): 205–233.

_____. "Peaceful Protest: Spanish Political Humor in a Time of Crisis." *Western Folklore* 36 (1977): 331–346.

_____. *Metaphors of Masculinity: Sex and Status in Andalusian Folklore.* Philadelphia: University of Pennsylvania Press, 1980.

_____. Gender Distinctions in Monteros Mortuary Ritual. *Ethnology* 20 (1981): 177–190.

Bouwsma, William. "Christian Adulthood." In Erik H. Erikson (ed.), *Adulthood*, pp. 81-96. New York: Norton, 1978.

Driessen, Henk. *Agro-Town and Urban Ethos in Andalusia.* Unpublished Ph.D. dissertation, Catholic University, Nijmegen (The Netherlands), 1981.

Freeman, Susan Tax. *Neighbors: The Social Contract in a Castilian Hamlet.* Chicago: University of Chicago Press, 1970.

Gilmore, David D. "Varieties of Gossip in a Spanish Rural Community." *Ethnology* 17 (1978): 89–99.

_____ . *The People of the Plain: Class and Community in Lower Andalusia.* New York: Columbia University Press, 1980.

Glick, P.C., and R. Parke, Jr. "New Approaches in Studying the Life Cycle of the Family." *Demography* 2 (1965): 187–202.

Goody, Jack. *The Development of the Family and Marriage in Europe.* Cambridge: Cambridge University Press, 1983.

Iszaevich, Abraham. "Emigrants, Spinsters, and Priests: The Dynamics of Demography in Spanish Peasant Societies." *Journal of Peasant Studies* 2 (1975): 292–312.

Lopata, Helena Znaniecka. "The Widowed Family Member." In Nancy Datan and Nancy Lohmann (eds.), *Transitions of Aging*, pp. 93–118. New York: Academic Press, 1980.

Moreno Navarro, Isidoro. *Propiedad, Clases Sociales, y Hermandades en la Baja Andalucía.* Madrid: Siglo Ventiuno, 1972.

Murphy, Michael. "Rumors of Identity: Gossip and Rapport in Ethnographic Research." *Human Organization* 44 (1985): 132–137.

Pitt-Rivers, Julian A. *People of the Sierra* (2nd Ed.). Chicago: University of Chicago Press, 1971.

Rogers, Dorothy. *The Adult Years: An Introduction to Aging* (2nd Ed.). Englewood Cliffs, NJ: Prentice-Hall, 1982.

Saunders, George. "Men and Women in Southern Europe: A Review of Some Aspects of Cultural Complexity." *Journal of Psychoanalytic Anthropology* 4 (1981): 435–466.

Scheper-Hughes, Nancy. *Saints, Scholars, and Schizophrenics: Mental Illness in Rural Ireland.* Berkeley: University of California Press, 1979.

Schneider, Jane. "Of Vigilance and Virgins: Honor, Shame, and Access to Strategic Resources in the Mediterranean." *Ethnology* 9 (1969): 1–24.

Schneider, Jane, and Peter Schneider. *Culture and Political Economy in Western Sicily.* New York: Academic Press, 1976.

Suarez-Orozco, Marcelo, and Alan Dundes. "The *Piropo* and the Dual Image of Women in the Spanish-speaking World." *Journal of Latin American Lore* 10 (1984): 111–133.

NISSA TORRENTS

Cinema and the Media after the Death of Franco

(In a pre- and post-Franco review of censorship, one finds there has been an expansion of civil liberties in moral and political issues since 1975, but in the area of newly emerged national cultures, news coverage free of censorship remains problematic.)

Two outstanding features characterize Spanish media and cinema after the death of the dictator: the end of a censorship that covered political, moral and religious issues and the upsurge of hitherto repressed national cultures.

Yet censorship has not been finally abandoned as the case of the Catalan journalist Xavier Vinader illustrates. Vinader was sentenced in November 1981 to seven years' imprisonment and a massive fine for an article in *Interviú* in which he alleged collusion between security forces and paramilitary organizations in the Basque country. Two of the people mentioned in his article were later shot by [the] ETA whereupon the Public Prosecutor accused Vinader of being an accessory to murder. A revision of his case under the Socialist government has not lifted the sentence and Vinader is now an exile in London, a victim of the persistence of habits of repression inherited from the old regime. Another example of this persistence is the confiscation in April 1983 of two issues of *Cambio 16*, the most prestigious Spanish weekly. An article on the Argentine security chief of Alianza Popular and bodyguard of

From Nissa Torrents and Christopher Abel, eds., *Spain: Conditional Democracy* (New York: St. Martin's Press, 1984), 100–114, by permission of the publisher. World rights granted by Croom Helm, London.

Fraga prompted a district judge, unbeknown to higher judicial authority, to order the confiscation of the magazine, an action contrary to democratic practice that will not enhance his tenuous democratic credentials. Since the death of Franco, over sixty journalists have been arraigned before military and civilian courts. Though the anti-democratic anomaly of military tribunals for civilians has faded away, the end of arbitrary measures against journalists is not yet in sight. The director of *Punto y hora*, a Basque magazine, began in April 1983 a hunger strike in the prison of Nanclares de Oca where he is undergoing a sentence of eighteen months for having published two articles on the Basque question. The notorious case of *El crimen de Cuenca*—a film of Pilar Miró, the present under-secretary of state for the film industry—reinforces the view that Francoist practices survive in the new atmosphere. A fictionalized account of an infamous miscarriage of justice by the Civil Guard at the beginning of this century, the film was banned by the military authorities for three years to become Spain's biggest-ever box office success when it was publicly screened in 1981.

The past weighs heavily on the present and will continue to do so until the machinery of the previous regime is finally dismantled. The Catholic Church and the Movement (which until 1975 was the only authorized party) were the principal ideological supports of the Franco regime and their influence was felt even after the relative liberalization of the 1966 Press Law. No allusion, however mild, that could be considered an attack on the Church, its moral codes and personalities was allowed; nor was the slightest attack on personalities and policies of the regime or its stated ideology. Western democracies were considered only marginally preferable to the Soviet Union; and liberalism, masonry and communism were treated by the official censors as synonymous. In Madrid a tribunal with the function of suppressing both masonry and communism—Tribunal para la represión de la masonería y el comunismo—watched over the frail morality and political health of Spaniards and imposed sanctions, both fines and imprisonment, upon offenders against Francoist legislation. The state imposed a thoroughgoing censorship of printed and film material. Two censors were employed: one almost invariably a priest to watch over moral and religious matters; the other often a civil servant from the Movement who decided about ideological content. Because all imported films were dubbed, the censors were free not only to cut "offending" sequences but to change dialogue at will. So, for example, adultery was banned from the screen with curious results. The adultery of Grace Kelly with Clark Gable in the film *Mogambo* was converted by the censors into an acceptable relationship as an engaged couple by compelling her screen husband to become her incestuous brother. Once the censors had finished their work, the "purity" of minds was indeed preserved.

THE PRESS AND PERIODICALS

After his victory in the Civil War Franco established a ministry of information and culture to supervise the cultural life of Spain. One of its principal tasks was the enforcement of his 1938 Press Law which borrowed heavily from the legislation of Mussolini and was predicated on the assumption that the main functions of the press were to promote controlled information and to indoctrinate readers in a Francoist worldview. State control of the press was facilitated by the direct appointment of newspaper editors in the private sector which was supplemented by the creation of the totally controlled *Prensa del Movimiento* (Press of the Movement), a nationwide network of newspapers and magazines. To further enhance the control of the media, the regime set up in 1941 a school for journalists. No one without formal school accreditation could exercise his or her trade and all journalists sympathetic to the Second Republic were prevented from exercising their profession. Since 1975 the *Escuelas de Periodismo* have faded away and have been replaced by university degrees in information sciences (*Ciencias de la Información*). Following the characteristic manner of the transition in which few Francoist institutions were specifically banned the *Escuelas de Periodismo* were just allowed quietly to vanish.

Francoist legislation was comprehensive. It covered all areas of information; it exalted the formal ideology of the regime; it aimed at instilling a stultified political and social culture—prohibiting, for example, in the name of the sanctity of the family, traditional mother-in-law jokes—and it kept a tight rein on the publication of new dailies and periodicals. Permission to publish was seldom granted. Rare exceptions aimed at improving the international image of the regime were made. In 1962 the intellectually prestigious *Revista de Occidente*, founded by the philosopher Ortega y Gasset, was revived. In the same year *Cuadernos para el Diálogo*, a Christian Democratic publication whose influence on the embryonic democratic groups was considerable was launched by the former minister of education and current ombudsman Joaquín Ruiz Giménez.

It could be argued that the first signs of liberalization coincided with the first wave of mass tourism in the early 1960s; multicoloured bikinis spelt the gradual loosening of the stifling influence of a reactionary

morality upon national life. Profits prevailed over old-fashioned morality. Spain needed a more progressive image if it were to draw tourists
from the European democracies. A new Press Law was devised in 1966
by Manuel Fraga Iribarne, the then minister of information and tourism,
a portfolio that disappeared under Suárez who established a new
ministry of culture while downgrading tourism and information to the
status of offices (*oficinas*) headed by under-secretaries. Fraga's Press
Law removed advanced censorship by state-nominated officials and
placed the full responsibility for the content of newspapers upon their
editors. Although the 1966 legislation was more liberal than that of 1938,
whole issues of newspapers and magazines were still confiscated, heavy
fines and suspensions of up to six months were imposed in order to
silence dissent.

The death of Franco opened the way for a cultural renaissance.
Spaniards discovered those features of their history from the Moors and
the Jews to Republican interpretations of the Civil War that had been
wilfully suppressed by the Franco regime. Spaniards threw themselves
into the passionate pursuit of political and sexual freedoms denied by the
Francoist oppression which gave rise to a publication explosion especially in the daily and weekly press. The colourful newspaper kiosks
were flooded with images from a denied past—like La Pasionaria and
Carrillo—which appeared side by side with photographs of splendid
females, defiant and a little surprised in their total nudity. Some
magazines had, even before 1975, opposed and mocked the regime. *La
Codorniz*, now defunct, was the most famous and popular. It codified a
kind of humour that owed much to the Spanish tradition of black
humour and liking for the scatological. Its first two directors, Miguel
Mihura and Alvaro de la Iglesia, lampooned the regime though they
were seldom overtly political. Politics and satire were combined in the
shortlived *Hermano Lobo* from Madrid and the more durable *Por Favor*
from Barcelona which was a victim under Suárez of the technique of
repeated suspensions and fines which bankrupted dissenting periodicals.
Por Favor modernized the humour of its predecessors and gave prominence to a new generation of cartoonists and satirists like Forges,
Perich, Nuria Pompeia, Fernando Savater, Manuel Vázquez Montalbán
and Juan Marsé who are now at the top of their profession. No social
historian will be able to ignore the cartoons of Forges who used the
private jargon of Francoist bureaucracy to coin new words and expressions that passed into everyday language.

Cartoons were easy rallying points for discontent. Quick and
effective, they had a large influence with a popular readership upon
whom most of the highbrow dissent in print had no impact. Like protest

songs, cartoons could speak a universal language and were, therefore, fiercely persecuted during the dictatorship and even during the transition. Their role in diffusing liberal views among Spanish public opinion should not be underestimated. Some serious magazines were published during the dictatorship. They included *Cuadernos para el Diálogo* and *Triunfo*, a weekly initially close to the Falange that specialized in bullfighting, that later assumed a left-wing position giving equal space to culture and international politics but carefully excluding comment on national issues because the government would not tolerate dissent. During the dictatorship Spaniards became adept at reading between the lines and learned to distrust information printed in the press. Magazines like *Triunfo* disguised comment on national politics in apparently innocuous articles on international affairs. In 1971 a newcomer joined the ranks of the serious press. *Cambio 16* began as a publication on economic and commercial affairs; but it soon extended its range to include matters of general interest and changed its presentation from an austere black and white on inferior paper to a glossy *Time*-magazine format. Well presented and readable, *Cambio 16* introduced to Spain a new style of weekly. This combination of lively journalism, attractive presentation and the successful blend of news, culture and up-market advertising caught the imagination of the increasing number of Spaniards who now perceived themselves as Europeans. *Cambio 16* projected an image of a "modern" Spain that seemed confirmed by economic growth in the 1960s. Its new journalism had many imitators; but in a very competitive market the fatality rate was high. One such casualty was *Opinión* which barely survived a few months after the death of the dictator. A splinter group of young journalists from *Triunfo* seceded and founded *La Calle*, a weekly associated with Eurocommunism, which began publication in 1978 and stopped publication in February 1982. A serious left-wing venture, *La Calle* was plagued in its last months by underfinance and the irritation of its readers at reading endlessly about the factiousness of the Communist Party and its inability to come to terms with the new Spain.

The magazine that best epitomizes the ambiguities of post-Francoism is *Interviú*, a glossily produced weekly which at the peak of its popularity in 1978 printed a million copies per week. *Interviú* aimed at a wide readership with a unique blend of left-wing politics without a party allegiance, serious investigative journalism, petty scandal, hot gossip, obsession with scatological detail and the hardest pornography to be found outside specialist publications. The success of *Interviú* meant that other weeklies lost many readers. Even the largely female readership of *Hola*, a typical Francoist weekly that followed the ups and downs of royalty, the international jet set and national high society switched to buying *Interviú* in spite of its explicit sexual content. Definitely down-market, *Hola* appealed to many Spanish women starved of glamour who were victims of the Francoist ideology of home and family. Since both sexes were heavily indoctrinated in the belief that women's work outside the home was evidence of the failure of men to fulfill their duty of providing for the family, homebound Spanish women eagerly followed the high life and the good looks of the privileged. Highly conservative in outlook, *Hola* was forced by competition to be less puritanical in content and presentation. It has survived the freer atmosphere of the democratic transition and the competition of both *Interviú* and weeklies like *Lecturas* that concentrate exclusively on the "private" lives and preoccupations of society and television personalities. At the bottom of the market, a spectacular range of ephemeral pornographic magazines, sold openly in kiosks both in the cities and outside, cater for all sexual tastes.

The expansion of civil liberties since the death of Franco has made possible the publication of weeklies in Catalan, Basque and Galician. Unable to compete with magazines in Castilian, few new non-Castilian weeklies have proved durable in spite of subsidies from the autonomous governments. Two factors—political disenchantment and radio and tele-vision—have been responsible for the loss of interest in serious jour-nalism and help to explain the growing reliance of the weeklies on frivolous themes in desperate attempts to sustain their readerships. These expedients were largely unsuccessful; and sales have plummeted since 1978.

The daily newspapers benefitted greatly from the substitution of new legislation for the 1966 Press Law, though they are now subject to ambiguous anti-libel legislation introduced in 1977. Permission to pub-lish new newspapers and periodicals was no longer required. News-papers of all political positions receive subsidies from the State and their readerships no longer need to exercise their skill at reading between the lines. In these circumstances the number and circulation of daily newspapers have expanded dramatically. In 1983, 120 dailies are published in Spain with an average sale of two and a half million; though it should be borne in mind that only nine of them sell more than 50,000 copies.

Daily newspapers owned by the parties do not exist. Each news-paper has a clear political position but retains the right to criticize policies and personalities of all parties. The Communist party tried to turn its periodical *Mundo Obrero* into a daily paper but the experiment soon failed owing to lack of funds and internal feuding. Recognizing the failure of the Communist experiment, the Socialists revived their pre-war daily, *El Socialista*, as a weekly.

No paper exemplifies better the new spirit of modernity and liberalism than Madrid's *El País* which after five years of preparation was published for the first time in May 1976. Owned by a co-operative of shareholders representing all the democratic political forces of the country, *El País* has a young director—José Luis Cebrián—up-to-date technology and a nationwide readership. *El País* has become the first national paper in a country which had previously only regional press. Unmistakably an up-market publication it sells over a quarter of a million copies on weekdays and more at weekends when it is accompanied by a well-produced supplement. The readership of *El País* is composed largely of professionals, executives and students. Two down-market newcomers are also available; *Diario 16* in Madrid and *El Periódico* in Barcelona. *Diario 16* is published by the same group as *Cambio 16* and *El Periódico* belongs to the Grupo Zeta, owners of *Interviú*. Both newcomers aim at readers of lower educational standards than *El País* and at the depoliticized youth that rejects the contents and presentation of the quality press. *Diario 16* and *El Periódico* use colloquial language, search for immediate news impact and resort frequently to sensationalism of a kind that is, nevertheless, more moderate than the British tabloid.

The revival of the daily press in the Catalan and Basque languages augurs well for the restoration of Spain's other cultures and their languages which were the victims of intense Francoist oppression. Under Franco no daily press appeared in a language other than Castilian. Catalonia has two dailies; *Avui* of Barcelona (founded in 1976), *Punt Diari* of Girona (founded in 1979) and two more are promised for 1983. In the Basque country, *Egin* (founded in 1977) and *Deia* (1978) are written half in Basque and half in Castilian, although recently Castilian has occupied a large proportion of the printed page, a development that suggests the difficulties experienced by Basques in recovering their national language. The surviving newspapers suffer from underfinancing and lack of competitiveness with the Castilian press in both news coverage and advertising; but despite their difficulties they have gained a place in the daily life of their countries.

Relics from the Francoist past persist. These are well illustrated by the organization of the main Spanish news agency Agencia Efe. Despite the fact that Agencia Efe is not a nationalized enterprise, its director is a government appointee, its running costs are budgeted for by the state and it enjoys a near monopoly of the distribution of incoming foreign news. The semi-official status of Agencia Efe is an obstacle to independent appraisal of international news.

A second relic of Francoism, the Prensa del Movimiento, survives precariously in provinces like Córdoba where a local democratic press has been slow to put down roots. Under Franco the Prensa del Movimiento controlled the press on Mondays when daily newspapers were not allowed to publish. Each large provincial capital published a newspaper on Mondays called *Hoja del Lunes* that had different content and editorial boards in each capital but the same title throughout Spain. The profits from the various *Hoja del Lunes* supposedly increased the pension funds of the widows and orphans of journalists. The collapse of the *Hoja del Lunes* was consummated in 1982 by the decision of the major newspapers to publish on Mondays.

Hoja del Lunes sold heavily on their sports coverage because football [soccer] in Spain is traditionally played on Sundays. They were complemented by a sports press which has continued to flourish during the transition. Barcelona alone has three sports dailies and sport features prominently in all other newspapers. Avidly read by a mostly male public, the continuing popularity of the sports press has surprised those observers who expected the sports fever to subside after the death of the dictator.

The astonishing proliferation of daily and—especially—weekly press that began in early 1976 was a major feature of the transition. The boom subsided in 1978 and the market stabilized after a series of newspaper and magazine failures that was symptomatic of twin features of the *desencanto*: a volume of publication that exceeded market potential and a widespread loss of public interest in political and cultural issues that followed Franco's death.

TELEVISION AND RADIO

Only 20 *per cent* of Spaniards regularly read newspapers and the majority obtain their news from radio and television. Spanish television (Televisión española—TVE) has two channels, allows a limited autonomy for local news, is watched daily by 60 *per cent* of the population and is financed by a combination of state funding and advertising revenues. TVE has been a state monopoly since its foundation in 1956. In spite of post-Francoist laws that aim to turn it into an autonomous body like the BBC, TVE remains an instrument of government patronage and the focus of endless disputes among the political parties demanding a fair share of television coverage.

Francoism exerted a heavy hand over television. The chairmanship of TVE has often been a launching pad for a political career, most notably in the case of Adolfo Suárez, chairman between 1969 and 1973. Suárez, a client of Carrero Blanco who was then at the peak of his political career, appointed to senior positions in TVE members and sympathizers of Opus Dei, an organization close to Carrero Blanco. The assassination of Carrero Blanco heralded a phase of uncertain *aperturismo*—some modest liberalization alternating with renewed authoritarian controls—in TVE. Changes in the legal status of TVE began under Arias Navarro in 1974 and continue. Television was declared by legislation in January 1980 to be an essential public service for which the state is ultimately responsible. The legislation was the product of consensus politics between the UCD and the Socialists and was fiercely opposed by the Communists and the Catalan minority in Parliament on the grounds that it did not contain sufficient safeguards for minority groups. The 1980 legislation is ambiguous: although it envisages the possibility of privately owned television channels, TVE remains a *de facto* monopoly even in matters of technological innovation both in the present—like cable and teletext—and in the future. With an annual budget of over 50,000 million pesetas and over 11,000 employees in 1981, TVE is an important source of patronage.

The autocratic habits of Francoism die hard. Shortly after taking power, the socialist government was accused in December 1982 of suppressing a controversial programme in the prestigious series *La Clave* that was supposedly critical of the socialist performance in the municipal councils. The state monopoly of TVE has been challenged, to date unsuccessfully, by powerful forces intent on breaking the centralist hold that range from national and multinational capital to autonomists of all political shades.

The main issue of contention between public television and private newspapers is advertising. The press accuses TVE of illegal competition and of using its pricing policy in such a way as to determine advertising rates elsewhere. The first channel has the popular programmes and takes the lion's share of the advertising. The second has less advertising, smaller audiences and "quality" programmes. Control of advertising content is in its infancy so that at such times as Christmas, alcohol and war and sexist toys are presented in a manner unthinkable in other Western democracies. Drinking is exalted as *cosa de machos* and women models with a distinctly North European appearance promote washing-up liquids and household appliances.

For its serials, TV films and films made for the cinema, TVE relies heavily on US and British imports that are dubbed in Spain. News and news-related programmes fill 26 *per cent* of viewing time; old films of which more than two-thirds are North American fill 18 *per cent* of programme time and sport, mainly football, 10 *per cent*. Drama accounts for only 5 *per cent* and classical music and education programmes are rare. Competitions and pop music programmes are popular; but, curiously enough, religious discussions do not enjoy regular slots, a fact that does not seem to concern the Church hierarchy.

The Basque and Catalan Autonomy Statutes made provision for national televisions but because the state is unwilling or incapable of financing the new channels and will not authorize private funding, a third channel for the autonomies remains a dream. Catalonia has had its own programmes in Catalan on the state channels since 1964, a result of Fraga's liberalizing measures; but although the present fifteen hours per week compares favourably with the once-a-month programme of 1964 it is insufficient for a country of 6 million people which enjoys the highest income and cultural level within the Spanish state. Basques, Galicians, Andalusians and other regional groups have fared even worse than the Catalans; and the Socialist government does not appear to be taking measures to redress the imbalances between the centre and the autonomies. A source of patronage, television is also a source of scandal; and accusations of fraud raised against the previous administration have still to be cleared up.

The degree of state control of television has reinforced the role of radio upon which 40 *per cent* of Spaniards rely for their news service. Although radio is also defined as an essential public service, this definition does not appear to have the same implications as for television because private radio stations have since the 1930s played a part in Spanish broadcasting. A state-controlled network, Radio Nacional de España, covers the nation in Castilian and the other national languages. Private enterprise represents a larger proportion of Spain's broadcasting; and since the death of Franco a myriad of radio stations has sprung up in the country. One chain, Cadena SER, claims 25 *per cent* of radio listeners. Alert to local needs and those of youth, Cadena SER with its nationwide network played a praiseworthy role in keeping the nation informed during the abortive coup of February 1981 when rebel soldiers occupied the main studios of TVE in Prado del Rey, Madrid. Radio news enjoys a greater credibility rating than that on television.

Radio is particularly popular for its all-night programmes which have a surprisingly large following and for its sports coverage which can be more extensive than television because radio can cover a larger proportion of local events, especially football matches. Radio is popular too because the language used by radio writers and presenters reflects more accurately the everyday idiom of Spaniards in the 1980s than the staid language of television.

CINEMA

The recent Oscar won by José Luis Garci for his film *Volver a empezar*, the first to be awarded to a Spanish film, has been received with the kind of triumphalist attitude that was standard under Francoism. Spanish cinema has suffered from a lack of clarity in cultural policies during the transition. Under Francoism those Spanish films that overcame the obstacles of moral and ideological censorship enjoyed a high degree of protection. A folkloric backward image of the country was fostered by those film directors who had not gone into exile and were either politically indifferent or willing to compromise. As in other cultural areas Spain had three cinemas; the cinema of exile in which Buñuel and Alcoriza were outstanding directors; official cinema which was subsidized by the state and responded to official cultural directives; and the cinema of internal dissent which played dangerous games with censors and other state officials. Among the dissenters Juan Antonio Bardem and Luis García Berlanga, currently the director of the National Film Archives, were the most prominent; and both directors continue to make films. Berlanga's *Escopeta Nacional*, a fierce satire of the bourgeois beneficiaries of Francoism, was one of the biggest successes of the transition. *Bienvenido Mr. Marshall*, directed jointly by Bardem and Berlanga, a box-office success in 1952 dared the unthinkable: to criticize Franco's foreign policy under the guise of satire. The best-known director under Francoism and the new democracy is Carlos Saura who though never overtly political has captured the everyday repressive mood of the Franco regime and touched on themes disliked by the dictatorship which wanted cinema to project a wholesome and happy image of Spain. Such moody and somber films of Saura as *Los Golfos* showed a face of Spain unwelcome to Francoist ideologues.

The courage of opposition artists despite the strong censorship and their persistence in making dignified films against all odds created a climate that made possible the explosion of film-making that followed the death of the dictator. Film directors, many of them very young, rushed in to film all those themes that had previously been forbidden. The recovery of the immediate past and the exploration, visual and thematic, of sexuality became the focal points of Spanish cinema which achieved for the first time a large and enthusiastic local audience. Spaniards had previously shunned their own cinema because they had difficulty in recognising themselves and their circumstances in a cinema that portrayed three principal themes: the glorious feats of past Spanish history—Columbus and the Catholic kings; religious themes—lives of saints, especially missionaries; and Andalusian set-pieces full of happy peasants given to flamenco dancing and singing.

The new cinema has explored recent history and problems of sexuality and broken personal relationships. The documentary and fictionalized documentary genre were very successful. Film-makers recovered the immediate history of Spain since the Second Republic: good examples include Basilio Martín Patino's *Canciones para después de una guerra*, *Caudillo* and *Queridísimos verdugos* and Jaime Camino's *La vieja memoria*. The directors Manuel Gutiérrez Aragón, Victor Erice, Jaime de Armiñan, Antonio Mercero, José Luis Borau, Eloy de la Iglesia, Bardem, Berlanga, Saura and Miró examined all the forbidden areas that for so long shaped the moral climate of the regime. Spanish cinema began to be recognized abroad for reasons other than its dissenting stance. No longer parochial it could compete with the cinema of the European democracies.

Among the films of post-Francoism one stands out, *Asignatura pendiente* by the youthful José Luis Garci. A symbol of all the political and personal frustrations of the previous regime, the film is understated and unashamedly sentimental. It had a great success among audiences who saw their own lives reflected in the private tragedy depicted. *Asignatura pendiente* is exemplary in its undidactic exploration of the destructiveness at a personal level, of the rigid attitudes of those in power. It is the story of a couple who after being in love in their student days during Francoism, meet again in the new permissiveness of the transition and try to recover the spontaneity smashed by oppressive Francoist morality. Their failure to recover their love and the lack of visible emotion with which they respond to this failure is symbolic of the relationships of many couples in Spain. *Asignatura pendiente* emerged as the key film of the transition.

In 1977 legislation aimed at regulating the film industry created ambiguities that did considerable damage. While the end of censorship was proclaimed, the state reserved the right to bring to the attention of the civil judiciary and military tribunals any film. *El crimen de Cuenca* of Pilar Miró was the first victim of this law. The removal of state protection and subsidies by the same law had a devastating effect on the industry. While it was acknowledged that this protection had constituted a means of ideological control under Francoism the sudden removal of protectionist measures and the end of the obligatory showing of Spanish films in national cinemas precipitated a profound crisis. Spanish cinema almost came to a halt because producers had used the guaranteed exhibition of their films as a means of obtaining loans to finance production. The multinational distributors invaded the Spanish market and many planned films were never made. In 1979 the First Democratic Congress of Spanish Cinema brought together producers, film-makers and distributors who pressed successfully for the restoration of the obligation to show Spanish films. . . .

The crisis of Spanish film production since 1978 is best understood in the light of the general economic crisis combined with the *desencanto* that has pervaded all areas of Spanish politics and culture.

Some films have nevertheless been produced that capture the atmosphere of disillusionment: *El desencanto* of Jaime Chavarri, *Opera prima* of Fernando Trueba. A feminist cinema has also appeared in such films as *Gary Cooper que estás en los cielos* of Pilar Miró and *Sesión de noche* of Josefina Molina.

The cinema of the other nationalities has had some successes. The Catalan cinema scored its first box-office hit with *La ciutat cremada* of Antoni Ribas Piera, a fictionalized reconstruction of the events leading to the "Tragic Week" of 1909 in Barcelona. An interest in exploring their own history is a constant theme in Catalan cinema because the Catalans suffered not only the general repression of Francoism but also the specific repression of their national culture. Josep María Forn in *Companys, procés a Catalunya* portrayed the fate of Lluis Companys, the last president of Catalonia before the Civil War who took refuge in France after the Civil War and was handed over by the Gestapo to Franco's government and shot. Catalan cinema also produces happy tongue-in-cheek soft pornography that reflects accurately the concern of the young with immediate pleasure. Francesc Bellmunt, director of *La orgia* and *Salut i força al canut* and Carles Mira, the Valencian director of films in Catalan like *La portentosa vida del Padre Vicente* are the best-known directors in this vein.

Basque cinema, spoken in Castilian because many Basques do not speak Eskera, is exclusively concerned with the fight for the recognition of their national identity. Three fictionalized documentaries, *El proceso de Burgos* and *La fuga de Segovia* of Imanol Uribe and *Operación Ogro* of Gillo Pontecorvo explore the violent confrontations between ETA and the central government from a perspective sympathetic to ETA. There is no room for other subjects in the Basque cinema.

Like in the press the new permissiveness has brought a spate of undistinguished pornography. Shown under the special classification of "S" films pornography fills too many screens but possibly it constitutes a necessary act of exorcism after Francoism. Pornography is severely threatened by both home video and new regulations aiming at "protecting" the public against possible corruption. Titles like *El fascista, la beata y su hija desvirgada* of José Coll Espona, *Mi mujer es muy decente dentro de lo que cabe* of Antonio Drove, *Trampa sexual* of Manuel Esteba and *Silvia ama a Raquel* of Diego Santillán indicate accurately the main themes of the national "S" film producers.

Desencanto is the common link in Spanish cultural production. The young rebels of the 1960s are the politicians of today; and the remnants of Francoism still exert a powerful influence in Spain. Many of the young try to distance themselves from the preoccupations of their elders by denying history and exalting pleasure; yet unemployment and the worldwide economic crisis are not shadows but a daily reality that darkens all our futures. To modify the slogan of Francoist tourist advertising "Spain is no longer different."

✳
DISCUSSION QUESTIONS AND ACTIVITIES

Giner

1. Identify some of Spain's antinomies, or inherent contradictions, that Giner identifies in his article on ethnic nationalism.

2. When Giner talks about cultural genocide during the Franco period, what exactly does he mean? What proofs does he bring to this assertion?

¢3. Trace the growth of ethnic nationalisms in Spain, as Giner presents them.

4. Research the Basque and Catalonian cultures: their history, their customs, their political power today, etc.

5. At the end of the article, how do you understand the term *nationalisms*? Is there anything comparable in the U.S.?

Driessen

6. Driessen describes the local bar as a focal institution. What are some focal institutions in your community?

7. How would you differentiate social gathering places you are familiar with by function, class, age, gender, or race?

8. To what extent are our kinds of focal institutions a reflection of the structure of our society and its values?

Brandes

9. Describe how a patriarchal system controls women in southern Spain.

10. Since the U.S. also remains a patriarchal system, what are the constraints that limit a woman's achievement in our society?

11. Interview a Spanish woman and man about the role expectations for women. How closely do their responses resemble each other? How closely do their responses coincide with Brandes's study?

12. Select one concrete image from the text that stands out. Put together the images cited by each member of your group. What connects these images? What does the list say about you, the readers? How does the list highlight the important points of the article?

Torrents

13. Play the role of one of the censors under Franco. In a first-person narrative, justify the Franco censorship policy.

14. Role-play the attorney who defends Xavier Vinader before the censorship board.

15. The threat of some degree of censorship is always present in contemporary societies. Present the facts surrounding the death threat against the writer Salman Rushdie after publication of his novel, *The Satanic Verses*. Research recent episodes of books banned from public schools in the U.S.: which books? for what reasons? Research the legal debate between evolutionists and creationists on science education in our public schools. Carry out a debate in which each side of the issue is defended.

16. View the videotape *Spain: Ten Years After*, from the PBS Series of the Press (1985, 60 min. VHS). What new information is shared with the viewer that is not found in the articles in this section? What new point of view is presented by the journalist who narrates the tape?

Addresses for Films
and Videos Listed in
the Discussion Questions

Amnesty International, 304 W. 58th Street, New York, NY 10019
Cinecom Entertainment, 1250 Broadway, New York, NY 10001
The Cinema Guild, 1697 Broadway, #802, New York, NY 10019
Films for the Humanities & Sciences, Inc., PO Box 2053, Princeton, NJ 10128
First Run Features, 153 Waverly Place, New York, NY 10014
Home Film Festival, 305 Linden Street, Scranton, PA 18503
New Yorker Films, 16 W. 61st Street, New York, NY 10023
Public Broadcasting Service/Public TV Library, 475 L'Enfant Plaza, S.W., Washington, D.C. 20024

Bibliography

Berger, Peter L. *Pyramids of Sacrifice*. Garden City: Anchor Books, 1976. 212–217.

Boorstin, Daniel J. "From Traveler to Tourist: The Lost Art of Travel." *The Image*. New York: Atheneum Press, 1962. 77–84, 99–109.

Brandes, Stanley. "Women of Southern Spain: Aspirations, Fantasies, Realities." *Anthropology* 9, 1–2 (1985): 111–128.

Carew, Jan. "The Caribbean Writer and Exile." *Caribbean Studies* 19, 1 and 2 (1979–1980): 111–132.

Connor, Walker. "Who Are the Mexican-Americans?" *Mexican-Americans in Comparative Perspective*. Ed. Walker Connor. Washington, D.C. The Urban Institute Press, 1985. 3–28.

Driessen, Henk. "Male Sociability and Rituals of Masculinity in Rural Andalusia." *Anthropological Quarterly* 56, 3 (1983): 125–133.

Fieg, John P., and John G. Blair. *There Is a Difference: Colombia*. Washington, D.C.: Meridian House, 1989. 41–48.

García, Carmen. "A Cross-Cultural Study of Politeness Strategies: Venezuelan and American Perspectives." Unpublished manuscript, 1990. 1–35.

Giner, Salvador. "Ethnic Nationalism, Centre and Periphery in Spain." *Spain: Conditional Democracy*. Eds. Christopher Abel and Nissa Torrents. New York: St. Martin's Press, 1984. 78–99.

Gudykunst, William B., and Young Yun Kim. *Communicating with Strangers*. Reading, MA: Addison-Wesley, 1984. 119–133.

Hansen, M. Eileen, and Robbie W. Peguese. *The Culture Capsule: A Device for Improving Cross-Cultural Understanding*. Ed. Eliane Condon. New Jersey: Intercultural Relations and Ethnic Studies Institute, Rutgers University, 1975. 1–34.

Hanvey, Robert. *An Attainable Global Perspective*. New York: American Forum for Global Perspectives in Education, 1976. 8–12.

Heath, Shirley Brice. "Language Policies: Patterns of Retention and Maintenance." *Mexican-Americans in Comparative Perspective*. Ed. Walker Connor. Washington, D.C.: The Urban Institute Press, 1985. 259–282.

Jofré, Manuel Alcides. "Culture, Art, and Literature in Chile: 1973–1985." *Latin American Perspectives* Issue 61, 16, 2 (Spring 1989): 70–95.

Paz, Octavio. "The Labyrinth of Solitude." Trans. Rachel Phillips Belash. *The New Yorker Magazine* (September 17, 1979): 136+.

Reati, Fernando. "Argentine Political Violence and Artistic Representation in Films of the 1980's." *Latin American Literary Review* 17, 34
(July–December, 1989): 24–39.

Sunshine, Catherine. *The Caribbean: Survival, Struggle, and Sovereignty.*
Boston: EPICA, 1988. 19–22.

Torrents, Nissa. "Cinema and the Media after the Death of Franco."
Spain: Conditional Democracy. Eds. Christopher Abel and Nissa
Torrents. New York: St. Martin's Press, 1984. 100–114.

Velez-I., Carlos G. "The Nonconsenting Sterilization of Mexican
Women in Los Angeles." *Twice a Minority: Mexican-American Women.*
Ed. Margarita B. Melville. St. Louis: C.V. Mosby Co., 1980. 235–248.

Zurcher, Louis A., and Arnold Meadow. "On Bullfights and Baseball:
An Example of Interaction of Social Institutions." *International Journal
of Comparative Sociology* 8 (1967): 99–117.

NTC SPANISH CULTURAL AND LITERARY TEXTS AND MATERIAL

Contemporary Life and Culture
"En directo" desde España
Cartas de España
Voces de Puerto Rico
The Andean Region

Contemporary Culture—in English
Spain: Its People and Culture
Welcome to Spain
Life in a Spanish Town
Life in a Mexican Town
Spanish Sign Language
Looking at Spain Series

Cross-Cultural Awareness
Encuentros culturales
The Hispanic Way
The Spanish-Speaking World

Legends and History
Leyendas latinoamericanas
Leyendas de Puerto Rico
Leyendas de España
Leyendas mexicanas
Dos aventureros: De Soto y Coronado
Muchas facetas de México
Una mirada a España

Literary Adaptations
Don Quijote de la Mancha
El Cid
La Gitanilla
Tres novelas españolas
Dos novelas picarescas
Tres novelas latinoamericanas
Joyas de lectura
Cuentos de hoy
Lazarillo de Tormes
La Celestina
El Conde Lucanor
El burlador de Sevilla
Fuenteovejuna
Aventuras del ingenioso hidalgo
  Don Quijote de la Mancha

Civilization and Culture
Perspectivas culturales de España
Perspectivas culturales de Hispanoamérica

For further information or a current catalog, write:
National Textbook Company
a division of *NTC Publishing Group*
4255 West Touhy Avenue
Lincolnwood, Illinois 60646-1975 U.S.A.